Manufacturing Against the Odds

D0611717

DATE DUE			
MAY 24 93'S			
NOV 06 1995			
I LL 15 84748			
WITHDRAWN			

Conflict and Social Change Series

Series Editors
Scott Whiteford and William Derman
Michigan State University

Manufacturing Against the Odds: Small-Scale Producers in an Andean City,
Hans C. Buechler and Judith-Maria Buechler

The Bushman Myth: The Making of a Namibian Underclass, Robert J. Gordon

Surviving Drought and Development: Ariaal Pastoralists of Northern Kenya,
Elliot Fratkin

Harvest of Want: Hunger and Food Security in Central America and Mexico,
edited by Scott Whiteford and Anne E. Ferguson

Singing with Sai Baba: The Politics of Revitalization in Trinidad, Morton Klass

*The Spiral Road: Change in a Chinese Village Through the Eyes of a Communist
Party Leader*, Huang Shu-min

*Struggling for Survival: Workers, Women, and Class on a Nicaraguan State
Farm*, Gary Ruchwarger

FORTHCOMING

*The Myth of the Male Breadwinner: Women, Industrialization, and State Policy
in the Caribbean*, Helen I. Safa

Literacy and People's Power in a Mozambican Factory, Judith Marshall

*Computing Myths, Class Realities: An Ethnography of Sheffield Workers in the
Information Age*, David Hakken with Barbara Andrews

Sickness, Healing, and Gender in Rural Egypt: A Political-Economy Ethnography,
Soheir A. Morsy

Manufacturing Against the Odds

Small-Scale Producers in an Andean City

Hans C. Buechler
and Judith-Maria Buechler

Westview Press

BOULDER • SAN FRANCISCO • OXFORD

Conflict and Social Change Series

This Westview softcover edition is printed on acid-free paper and bound in library-quality, coated covers that carry the highest rating of the National Association of State Textbook Administrators, in consultation with the Association of American Publishers and the Book Manufacturers' Institute.

All photographs taken by authors

Published in 1992 in the United States of America by Westview Press, Inc., 5500 Central Avenue, Boulder, Colorado 80301-2847, and in the United Kingdom by Westview Press, 36 Lonsdale Road, Summertown, Oxford OX2 7EW

A CIP catalog record for this book is available from the Library of Congress.
ISBN 0-8133-8448-6

Printed and bound in the United States of America

The paper used in this publication meets the requirements of the American National Standard for Permanence of Paper for Printed Library Materials Z39.48-1984.

10   9   8   7   6   5   4   3   2   1

To our fathers

*who knew about enterprise and
who fought, each in his own way,
for social justice*

Contents

List of Tables and Photographs   xiii
Preface   xv

1   Introduction: Three Firms   1

The Careers of Small-Scale Producers:
    Three Family Histories, 2
Aims of the Study, 13
Methodology, 16
Notes, 21

2   Consequences of the Debt Crisis   22

The Changing Headlines, 22
The Bolivian Situation, 22
The Effect on Small-Scale Production, 24
Supporting the Family in Hard Times: The Home, 25
Cutting Production, 27
Other Adaptive Measures, 27
Local Market Trade and Manufacturing, 33
The Impact on Family Relations, 34
Strategies from Below, 35
Notes, 36

3   The Actors: Rural-Urban Migrants
    and Long-Term Residents   37

Rural-Urban Migration and Small-Scale Industries, 37
General Characteristics of Long-Term Residents, 51
Multiple Occupations, 57
Conclusion, 59
Notes, 59

4   **The Actors: The Role of Foreigners**   62

Historical Roles of Foreigners in
   the Bolivian Economy, 63
Foreign Manufacturers, 66
Conclusion, 75
Notes, 80

5   **Learning the Trade**   83

The Transmission of Generalized Skills, 84
Transmitting Specialized Skills, 88
Urban-Based Economic Activities, 92
Conclusion, 104
Notes, 106

6   **The Social Relations of Production**   107

The Enterprise of Doña Flora, 109
Variants, 117
Work Relations in More Highly Capitalized
   Small Industries, 120
Conclusion, 131
Notes, 131

7   Financing Production   133

The Capitalization of Firms of Different Size, 134
Self-Financing, 135
Renting Equipment and Doing Without, 137
The Family as a Source of Capital, 139
Commercial Credit and Bank Loans, 141
The Acquisition of Real Estate, Capital Goods, and
   Raw Materials as an Investment Strategy, 147
Notes, 148

8   Production   150

Procuring Raw Materials, 150
Production in Smaller and Larger Firms, 154
Competition, 156
Work Hazards and the Risk of Theft, 158

Case Studies of Production, 161
Notes, 176

9   **Commerce**   178

Selling One's Own Goods, 178
The Personnel: The Importance of Kin, 178
Enculturation into Selling, 181
Commerce as an Entry into Production, 185
Retailing, 185
Wholesaling, 193
Production/Commerce of Goods with
    Low Added Value, 196
Mixed Strategies of Indirect Sales, 197
Attracting Clients, 197
The Crisis in Pricing, 211
Notes, 212

10   **Power and Empowerment**   214

The Role of the State in Development, 215
Producers' Unions, 217
Cooperatives, 225
Power, Empowerment, and Participation
    in the Fiesta System, 230
Notes, 240

11   **The Family History of an Artisan Couple**   242

Federico Gutierrez, 242
Mrs. Gutierrez, Federico's Wife, 250
Courtship, 255
Married Life, 257
The Two Daughters, 260
The Gutierrez Household, 263
Exercising a Profession: Federico Gutierrez, 267
Exercising a Profession: Rita Gutierrez, 271
The Forms of Work: "We Are Now
    into Everything," 273
Change: 1988, 275
Mrs. Gutierrez's Dreams, 277
Notes, 277

12   Conclusion   278

   Notes, 285

Appendix   288
Glossary   290
Bibliography   292
Index   302

Tables and Photographs

Tables

3.1	Occupations of Migrants from Two Lake Titicaca Communities	42
4.1	Foreign Industries in La Paz (Sample)	67

Photographs

Skirt maker sewing a *pollera* for a fiesta	3
Producing miniature hats in series	29
Electronically tuning a panpipe for professional musicians	90
Preparing the warp for woolen cloth	110
Women sorting coffee	122
Sidewalk shoe repairmen working with machines purchased with a loan from the World Bank	146
A sign painter and a confectioner working in a poorly ventilated room	159
A stall at the Feria de Alasita	189
Inaugurating a new street market	219
Costume makers dancing the *morenada* in the *entrada* of the Fiesta of Gran Poder	235

Preface

This book is the product of a long, manifold involvement with life in Bolivia in general and productive processes in particular. For Hans Buechler, dinner conversations about the state of the Bolivian economy, the politics of economic decision making and competition among importers in La Paz were a daily aspect of his childhood in that city, where his father worked for an international mining and import firm. Later, small-scale production became a concern of his family when his mother founded a crafts shop for handicapped children, with which his sister continues to be involved today. Professionally, he has researched a variety of rural Bolivian themes since 1961 and has conducted urban research since 1965. Judith-Maria Buechler became involved with Bolivian economic themes in 1965 through her dissertation work on rural and urban marketing patterns. We initiated joint research focused more specifically on small-scale manufacturing enterprises in 1981 and made subsequent visits to Bolivia in 1984 and 1988.

In our joint research, we received the assistance of too many persons to adequately acknowledge. Our research in 1980 would not have been possible without the generous financial assistance of the National Science Foundation (BNS 80-24513), sabbatical leave from Hobart and William Smith Colleges and several months' salary from Syracuse University. The follow-up study in 1984 conducted by Hans Buechler was supported by a research grant from Syracuse University, and Hobart and William Smith Colleges paid for Judith-Maria Buechler's traveling expenses in 1988. In the field, we were assisted for a number of weeks by Sofía Velazquez in locating and interviewing migrants from Compi/Llamacachi, her mother's community of origin. She also transcribed some of our tapes, while Jeannette Barnette de Alarcón undertook the task of transcription during most of 1981 and again in 1988. Teresa Johnson transcribed our tapes in 1984. Hans Buechler's parents, now deceased, assisted us in countless ways, from providing us with a place to live in La Paz to sending us newspaper clippings when we were back in the United States. His sister, Rosemarie, also put us up, keeps us abreast about events in Bolivia and maintains the extended family's aging vehicle, without which our urban research would have been practically impossible. Judith-Maria's mother kept our household running while we were away on field trips and has cheerfully suffered the trials that arose from our producing a book. Our daughters, Simone and Stephanie, accompanied us to Bolivia in 1981 and in 1988 and have provided valuable insight into the workings of the Fundación para la Promoción y Desarrollo de la Microempresa (PRODEM), the development agency in which they had an internship in 1988. Dorothy Densk and Simone Buechler assisted us in the final editing of the manuscript. We also thank Beverly LeSuer, copy editor for Westview Press, for her careful, clear, and insightful editing, and Mike Sedore and John Koegel at Academic Computing Services at Syracuse University, without whose help and understanding the production of camera ready copy would have taken even longer than it has.

Portions of two chapters are reprinted, with permission of the publishers, from two articles by Hans Buechler. They are: "Doña Flora's Network: Work Relations in Small Industries in La Paz, Bolivia" in *Urban Life: Readings in Urban Anthropology. 2d ed.*, edited by George Gmelch and Walter Zenner. Prospect Heights, Illinois: Waveland Press, 1988 and "Apprenticeship and Transmission of Knowledge in La Paz, Bolivia" in *Apprenticeship: From Theory to Method and Back*, edited by Michael Coy, Albany: State University of New York at Albany Press, 1989.

Last, but not least, we wish to thank the many artisans and other manufacturers whom we interviewed often repeatedly over the years. Without their willingness to share with us the intricacies of making a living in Bolivia, this study would not have been possible. In deference to the privacy of our informants, all names except for that of one artisan, already identified in the literature, have been changed.

Hans C. Buechler
Judith-Maria Buechler

1

Introduction: Three Firms

Small-scale manufacturing continues to provide a large part of the consumer goods in Third World countries. Economic and political conditions in Bolivia may be particularly well suited for such enterprises. High transportation costs make imports expensive, while large industries have difficulties surviving because of the small internal markets and difficult access to external ones. In addition, small-scale producers may in some ways be more flexible than large industries in the face of political turmoil and periodic downturns in the economy.

The primary purpose of our study was to understand the range of problems faced by these small-scale enterprises; the manner in which they were organized; their development over time; their linkage to rural-urban migration; and their relationships both among themselves and to larger firms within the nation and abroad.

The small-scale industries we studied ranged in size from one-person operations to factories with around fifty workers. Their capitalization ranged from less than US $100 to several million dollars, but most were in the lower range.

The persons involved in these industries come from a variety of backgrounds. Some are artisans, cobblers, tailors, and tinsmiths who have continued their trades with little transformation for generations within the urban context. Others, such as the flute makers, some of the costume makers, gold- and silversmiths, are recent arrivals from the surrounding rural areas who have brought their traditional trades with them. Still others, with a wide range of origins, have found niches in the production of more modern types of goods. For example, the high cost of importing spare parts for imported machinery and vehicles and regular shortages of such parts have resulted in work for skilled mechanics capable of remaking or copying parts. On a more capital-intensive level, small factories with but a handful of workers produce everything from Styrofoam to synthetic knit materials for jogging outfits.

Geographically, the enterprises were dispersed throughout La Paz. There was a clear tendency, however, to move away from the congested traditional commercial center to the burgeoning satellite city of El Alto.

In terms of work relationships, the industries ranged from family firms to formally constituted corporations with full employee benefits prescribed by law as well as traditional patronage benefits, such as soccer clubs and annual outings.

Some of these firms produced only for the local urban market. Others had a regional and national distribution and a few enjoyed an international clientele. Most suffered from the uncertain economic conditions, the scarcity and unpredictable nature of capital and supply of raw materials, the intense competition, and the pressures of dealing with unwieldy government bureaucracies with complex and arbitrary regulations which limit or even impede normal functioning.

The Careers of Small-Scale Producers:
Three Family Histories

Three family histories ranging from a relatively poor to a relatively well-to-do family will provide the reader with an initial orientation to the place of small-scale production in the socioeconomic fabric of La Paz life. The relationships among family members and their ways of coping will serve to introduce and illustrate the adaptive nature of these enterprises, their connection to other sectors of the economy and to the world economic system, and the manner in which such work and family/gender relationships contribute to the development of class consciousness and mobility.

The Condori Family: Carpenter and Dressmaker

In the corner of a warehouse, in makeshift quarters near the central cemetery of the city, we interviewed Marcelino and Maria Condori, a couple in their sixties who migrated to La Paz from a Titicaca lakeshore community before the Chaco War--that is, in the early 1930s. Marcelino, an orphan, was raised by his granduncle on his mother's side. His older brother, who was working as a servant in the city, urged Marcelino to join him there. At the time, Marcelino was working as an assistant to a truck driver and for the owner of the landed estate of the community. Some time later, his brother was inducted into the army, where he died in a dynamite accident. When the authorities tried to draft Marcelino, his granduncle persuaded the officer in charge to take his youth (he was 17) and his only brother's death into account and thus to postpone his conscription. Five years later Marcelino joined

Skirt maker sewing a *pollera* for a fiesta

the Lanza regiment in Guaqui. A year later, he married and went into the reserves. Then he was employed for 12 years as a lathe operator in a glass factory. But in 1950, after a military coup to prevent the installation of a left-of-center regime, he was fired without benefits for his alleged support of Victor Paz Estenssoro of the MNR (Movimiento Nacional Revolucionario). At that time he also suffered an accident that left him on crutches; thereupon he began working as an independent carpenter.

In spite of the loss of two fingers on his left hand in another accident in 1958, he now fashions wooden doors, window frames, tables, counters, shelves, wardrobes, and other similar items for private homes. He buys the wood, which is imported from Santa Cruz, from two La Paz lumberyards that also rent out the use of Brazilian and Czechoslovakian machinery on the premises to some ten carpenters at a time. Although the cost of the lumber is a bit higher here, Marcelino calculates that the convenience of the location, the savings in transportation and his close relationship to these men--one of whom he calls *compadre*--compensate for the difference in price.

He is concerned that he has to work with second- or third-grade materials, since the first-class wood, much of which is monopolized by the government, is exported to Argentina and the United States. Since he has to rent machinery and pay for transportation, he earns little; for the large contracts go to large construction firms who some-times subcontract or hire carpenters like him. He is also plagued by the inflation in the cost of raw materials and the lengthy delays in payments by his clients who, in turn, are waiting for long-promised bank loans.

This household, like many others, depends on the income derived from the wife. Maria, a monolingual Aymara speaker, orphaned in the same lakeshore community as her husband, came to La Paz in 1930-31 when she was about ten. An aunt, who traded in foodstuffs from Desaguadero, on the Peruvian border, found a job for her as a personal servant. When Maria married, her sister-in-law taught her to become a seamstress specializing in *polleras* (the traditional gathered and pleated skirts worn by rural and urban Aymara women). She has both hand- and machine-sewn these skirts of imported German and American polyester brocades and velvets for primarily (but not exclusively) rural clients, who are well attuned to the subtle annual variations in style, skirt length, width, kind and number of pleats or tucks, color and material.

At one time she worked with two apprentices, subcontracting for two large establishments that make and sell skirts, but now she works alone or with her daughter for private customers. She is particularly busy just before the major fiestas in town and in the country and before the weddings of meat vendors. These relatively well-to-do traders pride themselves on the number and quality of *polleras* in their dowries, which are on display during the festivities. On these occasions, she can earn about two dollars a day, which is equivalent to earning the wage of a factory worker (i.e., US $90-100).

This couple had five children, but one died in a traffic accident. Their youngest son is helping his father and studying. He thinks that his experience as a truck driver and mason/carpenter for his father's cousin in Tarija, who owns a hotel and construction firm, will provide him either with entry into a military school or a job in a tractor factory. The second son worked in a tailor shop and is now married to a migrant from nearby Laja who sells condiments in an open market. A married daughter lives in a lakeshore community (near her parents' community of origin) where she occasionally sews *polleras* and runs a small store-*cum*-restaurant. She and her husband own a motorboat that ferries travelers across the straits of Tiquina. Her husband is also employed as a barber and chauffeur at the naval base. Another widowed daughter, formerly married to a tailor from a rural community near the city, sews and helps her mother, who in turn is helping to educate her 14-year-old granddaughter.

The old couple dream of moving to the warm fruit-filled valleys of Tarija, where Marcelino has worked before and where a rich cousin has offered them land to build a house. Maria is particularly reluctant to leave her children, and they both fear the cost of the move. However, they also feel vulnerable living as renters in an unprotected space where they have already been robbed twice. They are also hard hit by hyperinflation and devaluations accompanied by the cessation of construction and the curtailment of expenditures for clothing associated with the recent debt crises.

This family history illustrates the classic migrant pattern. In this case, an orphaned, landless male who became acquainted with the city through trucking and military service, migrated to the capital, following a brother who worked as a domestic. He was lucky to land a job in a factory using skills common to every rural male. After twelve years he invested the savings from a salaried job into an independent enterprise, with the goal of educating his children and providing them with the means to establish themselves in the country or city. Maria illustrates the female version of the pattern. Orphaned and poor, she also moved to the city to join a female relative, a trader, and worked as a servant until marriage, whereupon she apprenticed to another relative, her sister-in-law, in order to learn a traditional skill that enabled her to set up her own workshop. Both maintain strong social and economic ties with the countryside that continue to be valuable for their children. The strength and importance of these ties is reflected in the marriage of three of their children and their choices of profession.

Both Marcelino's and Maria's work can expand in good times and contract in poor. In times of relative prosperity they can expand by hiring assistants and by working overtime for larger construction or clothing firms. In poor times or slack months they work alone on repairs. They require practically no capital investment in machinery or stock, and they pay no business taxes. Marcelino owns some trade tools but rents machinery and buys wood as needed. Maria frequently still sews by hand and owns only one sewing machine. They tend to work on a cash-and-carry basis and thus are less subject to capital loss due to inflation and devaluation.

The linkages to "services" and formal sectors of the economy are also apparent in this case. Both Marcelino and Maria began their working lives in "service" (transportation and domestic service, respectively). Marcelino then worked for more than a decade in the "formal sector" and is in competition with larger firms or carpenters who subcontract. Maria has been subcontracted by stores. Other seamstresses work for particular vendors who sell in the market. Marcelino's and Maria's children and in-laws trade and work in their own enterprises and in salaried service occupations for the military.

Both enterprises--the carpentry and skirt making--are subject to events beyond their control. Marcelino has to work with poor-grade wood because the first-quality materials are monopolized by the state for export. He must rent the means of production, the imported machinery, and buy the material at a higher cost because he has never been able to amass sufficient capital to invest in costly machinery or in the transport of the wood. His clients from the private sector are also disadvantaged, since they enjoy less access to bank credit for home construction and improvement than larger or state-run enterprises, especially during times of enforced austerity and scarcity of capital.

Maria works solely with imported cloth, thread, needles, and machines. Successive devaluations, the stricture on imports, and stricter controls on contraband have increased the cost of new skirts immeasurably. (The cost of a skirt tripled in a single year.) Her best clients, the meat vendors, have been hit by both a natural disaster--swine pest--and the decrease in sales, since most people have had to sharply curtail their consumption of meat. All the enterprises associated with fiestas are suffering similar declines.

So orphaned Marcelino and Maria, although still "propertyless," have gained independence. They see their children enjoying property, education, skills, and salaried job prospects in a number of areas, and they have a wide network of kin in the city and two regions. They are lucky in two respects: They have remained together and can expect a joined income, and they have been spared major accidents and ill health. It is these two threats, abandonment and catastrophic medical expenses, that reverse the fortunes of persons, especially women, on this level. Maria and, to a lesser extent, her daughters enjoy less education and are more involved in commerce than their male counterparts, whose opportunities are more varied.

The Mendoza Family: Jewelers

This couple in their late forties owns a two-story building with a jewelry store/workshop below in one of the busiest central thoroughfares of La Paz, the Buenos Aires. The husband, Luiz, comes from a long line of metalworkers, both urban jewelers and bronze casters from Jesus de Machaca. His wife, Leandra, is a Peruvian, descended from a family that gave many sons to the church as priests. When they were both younger and in better health, the the husband and wife created pure and plated gold and silver jewelry, primarily stone-encrusted pins and earrings in the form of flowers, baskets, llamas, etc., for *cholas* (or *de pollera*), urban-born women who continue to dress in the traditional garb that includes the *pollera* (skirt), *manta* (embroidered shawl), and felt bowler hat. Luiz learned his trade from his father's brother, who apprenticed him with his cousins. He, in turn, taught his wife when they married. They design the pieces on the basis of illustrations in trade magazines from abroad and from their own inspirations, adapted to the rapidly changing styles in vogue among their fashion-conscious clientele.

The raw materials, such as faux and real pearls and semiprecious and precious stones, are imported from Japan, Brazil and Switzerland, while the gold and silver are bought directly from the Banco Minero (Bank of the Mines), from traders who travel from the mining sites, and from dealers in old coins. The couple work by hand and with both imported and national machinery to chisel, plate, bathe, magnify and polish. They hope to import an American plating machine similar to the one that an uncle owns and permits them to use from time to time. Most of the time they put out gold and silver to subcontractors (all but one of whom are relatives), who prepare the pieces in their own quarters in outlying barrios. The pieces are then finished in the main shop, where the stones and pearls are put into place. Sr. and Sra. Mendoza specialize in fretwork and the setting of stones.

They have six children, three sons and three daughters. Two sons studied medicine, one of whom has completed his oft-interrupted studies, and the third son is an accountant. The eldest daughter became a nurse, the middle one is an accountant and the youngest is still in school. All of them have worked in the shop on occasion, but it is the daughter-in-law (the oldest son's wife) who is most actively engaged in the profession.

With capital and encouragement from her mother-in-law, she has established a small store, near a central market, that belongs to an uncle who has as yet not charged any rent. She is the daughter of a tailor and a trader. After leaving school (having completed only four years of secondary education) she became a machine operator in a thread factory, then graduated to a white-collar secretarial position before marrying and learning the jewelry business from her in-laws. While her twelve-year-old sister-in-law takes care of her three preschool children, with the occasional help of her husband, who is at home because the university was shut down, she attends the store and repairs jewelry. She lives with her in-laws and maintains a close relationship with a sister who is a teacher and a brother who drives a car for a military officer in La Paz. She hopes to continue this business even after her husband finishes his medical internship and residency.

The years of working with acids and strong lights have affected Sr. and Sra. Mendoza's health. He was incapacitated recently, and she was ailing. They were thinking of transforming their shop/workshop area into a pharmacy/clinic where the two sons, a daughter, and they would be employed as doctors, nurse, receptionist and business manager, respectively. They hope for funding for this project from the Brothers of the Cross, an American-based religious sect.

In addition to the fluctuation in the access and price of gold, silver and imported stones and machinery that has severely hurt their business, Sra. Mendoza also fears the increase in street crime. They have had stones thrown at their windows three times during recent strikes and demonstrations. The volume of their sales has also decreased considerably, since few people can afford to buy jewelry for fiestas. Most of their work is now in repairs, which earns much less money. They have even sold the truck driven by Sra. Mendoza's cousin because they still owed money on it, and it was beginning to show the wear of traveling the rut-filled, neglected roads of the country.

This family illustrates the condition of a "middle-class" family of comfortable means who have worked as traditional artisans for generations. They have invested in the property in which they live and work, in a truck from which they enjoyed additional income, and in the private education of their children, whose training they hope will support them and provide them with alternative, less strenuous and healthier work in their old age. They have been able to adjust to the fluctuations in demand by curtailing their own consumption. They are still using a twenty-five-year old national plating machine and borrowing time on their uncle's American one that costs anywhere from one to two thousand U.S. dollars. They put out much less work than in the past and devote themselves more to repairs. To help support the oldest son, his wife and three children, the family has provided the start-up capital for a second store near a busy market.

The possibilities available in this "class" are best illustrated by the daughter-in-law, who, born to a modest tailor and trader, became a shopkeeper-artisan married to a professional man from an established urban family and is now his assistant in his medical practice. This young woman and her sisters-in-law enjoy a much higher education and white collar work experiences denied their migrant sisters in the Condori family, but they are still less well educated than the male members of the family. Again, in this generation, a woman is taking on the commercial aspect of the firm.

The manufacture of jewelry is heavily dependent on mining, which has suffered neglect in technological improvements and work conditions, as well as on the internal and external fluctuations in the price and availability of metals and stones. Successive devaluations have increased the price of imported stones, machinery, and chemicals and decreased the cost of exports. Jewelers compete for these materials. The same international pressures to devaluate have also led to the restriction on imports in general which jewelers require.

In their role as jewelry merchants, the Mendoza family members are embedded in commerce. Specialized as they are in making "traditional" jewelry--a luxury item for a specific class of women who trade in the market--keeping shop or running other small enterprises, they are particularly vulnerable to downturns in the economy.

The economic dependence of Bolivia on the world economy results in considerable under-employment and economic distress and its concomitant social and political unrest, which in La Paz has resulted in more petty crime against property and persons than before. This family sees its best hope in "joining together" in a professional concern assisted by foreign aid.

The Salases: A Family Factory

The Salas factory is owned and run by five siblings and their mother. In 1930 (when he was 17 or 18 years of age), the deceased father, a Spaniard from a small town near Burgos, migrated to La Paz. He came to join some other Spanish businessmen, all of whom were working for a Bolivian company that dealt in cinchona bark in the Yungas, the semitropical valleys near La Paz. The father later formed an association with the foreign head of a laboratory in La Paz, and they began to sell cinchona bark. He met his future Bolivian wife in the Yungas, where her parents owned some landed estates and where she spent her holidays while studying nursing in Argentina. She later became an instructor in the School of Nursing in La Paz. In 1942, the couple bought a small factory and made candies, pasta and bread under the husband's direction until 1970, when his health began to deteriorate. By then, the oldest son had already been working in the plant for three years and could take over. This son had been sent abroad to Barcelona to study and had worked in a similar plant in Italy for a while. In the meantime, his brother studied electrical engineering and mechanics in the Pedro Domingo Murillo School of Industrial Arts in La Paz, but he was sent to Germany and Panama for similar internships. When the father died, the brothers formed a partnership with their two sisters and mother. One sister received her doctorate in history in Italy, where she is now teaching Spanish and Latin American history at the university. The other married sister lives with the mother, and they take turns working in the office and warehouse of the factory. The mother and children share in the profit according to their work input and responsibilities. The older son is more involved in the business and financial aspect of the enterprise, and the younger one is involved in the technical part.

The factory expanded from twelve to fourteen workers in 1967 to twenty-eight in 1981 and is in the process of moving part of its production facilities to El Alto, the growing working class satellite city of La Paz, located on the high plateau, while maintaining its offices in town. This expansion in size will be accompanied by the addition of new machinery and 30% more personnel. In 1981 the factory was producing two thousand kilos of sweets and 10,500 kilos of noodles a day, but the Salases hoped to increase the capacity by 60%. Like the preceding cases, this factory is largely dependent on imports. In the 1980s the machinery was imported from Argentina, Italy, England and East and West Germany. The East German machines were not considered as good as some others, but the East Germans had the advantage of a tradition of making sweets and extending the best terms of credit. For pasta, the firm preferred machinery made in Italy or by Italian companies in Argentina and Brazil. The principal components of the machines and the presses were bought directly from Italy, while some parts were bought in Brazil and Argentina, where the quality of the merchandise was said to be inferior. All of these sources for machinery offered credit for below the 32% interest charged by local banks, which also were very slow to process loans.

Some of the raw materials and packaging are also imported. The government-subsidized flour for noodles comes from Argentina, while the essences, colors, sugar substitutes, and the imprinted paper packaging come from England and Argentina because these materials are either unavailable in Bolivia or too expensive there. For example, the factory imports cellophane candy wrappers embossed with its trademark from England because similar wrappers made by the local paper monopoly would cost more. Similarly, the price of sugar from Santa Cruz fluctuates wildly in the international market and from harvest to harvest.

The Salas family markets their wares in La Paz, its surrounding towns, Cochabamba, Santa Cruz, and Oruro. Demand fluctuates seasonally. Right after the potato harvest, when prices are low, sales for noodles drop by about 25%. Similarly, the sale of sweets decreases 15% when schools are closed and increases 100% during the Christmas season. Noodles are considered a staple by townspeople and are very much in demand for daily soups and feasts in the countryside.

The factory sells its goods wholesale to traders in markets and stores. The Salases prefer to sell for cash, but they allow some exceptions for long-term customers, who are granted thirty to forty-five days of credit. The factory has its own truck, which is used for distributing the products to the market stalls and shops; the driver collects the payment at the same time as delivery. Twenty other pasta factories and stores of small candy makers, some of whom once worked for the company and have now set up independent firms, compete with the firm.

Employer-employee relationships are patronal and personalistic in character. During the military regimes of the recent past, the workers negotiated wages and work conditions via the half dozen "old-timers"--persons who had worked with the company for decades. These old-timers enjoy close paternalistic ties not only with the owner-family but with more recently hired help, all of whom share a common community of origin on the altiplano and many of whom are related. The workers are paid relatively well (about US $125 a month in 1981) and have access to a reasonably priced hot lunch from the company canteen. The normal work week is 48 hours, but many work "extra" hours at regular pay. The company celebrates a fiesta on New Year's Day, and workers and managers play soccer together.

By 1984 this relatively amicable relationship had deteriorated due to the succession of economic crises. One employee, the secretary-general of the union local, spoke with some passion of how the cost of living had gone up 300% to 400% yet the government had allowed factories to pay only 100% in salary increases. He and some others have entered into a series of hunger strikes that have put pressure on the government to allow another 30% increase. Even so, the purchasing power of these workers decreased by half between 1981 and 1989.

The factory itself has been hard hit by the continuing inflation and devaluations. It is said that many candy factories sold their products at black market prices to the highest bidders, far above the government fixed prices. They have also had to compete for scarce flour and sugar and have been affected by contraband as well. In 1981, candy from Brazil smuggled into Bolivia was cheaper than candy made in Bolivia, and at times Bolivian marketers even sold staples clandestinely to Peru, where they fetched a higher price. The cost of imported goods skyrocketed with each devaluation. The devaluations, part of the austerity program of the International Monetary Fund (IMF), have increased inflation and decreased wages and thereby have decreased the demand for merchandise. The negative effect on living conditions, especially nutrition, has led to strikes and riots.

Analysis

These cases, illustrating as they do three levels of "well-being," share a number of features. All three firms are basically family-run, with loose partnerships among female and male members. In the first case, the husband and wife work independently but contribute to a joint purse; in the second, the original pair work together and expect female and male members of the next generation to cooperate in a joint enterprise; and in the third, a joint enterprise has been established, but one professionally trained daughter has opted out and her more traditional mother and sister "mind the store."

The relationships between employers and employees in terms of recruitment and treatment are familistic at present but may become less so if the union movement expands again as it seems to be doing. Each firm attempts to meet downturns in demand by curtailing the work force, either by putting out work to fewer persons or, in the case of the pasta company, by adding machinery. The dependence on external sources for raw materials and machinery is common to each firm, so they are all subject to the pressure on prices associated with devaluation. At the same time, they suffer from seasonal variations in demand and the drop in the local demand that has resulted from inflation and the decline in wages and thus purchasing power of those still employed and those under- and unemployed.

The primary members involved in each case differ in the level of education attained. In the first case, the carpenter and his wife are uneducated, and the wife is monolingual; in the second, the jewelers, both female and male, attained more years of an urban education; and in the third, the senior members of the factory already had been university trained and one sister, a professor, does not work in the firm. A higher level of education is associated with greater movement in and out of professions that provide more security. We also see a progression from renting to ownership of a house and from owning a few basic tools but renting the means of production through joint use to ownership of large, complex machinery. Ownership of housing and machinery, in turn, provides access to credit from local banks and foreign firms. The size of the market and its geographic dispersion expand correspondingly. The class composition of the clients is more mixed and general. With growth, the production may become more class-specific, but that is not always the case. Some small enterprises serve a wider spectrum of classes.

The variations in origin, education and capital as well as access to credit and markets are the basis for the class differences among the cases, which are reflected in the kind and variety of social ties each enjoys, their general financial standing and their geographic orientation. But the class boundaries are not clear-cut or impermeable. Viewed over three generations, we can see these classes in the making as individuals gain access to skills, capital and social ties, which in turn changes their definition of themselves and their relationship to others. Social mobility is not a simple progression within the lifetime of an individual. Orphaned persons (who are often at a considerable disadvantage) might be aided by their newly skilled children, and persons from a family with low social standing may continue to work in a business that lays the basis for another enterprise which will support an entire family's hopes for upward mobility. Similarly, a person with professional aspirations may stand on the shoulders of family members who run a factory.

Aims of the Study

In recent years the interest in small-scale enterprises has risen exponentially all over the world. An increasing number of economists as well as development agencies and, to a lesser extent, the government agencies in Third World countries have become disillusioned with models of development based on trickle-down mechanisms. The debt crises in many of these countries, which, in part, resulted from the blind concession of government guaranteed loans to corporations, have led to a reevaluation of the wisdom of staking all hopes on larger enterprises.

Concomitant with the decline of larger enterprises has been a rapid rise in the number of smaller ones. Lending agencies are taking a new look at lending policies and are providing funds to both governmental and nongovernmental organizations to facilitate credit to such enterprises. To be sure, this shift in thinking has yet to be translated into a shift in funds commensurate with the relative importance of smaller firms in the national economies of Third World countries. For example, in 1988 the U.S. Agency for International Development (USAID) budgeted some US $50 million for work on microenterprise development (Levitsky 1989:xv). Similarly "it is estimated that $500 million of the $3 billion or so lent for more than 60 small enterprise projects since 1975 have benefited the microenterprise sector" (p. xvi). The trends are nevertheless promising.

A reevaluation of the practical role of small enterprises is beginning to lead to a rethinking of the theoretical assumptions underlying economic programs, many of which have heretofore been accepted as articles of faith. For example, a recent study of agricultural production in Bangladesh concluded that, contrary to accepted wisdom, the savings rate of agricultural producers was *inversely* related to the size of their holdings (Manwar 1990). And the argument that economies of scale must invariably lead to the demise of smaller units of production can no longer be accepted as a given.

One of the major theoretical problems with the rethinking of economic categories has been the tendency to employ traditional rubrics as a base. First, small scale has been assimilated with traditionalism. Third World economies were said to consist of a dynamic modern sector and the vestiges of an earlier economic order, leading to the concept of "dual economies." When it became apparent that this so-called traditional sector produced modern goods and services, the concept was replaced with "informal sector." This concept retained the notion of a separate economic sphere. The high degree of interlinkage between smaller and larger firms through the movement of personnel from one to the other, through putting-out systems and so forth, has led to questioning of the utility of economic spheres as well. And, as Redclift and Mingione (1985:2-3) put it, the informal and the formal sectors "proved to have shifting parameters that varied according to context. . . . Physical areas were not always coterminous with types of work, and households themselves were difficult to characterize along sectoral lines making use [as they do] of multiple strategies to ensure their survival."

The lack of valid criteria to divide the economy into separate spheres has led some researchers to focus on what are considered to be prevalent attributes of small firms, with the recognition that these attributes may also characterize many larger firms as well. A number have focused on unregulated activities. Thus Castells and Portes define the "informal economy" as income generation "unregulated by the institutions of society, in a legal and social environment in which similar activities are regulated" (Portes et al. 1989:12). They argue that the informal economy should be regarded as a process rather than as an object, and they wish to depart from "the notions of economic dualism and social marginality" (p. 11). But the very concept of informality suggests its opposite, "formality," a concept that misleadingly implies legitimacy and consistency resulting from a process of decision making on behalf of a collectivity including both actors acting "formally" and those acting "informally." Thus, progressive labor legislation would be placed under the same denominator as bureaucratic red tape whose sole effect might be to provide protection for a small elite of producers.

An interpretation of formality and informality in terms of the power relationships involved leads to a different assessment. Laws tend to be instruments of particular groups. To be sure, some laws can be regarded as compromises reached as a result of a struggle between groups, but even then each group employs them to its own advantage. Changing political configurations lead to changes in the enforcement and in the outcome of the application of laws. From this perspective, formality and informality form part of the same process, a process that in Bolivia (as elsewhere) is often dominated by the interests of the middle-class and the elites. Social welfare legislation was enacted by governments seeking the political support of organized workers in larger enterprises. But together with tedious processes of achieving legal status,[1] the laws become a tool for securing the loyalty of skilled workers, who might be tempted to (and indeed often do) set up enterprises of their own. At the same time the laws enhance the viability of larger firms by limiting the the workers' incentive to engage in capital-intensive activities, thereby discouraging competition. The resulting oligopolies often are able to dictate the kind of activities that smaller firms are able to engage in. Viewed in this light, informality can be regarded as a means, engaged in various ways by both smaller and larger firms, to counter such mechanisms. Some smaller firms and those involved in the production of illegal goods can do so through bribes and clandestine production, and larger firms can do so through special connections with governments in power. It should be noted that similar mechanisms operate to limit private sector competition with state and/or mixed enterprises.

Harding and Jenkins (1989) have lent the concept of "informality" more flexibility. While accepting the central role of state intervention "as the major criterion of formality," they argue that the major differences that exist in the nature of state intervention in planned socialist nations, social democracies of Western capitalism, and developing nations warrant separate treatment. In addition they argue for a flexible contextual definition of formal and informal activities even within Western societies, which are the focus of their analysis: They regard formality and informality as "ends on a continuum," with no clear criteria separating one from another, rather than as "separate domains of social experience."

However, even this refinement would not alter the fact that an analysis based on distinguishing formal and informal activities would differentiate small-scale firms that, apart from their legal status, would be almost indistinguishable. For example, the dichotomy would place highly regulated small-scale activities, such as selling goods on sidewalks in La Paz, and very similar activities engaged in the same streets by ambulant vendors in different categories. Authors writing about the "informal sector" ultimately can circumvent such problems only by explicitly or implicitly conflating small size and informality.

The fact that small scale, or at least very small scale (for which the term "microenterprise" has been coined), is often confused with or dealt with in the same breath as informality, particularly in the study of Third World situations, has detrimental repercussions on the manner in which they are viewed by social scientists and government agencies alike. Small scale is frequently regarded essentially as a means of competing with "legitimate" and "economically sound" larger enterprises by circumventing taxation and labor laws. It thereby receives a connotation of illegality and residualness.

Acceptance of residualness leads to the treatment of small-scale industries as welfare beneficiaries at best rather than as full contributors to the national economy. In contrast, similar support to larger firms continues to be regarded as a means of securing a country's economic future.

If the intrinsic superiority of larger, more capitalized firms is no longer accepted as an article of faith, a series of questions must be asked to determine the range of strategies producers adopt under different economic circumstances and why. In order to succeed in this endeavor, it is important to broaden one's definition of "the economic" to include many kinds of behavior that are usually not included in economic analyses. Social and political capital, for example, may constitute a major determinant of a firm's success. Even the very notion of what constitutes a firm and hence what constitutes success or failure of such an entity may require revision. More specifically, the kind of study envisioned and subsequently undertaken refocuses the questions asked to include the following, among others:

1. What strategies enable producers to survive during periods of economic crisis and/or political instability?
2. What are the range of economic activities individuals engage in simultaneously and consecutively and under what circumstances?
3. What are the roles of social class and gender in influencing economic decision making?
4. To what extent and how do producers from different social backgrounds circumvent policies they find inimical to their interests?
5. How are governmental policies and those of lending agents and banks manipulated to favor certain categories of individuals?

We hypothesize that small size, flexibility in size and in the nature of work relationships, and low indebtedness are among the strategies that have enabled many firms to survive the economic crises of the 1980s in Bolivia. And further, we hypothesize that these strategies involve cooperation as well as conflict between members of different social classes. Social class may, in fact, be as context-dependent as "informality" and may be experienced differently depending on gender, place in the family, and background (e.g., rural or urban origin and ethnic identification).

Methodology

The Scope of the Study

We estimated the number of small-scale enterprises in La Paz by means of a number of approximations. The *Censo nacional de población y vivienda* 1976 (the 1976 National Population Census and Study of Living Conditions for Bolivia) breaks down occupations according to locality, employment category (employers, self-employed workers, unremunerated family members, wage earners, and salaried workers), broad occupational groupings, and sectors of the economy (Bolivia 1976). Based on data from that census, out of a total population of 635,283 in Bolivia in 1976, of whom 221,685 were economically active, 36,759 were occupied in manufacturing industries. Of these, 11,123 were listed as self-employed and 920 as employers, while 12,966 were counted as wage earners, 10,976 as salaried employees and 366 as unremunerated family workers. By comparison, a survey taken in 1980 by the United Nations' funded Proyecto de Migraciones y Empleo Rural y Urbano, which employed somewhat more inclusive occupational criteria than the 1976 census, arrived at a much higher industrial employment figure. Out of a total population in 1980 of 757,933, 56,900 (or 20.4%) of the economically active population (vs. 17.6% in 1976) were employed in the industrial sector. However, the breakdown of occupations in the 1980 survey is not sufficiently detailed for our purposes, and the figures in some categories, such as the number of unremunerated family members, are probably useless because the persons interviewed may not have understood the questions (Escobar and Maletta 1981).

The municipal tax records of 1981 listed 8,974 enterprises in 49 categories, excluding construction and demolition industries and those oriented to service alone, such as car repairs. If one adds construction, demolition and service industries, the total is 12,273 in 54 categories. These records provide a better breakdown for some of the more visible industries (which are therefore more easily subject to taxation).

These records do establish approximate numbers, growth and decline, location, relative capitalization, and tax assessment. However, the records have to be read with caution. For our purposes it was difficult to segregate productive from primarily service or commercial enterprises. This difficulty can be shown by category 62015, listed as jewelry, watch and silver establishments that include manufacturing. In this case, repair, sales and production workshops are combined. In contrast, carpentry and machine shops (category 95103) are distinguished from sawmills, which, in fact, may also rent out their equipment to carpenters and hence are also involved in manufacturing. So the principles that govern the separation of categories is not always clear or consistent.

The total number of enterprises subject to taxation should also be read with caution because establishments are sometimes not removed from the list even after years of nonpayment of taxes. We attempted to correct the total number by subtracting the number of enterprises that had never paid taxes and those that had defaulted over the past seven years, at which point the municipality considered them defunct (i.e., 1,810 in 49 categories). If these are subtracted from the total, we arrive at the figure of 7,164 enterprises for 1981. In the forty-five categories where the records for 1980 and 1981 were available, the number of enterprises increased from 3,485 to 3,924, or a 12.5% addition.

We tried to substantiate this increase by comparing the number of enterprises established in 1970 (597) to the number founded in 1980 (666) in 49 types of industries. This increase of 69 is 11.5%, which is comparable to the 1980 and 1981 figures.

We grouped all the addresses listed in the records into districts and then plotted these on a map of La Paz. The distribution points to both concentration and dispersion. In each category, one district has a greater cluster of a particular type of industry, but at the same time single workshops can be found in many dispersed locations. In general, although there still are small industries even in locations where one would least expect them, such as in garages of upper-class dwellings, there has been some movement away from the center of the city to El Alto, which has also become a residential area for workers and the site of almost all new large-scale industries. By 1988 El Alto had become a separate municipality.

The Sample

In 1981, we interviewed 196 individuals in open-ended taped interview sessions, ranging from single sessions of between 30 minutes and three hours to a small number of multiple sessions that in one instance amounted to a total of over 25 hours. We revisited about half of these informants in the summer of 1984 and a smaller number (mostly of those already revisited in 1984) in the summer of 1988. Our sampling techniques reflected the principal concerns of the study. We attempted to select at least two cases for almost all the manufacturing and repair activities we were able to identify. Where the complexity of the work process and division of labor warranted it, we interviewed more individuals. Where both small and large firms engaged in the same activities, we selected examples of small, medium and large ones. We thereby were able to determine the influence of both size and the nature of the activity on the characteristics of firms. We were also careful to examine well-established and more recently founded firms and legally registered as well as clandestine operations. And we studied the work history of the owners of existing firms to obtain data on the reasons for firm failure.

Firms were also selected in terms of their geographical location: the older sites in the center of the city and the more recent ones on El Alto, the rapidly growing satellite city on the high plain to the northwest of La Paz. Finally, our interest in migration and its relationship to entrepreneurial activities led us to employ snowball sampling methods to interview migrants from Compi/Llamacachi, two neighboring Lake Titicaca communities we had studied intensively in the 1960s and early 1970s. This technique also offered a correction to the bias resulting from interviewing mainly owners of firms, a choice mandated by the suspicion and potential distortion an interview with a worker in the presence of his or her master would have created. Similarly, a snowball sample made it possible to interview producers whose workshops were not visible from the street. We do not claim, however, to have eliminated the bias toward more visible, and therefore presumably more successful firms. Finally this approach permitted us to compare small scale manufacturers with market vendors from those communities, now residing in La Paz, whom we studied between 1967 and 1976. Our long-term assistant Sofía Velazquez, who is from Llamacachi, was helpful in this endeavor.

Intensive Open-Ended Interviews

Informants were asked biographical information and their work histories, including multiple activities and plans for the future, as well as the activities of their parents and siblings. They provided data on the organization of the firm and its development; the work process from the procurement of capital and acquisition of machinery and raw materials to the commercialization of the finished product; labor relationships, including putting-out practices, temporary and permanent employment of workers, and involvement of other family members in the firm; health conditions; salaries; and benefits. We investigated the relationship of the firm to the municipality by means of taxation and various regulations and the role of the national government in terms of labor laws, protectionist legislature (including import tariffs), projects funded by international agencies to promote small businesses, and the relationship between private and public enterprises. For reasons already indicated, we were unable to study producer organizations (*sindicatos*) during our initial fieldwork; however, we were able to attend a few meetings and interview *sindicato* leaders in 1984.

In contrast, during all phases of our study we were able to include cooperatives of various kinds which were sanctioned by the government. The longer and more intensive interviews also included questions on social life, sports involvement, and, most important, participation in the fiesta system and rites of passage. Interviewing the same individuals two or three times over an eight-year period made the changes and continuities manifest, and the long-term contact permitted a greater depth in the interviews. Our informants often welcomed the chance to pour out their travails to persons who were strangers but at the same time familiar with their problems.

Family Histories

In addition to obaining individual life histories and family histories of the informants which typically involved recording sessions of one to three hours, we spent many hours observing the activities and interviewing various members of a family engaged in the production of woolen goods for export. The life histories of a tinsmith, his seamstress wife and daughters were also recorded during thirteen one- to three-hour evening sessions at their home over the entire study period, and we observed the couple at work. This intensive method of data gathering provided much greater depth in understanding the learning process involved in becoming an artisan, the role of an individual's social network in his/her economic activities, the mechanisms of competition, the relationship of economic decision making to other aspects of life, the nature of social stratification and economic and social mobility, and many other topics integrating different aspects of our research. Most important, the impact of the economic crisis over an eight-year period and of the changes in the role of artisan production could be examined in detail.

Our study suggests that small-scale enterprises may well remain a major and indispensable component of Third World economic niches which large industries find too risky and that they generate links among different activities to promote new types of enterprises.

We discovered that an orthodox Marxist model which views "simple commodity production" as a vestige of a precapitalist past destined to disappear under the pressure of advanced capitalism was inadequate to describe the Bolivian situation. Instead of an inexorable unilineal evolution toward greater and greater capitalization and increasing loss of autonomy on the part of the worker, we found a mutual accommodation among firms of widely varying nature. Development did not proceed from independent producer to dependent worker. Capital generated by the wages of a dependent worker may be invested in small-scale production. Thus, individuals who began their careers as workers in large factories (the so-called formal sector) used their accrued benefits to establish owner-operated industries. Indeed, bureaucrats could become artisans and professionals could become managers of small firms.

Consequently, in order to understand the development of firms, we found it imperative to trace the interdependencies of firms both of similar size and of different sizes. A simple typology based on size, capitalization, product, labor process and market would have been inadequate. Firms were interconnected through putting-out systems; rental or borrowing of space and machinery; complex division of labor among otherwise independent producers based on differences in skills and access to means of production; and partnerships involving various kinds of arrangements among other things. So, particular producers may engage in a number of different aspects of production--i.e., they may at the same time be managers; engage in skilled, more highly remunerated aspects of production; and take part in relatively unskilled, low-margin work. They are thus simultaneously exploiters of the labor of others and exploiters of their own labor and that of members of their families.

Marxists often assume that highly capitalized industries are necessarily more centralized in terms of the control over the labor of others. However, we found that relatively highly mechanized industries could permit relatively decentralized production. Thus, lumberyards rented their expensive machinery to carpenters by the hour. The rates were probably not much higher (and, under the present conditions of falling exchange rates, perhaps even lower) than amortization costs of a privately owned machine. Some informants cited convenient access to machinery rather than returns on capital and labor as their reason for wishing to acquire their own machinery. The progression from smaller to larger firms postulated by orthodox Marxist models as well as developmentalist ones is also far from universal. In fact, we found that in Bolivia the dissolution of a large firm often is the basis for the creation of a number of smaller ones, as long-term employees receive pieces of equipment in lieu of severance pay and in this manner set up their own shops. At the time of our 1984 revisit, this process was accelerated by the economic downturn, which forced larger firms to lay off large numbers of workers.

Notes

1. Cf. the example reported by De Soto (1989). In order to experimentally, formally register a small firm in Lima, Peru, he had to engage a lawyer and four assistants for 289 eight-hour days.

2

Consequences of
the Debt Crisis

The Changing Headlines

The view on Third World debt, especially Latin American debt, changed from one of alarm in 1984 to cautious optimism in 1985. Journalists, social scientists, and financiers in 1984 typically described such debt as a "ticking bomb" and the "Vietnam of the international financial system." In 1985, they claimed that "the worst [was] over." Even Michel Bouchet, a more cautious, tempered economist, of the Institute of International Finance, stated that "the debt crisis in its short-term sharp manifestation is over" but "the debt difficulties are not" (*New York Times*, 2/4/85).[1] From our perspective, such suggestions are most misleading. For the New York banks, the "unease may have lessened" since, for them, the "relatively small" debt of smaller countries like Peru, Chile, and Bolivia poses less of a problem than debts of larger countries, especially if the smaller countries do not default all at the same time. But from the vantage point of one of those countries, Bolivia, the crisis was hardly over even in 1991.

The Bolivian Situation[2]

By the mid-eighties, Bolivia had accumulated a total foreign debt variously calculated at $3.1 billion and $5 billion and a debt to U.S. banks of $300 million (Pastor 1984; Dunkerley and Morales 1986). In May of 1984, Bolivia stopped all payments on interest and principal, instituting a moratorium on debt which is attributed to a general strike by the Bolivian Federation of Workers (Pastor 1984:2). The country was subsequently cut off from loans from the World Bank and the IMF. The country then lost additional international credits. By January of 1985, the rate of inflation had reached 50,000 percent.

The Bolivian economy seemed to be collapsing. The gross national product grew by only 0.5 percent from 1983 to 1984, and the trade surplus was a mere $200 million. Pressured by creditor banks, the IMF, and the U.S. State Department for defaulting and for failing to adhere to even more severe austerity measures and pressured to curtail or eradicate the growth and export of coca and cocaine, the Bolivian government was threatened by the loss of credit and foreign aid and the freezing of U.S. accounts. Given this scenario, it is perhaps not surprising that Bolivia has been called a basket case (*New York Times*, 2/4/85) or that one non-Latin banker said in New York that "most of us have already given up on places like Bolivia" (*New York Times*, 5/21/87:D7).

The present debt crisis has deep historical roots. At its inception, the young republic agreed to recognize and assume the private debts of Bolivian citizens to Spain. In the nineteenth century, the state again borrowed from international markets on disadvantageous terms to meet annual deficits and to build railroads; it also made mining concessions and lost or ceded territories to neighboring countries. In 1931 and earlier in the twentieth century, when mining exports fell, Bolivia discontinued its foreign debt payments (Gomez 1976:466). Bolivia has, in fact, long depended on tin mining for foreign currency provided at special exchange rates to purchase essential imported raw materials (Canelas 1966:30). Later, foreign credit sources played this role. When the United States entered into the world financial markets as a debtor nation, credit sources dried up and interest rates rose (Pastor 1986). Bolivia lost its financial support at the same time that it faced declining tin prices and bad harvests. Due to the precipitous decline of the world market price, tin mines, once Bolivia's main source of income, now had become a liability. It cost Bolivia more to operate the mines than it could earn from tin exports. All other industries followed into a deep recession.

In 1986, Bolivia embarked on an IMF-directed New Economic Policy under the newly elected president, Victor Paz Estenssoro, whereby the government received an IMF standby loan. The 1986 economic austerity program included the elimination of government subsidies that had been used to keep costs low for some basic staples; the removal of restrictions on exports and imports; the elimination of most price controls; and a freeze (with controlled thaws) on public sector wages. It also cut back public services, including the operation of low-cost rural pharmacies. In addition, major banks were closed. Over 23,000 miners from the State Mining Company lost their jobs. Many mines were privatized. The remaining miners lost many of the benefits they had fought so long and hard to obtain. The mining company stores no longer sold subsidized food and basic supplies, and the school lunch programs were terminated. All of this resulted in extreme hardship. In August 1986, the wives organized a March on La Paz for Life and Bread, in which 7,000 persons participated. However, government troops interfered, and none of the petitions were granted.

In July 1988, Bolivia agreed to an Enhanced Structural Adjustment Facility Arrangement with the IMF. The World Bank renewed its lending, and in a three-year period through May 1989 approved a dozen soft-term credits reaching approximately US $340 million. However, most of the funds to "reactivate" the economy did not go into increasing Bolivia's productive capacity but only served to pay back foreign investors. Strikes to protest the layoff of fellow teachers as a result of the government austerity program as well as long arrears in the payment of wages have seriously undermined public education. More than 7,800 teachers abandoned their jobs during 1987-1988.

The Effect on Small-Scale Production

Arensberg has argued that cultural regularities emerge out of interpersonal behavior rather than from "purposes" and "essences" (1972:11). Such a perspective can provide insight into the process of industrialization in Bolivia, one of the poorest countries of Latin America and one whose economy is highly dependent on trade and financial relationships with the core industrial nations and its more prosperous neighbors. We shall focus on the detrimental effects of the crisis on small-scale producers in La Paz and examine the adjustments they made to the deepening depression. It is our contention that these adaptations may provide a key to the functioning of such enterprises in more normal times as well.[3]

The emerging characteristics of industrial development in Bolivia can be regarded as the outcome of both long-term and short-term adaptations to the vagaries of external domination. The dependency of the country's economy on narrow international interests and associated national elite interests has rendered it particularly vulnerable to downturns in the world economy, resulting in a long chain of economic crises.

Our research in 1981, 1984 and 1988 enabled us to observe the effects of the crisis at three stages of its unfolding: an incipient stage, where the effects of mounting debt were compounded by the ravages of a series of corrupt military regimes; a second stage, when the government was obliged to technically default on the servicing of part of its foreign debt, when foreign sources of credit dried up completely and when hyperinflation was in full swing; and a third stage, when structural adjustment measures had decreased inflation but had done little to improve living conditions.

Our data confirm the progressive drop in production and in individual purchasing power shown by the official statistics.

Supporting the Family in Hard Times: The Home

Hyperinflation, combined with wage controls, forced women, who generally are entrusted with the family purse--*chola* women literally hold the purse strings under their shawls or skirts, and lower and lower-middle-class women, in general, distribute their families' pooled resources according to the needs joint and individual needs of the members of the household--to cut out or cut back on food, shelter, clothing, utilities, and services and to provide by their own labor goods and services they once purchased. Their goal was to provide bare sustenance during the week and, if at all possible, one "good" meal on Sunday. To that end, they went to extraordinary lengths. The number of meals per day was reduced and their content drastically altered. For breakfast, it was not uncommon to make do with coffee (brewed from the dried pulp and skin of the coffee berry). When bread vanished from the stores, oatmeal, distributed by CARITAS, a Catholic relief agency, for a nominal fee, was substituted, or the women began to bake bread themselves if they owned an electric stove and if they had legal or illegal access to both imported flour and yeast. Often, when one of the ingredients became available again, the other was not. As one woman interviewed said, "The children cry for bread. Why did we let them get used to bread? They beg and beg. How can I deny them?"

For the one other meal of the day, bananas, yams, yucca and oca (a tuber) often took the place of the favored potatoes, rice or noodles, and a few eggs, some fish or cheese were often substituted for meat--now considered a luxury. Family members were up at dawn, taking turns on long lines for rations, which the poor were often forced to sell for cash. When buying food, women calculate into their decisions the subsidized meals and additional rations given to of working members of the family. A once-proud baker was relieved that her older son could eat at the factory, and she reluctantly accepted domestic service at "starvation" wages because she and her school-age son were given lunch and tea (when he helped around the house too). She had accepted this job in part because her older son feared that her baking and selling in a kiosk might endanger his salaried position. He preferred that she engage in "hidden" work.

Everyone tried to activate or reactivate the kin and community ties to inherited furrows of land or to obtain produce from the countryside. Even charitable donations of staples distributed in the countryside were carried back to and sold in the city. There, relations with officials and storekeepers were assiduously cultivated. In stores, the shelves that were conspicuously empty of dry goods during the day filled up miraculously after 8:00 p.m., when the police left. Hoarding on all levels was commonplace. Peasants held back, selling only to selected intermediaries who paid well. They, in turn, favored select clients who had sufficient cash at the right time and enough space to accumulate sizable reserves.

With regard to shelter, extended families crowded together. Young married persons often did not live with their spouses but instead lived with their families of origin. Every conceivable space was rented out. For instance, a former dressmaker and her two daughters hauled stones and molded mud bricks to construct extra rooms to accomodate "hippie" tourists. And a well-established market vendor rented a tiny repository, "where evil spirits have resided for generations," to members of her union as a meeting place. Clothing was altered, mended, and handed down and around. Utilities were paid at the end of the month with inflated money. To resist the price hikes in transportation, workers walked, hitched rides and resorted to violence, road blocks and strikes.

Perhaps the most detrimental consequences of the crisis were the deterioration in education and health care. Students had to interrupt their education due to school closures and/or costs. Even in normal times, mothers complained about the expense of school fees, supplies and "donations"; the cost now seemed preposterous. As Silvia, the cookie baker turned laundrywoman, put it:

> Those teachers are always asking for money. . . . Last year I spent a lot of money on the public school. . . . The teacher kept asking for money until one day I got angry and said: "What does your teacher think? That I'm made of money? Tell her that!" So he didn't bring any money to school, and he was kept back and lost a year. Added to that, she had him buy gas, sell her things and help her at home. But he still didn't pass. It was as though the lady took revenge on the child, and so I put him in night school where he is getting good grades and they understand the situation.

Medical care was postponed or neglected. Western medicines, many of which are imported, were either unavailable or commanded exorbitant prices. In the recent past, health care consisted of a judicious mix of modern Western and traditional Aymara treatment. Now, there seemed to be more reliance on self-help. In 1983, Doña Flora almost died of diabetes. She had received injections in Argentina to no avail, so she cured herself with *jamakara*, an herbal tea. The story goes that she learned about this remedy from a gentleman who for three years had unsuccessfully sought treatment in the United States. On a trip to Cochabamba, this gentleman had chanced on a Tarabuco sweater vendor who cured him with *jamakara* when he collapsed. In 1984, Doña Flora claimed to be healthy again except for her failing eyesight, but in 1988 she blamed her continued poor health on the fact that her business had not prospered in recent years. She continued to visit curers and was confident that she would be able to become more active again.

Cutting Production

Between 1980 and 1985, industrial production dropped at an annual average of 9.6% (Müller y asociados 1988:4). Our data confirm this progressive drop in production. For example, in 1984 Don Alfonso, who produces peanut butter, not only was receiving somewhat less money for his peanut butter in inflation-adjusted terms per unit than in 1981, but he also had to contend with decreasing demand for his product. At its apogee in 1980, the fledgling industry had produced some forty 600-gram jars a month. In 1981, a drop in the number of foreigners, recalled by their governments because they were opposed to the military regime of President Luís García Meza, led to a parallel drop in demand for Don Alfonso's product to 25-30 jars a month. Finally, in March 1984, he sold nothing at all. His recent clients, the cookie factories, were forced to cut production themselves, and his traditional customers, the retail stores, insisted on buying on consignment and paying him later with devalued currency later, a condition Don Alfonso found unacceptable.

The poorest artisans were often the most severely affected by the crisis. Hardest hit were the large number of knitters who knit sweaters by hand for export. Tourism decreased in 1981 due to the actual and rumored coups d'etat and decreased in 1984 because of frequent street demonstrations. Exporters were reluctant to ship goods to other countries when they were legally bound to deposit the foreign-currency proceeds in the central bank in return for pesos bolivianos at the low official exchange rate. Thus, one producer-exporter, who had made shipments of several thousand woolen knit sweaters, woven jackets and ponchos in 1980, sold far fewer in 1981 and had ceased producing altogether in 1984.

Other Adaptive Measures

Most of our informants were able to alleviate the effects of the crisis somewhat by taking a number of adaptive measures. Some made the principal adjustments early in the recession or even applied lessons learned during previous crises. Don Alfonso, the peanut-butter maker, and his wife, Doña Carmen, are a case in point. In 1972, he lost some money that he had deposited in a bank when there was a sudden devaluation of the peso. He never deposited money in a bank again. In addition, he and Doña Carmen were able to protect themselves against periodic shortages of foodstuffs by buying staples when they were plentiful and the price was right. Indeed, some of their many activities were launched during times of scarcity, for example, during actual or rumored coups d'etat.

The couple first began to make bread in their small oven when no other bread was available. They found that even the hard loaves that were the product of their first experiments sold extremely well to middle-class customers. So did the more lucrative small sweet cakes. As the crisis progressed, they refined these tactics further. When flour became so scarce that existing supplies were in danger of running out, the couple ceased to bake bread and sweet cakes and concentrated instead on filling special orders for fancy party cakes.

Other small-scale producers made few adjustments in the early stages of the crisis other than to reduce production, but by 1984 they were forced to adapt to the deteriorating situation in more creative ways. For example, sweater knitters and furriers resorted to substituting or mixing alpaca with inexpensive sheep wool.

Similarly, Alcides, a highly skilled goldsmith, did not mention any major difficulties in 1981. He had stockpiled the few essential imported means of production long before and had enough casting plaster and wax for another seven years. As a result, he was immune to rising costs and scarcities of imported raw materials.
In fact, he was planning to take a trip around the world with his wife. By 1984, however, Alcides had to reduce his work force from its 1980 maximum of ten to two workers. And yet his enterprise continued to prosper. He had moved part of his operations to a centrally located office building where he was catering to clients (mainly Japanese) referred to him by the embassies. Often his workers worked at home rather than brave transportation strikes and slowdowns, giving him time to work alone in his other workshop. On occasion, some of the workers whom he had let go also continued to work for him. Alcides had helped them to establish their own workshops, and they would take in work "in gratitude," as he put it, for the assistance they had received. In addition, Alcides set up his wife in a glassware store. Glasses, he figured, would not be likely targets for thieves, whose number had multiplied during the crisis, making his neighborhood increasingly unsafe. His trip around the world never materialized, in part for family reasons, but he still expected to make a shorter trip to other Latin American countries in the near future.

In 1988, he was uncertain whether his jewelry production was still a viable enterprise. He had been engaging in a variety of commercial deals that kept him afloat and had set up his wife in a copy-service center, although store he had originally intended the store to be for jewelry sales. For him, as for many others, service and commerce appeared more lucrative than manufacturing.

Some artisans included international migration in their strategies. Thus, when the crisis was in full swing, a lamp-shade and chandelier maker migrated to Costa Rica, first with the intention of learning new skills and then returning when conditions improved but then deciding to remain permanently. By 1988 he had sold his business.

Some of the craftsmen initially sought more lucrative product lines within their specialty, and others diversified into a number of unrelated activities. As the crisis progressed, they then attempted to

Producing miniature hats in series

rationalize production to cut costs. Thus a manufacturer of miniature hats, replicas of peasant styles worn in different parts of the country, switched from making regular-sized hats to making miniatures on a full-time basis in the late 1970s because his previous business had been hurt by clients who would order new hats or have them remade and then would disappear for lengthy periods of time, leaving him with his capital sitting idle on the shelf. In 1981, when sales of miniature hats were slow because of the low number of tourists, he visited an artisan fair in the United States and attempted to sell his hats there and to find more reliable outlets. Unfortunately his trip was not as successful as he had hoped: The gringos were mainly interested in his replicas of Mexican sombreros. Finally, in 1984, although sales were no better, he achieved economies of scale by making longer runs of the same models instead of keeping a stock of a larger variety. This strategy was a further development of his practice of rationalizing production by segmenting the work process into small steps, some of which, like making tassels and hat bands, he put out to kinswomen, while others, like shaping the felt, he reserved for himself or, as in the case of decorating the hats, entrusted to his wife.

A woman whose principal activity is baking cookies sought to solve a similar drop in demand in 1981 but did so in a diametrically opposed manner. Rather than further narrowing her activities, like the hatmaker did, she diversified by adding a few sidelines, including cooking for fiestas, serving meals to workers in the lumberyard next door and running an ice-cream concession. In addition, she engaged in an entirely unrelated trade, the manufacture of machine knitted sweaters. In 1984 she again employed this strategy of diversification, but this time she also rationalized production. By now she had expanded her clientele but could not fill their orders because of a scarcity of practically all ingredients, so she began selling crocheted garments, that were made to order by other women. Since this is a more middle-class activity than knitting, we assume that she was taking advantage of the fact that women of more privileged backgrounds were now also beginning to seek ways of adding to dwindling household incomes. Once staples became more available again, she resumed her baking activities. Later, she switched to a smaller (and presumably more energy-efficient) oven.

To be sure, a few artisans did benefit from the crisis (even if they were not involved in the lucrative illegal production and trade of cocaine). Thus a mechanic who repaired truck engines had as much work in 1984 as before, and a metal-lathe operator had more work than he could handle rebuilding vehicle parts that could no longer be imported because the government could not satisfy the demand for foreign currency at the official exchange rate. But unless an artisan was extremely shrewd, he could still end up with heavy losses. The lathe operator mentioned lost a large part of the assets he had deposited in a bank and had hoped to use to buy a small car. When the car finally was ready to be delivered, the official exchange rate had dropped, and he could no longer afford to buy it. The same thing occurred when he decided to purchase a second lathe. Because of these steep, unpredictable devaluations, obtaining bank loans for new equipment was out of the question by 1984. By the time the lengthy paperwork had been completed, the loan could no longer purchase the item for which it was intended.

Cutting Costs, Cutting Profit Margins, and Converting to Other Activities

Few producers had the option of cutting costs by substituting local raw materials or goods for imports. In fact, some national staples such as rice and sugar also became scarce because agro-businesses and larger farmers were keeping them off the market in protest against prices decreed by the government.

Obviously, the decreased purchasing power of the wage earner *did* force the artisans and at least those factories producing cheap consumer goods to lower their prices and content themselves with much lower profit margins than before if they were to make any sales at all. A furniture maker and upholsterer was forced to cut his profit margin substantially in 1981 and again in 1984 because customers could not pay prices commensurate with the increase in the price of imported raw materials. Due to speculation, these prices had risen considerably even when calculated in U.S. dollars. In addition, by 1984, although he had begun to charge 50% in advance, he still lost a large part of the original value on the balance by the time the furniture was picked up. Some clients were willing to cover the loss resulting from inflation, but others refused to pay more than the original price.

Similarly, as a result of the glut of woolen knits, a knitter in 1984 earned a dollar or less on a sweater that took from two days to a week to complete by hand or a day and a half with a hand-powered knitting machine. In 1981 this same work typically brought in between four and five dollars.

Petty artisans purchased storable staples and raw materials, while larger producers also converted their pesos bolivianos into U.S. dollars in the black market and/or invested in larger consumer items such as furniture and cars. Whether or not they were converting their pesos bolivianos into dollars, producers and vendors alike set their prices with the daily changes in the black market rate in mind. The dollar was the only reliable gauge of value because imports, that must be paid in dollars, enter into most Bolivian production. The lack of hard currency entering the country through *official* channels could have made the demand for dollars a moot point. However, a steady *illegal* flow of dollars continued to enter the economy through the cocaine trade; the black market rate reflected this flow.

With some exceptions, many of the adaptations described above could be predicted from recent analyses by political economists. The "dolarization" (see Dunkerley and Morales 1986:97) of the economy under the influence of the cocaine trade is one such exception. However, the adaptations to devaluations cum price increases and wage controls were often much more complex than those that have been described. One such mechanism of adaptation, which we will explore in more detail in Chapter 9, was for the government to allow foreign currency earned through export to be used only for importing specific consumer goods. Others included the formation of neighborhood cooperatives designed to enable the consumer to bypass the middleman and the establishment of neighborhood committees to control the distribution of bread made in local bakeries. These systems had some success. In fact, for a time, bread was more readily available in poorer neighborhoods of La Paz than in upper-middle-class Calacoto.

Nevertheless the "arbitrage" between the price of goods pegged at the official exchange rate to the dollar and the street rate continued unabated both from the upper and the lower rungs of the social ladder. Residents of Calacoto bought bread and even bags of sugar at a premium from working-class contacts.

Many informants adapted their work in ways that they hoped would counteract inflation. For example, a truck driver for a noodle factory hoped to stretch the purchasing power of his meager wages by having his wife switch from the sale of onions to the sale of staple foods. He planned to buy noodles from the company at a rate which he implied was already above the legal price and transport it clandestinely with the company truck to the store he would open. Don Alfonso, the newspaper vendor/peanut butter manufacturer mentioned earlier was allowed to buy enough scarce kerosene at the subsidized rate for his backyard industry and even jump the line at the pump because the policemen in charge of controlling distribution knew that he did not abuse this privilege for speculative ends.

In contrast, the ultimate in windfall profits from inflation was reserved for what was undoubtedly a select group of fortunate or well-connected mine owners and manufacturers. According to newspaper reports, they were allowed to borrow pesos at a subsidized rate of 110% (i.e., 30% below the rate paid to depositors). By converting the loans into dollars, subsequent hyperinflation permitted them to pay back their loans at a small fraction of their original value. Thus one private miner who suffered an operating loss of $7 million made a $12 million profit in financial deals and ended up with a net gain of $5 million (*Wall Street Journal*, 8/13/85).

Some of these adaptations form part of long-term economic strategies, as permanent hedges against potential crises. Thus capital has fled Bolivia even under favorable economic conditions, and those Bolivians who can afford to do so have always held part of their assets in the form of real property. But, in addition to preventive measures, crises require inventiveness and an extreme degree of flexibility if one is to survive the abrupt changes in economic constraints.

A few years before the debt crisis reached its peak in 1985, dollar accounts had suddenly been disallowed and assets were converted into pesos at the low official rate. Within weeks of our interview with a shirtmaker, a further acceleration in the rate of inflation would have doomed him to assured bankruptcy. He was still relying on the strategy of payroll deduction sales of shirts to factory workers (see Chapter 9). Unless all the transactions took place on payday, he would have lost his capital, for he would have been paid with inflated money and would have had to pay salaries at a higher rate. It remains a mystery to us how the numerous artisans survived who sold their goods to middlemen on consignment.

In 1985, a year later the new president, Paz Estenssoro, permitted the official exchange rate to float, froze public salaries, and allowed employers to discharge workers and set wage scales through direct collective bargaining. Subsequently, real estate, which had been sacrosanct, was subjected to a steep one-time tax levy. Even the seemingly inexorable decline of the peso boliviano could not be counted on at all times. At one point in 1984, the central bank ran out of bank notes. (They were imported from Brazil and eventually became Bolivia's third largest import.) As a result, salaries could not be paid for a few days, which had the effect of improving the exchange rate to the dollar. Later, Paz Estenssoro's stabilization plan appears to have had a similar temporary effect on the exchange rate. So the producer had to be on guard constantly.

These uncertainties and the tendency for each actor to interpret events in his or her own favor have led to contradictory assessments of the economic situation. Next to the lucid interpretation of Don Alfonso, the peanut-butter manufacturer, who discussed his strategies with the detachment of the true savant, there were the puzzling claims of the equally experienced Mr. Gonzalez of Cafe San Isidro, who said that excessive wage demands would force producers to either increase mechanization or put their money in bank accounts where it would earn high interest. Apparently, the opportunity to criticize organized labor was sufficient to make him forget the effects of inflation he had bemoaned earlier in the same interview, when he admitted to having lost part of his working capital in precisely this manner.

Local Market Trade and Manufacturing

Both women and men pursued mixed strategies (Uzzel 1980), or what Scott Whiteford aptly refers to as the strategy of least vulnerability (1981). Vendors and producers accepted every opportunity to secure scarce goods, to limit the cost of labor, to find markets and to invest in something or someone of durable value. Market vendors ventured farther, with more danger, to obtain limited quantities of legal and contraband goods of questionable quality. Goods and bundles of inflated money had to be safeguarded from robbers. Buses ran irregularly, if at all because their owners were not allowed by the government to raise fares to keep pace with inflation.

Leaving prized stalls empty, vendors sought to sell directly to establishments or to persons with cocaine wealth. Longer-term vendors of vegetables have all tried to establish dry-goods stores where, with careful manipulation of price and availability, they could turn a small profit. Credit, even for long-term *caseras*, or favored clients, was shortened or eliminated. Cash was invested immediately in durable goods. One market trader said: "I don't even know whether I am really making anything. I just take my extra cash and run to buy shawls. I have twenty now. I bought them at 10,000 pesos, and now they cost 40,000, so I feel happy. I have a little something, a little protection." Her sister-in-law bought beer, but her "donkey of a brother" lost his retirement benefits even though she had urged him repeatedly to buy a truck as a hedge against inflation (see Chapter 7).

The Impact on Family Relations

The struggle for material support was accompanied by the effort of coping with the fear, frustration, loss and anger experienced by family members. Our findings support those of Milkman (1976:84), who wrote that "the impact of crises was to exaggerate previous family patterns." Sheer necessity led to increased economic interdependence and cooperation and emotional support in close families, as can be seen in the life history of the Vizcarra family, which is recounted at greater length in Chapter 5.

> In our old age my wife and I take care of one another. I give money to my wife, but my daughters don't want us to spend. They serve us a plate of food, or when they have a small celebration, they never forget us—they always send us something. And my son, who lives in Santa Cruz, also remembers us. He knows that we don't have any sugar here, so he sends us what we need. Here, one can't get any sugar. There is some at the corner store, but they sell it for 550 pesos a pound, while the government has fixed the price at 350. They earn 200 (above what it should cost), but we have no choice but to buy at that price. For bread too, we have to go out at 3 or 4 in the morning and wait until the bread comes out of the oven. Since we are only two persons, they only give us four buns with our ration cards. So we have to create miracles to survive another day. That's why we no longer spend much. We lack rice, meat, and many other things. Now when there is food, it is extremely expensive. What we have budgeted vanishes like dust. So we look for ways of saving. In order to live more comfortably, we are depriving ourselves of fiestas. We no longer attend dances or invitations.

Relationships deteriorated markedly in those families where alcohol-related violence, infidelity or class differences had already created strains. Thus, an erring husband, who was better educated and enjoyed more official connections than his young wife (an artisan), finally deserted her and their two young children to take up with a store owner. The wife continued to live with her extended family, engaged in trade, and sold all extraneous items. "If you have two tables, you just sell one," she said. She and her family were very embittered by the loss of his support and the fact that he had ruined a number of deals for them. Younger single women with children and with less familial support established new unions. Making it alone is now nearly impossible. Older women relied on kin, mostly children of both sexes, for economic and emotional support. One artisan proudly related that her son, who had migrated to Australia, had spoken to her by telephone for more than half an hour. He told her not to worry so; he was working three jobs. When her husband had died in a drunken accident she had slaved to take care of the children; now, she was being repaid in kind.

Strategies from Below

The way that owners and workers have dealt with inflation, devaluation, shortages of capital and raw materials and the shrinkage of markets might shed light on the manner in which the nation could overcome problems of the debt crisis. We turn once more to a case discussed in part earlier, the case of Don Alfonso, his wife, Carmen, and their two daughters, aged 9 and 10. Don Alfonso is blind. He grew up in a state institution where he was visited one day by the daughter of the owner of a poultry farm and feed factory. On her first visit she asked the children in the institution what they wanted. Some wanted clothes, others food, but Alfonso wanted some books. She was so impressed by this request that, upon her return, she asked whether there was something else that she could do for him. He replied that he wanted to work. She then persuaded her father, who was most reluctant, to give Alfonso a chance to prove his ability. He rose from chicken dresser to mechanic and salesman. Today he and his family are still involved in feed sales and occasionally raise of young chicks for market, but they also manufacture peanut butter, make cakes and run a kiosk for periodicals and notions for schoolchildren.

The last few years have been tough, but Alfonso and his wife are optimistic. They claim that they have seen bad times before and talk about the depression in 1956 that followed the revolution when they were children. In 1977, Alfonso bought a Bolivian machine to make peanut butter and had it reconstructed by bringing parts to local mechanical workshops to be custom made to his specifications. By doing so he saved 30% of the price of the usual imported machine. His skill and capital were derived from his work experience in the chicken-feed factory.

Alfonso and his wife obtain the peanuts from a long-term *casera*, a market trader, who assures the supply from Caranavi or Santa Cruz even in times of scarcity because the peanut-butter manufacturers are faithful customers and because they pay her a just price above the official posted rates. The peanut-producing areas are, of course, also the ones where coca is grown with increasing frequency and profit. Alfonso and his wife buy on a cash basis and used to sell on credit, but since the severe devaluation they try to be paid immediately. For reasons explained earlier, they distrust banks. Alfonso has a similar attitude toward credit. Once, he acted as a guarantor for a friend who then disappeared. He quotes the saying, "*Cuando alguien te pide que lo garantices, regalale el pasaje de regreso*" ("When someone asks you to be a guarantor, pay for his trip home").

He and his wife counter inflation and devaluation by curtailing all unnecessary consumption, by relying on wood, charcoal and agricultural goods acquired through friends and kin in the country and charitable contributions, such as milk from Caritas, which is distributed by Mothers' Clubs and by investing any cash they earn immediately into goods and/or services. All savings go into the construction of a house in Alto Següencoma. They never buy things when they are expensive, i.e., when they are scarce, or before a devaluation, but they do buy goods just before they disappear because at that time people sell goods at the real value. They are self-exploiting and have curtailed their various enterprises to meet lower demands.

With regard to their peanut-butter business, the lack of imports has benefited their sales in La Paz and as far away as Peru, but the decline of wages has left many customers without resources to buy nonessential foods. Also foreign clients have left. They complain about the bureaucratic red tape to get permits to run their firm. If they complied with all the regulations, they claim that they would make no profit whatsoever.

In a year or two, they plan to put their two daughters to work in the kiosk. They hope to live in their own house and add salted nuts to their product. They are also negotiating with a large cookie factory to set up a deal in which they will supply the factory with peanut butter for cookies. When they grow up, the daughters hope to open a restaurant and pastry shop and to relieve their parents of the extra work involved in selling magazines.

The lesson then to be learned from Don Alfonso and his family and the other cases described is the importance of fostering intellectual agility and low-cost, labor-intensive enterprises that do not require external financing, that have a multiplier effect, and that are geared to a local market but can expand to include exports or tourist demand but are not dependent on them. We will explore these options in greater detail in subsequent chapters.

Notes

1. By 1987, the *New York Times* was reporting again on the new "acrimony over world debt" and the tougher obstacles in new Latin borrowing (*New York Times*, 5/21/87).

2. We wish to acknowledge the contribution of Simone Buechler to the writing of this section.

3. Although Arensberg has criticized models built on economic decision-making, such as Barnes's transaction model, because they tend to deal with economic actors in pairs while "cultures shape numbers far larger than pairs" (1972:4), this objection would not apply to models that take much more complex arrangements of interacting individuals as their points of departure.

3

The Actors: Rural-Urban Migrants and Long-Term Residents

In this chapter we will deal with the general characteristics of small-scale producers are discussed, particularly in terms of the social resources they employ to enter into activities and further their careers.

Significant differences exist between first-generation migrants from rural areas and longer-term residents in La Paz. Some of these differences, particularly those related to the learning of skills, will be dealt with in greater detail in Chapter 5.

About the same percentage of migrants and persons born in La Paz are engaged in commerce, but more migrants are salaried (Escobar de Pabón and Maletta 1980:56), and as a corollary, at least among recent migrants, fewer are engaged as independent workers (Casanovas 1985:223-224). A higher percentage of migrants are employed in manual work, especially in construction, and they are twice as likely to be in domestic service (Escobar de Pabón and Maletta 1981:48,49,56). In contrast, fewer are employed in industry (Escobar de Pabón and Maletta 1981:48). They work more hours than their nonmigrant counterparts and are more likely to be "underemployed," in the sense that they not only wish to work more but are actively searching for additional work (Escobar de Pabón and Maletta 1981:57,59). However, migrants are less likely to be unemployed (7.7% versus 12.8% of the nonmigrants), and their primary income does not differ appreciably nonmigrants (1981:64,66).

Rural-Urban Migration and Small-Scale Industries

The special role of rural-urban migration in Andean industrialization has been underlined by many researchers. Not only do Andean countries like Bolivia and Peru share in the massive global movement to the cities, but perhaps in Andean countries more than in other areas, the rural communities of origin continue to play a major role in the migrants' economic strategies. Thus Laite (in Long and Roberts 1978:73-

95) concludes that the Peruvian solution of "circulatory migration to handle problems of industrial change in Peru is in marked contrast to the creation of an urban-born proletariat in the industrialized nations" (p. 95). Indeed, in some villages in the Mantaro valley, "more than half the economically active population were engaged in non-agricultural activities as their principal source of income. These families continue to retain and work land and regard it as an essential component of their household economy; at the same time, it is often the opportunity for external urban work that enables them to continue in the village" (Long and Roberts in Long and Roberts 1978:319). Similarly, Doughty describes the sharecropping arrangements that emigrants from Huaylas in Lima make with siblings and other relatives to cultivate land in the village (1968:102). In return, the migrants send presents to their relatives back home, participate in fiestas, in the home community, and give public gifts for town improvement (1968:180,232,234).[1]

In Bolivia, the situation is in many ways analogous. Rural-urban migrants continue to visit their communities of origin at least during fiestas and many retain or attempt to retain economic interests there (Buechler and Buechler 1971; Preston 1978). At the same time, migrants transform the economy of cities, a fact that has often been overlooked or even denied by social scientists.[2]

Migrants to cities in the Third World are often described as entering into preexisting niches in the urban economy that may, or may not, be able to absorb them. We deem this view as simplistic and, indeed, erroneous. We argue instead that migrants create networks that help to shape the urban economy by introducing and organizing new activities and transforming traditional urban ones. Although the cultural contribution of migrants has been acknowledged in such concepts as "the peasantization of cities" or "retribalization in cities" (Eames and Goode 1977:50-51) and the concept of "circulatory migration" (Trager 1988), their economic innovations have received less attention. This is perhaps due to the fact that their economic innovations cannot be accounted for adequately by models of diffusion or adaptation, predicated as those models are on the initial distinction and isolation of the rural and the urban. In reality, many of these processes of economic innovation and transformation are the result of bidirectional rural-urban linkages that have become more prominent as a result of the recent massive inflow of migrants to Third World cities.

The Scope of the Migratory Process

According to a study by Escobar de Pabón and Maletta, about half (47%) of the La Paz population, aged 10 and above, has had migratory experience (1981:7).[3] Almost two thirds of the migrants (62%) come from rural areas (Escobar de Pabón and Maletta 1981:20).[4] Of these migrants, 43.6% have been in La Paz for less than 10 years (1981:8). In addition, the rate of migration to La Paz has increased in recent years.

The average annual increase in the urban population through migration was 2.27% between 1976 and 1980, which exceeded the rates of 1.14% for 1950-1971 and 1.46% for 1971-1976 (1981:15). Albó's figures (Albó et al. 1981:51) are even higher. He and his co-workers calculated that out of a total of 1,385 migrants from rural areas interviewed in La Paz, the average annual rate of migration was 1.3% between 1946 and 1951, 2.3% between 1962 and 1964, and 6% between 1971 and 1976.

The magnitude of migration is equally salient when viewed from the point of origin. The 1976 census indicates that in almost every province of the department of La Paz, one out of every four to five persons was forced to migrate (Albó et al. 1981:44-45). In some rural communities such as Ojje, located in a particularly crowded area on the shores of Lake Titicaca, the total number of migrants amounts to almost half of the community's recent population.

Most of the migrants to La Paz (89%) come from within the department (Escobar de Pabón and Maletta 1981:19). In contrast, in other Bolivian cities only 1/3 to 1/5 of the migrants are from the same department (Albó et al. 1981:44). Migrants constitute a high percentage of the economically active population, i.e., 61.2% (Escobar de Pabón and Maletta 1981:48).

The History of Migration

The earliest migrants tended to be mestizo townsmen, *vecinos*, rather than Aymara and Quechua peasants, who traditionally lived in dispersed settlements (Albó et al. 1981:39-40; see also Mc Ewen 1975:119,147,185-186). Since the 1940s, peasants have migrated in increasing numbers as well.[5]

The social revolution and agrarian reform of 1952-53 had a major impact on migration patterns. The reform led to the dismantling of haciendas (landed estates run according to a semi-feudal system), which freed the peasants who had cultivated the landlords' lands for up to twelve man labor days a week per family in return for subsistence plots, and resulted in the distribution of most of the land among the former serfs. The latter, as well the *comuneros*, the peasants from *comunidades*, communities that had managed to remain free from the large landowners, also benefited from communal suffrage, a massive rural education program, and an increased political voice in local governments and in peasant unions. Peasants from both ex-haciendas and *comunidades* were also able to take advantage of easier access to urban markets. Rather than going through traditional middlemen or middlewomen, they could now sell their produce directly in large weekend fairs established throughout the city.

Both before and after the agrarian reform, migration patterns appear to have been influenced by a community's status as an hacienda or *comunidad*. In an extensive study of Compi, a former hacienda on the shores of Lake Titicaca, and Llamacachi, a neighboring *comunidad*, and a survey of nearby neighboring *comunidades* (H. Buechler 1966), we found that *comuneros* were more likely than the peasants from the haciendas to suffer from the lack of land when they migrated but at the same time were more flexible and more able to diversify their activities and were able to plan their moves to the city or to the subtropical Yungas valleys. Hacienda peons often left for the city abruptly, as a result of some misfortune: the loss of sheep from the hacienda's herds entrusted to them; a shortfall of *chuño* (frozen dried potatoes) processed from the landlord's potatoes, which they were forced to make up with their own; or a particularly abusive overseer, who made it impossible or at least even more arduous than usual to fulfill the onerous obligations toward their landlord (Buechler and Buechler 1971:12). On the ex-hacienda we studied in depth, most of the early migrants left between 1935 and 1943, when work conditions seem to have been particularly severe, even though land was abundant. In some instances, such as on a small hacienda on a nearby island, the landlord arbitrarily forced families to leave when he felt that there were too many families on the hacienda.

From the foregoing, one would expect to find a high pre-reform migration rate from haciendas. In fact, haciendas had smaller population densities and larger plots per family than *comunidades* in the same areas. But Albó et al. (1981:39,51) found that migration rates to La Paz were similar from both kinds of communities. One explanation for the apparent paradox may be the practice we found in the hacienda of Compi of peasants going to live with kin in the neighboring *comunidad* enclaves. This practice would have put additional pressure on *comuneros* to migrate. In addition, the figures reported by Albó et al. may not take into account a long enough time span for an adequate comparison of migration trends. Whatever the case may be, the more unpredictable timing of migration from haciendas resulted in a different migration process.

Migrants from *comunidades* (and presumably from towns as well) often employed chain migration tactics to establish themselves in the city. The process would begin with the move of a pioneer member to the city, who eventually became established in artisanry or in small-scale production. This migrant was soon followed by kin and former neighbors, some of whom became apprentices and, in some instances, boarders as well. A group of communities on the shores of Lake Titicaca provides a good illustration of this process. Migrants from these communities tend to specialize in similar trades or to migrate to the same rural areas. Thus, in the 1950s or 1960s, one or two migrants from Amakari became tailors in La Paz. In 1965 the number of migrants who were their kin or former neighbors from Amakari had increased to around 50, representing three quarters of the migrants from that community in the city (H. Buechler 1966:130). Their neighbors from Ojje engaged in this trade as well in baking. In 1977, Sandóval et al. found that out of 162 male migrants from Ojje, 59%

were engaged in the garment industry and 14% were bakers (1978:85). The same phenomenon is true for migration from other places. Many persons from Tiquina go to work in the mines in order to save money to invest in car ferries and passenger boats to transport travelers across the straights. From Chiquipata, many travel to La Paz and to the subtropical yungas valleys to transport and deal in coca, whereas many families from Chicharro have migrated to San Agustin, an hacienda in the Yungas. The "founder effect" can also be seen with jewelers from Chajaya. Jewelry making is not traditional to Chajaya, but a number of migrants have taken up the trade in La Paz and in other cities. They followed the example of one *paisano* (person from the same community of origin) who initiated the activity.

In contrast with migrants from *comunidades* who employed this process of chain migration, migrants from ex-haciendas (if Compi is at all representative) entered a wider array of occupations (see Table 3.1). Early migration from Compi was abrupt. Deteriorating conditions on the hacienda set off a migratory wave. Few migrants could therefore rely on already established kin or former neighbors for jobs. Their first jobs were often the most menial kind, particularly carrying and distributing bread to stores. This occupation required only a minimal knowledge of Spanish, an important consideration for these early migrants, who were unable to attend schools. In time, they sought more varied jobs and gradually improved their lot. Thereby they broadened the career choices of later migrants, whom they took in as apprentices or for whom they found employment. The contrast between pre-reform migration patterns in *comunidades* and haciendas should not be overdrawn, however, for as Sandoval et al. have pointed out (1978:85), 76% of the men from the *comunidad* of Ojje have been engaged in more than one occupation since their arrival in La Paz, and 34% have changed their occupations three or four times. In addition, Albó et al. (1981:130) found that a high percentage of both very recent and longer-term migrants claimed to have found their present job without any assistance.[6]

After the agrarian reform, migration processes probably did not differ for *comunidades* and haciendas. However, the fact that haciendas were, at least initially, less crowded led to a slower rate of emigration. In the first 12 years after the agrarian reform, 68.1% of the migrants in Albó and co-workers' sample of 1,083 migrants to La Paz (1981:51) were from comunidades and 31.9% were from ex-haciendas, with only a slight lessening of the differential thereafter.

Linkages with the Community of Origin: Fiestas, Marriage, Residence, Jobs, and Land

Fiestas. Chain migration is an aspect of a much wider phenomenon of linkages with the place of origin. Out of 23 Compi migrants interviewed in 1966, 17 had regular contact with fellow migrants from

Table 3.1 Occupations of Migrants from Two
Lake Titicaca Communities

	Compi/Llamacachi N = 106		Ojje N = 162
	N	%	%
Artisans	45	42.5	
Tailors	23		59
Bakers	8		14
Bread Distrib.	7		
Carpenters	4		
Shoemakers	3		
Other Artisans			4
Factory Workers	17	16.0	9
Construction Trades	14	13.2	
masons	10		
painters	3		
adobe makers	1		
Students	not included		3
Public & private employees	16	15.1	4
policemen	5		
musicians in the army	4		
military	1		
cemetery work.	2		
municipal work.	1		
radio announcer	1		
teacher	1		
driver for soc. security	1		
Merchant	1	0.9	4
Store helper	5	4.7	
Transportation a.	3	2.7	
Owner of rice peeling mach.	1	0.9	
Stevedore	4	3.8	

a. 1 truck owner, 1 driver, 1 *assistant*.

Source: Compi and Llamacachi data from 1966 survey by H. Buechler.
Ojje data from G. Sandóval, G., X. Albó and T. Greaves
*Ojje por encima de todo. Historia de un centro de residentes ex-campesinos
en La Paz*. La Paz: Cuaderno de Investigación CIPCA, No. 16.,1978,
p85.

the same community, or *paisanos*; 4 claimed that such contacts were rare; and only 2 said that they had lost practically all such contacts. Of the 21 who maintained contacts, 8 specifically mentioned fiestas, especially rites of passage, as major occasions for contact. Indeed, some *paisanos* who rarely see one another during the year invite fellow migrants to attend rites of passage (H. Buechler 1980:158,188,301). Migrants also organize dance groups composed mainly of fellow migrants. Especially in the past, migrants participated in La Paz neighborhood fiestas in this manner (H. Buechler 1980:298). Today, organizing or participating in dance groups in the community of origin still constitutes a major means of keeping up ties in the home community and at the same time reinforcing ties among fellow migrants in the city (H. Buechler 1980:320). Even persons who fled from intolerable conditions on haciendas organized such dance groups. Participation in the same soccer club in La Paz or in the home community has similar functions. Thus many Compi migrants participate in the regional soccer matches held during the Easter week back home.

Kin Ties. Due to the frequent contacts between *paisanos*, marriage between members of the same rural community of origin remains frequent even after they have migrated. Out of the 55 migrants from Compi we studied in 1965, 9 were married when they arrived, 14 married Compeños after migration, 6 married migrants from nearby communities, and 26 married persons from elsewhere on the altiplano and from La Paz. As in Compi itself, relatives remain the most important links in an individual's social network. Out of 25 persons questioned, all but one lived with one or more relatives or ritual kin in the same compound or next door. The main difference between residential patterns in La Paz and those in the home community is that in La Paz a wider range of relatives live together. Most of these are close relatives, i.e., siblings of either spouse, parents, nephews and nieces and, more rarely, cousins. Changes in residence are also more frequent for migrants in La Paz than in the home village. Thus, in La Paz, one Compeño first shared a compound with his sister, then with his wife's brother and finally with his wife's brother and his wife's mother. Another lived first with his uncle, then with his father and brother and finally with his godchild related to him as a father's brother's son. Still another stayed with a cousin when he first came to La Paz and then with a father's brother's son and a *compadre* from Chua. Later he allowed his father's brother's daughter's son to come to live with him so that he could study in the city.

In Compi, kin ties through one's wife can receive equal recognition to kin ties through the male only under certain circumstances. A man lives with his wife's relatives only when she has access to substantially more land than he. This is rare, since males inherit the largest share of the land. Bilaterality would increase the already considerable fragmentation. In contrast to patrilineality in rural communities, the wife's relatives are as important as the husband's in the city. In our La Paz sample, 10 male migrants were living or had lived with relatives of their wives, especially wives' brothers, wives' mothers and wives' fathers, an observation which explains the prominent position of the wife's relatives in La Paz fiestas. The greater flexibility in kin relationships in the city is not surprising. It has been observed in similar contexts elsewhere. Complete bilaterality greatly increases the network segment associated with finding scarce lodgings as well as jobs. Furthermore, women frequently continue to sell goods in the market after marriage, inheriting their market locations and clientele through their mothers. Thus the husband's ties with his in-laws are strengthened.

Continued Access to Land in the Home Community. Access to land in the home community can mean anything from a safety net during a recession to a small, sporadic supplement to the household economy, a regular part of an urban household's subsistence strategies, or a basis for fairly ambitious entrepreneurial ventures.

Reliable quantitative studies of the extent to which migrants continue to have access to land are as yet unavailable. In our study of migration from Compi to La Paz in 1965 and 1967, 13 out of 22 migrants retained access to either land or a share of the harvest and two others hoped to obtain some land in the future. In a wider survey of market vendors undertaken in 1967, we included questions regarding access to land. However, since the informants rarely specified whether they obtained products from the land and whether they returned to work there, the exact nature of their access to land remained unclear. Such responses as "Yes we have land; my siblings cultivate it" could mean, for example, that the informant had sharecropping arrangements with siblings, that siblings gave the informants gifts of produce in exchange for bread, fruit or dry goods bought in La Paz, or that the informant had not entirely given up the idea of claiming a share of the family land. With these limitations in mind, it is nevertheless significant that only 22.6% of the 133 migrant vendors to whom the question was addressed did not make any claims on land. For the first generation of La Paz-born vendors, this figure increased to 64.4%, and for subsequent generations, to 87.8%. A person's access to land definitely appears to decrease with increasing length of residence in La Paz. The figures, however, may not tell the entire story, for migrants may send a child to live with rural-based kin during an emergency situation, or they may attempt to regain a stake in the land after many years by sending a family member to assist close kin during the harvest.

Aymara Land Tenure Patterns

An understanding of access to land requires a fairly lengthy exegesis into the complex arrangements among altiplano peasants. Access to land is not simply a matter of individual ownership. Nor can such distinctions as ownership, sharecropping and cash rental adequately describe such relationships. Rather, individuals make varying claims on land depending on their status as community members and their descent from, or marriage into, land-holding families and/or depending on their active participation in community affairs and in the exploitation of land. Jural status as community or family member is important. Outsiders who have acquired land in a community through purchases risk being dispossessed.[7] Even outsiders who acquire rights to land through marriage may find their access contested by a spouse's male kin. Yet jural status does not guarantee an individual's rights. These must be maintained and consolidated by fulfilling obligations toward the community and one's kin. Failure or inability to do so lessens a person's hold over land. Conversely, an individual who sponsors dance groups, holds leadership positions, or regularly assists others may thereby acquire certain rights. As we have described elsewhere, (Buechler 1980:20-21), children typically acquire land as follows:

> Inheritance predominantly follows the male line. Each son receives a share of land usually after (but today sometimes even before) he marries. Often sons remain partly dependent upon their fathers for some time after their marriage, entering into a wide variety of agreements with them. Either the youngest son or the last son to marry usually inherits the parental home, but assumes the obligation to take care of his mother should she survive his father. A provisional division of the land between the last remaining son and the father may occur while the father is still living. Married daughters or daughters about to marry usually receive only *chiquiñas*, i.e., the usufruct right to a specified number of furrows in each plot owned by the family, or sometimes one of the smaller plots either from the father or, especially when the father has died, from the eldest brother. Women are entitled to the produce from these furrows or plots for as long as they aid their fathers or eldest brothers with the agricultural tasks associated with plot in which the *chiquiñas* are located. On the other hand, daughters inherit the land when there are no sons in the family. In this case a father often prefers one of his daughters to marry a man with little access to land in order to secure a partner in all agricultural tasks, inducing him to move into or close to his compound. A daughter or even a granddaughter who has taken care of her mother in her old age may also be favored. All these arrangements are very flexible and depend on the particular circumstances.[8]

As we have indicated, all arrangements concerning land are associated with work obligations. A group of persons we observed harvesting barley may serve to illustrate these relationships. It consisted of Agapito; his wife; Marcelino, who is one of Agapito's married sons;

his wife and their seven-year-old son; the husband of Agapito's eldest daughter; an unmarried daughter; and a *comadre* (the mother of his wife's godchild). Marcelino received 2 to 15 furrows in each plot as did his brother (who was not present that day). The son-in-law and the unmarried daughter each received a certain amount of barley, as did another sister who came only for an hour or so at the end of that day. The *comadre*, who was not closely related, received a much lesser amount. Arrangements concerning access to land can thus be seen primarily as flexible working agreements in which children and their spouses play a prominent role.

Family ties are not the only basis for arrangements concerning production. As seen in the above example, ritual kin or other individuals may aid in the field in return for some produce or may rent or sharecrop land. Ritual godparenthood, customary for baptism rituals and marriage, is usually established on the basis of a preexisting tie which it confirms or strengthens. The godparent may have been a neighbor, an acquaintance in La Paz or in the Yungas, a person who has served in the same capacity to other individuals and is known to fulfill his ritual duties well, or a colleague in a music band.[9]

A few landless individuals, including illegitimate children, gain access to land by offering their aid to persons with more land than they do in return for a household plot and *chiquiñas*. Thereby they become *utawawas*, (literally "children of the house"), which are adopted children.[10]

The hacienda system itself was an important influence on inter-familial relationships concerning land. In many instances, two families which were often but not necessarily related shared a portion of land allotted to them by the hacienda. Finally, many peasants who had left the hacienda previous to agrarian reform attempted, after the reform, to claim the parcels they had cultivated. A handful succeeded in obtaining at least some land. Some claims were never settled completely, which resulted in sources of conflict among many Compeños.

In some *comunidades*, particularly on the peninsula of Copacabana, where land shortage has made it impossible for all but a few families to live entirely from agriculture, sons and daughters inherit equal shares of land. In others, all daughters together receive a share equal to that of a single son (Carter 1964:55).

An individual's move to La Paz or elsewhere further complicates the land tenure situation. Persons who had full access to a plot of land previous to their departure for the city, e.g. through inheritance, usually find it easier than other migrants to retain access. They may cultivate the land by sharecropping or rental, or they may even continue to undertake some of the major agricultural tasks themselves. Thus, of the 13 Compi migrants in our 1967 study with access to land, 7 still helped at least during harvest time, while 3 sent their wives to help in harvesting the crops. J.-M. Buechler's study of market

women (J.-M. Buechler 1972) revealed that out of 17 vendors with full
access to land who provided detailed enough information, 7
sharecropped their land, receiving half of the production minus seed
reserves; 5 rented it; and 5 either attended to the production personally
or received an unspecified share of the produce. Finally, in a survey
of migrants to La Paz from communities near the southern end of Lake
Titicaca, Preston (1978:98-99) found that the respondents disposed of
land differently in each community. In one community, 82% of the
respondents sold their land, almost invariably to the members of the
same community and 18% usually rented or sharecropped it. In
another community, the corresponding figures were 37% and 63%. In
the remaining two communities, informants claimed for the most part
to be renting or sharecropping their land.[11]

Our 1981-88 study provides indications that these patterns of
ownership of land by migrants continue. For many migrant households, access to agricultural land forms a significant part of their
economy. For example, a candle maker who received a parcel of land
from his father was able to obtain five *cargas* (750 kilos) of potatoes
from his field, two of which he has set aside as seed potatoes. The
father and son assist one another in their work. Similarly, Mr. Chok'e,
a jeweler from the area of Charazani, helps his father's sister cultivate
land in the tropical Caranavi area. In addition, he owns some land in
his home community that a relative works for him on a sharecropping
basis. In return for access to land, he has sponsored a fiesta in the
community.

A spouse's ties with his or her rural community of origin may
lead a person with few rural ties to become involved in agriculture.
An example is a woman in a weaving cooperative in one of the
neighborhoods in El Alto: she is a Paceña (a woman born in La Paz)
married to a migrant. Her relatives are upwardly mobile but have cut
her off. She continues to work her husband's land (or land to which
her husband has access) in a community that is heavily involved in
bayeta (handwoven woolen cloth) production. Her father-in-law is also
involved in *bayeta* making. She says,"We only have small pieces of land
because they have been subdivided."

For those who moved to La Paz before they were allotted a share
of the family land, access to land is often problematic. The migrant
members often resent the fact that their siblings back home have been
allocated land permanently, while their own claims remain tenuous. For
example, Manuel Mena, a baker who originally came from the
lakeshore community of Llamacachi, resents the fact that his father
gave land to those brothers who remained in the community while
giving him access to land only on an ad hoc basis. He is still thinking
of retiring in his home community, which would be more feasible if
he had land of his own there.

Both men and women may be allotted *chiquiñas*, often in return
for their or their spouse's assistance during harvest.[12] The reciprocal

arrangements include the exchange of gifts. The migrants bring home tropical fruit or processed foods, such as flour or lard, and the rurally based kin bring homegrown produce on their visits to their urban kinsmen. Such arrangements are often discontinued upon the death of one or both parents. The case of a tailor from Compi we interviewed in 1981 is typical: When his father was still alive, he received a furrow or two of land in each of his father's parcels and in return brought his rural kin fruit from the city. When his father died, he no longer insisted on sharing access to the family land in this manner.

> I prefer those who live there to cultivate the land for themselves. I can live from what I earn with my work. Of course, when I go there they take good care of me. They invite me and give me at least a pound or so of potatoes and broad beans. And I, in turn, bring them fruit. Now, if I went there and asked for land from my parents and did not cultivate it, that would harm them. And since I live here, I can't work it. Of course, when my father was still alive, both I and my brother had access to produce. [He would tell me:] "I am cultivating this for you." But he died four years ago; only my mother is still living. And it is she who needs help because she is not well. Now my mother cultivates in two or three places, and when there is a fiesta, she waits for me with a little lunch, and she tells me: "The land has produced a little something; let's cook for ourselves." And so we cook for two or three days, and I get some rest. Then I return to La Paz. I only go there three or four times a year. In contrast, my brother goes there every Sunday because he is in charge of the civil registry there. So he goes in my stead.

Attenuated access to produce from the community of origin takes many forms. In some instances, like in the foregoing example, goods flow both ways. In other instances, no specific reciprocity is expected from the migrant household member. The parents or sometimes siblings simply send some produce at harvest time. Six out of twenty-three migrant vendors in the 1967 study mentioned earlier benefited from such arrangements. Similarly, a tinsmith we interviewed in 1981 from Compaya does not have direct access to land in his community of origin, but his brother and sister bring some produce when they come to visit him in the city.

A migrant may be able to gain access to land even when he can make no direct claim on family land. With roots in a community, he is much more likely to be allowed to purchase a plot of land. For example, Raúl owns some land in Compi, his home community, that he purchased from the former owner of the hacienda. In addition, he rents land and helps relatives in return for access to land. Since his wife commutes between La Paz and Compi, where she has a store, she can keep an eye on the land. She also raises pigs, which she sells in La Paz.

Similarly, Pedro, whose father had been expelled by the patron of Compi in pre-reform times and who had become a baker in La Paz, was able to purchase land in Compi. His wife and children remained in Compi for some years, occasionally traveling to La Paz with produce from the fields, which Pedro's wife continued to cultivate. A few years later, the family moved to La Paz permanently. After the social revolution of 1952, the MNR party, which took power, encouraged the formation of all sorts of cooperatives and other organizations, and Pedro organized a credit union in Compi. After a while, he left his job in the Ministry of Peasant Affairs because he was disenchanted with the manner in which peasant leaders in Achacachi, the main center of political activism on the altiplano, were conducting and threatening to conduct raids in the general Compi area. Then, he helped form a cooperative with the former patron's son to cultivate the land which had not been expropriated. Later, he was instrumental in liquidating the property by purchasing some land for himself and securing some for his migrant brother as well. The brothers cultivated these lands through sharecropping arrangements with neighbors. Finally, Pedro built a house on his land.

Since that time, the family has maintained one foot in the city and the other in Compi. They moved back to La Paz and opened a dry goods-store there, but they also raise pigs with hired help in the home community. Before an epidemic killed Pedro's pigs, he was reputed to own some 400 pigs. In a community where very few families traditionally raised more than a dozen pigs, his was an innovative venture indeed. Disillusioned with raising hogs, his plans in 1984 were to buy reed plots in the lake, raise dairy cows and manufacture cheese.

Finally, Celestino, who began his career as a stevedore in La Paz and the tropical Yungas valleys, decided that commerce was a better option. He was able to acquire some land in Compi from the former landlord, where he planted onions that he sold in La Paz. Even after a long and successful career that has made him the proud owner of a lumberyard, he continues to incorporate this land in his household's economic strategies. To show his neighbors in Compi, who had laughed at his previous small house, that he has arrived in the world, he built a two-story house there that far exceeds his present needs. His wife still works the land regularly with the assistance of hired help and sells the onions in La Paz.

By maintaining access to land in the community of origin and keeping up ties with that community, the migrant leaves open the option for an eventual permanent return. The migrant returns when he has not been able to find a satisfactory livelihood in the city or when he has found that a biresidential existence with the home community as his principle base is advantageous. Although most of those we interviewed who returned were short-term migrants who worked in La Paz for a few months, a handful came back after many years in the city because of a landlord's request in pre-reform times or because the death of a father without an heir enabled them to obtain land after the agrarian reform.

Our 1981-1988 study indicated that migrants now sometimes see the place (or region) of origin not only as a source of food and marriage partners and as a place to visit during festive occasions but as a potential site for entrepreneurial activities as well. Celestino, whom we encountered earlier, planned at one point to leave the lumberyard to his sons, retire to Compi and open a small tourist hotel there. Similarly, one quite successful furniture manufacturer, in spite of economic setbacks occasioned by familial litigation and by nonpayment for furniture delivered to military officials, intended to invest the profits of his enterprise in a hotel/pension in his native Copacabana, a famous pilgrimage center on Lake Titicaca. In 1981, his only access to land there was in receiving some produce from the family land when he visited his home community. But he planned to buy a building lot in Copacabana from his parents and then sell half of it to raise the capital to build the hotel. When we attempted to look him up in 1984, he was no longer working there, but his neighbors claimed that he was still working in the city. Another migrant, a tailor, who was unable to prosper in the city, returned to claim his fields in his home community, although his wife remained in La Paz.

In conclusion, continued claims to land, as tenuous as they may be in many instances, remain an important factor in the life strategies of Bolivian rural-urban migrants in general and small-scale producers of rural origin in particular. With the deepening of Bolivia's current economic crisis, it is likely that more and more migrants, both in cities and in the even more profoundly affected mining areas, will attempt to reactivate their rural ties in order to contribute to their dwindling family incomes.

Families engaged in small-scale production would be particularly likely to take advantage of these ties, for they could gradually increase their involvement in farming during the slack periods in their workshops. The more dispensable household members could be sent first, followed--at least during the busiest period in the agricultural cycle and certainly for the harvest--by the shop owners themselves, who would not ordinarily have the time and incentive to visit their communities of origin. In 1984 we found some evidence that this was indeed taking place. As we shall see, ties to the countryside symbolized by claims to land are also vital for access to the means and social relations of production: raw materials, skills and labor.

Conclusion

The manifold and multifaceted casual to intense links that migrant small-scale producers continue to maintain with their communities of origin, which provide economic and social sustenance, provide ample evidence of a multilocal regional field of activities. This model refutes a biologistic notion of adaptation to a niche in a new locale, i.e., the city, and looks toward a model that captures the multicentered flows of persons, goods and experiences. The transfer of rural crafts to the city, the use of commonly held rural skills and the reliance on fellow migrants to initiate new skills are all processes incompatible with the view of migrants as persons filling preexistent niches. Migrants create networks that help to shape the urban economy by introducing and organizing new activities and transforming traditional urban ones.

General Characteristics of Long-Term Residents

As we have noted, at least over several generations, long-term residents in La Paz gradually lose access to land in their ancestral communities of origin. At the same time, they also lose a ready-made potential support network based on home ties. New networks are gradually created in La Paz. Some succeed in establishing strong ties in their residential neighborhoods, particularly if they also work there. These networks may be consolidated through fiesta sponsorship. But as one of us has shown elsewhere (H. Buechler 1980), even neighborhood fiestas include large numbers of participants from other parts of La Paz. Networks, then, are more geographically diffuse than in rural areas. As in rural areas, kin networks play a major role. Freed from the patrilateral bias present in rural land transmission, these networks become more bilateral even in the first migrant generation.

Perhaps the major difference between *Paceños*, or longterm residents, and migrants with regard to their potential for a successful career is the fact that *paceño* parents are often the most important resource for learning a trade (a matter we shall deal with at greater length in Chapter 5) and for obtaining the capital and materials to start a business; they also provide continued support in running it. Similarly, a spouse or his/her family may provide such support. As a corollary, being orphaned at an early age--a frequent occurrence in a Third World country--may place a particularly heavy burden on an individual.

Because parents and other close kin are such important economic resources for   the small-scale producer, individuals will often engage in the same trade as their siblings. Particularly in larger industries, a number of children may be employed by their parents and may eventually run the business as partners when their parents retire or die. However, individuals from established *paceño* families, also often enjoy considerably more life choices. They may enjoy a better education than their migrant counterparts, and a sibling set may follow a variety of career paths.

The economic linkages of *paceño* children with parents are readily discernible in the case of an artisan/vendor who produces and sells colonial-style furniture. His grandfather carved minuscule table settings out of wood and enclosed them in wooden eggs. His father sells antique weavings. His mother and he also play a number of musical instruments. The informant worked in the United States for a time as a "teacher in commercial pictures" and then came back to engage in his present trade. Like his father, he also sells antiques, and his mother is involved in the business by bringing things to sell in the store.

Another example, the case of a woman who has opened a small printing enterprise, illustrates the influence of spouses in selecting an activity and in running a business. Señora Patricia Guachalla was originally an executive secretary. But she lost two good jobs: one when the medical supply importer she worked for went bankrupt, and the other when the university at which she worked closed during a period of political strife. Then, she decided to establish a printing firm for cards, letterheads and calendars. Her husband works as a skilled supervisor and mechanic for a large printing press during the day. They bought a second hand printing press on credit, in U.S. dollars, at an interest rate of five percent per month. Her husband has access to an offset printing machine at an advantageous rate and, in return, does not charge for repairing the machine whenever it breaks down. They are also dependent on a private semimonopoly for imported paper that is subject to constant price increases.

Señora Patricia solicits clients in the neighborhood and from offices, banks, associations and acquaintances and designs, prints, loads and delivers the stationery herself. In a good month, with many subcontracts from larger firms and orders from private individuals, she can earn as much as US $240. But in a poor month, her earnings may fall as low as six dollars. Not only does demand vary, but payments are often delayed for as long as six months, especially for government contracts.

To understand this woman's work, we must analyze the family resources in terms of labor and capital. Patricia's husband earns US $250 a month as a printer for a large printing press. He helps her at night and during the weekend. They live in two rooms in her parents' home, "practically rent free." Her father is an inspector for Bolivian Power and spends a grueling twelve-hour day checking meters. Since he is exhausted when he comes home at night, her father does not help her with her printing, but he does solicit clients. Her mother rents out a room as storage space for electric stoves. She also works at home, cares for her grandchildren and assists in loading and delivering the heavy stacks of printed materials and delivering them to their destination.

This example shows how the family, by pooling its resources, provided a cheap source of shelter and maintenance, expanded its services to cover the unemployment of the wife and the under-employment of the husband and father, and made it possible to live on low wages. By filling subcontracts, Patricia's small firm also serves as a crisis buffer for larger firms, but at the same time it suffers from an inability to obtain reasonable credit, inflationary prices for its raw materials and long, bureaucratic delays in payments.

Both in-laws and members of the extended family played a crucial role in Poleras Muñoz, Muñoz T-shirts, a case that also illustrates the manner in which close kinsmen become involved in the same trade. Mr. Muñoz was originally a tailor. In 1970 he purchased a knitting machine from his father-in-law and obtained an army contract worth $200. Then he gradually enlarged his firm, and by 1981 he had at least four machines, including a circular knitting machine imported from Germany. His total weekly production amounted to some 70 dozen garments. One of his brothers works for him (after working for his other brother), and the other two work independently in the same trade but with smaller machines. Two brothers-in-law are also engaged in the same occupation. The brothers sell or even give one another equipment they do not need.

A negative instance further illustrates the importance of kinship over several generations. Here, Mario, an orphan, has *few* long-lasting ties to fall back on in times of adversity, while the wife, despite serious economic hardship, has managed to cope, in part thanks to her kin network. When we interviewed Mario in 1981, he painted signs and metal furniture. He worked in a tiny room with a bedroom partition, where he lived alone. His wife and stepchildren lived in another part of the city in a much nicer house, belonging to the wife's extended family. She came regularly to make cookies that she then brought to a nearby baker's oven. Their marriage was on the rocks and was soon to dissolve.

Mario had always liked to draw and paint. In school he always had a beautiful *carpeta*--a notebook in which he, like generations of Bolivians students, copied standard lectures from a blackboard for hours on end and then illustrated them at home with drawings and cut-outs from magazines. Grades were not only based on the student's ability to memorize the contents of these lectures, but they were also based on the neatness of the student's handwriting and the quantity and quality of the illustrations. Mario excelled in the latter and had always wanted to become a painter.

One day, when he was working as a messenger in the advertising firm of a foreigner, his boss asked him to draw a sign with a paintbrush. The boss was impressed. Mario, who had already been observing the sign-painting process, learned rapidly. He stayed on for two years and then opened his own shop. He painted signs for workshops, advertisements on white-washed sign walls, and cribs and other metal objects that other artisans brought to be spray painted. In addition, he had a regular job as a ticket controller in a cinema, where he also re-lettered the advertising posters sent by the film producers. These were often in other languages, so the original lettering had to be covered over (sometimes twice) with paint and new lettering added.

Mario's major problem was a lack of adequate working space. Not only was he poisoning himself with the paint thinners (a problem we shall analyze in greater detail in Chapter 8) because his room lacked adequate ventilation, but he had little space in which to hang the signs to dry. He lost a lot of time because he had to wait for each small batch of posters to dry on the clothesline just outside his room before he could paint another batch. And, of course, on rainy days the logistics became even more complicated. Sometimes his fifteen-year-old son came to help him after school: "The boy has learned a lot. He is already better than I am. He already knows how to draw figures and things like that." Mario was hoping that his son would study at the university. To ensure his success, he and his wife were planning to send him to two schools, one public and one private, at the same time, so that if he failed in one, he might still have a chance to make the grade in the other. Mario earned between $b. 2,000 and 4,000 (US $80 to 160) per month. In addition to his regular activities, he made decorations out of paper for Carnival. But in 1980 he did not have the time to make any. In 1981, other decorations made out of plastic film became fashionable, and with so many persons making them, the market became glutted. For the Christmas season, he makes small artifical trees.

Silvia, Mario's wife of six years, was 36 years old in 1981. She had been divorced before (her first husband, who worked in a leather shop, later died in an accident), and she had two sons, nine and fourteen years old, both from her first marriage. Mario's assertions to the contrary, she claimed that he did not provide any financial support for her children. Her father came from Potosí and ran the veteran's benevolent association until his death in 1973. Her mother's family have been *paceños* for at least three generations. Fortunately, Silvia was able to live in a pleasant house located in a narrow alley within a fifteen minute walk to downtown La Paz. She and her two brothers inherited the house from her mother, who had died four years earlier. We were received in an airy, well-furnished living-dining room decorated with her husband's posters.

Her brothers ran a successful workshop, where they made high-quality furniture. A cousin, who rented a room from her for $b. 150 (US $6) per month, also lived in the compound. In addition, she rents out a store and an extra room on the ground floor for $b. 500 (US $ 20).

Silvia engaged in a number of economic activities, the most important of which was baking coconut cookies. She learned to bake these sweets when she was only seven by watching a neighbor who owned the oven where her mother roasted peanuts. She then began making some of these sweets for her mother to sell. In addition to baking cookies, she worked in a canning factory during the week. She worked there from the age of fourteen until she was twenty. She also engaged in dressmaking for two and a half years, but she had to stop when she married and was pregnant with her first child. Sporadically, she still sewed some aprons and furniture covers for people in the area. At one point, she also worked as a servant for a Spanish family for a year and a half. They had wanted to take her with them to Spain, but she was unable to leave her mother.

In 1981, she made some fifty pounds of cookies a week, earning about $b. 1000 (US $40). She sold them wholesale to sweet vendors and also retailed them in her own two stalls, one of which she ran herself. For the other, she hired a young woman who had a three-month-old baby. This woman could not find a job as a servant because families do not want to be bothered by small children. According to Mario's landlady, Silvia took care of herself and was not dependent on her husband for money. Like her husband, she also made special goods for fiestas, including sugar coated almonds for Carnival which she sells on the street. For Alasita, the fair at which miniature objects are sold, which we shall discuss later, she crafts miniature containers with food, a skill she learned from her mother.

While Silvia was managing reasonably well in 1981, her luck had changed for the worse when we interviewed her again three years later. As we saw in Chapter 2, the deepening economic crisis was hitting her particularly hard. In addition, as we shall see in Chapter 8, she had lost much of her capital through theft. To tide herself over, she was forced to sell her kiosk, although she retained the right to reopen it. Mario, with whom she had been quarreling constantly because of his frequent drinking bouts and the fact that he rarely gave her any money, had abandoned her for another woman, who not only sold his equipment, to which Silvia had contributed, but also sold some of Silvia's personal belongings, including a liquifier, dishes and furniture that she had left in his room.

Silvia then started to work as a cook for a woman from the Beni. But she could not stand her boss's vulgarity. In addition, the pay was very low and the work hard. She developed a back problem, which dissuaded her from returning to making cookies, an occupation that involved a lot of heavy carrying. Also, she simply could not come up with the capital to do so. When we interviewed her in 1984, she was doing the laundry for several families.

Silvia's sons, however, were doing well. The eldest was going to evening school so he could get his high school degree and was taking two hours of mechanics as well. She hoped that with a high school degree he would be "somebody" and could get a job in some office or ministry. His desire was to become a pilot, if only he could earn enough to cover the cost of training. At the same time that he was going to evening school, he was working as a mechanic at the military airport and was contributing economically to the household. W h e n Silvia went to do the laundry, she took her younger son along. He helped her with one thing or another, thereby earning lunch and tea. Her base, with a secure house and fraternal relations, and her "investment" in her sons for the next generation should provide her with the necessary cushion for economic shocks now and in the future.

A father's successful occupation and/or enterprise may enable his sons to engage in activities that are related to his own in various ways or, alternatively, may make it possible for them to choose different careers that require more education. The Blanes family serves as an illustration. The father, who works as a mechanic for the air force, also owned a bus. One son worked for some Argentinians making bus bodies and then opened an independent body shop when the company went broke. He had capital totalling approximately $b. 60,000 (US $2,400). Another son was a head of personnel for a printing shop. A third son worked for his brother at the body shop for a commission while he was studying. He seemed to be an eternal student. His father sent him to Argentina to study, but he played in a folklore group instead. At that time he became a Mormon. In 1981, he earned a living making insignia for the air force, a contract he obtained through his father. When there was no work, he operated his father's bus. No one else drives the bus. In this case, then, one son followed in his father's footsteps but in a more independent way; another chose a different occupation; and the third was able to coast along without much concern about his future career, but depends on his father for some work.

More prosperous producers rely on family ties in a similar manner. The main difference is that in these families a number of siblings or children may be employed in the same enterprise. The background of one such producer included landed wealth and professional status. The maternal grandmother had property in Sorata. She was a *Paceña*, but she and her family lived on the Sorata property. The paternal grandparents are teachers in Peru. The informant works in her father's upscale jewelry shop. One sister studied commerce and another economics. The older sister opened a store, but because her husband's trade is not connected to jewelry, she was not able to continue in the family tradition. Her brother is studying geology and working in a store in Geneva, Switzerland. He plans to come back and work in the jewelry trade as well. Another brother is studying to become an architect in Fribourg, Switzerland. But, as the woman we interviewed says, all her siblings have commerce in their blood.

Although siblings from wealthy families may work in the same enterprise, the range of activities engaged in by such sibling sets is often even more varied than the activities of siblings in less-wealthy families, a fact which is apparent in the case of a man who heads the tanning section of a factory started by his father. The factory produces only riding boots, mainly for the army. It has 35 workers and yearly earnings of about 200,000 pesos. The informant's mother helped in the factory, and two of his siblings are also involved. The factory is owned corporatively. The informant began at the factory at age sixteen. He learned from his father and attended schools for tanners in Brazil, Argentina and Peru. However, one of his brothers is a physician, two of his siblings "*pasean las calles*" (are not economically active) and his wife is also not involved in the factory.

Middle-class and elite producers may also use ties outside the family (for example, those established during their education) to start enterprises. A former director of a university who taught at the university joined with two other individuals, who were not family members to open a ceramics factory.

Multiple Occupations

The high competition and low earnings in many occupations and the economic and political uncertainty in Bolivia have forced many small-scale producers, or at least their households, to engage in more than one economic activity at once, either to increase their income or to spread the risk.

When individuals personally engage in more than one activity, they may do so at only certain times of the year or year round. Small-scale producers (and others who are not usually engaged in production) often set aside a number of weeks or months to produce miniature objects for the annual Alasita and/or Christmas fairs. What they produce for the fairs may not be related to their usual trade. For those who engage in more than one occupation year round, the occupations may be at least vaguely related, as seen in the cases of a woman who helps her husband produce and sell shoes for fiestas and is also selling contraband goods she fetches at the Peruvian border; a jeweler also repairing watches; a mechanic who repairs stoves and makes windows also repairing television sets; and a cookie baker also making cakes, selling ice cream, making hors d'oeuvres for parties, and cooking meals for workmen in a neighboring workshop. Or the occupations may be quite unrelated, as seen in the cases of the cookie baker just mentioned, who is also knitting sweaters; a motor-vehicle painter also driving his father's bus; a wood-carver also working as an architect; a producer of woven willow chairs also studying law;[13] a printer also selling used cars; and a candle maker also working as a construction worker.

Such flexibility makes it possible for an individual to temporarily or permanently abandon a trade and switch to another one. Thus, a number of artisans we interviewed in 1988 had recently switched from producing goods for the tourist market to selling imported goods. Again, the switch may be into multiple activities. We encountered such a switch in the example of the cookie baker who has become, among other things, a washer woman. She was at one point thinking of also selling pressure cookers, mixers and other small electrical appliances and blankets outside the shops that sell these items (because a *compadre* in the military could furnish her with these goods). And she also made aprons and furniture covers.

The shift from production to commerce need not be abrupt. At least in one case, the artisan himself apparently was unaware of the extent to which such a shift had occurred. Alcides, a jeweler, had always engaged in commercial transactions and worked as an appraiser of jewelry, gold and precious stones. But by 1988 these activities, which now also included acting as an intermediary for antiques of all sorts and running a copy center, were bringing in more revenue than jewelry making. "Out of curiosity," he said, "I said to myself, 'Well, this year let's be organized and let's see what we are spending and what is flowing in.' Well, my accountant told me: 'Don Alcides, you are spending more [in your jewelry business] than you are earning.'"

Both spouses may engage in a joint subsidiary activity. As we saw in our discussion of rural-urban migration, many artisan couples cultivate a few plots of land in their community of origin. One informant accompanied his wife on her trips to purchase potatoes on the altiplano for resale in the city when his shoe sales were slow. Another informant, a mechanic, built a large oven for his wife's cookie and *empanada* (cheese and meat turnover) business.

The array of economic activities engaged in by a couple may become impressive indeed. Don Alfonso's and Doña Carmen's household economy stands out as an example of economic complexity (see Chapter 2). Carmen is a caretaker for an upper-class family. For this she receives a small salary and lodgings for the entire family. In the past, she also sold chickens for the family. In addition, she makes cookies and, on occasion, bread. Her husband, who is blind, produces peanut butter, sells bread, and, more recently (1988), provides access to a telephone on a busy street. In addition, he owns a small kiosk where an employee sells newspapers and candies. Although the latter does not bring in much money (some $b. 2,500 [US $100] per month), he keeps it as a safeguard in case he should have to move out of his present economic activities.

Household heads may furnish other members of the family with a means of securing a livelihood while at the same time contributing to the household economy. As we have already noted, parents, for example, may provide employment for a son by investing their savings in a truck or bus which is then driven by the son. Thereby, they also gain an additional source of income for themselves. Similarly a cookie maker purchased a knitting machine with which her son was able to finance his studies in medical school. And a mechanic who builds bus bodies owned two stores: a beer distributing point and a grocery store run by his daughter. In addition, he owned two small buses and one large public transportation bus.

While investing in a bus or truck does provide a hedge against at least short-term inflation and does enable a producer to diversify, it is also highly risky. Motor vehicles depreciate. In addition, insurance premiums are very high, and reliable coverage is difficult to obtain. Few vehicle owners in Bolivia carry any coverage at all. Accidents on poorly maintained roads often lead to the total loss of the vehicle and major personal liability expenses. The risk in this investment is compounded by the loss due to devaluation and inflation. Payments for vehicles must be made in U.S. dollars, subjecting the vehicle owner to exchange-rate risks during the numerous devaluations. Furthermore, passenger fares are fixed by government decree; therefore, the increased debts can not readily be passed on to the passenger.

Of course, the most common form of multiple income in a household is for a husband and wife to engage in separate economic activities. Often the wife's contribution through selling in the market, running a store or a shop with copying facilities, or managing a rotating credit union (*pasanaku*) is quite substantial. Some activities bring in very meager earnings and are feasible only if the husband has income from a more lucrative activity. Knitting, for example, brings in small earnings. A woman who depends on knitting to make a living complained that women were charging so little for making a sweater that their profit was practically nonexistent.

Finally, producers may invest in a capital good such as a bus or truck and hire someone outside the immediate family to run it. Or they may speculate in real estate to provide an alternate form of investing and earning a subsidiary income.

Conclusion

The process of becoming a settled producer, then, is characterized by a change in the source of security from land, with its rewards and obligations, to social ties based on bilaterality, neighborhood and occupation. Women benefit from the lessening of the patrilineal emphasis connected with the inheritance of land, but they remain dependent on males, especially brothers and sons. Increased prosperity leads to the clustering of sibling sets in the same enterprise and the expoitation of education for the discovery of new sources of work and network contacts, which are not unusual occurrences in Latin America (see, for example, Lomnitz 1987).

Notes

1. Similar observations were made by Stein regarding migrants from Hualcán who work in coastal plantations (1961:43,68,232) and by Brush for Uchucmarca (1977:146,161,162).

2. Exceptions to this tendency include Abu Lugod and Simić (in Gmelch and Zenner 1988).

3. According to 1976 census figures, La Paz had a total population of 635,283 of whom 561,188 were nationals 10 years and older (Bolivia 1976).

4. However, the *rate* of urban-to-urban migration is higher than the rate of rural-to-urban migration (Escobar de Pabón and Maletta 1981:25).

5. In anticipation of and after the agrarian reform there was an even more pronounced exodus of town mestizos (McEwen 1975:147; Albó et al. 1981:39-40), who were replaced by upwardly mobile peasants.

6. Albó et al. (1981) found that 47.9% of the men and 31.7% of the women with less than four years of residence in La Paz found jobs without any assistance; the figures for the total sample of rural-to-urban migrants were 50.5% of the men and 38% of the women.

7. Thus, several years after Llamacacheños purchased land from the former landlord of neighboring Compi, the ex-hacienda peasants decided to take these lands over again.

8. For examples of the arrangements among close kin concerning access to land see the Appendix to this volume.

9. In 10 out of 26 cases on which information was gathered, interaction between *compadres* was limited to occasional visits. In the remainder there was a variable degree of cooperation. In 4 instances where the *compadre* was either from La Paz or from the Yungas valleys, mutual gifts of food were proffered. In the others, the *compadres* helped each other in the fields, the most usual arrangement being for one partner in the relationship to work for the other in return for food and, at least during harvest time, small quantities of produce.

10. Some of these individuals came from other communities, others left the hacienda to become *utawawas* of a relative in Llamacachi, and still others received practically no inheritance because they were illegitimate children whom neither their father nor mother's husband recognized. One such case was Eustacio, who lived in the house of his deceased mother's father, which stands on a plot inherited by relatives of his stepfather. He also received a small plot from his father on a temporary basis and *chiquiñas* from another member of the same section of the community, whom he helped.

In four of the hacienda sections alone, we counted 32 women who had borne illegitimate children without expecting to marry their fathers. Others are legitimate children who for various reasons are raised by relatives. Out of 13 recorded adopted children in Compi proper, 2 were waifs; 3 were illegitimate children; 3 were grandchildren given to their grandparents to keep them company and to provide them with help in their old age, a frequent practice in the community; 1 was a twin whose aunt took custody of him because she had just lost a child of her own and because his mother would not have been able to breastfeed two children; 1 was the child of a woman who remarried and did not wish to be burdened by her child from a former marriage; 1 was adopted by her childless godfather; and 2 came from very poor families. While some adopted children are treated like servants, others become full members of the household and eventually heirs. Such arrangements often create conflicting claims on land resulting in inheritance squabbles (see Buechler and Buechler 1971:41-42).

11. The total number of informants in the four communities was 43.

12. For example, Pablo, who lives in La Paz, does not receive *chiquiñas* from his father, but the latter plans to give him some when he marries. Should he return to the community he would receive entire plots of land. In contrast, Gerbacio is married, so he receives 3-4 furrows of *chiquiñas* in each of the family plots. His father tends the land and sends him the produce, retaining only enough for seed. In this case neither Gerbacio nor his wife help, although they do come for the patron saint fiesta. Instead, Gerbacio sends his father gifts of sugar and other goods. When he left for Arica, Gerbacio told his father that he would sharecrop the land with his brother so that his father would not have to work hard in his old age.

13. Like his father, who worked half-time as a procurator in the courts and half-time in the same trade as his son, he expects to continue in both fields after completing his studies. Two of his brothers, who are still in Buenos Aires, also have two occupations.

4

The Actors: The Role of Foreigners

One of the major concerns in the study of Third World countries is the impact of the more industrialized countries on their economies. To what extent are these relationships exploitative and to what extent have they contributed to development? More specifically, to what extent, if at all, have they led to the long-term improvement of the living conditions of a majority of the population? Only after a careful examination of the range of roles foreign interests have played in a country, and conversely of the roles nationals have played in the wider world economy, can we begin to answer such questions. Here we will examine the role of independent, foreign small-scale producers in promoting industrialization in Bolivia, a "lesser developed country" with an economy based primarily on public and private, large- and medium-scale extractive industries and based secondarily on commercial agriculture supported by governmental and international financing.

The foreign firms in Bolivia represent several migration waves. The earliest factories, established by the parents of some of our older informants, were among the first set up by foreigners in Bolivia. Others were established during and after World War II. The latest foreign firms represent a recent industrial boom period in Latin America, in which Bolivia participated marginally. Koreans were prominent among this latest wave of migrants.

At present, these foreigners and their descendants are involved in perhaps a third of all medium-sized and larger manufacturing firms in Bolivia and engage in varied production.[1] We shall compare the role of these producers with that of other foreigners: merchants and miners whose original base was Bolivia but who subsequently internationalized their operations. We shall also compare their role with that of multinationals in countries that have been more attractive to massive private investment in industry, and we will place the foreign industrialists into the context of Bolivia's massive foreign debt. The analysis will reveal that while the foreigners share some characteristics that distinguish them from their local counterparts, their role is as much defined by the nature of their insertion in the local, national and international economy as by their foreign status per se. We shall therefore analyze the foreign manufacturers' role in the context of the history of Bolivia's international economic ties.

Capitalism, according to Wolf (1982:298), is the process whereby surplus generated by labor is reinvested in tools of increasing productive efficiency plus more labor power. This process depends on access to a pool of labor that can offer its services "freely" as a commodity on the market. The industrial revolution accelerated production and, hence, the process of surplus extraction as well as reinvestment. The process of capitalism is directed by a market which determines what must be produced and the rate of accumulation.

It has generally been recognized that capitalism in Third World countries is not simply a smaller-scale copy of capitalism in industrial nations. Rather, Third World capitalism entails the exaggeration of certain aspects of First World capitalism. Social scientists stress the fact that Third World countries are suppliers of raw materials for goods produced elsewhere, a role that is now further complicated by the new international division of labor, whereby these countries also serve as a cheap source of workers. From this they deduce that such countries become the victims of forces beyond their control. It follows that the national elites, while playing into the hands of international capitalism, nevertheless have little choice. Local capitalists are regarded as "super-exploiting" workers because they not only extract a surplus in the manner of all capitalists, but they are themselves subjected to unequal exchange relations with consuming countries and make up for this fact by doubly exploiting their workers. Some Marxist economists, such as Carlos Johnson (1979:1), regard this model of Third World capitalism as too positivistic and mechanistic. Johnson argues that dependency theory "requires explanation in terms of capital/labor relations in order to understand its historical and socio-political meaning for class struggle." Similarly, we would argue that the *dependistas* neglect the fact that the entrepreneurial activities of local and immigrant elites shape and often serve to perpetuate the relationships between national and world economies.

Historical Roles of Foreigners in the Bolivian Economy

In the case of Bolivia, the intensification of a feudal land tenure system from the mid- but more particularly the end of the 19th century to the beginning of the 20th century may have contributed substantially in providing cheap labor to the capitalist mining industry. In fact, the period when the largest number of peasant holdings were encroached upon and converted into haciendas coincided with a revival of silver mining and the development of tin mining (see Mörner 1985:160). In other words, mine owners were indirectly able to extract surpluses "by other than economic means," characteristic of what Wolf (1982:267) calls preindustrial "mercantile domination."

The early foreign and national capitalist entrepreneurs in Third World countries producing raw material had, in some ways, a relative advantage over their First World counterparts. While it is true that dependence on world demand for raw materials generated unequal exchange, the fact that the producers of raw materials did not have to develop a local market for the goods they produced enabled them to perpetuate inequality and to give their support to political systems that fostered the interests of a tiny minority. They did so by, among other things paying low wages, supporting regressive taxation and putting pressure on governments to borrow from foreign lenders in order to finance the infrastructural development necessary for their enterprises. In addition, the most powerful local entrepreneurs were able to expand outward by investing abroad and becoming international capitalists in their own right. Thereby they contributed in a very active manner to a process of extraction with minimal reinvestment in their country of origin.

Foreign involvement in manufacturing seems to have occurred late in Bolivian history, but Europeans other than Spaniards have played major roles in the country's economy since the middle of the 19th century. A major arena of foreign influence was commerce. By the end of the colonial era, Bolivian silver miners obtained British goods through Buenos Aires, where the British had succeeded in coercing Spain to permit British ships to land. By the beginning of the twentieth century, British and American firms dominated importing; later in the century, Middle Eastern firms gained prominence as well.

But the most significant impact of foreign economic interest was in government finance and in mining. The Bolivian government was saddled with a foreign debt right from the republic's inception, when it agreed to recognize and assume the private debts of Bolivian citizens to Spain. Then, from the mid-19th century onward, the government borrowed money on the international market to build railroads and to cover annual deficits in the budget. These loans were often made under extremely disadvantageous conditions for the country. In addition to these loans, Bolivia made mining concessions to British-financed Chilean firms in its coastal territories, for which the state obtained practically no financial returns. With the loss of the Litoral to Chile, even these revenues were lost. In the meantime, silver mining, which had provided Bolivia's fiscal base, suffered from declining prices as a result of major silver finds in the United States and elsewhere, and the concomitant move to the gold standard, in turn, reduced the demand for silver (Peñaloza 1953:103-104). Although tin rapidly supplanted silver as the country's principal export, the state taxed it at such a low rate that Bolivia continued to depend on foreign loans and the compensation for Bolivian territory ceded to Brazil to finance railroad development, refinance internal debt, etc. Bolivia's present debt crisis has deep historical roots indeed.

Highland mining presented a very different pattern of foreign involvement. In contrast with coastal mining, highland silver mining and later, tin mining were not dominated by foreign interests until the 1920s, when Patiño incorporated his firm in Delaware and sold a part of his holdings on the stock market, a move precipitated by a temporary increase in export taxes on tin. From then on, the company of the largest tin magnate in the world invested mainly in smelters abroad and even in mines in competing regions, i.e., Malaya (Peñaloza 1953, vol.II:314; Nash 1979a:326; Irvin 1979:114). Bolivia not only continued the colonial tradition of an economy based on extractive industries, it also mortgaged its future through international debt, the benefits of which went principally to a sector of the economy that did not produce state revenues commensurate with its profits and did little or nothing to develop the rest of the economy.

The situation in the mid-1920s, when some of our manufacturer informants arrived in Bolivia, can be summarized with a quote from a Swiss businessman who arrived in Bolivia in 1924.

In 1924-29 the Bolivian economy was based almost exclusively on the export of minerals (tin—perhaps 90% at that time—but also silver and lead), which provided the greatest part of foreign exchange to cover imports and give the government an income through export taxes to cover its budget, which naturally was bolstered through duties on imported goods, a sales tax and direct income taxes.

There were no obstacles in trading. Any firm properly registered and with adequate capital and connections could dedicate itself to the importation and distribution on a wholesale or retail basis. [We should add that this openness was reflected in the dominance of foreign import firms. In 1925, out of 23 La Paz-based import firms listed in *Bolivia en el primer centenario de su independencia, 1825-1925* (Alarcón 1925), only six were owned or run by individuals with Spanish surnames. Other cities had similar ratios.]

Early in the 20th century, to cover a growing demand, a few foreign trading firms established themselves in Bolivia with capital and experience acquired in other countries, such as W.R. Grace & Co. (American); Duncan, Fox & Co. (British); and E. & W. Hardt (German). These turned into wholesale importers and distributors. In those years, a growing colony of European small traders who had left their home countries for political or economic reasons established themselves all over Bolivia as retailers opening outlets for general merchandise. Syrians and Lebanese took over the dry-goods trade (cloth, bazaar articles), while hardy Dalmatians (from Yugoslavia), who had migrated to Bolivia in order to avoid military service under the Austrian regime, became retailers of foodstuffs, enamelware, agricultural implements and other related articles. The former would soon be found all over Bolivia, whereas the latter appeared to prefer the mining districts and the cities of Sucre and Cochabamba. [In 1925, all eleven dry-goods stores listed by Alarcón (1925) were owned by individuals with Yugoslav names.] La Paz was left to merchants from neighboring Peru.

Industrial enterprises were limited to a brewery and a few alcohol distilleries and soap factories [to which one should add a modern shoe factory, a paper factory and a large number of semi-industrial concerns, such as pasta, sweet, candle and furniture factories and brick kilns]. Lumberyards depended on Oregon pine imported from the North Pacific Coast of the United States. Wheat was milled locally in producing areas but in insufficient quantities to cover the demand. Sugar production in the Santa Cruz area was insignificant, being limited to *chancaca*, a product that contained all the cane's molasses. It had little acceptance, in part because of excessive transportation costs. The foregoing meant that practically all consumer goods had to be imported, including flour and sugar. The only agricultural produce available in adequate quantities were potatoes, beans (*habas*), oca, quinoa (a protean-rich cereal) and barley (for animals). Sheep, alpaca and llama wool were in abundant supply and led to the establishment of the first textile mills in La Paz, which produced cheap blankets for the army, the peasants and the lower classes. All cotton goods had to be imported.

In the first quarter of the twentieth century, industries were established both by foreign individuals and corporations that had previously engaged in other activities, especially commerce, and by newcomers. Just as their predecessors specialized in the import business, transportation (railroads) and retailing, the foreign manufacturers tended to specialize in certain types of industrial activities. The spread of, and even the association with, particular activities varies according to the migrants' origin and, perhaps, length of residence in Bolivia. Perhaps most specialized are the Koreans, who are almost exclusively engaged in clothing and textiles. The Italians seem to be highly specialized as well. They are involved predominantly in manufacturing pasta, bread and quarry tiles. Least specialized are the Yugoslavs, who, as we have seen, began their Bolivian careers in commerce but are presently involved in a whole range of manufacturing activities. Between the two extremes are many migrant groups who are quite diversified but also dominate certain businesses. The Germans and the Swiss are involved with many products but dominate the pharmaceutical, paint, sausage and beer industries. The Arabs are associated with an equally wide range of occupations but appear to have a particular interest in the cosmetics industry.

Foreign Manufacturers

Among the early foreign manufacturers was a German sausage producer who arrived in Bolivia in 1910. His example will provide the basis for an analysis of the reasons why foreigners established factories in Bolivia.

Mr. Stein was one of eleven children, and since his youngest sibling inherited the family farm, he had to earn a living by other means. First, he learned sausage manufacturing in Braunschweig, Germany.

Table 4.1 Foreign Industries in La Paz (Sample)

Type of Establish-ment	Date Established	Type of Ownership	National Origin of Owner	Condition of Equip-ment	Number of Workers	Production in 1981
Sausage Factory	1910 later corp.	individual	German	mostly old	41 workers, 11 empl.	1,000 kg of meat per day
Sausage Factory	1980	3 partners	2 Swiss 1 Boliv.	modern, worth $1 million	4	2 head of cattle, 7-10 pigs per week
Noodle & Sweet Factory	purchased by father of present owners, 1942	family	F = Spanish M = Bolivian	partly new, major renovations in progress	28	10,500 kg pasta 2,000 kg sweets per day
Plastic Containers & Film	1960s	corporate	German	modern worth ±$4 million	100	N.A.
Shirt Factory	1946	individual	Polish	old	35 (10-15 are homeworkers)	± 4,000 shirts per month (2,500-8,000)
Knits	1960s	individual	Corean	fairly new	21 (15 at home)	
Furniture	1976	individual	Chilean	new	15, out of whom 6 mainly at home	foam rubber: 4 tons per month furniture: N.A.

Source: own interviews

N.A. = data not available

Then he managed farms, first in Kenya and later in Peru. When his Peruvian employer went bankrupt, Mr. Stein followed the example of other Germans who had moved from Arequipa, Peru, to La Paz. In La Paz he found a German partner and began sausage production with two workers. He slowly increased production until the number of workers reached 41 and then bought out his partner. Mr. Stein's first customers were fellow migrants, but slowly Bolivians became interested in sausages and cold cuts as well. Today, cold cuts form a part of even lower-class urban fiestas. There are presently three medium-size producers of sausages and cold cuts in addition to some home industries.

Mr. Stein's example illustrates a number of processes that were, and often still are, characteristic of the implantation of foreign manufacturing firms in Bolivia. For example, the elder Stein was initially involved in activities that were more characteristic of the colonial and early republican experience, i.e., agriculture and trade. (We found little evidence of shifts or diversification from mining into manufacturing at any time.) He became a manufacturer only after a stint as a farm manager in two colonial settings in Africa and Peru. Parallels can easily be found to Mr. Stein's example. The case of Mr. Salas described in the introduction is one such case.[2]

Some of the recent immigrants to Bolivia have also followed this pattern. In their cases, however, the initial move into traditional sectors, specifically agriculture, was made necessary because of Bolivian immigration policies. For example, in 1964, when its condiment factory failed, a Korean family of twelve migrated to Bolivia, impelled in part by the fear of the dominion of North Korea and enticed by the promise of a partnership in a firm owned by another Korean and a Japanese, who was married to the daughter of a former Bolivian president. By the time the family arrived, the business was on the decline. Furthermore, they could obtain only a visa to work in agriculture. As a result, the family migrated to lowland Caranavi, where they could take advantage of government grants of frontier lands. After a year, one son and one daughter decided to move to La Paz, where they purchased two knitting machines and, despite considerable discrimination, began production in a tiny rented room. They were later joined by the remainder of the family, all of whom entered into production.

Returning to our point of departure, the example of Mr. Stein, we find that his case also exemplifies a second pattern in that he moved from a more developed neighboring country to Bolivia. In this case, the country of origin was Peru, a country which was a step ahead of Bolivia in commercial and industrial development. Many Bolivian firms of both European and Peruvian origin have roots in Peru. For example, the first large-scale textile manufacturer, H. Forno, managed a textile factory in Urcos, Peru, that sold blankets to the Bolivian Army before he set up a factory in La Paz (Alarcón 1925:769). In recent years this process has continued. The largest cottonseed and soybean oil factory in Bolivia is owned and managed by a Peruvian corporation. The pattern is shared by some of the import firms as well. W. R. Grace was commissioned to bring a group of Irish farmers to Peru, where he became involved with a Scottish shipping firm that he and his brother took over in the late 1860s. From shipping and commerce, which the firm extended all over South America, the firm also went into banking and finally into sugar and textile manufacturing. It was only in 1905 that the firm established a subsidiary in Bolivia (Alarcón 1925:761), where, in addition to import-export, it became active in mining and cement manufacture. Thus the firm also exemplifies the evolution from involvement in traditional sectors to involvement in manufacturing.

The establishment of manufacturing firms in Bolivia has been a gradual process. The persons involved moved from agriculture, the gathering of wild products, commerce and shipping into industry, and they moved from the more developed to the less developed countries of South America (see Schoop 1978:1 for the modern counterpart of the latter process). Why, however, did this process take place? Why were national firms not attracted to manufacture? Why were foreign enterprises attracted into an underdeveloped sector of the economy of a Third World country? Probably the major attraction of Bolivia was the fact that many of the early foreign industrialists had no local competition at all when they first came to Bolivia.

For Bolivians in the nineteenth and early twentieth centuries, agriculture and highland mines, both highly labor intensive, were regarded as much more secure and lucrative areas for investment than manufacturing industries. Perhaps as a result of the massive Indian community land sales that the government carried out from the mid-nineteenth century into the present century, with their promise of perpetual returns from a serf labor force for only a small initial investment and low management costs, wealthy Bolivians did not even invest in the booming mines of the Litoral when it still belonged to Bolivia (Peñaloza 1953, vol. I:291). Eventually, major investments *were* made by Bolivians in *highland* mining, particularly tin mining. But once the necessary road and railroad links were established, concentration plants built, etc., few of the profits were reinvested beyond maintenance and, to a degree, exploration. Cheap labor, rather than capital investment, continued to be the mainstay of the industry. Profits fled the country and were not reinvested even in activities subsidiary to mining, such as smelting.

At the same time, the small foreign manufacturer was relatively protected from the competition of large multinational corporations, for the small internal markets, high transportation costs and trade barriers discouraged large-scale investments in all except a few activities, such as sugar and cement production. As a result, it was mainly the small manufacturing firms with modest capital that were established in Bolivia. Elsewhere, the market was often monopolized by a few larger firms, whereas in Bolivia it was possible to corner almost exclusive rights to small specialized markets for generations. The attraction of such exclusivity can be illustrated by the example of a Swiss sausage manufacturer.

Mr. Grob decided to settle in La Paz while he was taking a motorcycle trip through South America. He was born into a butcher family (his grandfather and four brothers are butchers) and learned to butcher meat in Switzerland. His search for adventure first took him to South Africa, where he worked as an expert in a large meat-processing factory. After ten years, he was ready for something new. Starting a firm of his own in that country seemed out to the question. The industry was too modern and mechanized and already too highly competitive for a small entrepreneur to survive. Three or four large firms with branches in neighboring countries completely dominated the market. One option was to take over his aging father's restaurant in Switzerland. However, when he reached Bolivia on his trip, he met a Swiss restaurant owner who casually mentioned that a sausage manufacturing plant was up for sale. The equipment had apparently been imported for an exhibition that had never taken place because of political unrest. A few days later, the two Swiss went into partnership with a Bolivian army general (a move perhaps designed to cut through governmental red tape) and purchased the factory. In addition to the fact that the equipment was available, they were attracted by the central location of the plant; because it was located near a major public produce market, the manager could retail his products while keeping an eye on his workers. After only four and a half months in business, Mr. Grob and his partners had already expanded their operation. His clients included a store run by an Eastern European immigrant and both foreign and elite Bolivian retail clients.

When we returned in 1984, Mr. Grob had hired a foreign woman to run the store, while he was involved in running the much larger plant of his competitor--Mr. Stein's successor--as well as continuing his own business. In spite of the increasingly difficult economic climate, he was apparently quite successful. Although he was not the first to engage in sausage manufacture in Bolivia, that disadvantage was mitigated by the demand his competitor had been able to develop. In addition, as one of the few specialists in this branch, he became an asset to his competitor.

Mr. Grob, then, was able to achieve financial independence in a much shorter time than might have been the case in his native Switzerland. In a period when the Bolivian economy was already very unstable, and individuals willing and able to invest substantial sums were particularly rare, his savings could go much farther than at home, albeit at much greater risk. His choice also gave him a degree of personal freedom which he might not have enjoyed had he taken over his father's restaurant. He might have had to compete with his brother, who was living in Brazil at the time, for the position of running the restaurant and perhaps would have had to submit to continued supervision by his parents.

A lack of large-scale foreign investment (as start-up capital) was also the case in the mining industry, probably because of the long history of Bolivian entrepreneurship in this sector. Indeed, the major attempt in 1922 by a U.S. mining company financed by Guggenheim Brothers to establish itself in Bolivia, making large investments in road construction to link its mines with the railroad system, failed due to excessive costs, and its assets were acquired for an insignificant sum by a firm with Bolivian capital, Aramayo (Peñaloza 1953, vol. II:318-319). In contrast, the Chilean-based firm of Mauricio Hochschild was able to acquire controlling interests in a Bolivian mining firm and from this base expanded until it became one of the three major mining concerns in the country. This firm too, however, was dependent on foreign capital only initially. Hochschild appears to have made his major acquisitions with capital earned from buying and selling minerals (Peñaloza 1953, vol. II:319-323; Alarcón 1925:933).

In contrast, there was room for foreign entrepreneurial activities in medium-sized mining operations, either in consort with Bolivians or separately. Thus W.R. Grace & Co. shared the ownership of one mine with one of its employees and introduced a system of dredge mining with cast-off American equipment in another. A number of other foreign firms and individuals also owned medium-sized mines. However, the dominant mode of foreign involvement in mining was (in addition to the obvious fact that industrialized countries were the sole consumers of most ore) of a different nature from that in manufacturing industries. We shall return to this point later.

The observations we made regarding investment opportunities also apply to skills. The foreigners often came from long traditions of small-scale artisan, semimechanized, or mechanized production. Even after they had transmitted these skills to their Bolivian workers, the latter did not necessarily become potential competitors. For reasons that will become apparent later, Bolivian workers who could have acquired the technical skills would have had neither the capital nor the ability to acquire the managerial experience to run such firms as Mr. Grob's meat-processing plant. With a long family background of small-scale butchers and managerial experience, Mr. Grob possessed an ideal combination of skills. Other foreigners arrived with similar combinations of skills that could be modified readily in Bolivia, since no change in the scale of operations was required in the transfer. For example, Mr. Stein had a similar combination of butchering and managerial skills, and the Korean immigrant described earlier had worked in and managed a condiment factory.

We can conclude that manufacturing was very much a residual sector of the Bolivian economy for both nationals and foreigners. Moreover, the local artisans who had produced such goods as cloth and boots on a larger scale had been displaced by foreign imports as early as late colonial times, when the region was first opened to cheap British manufactured goods (see e.g., Peñaloza 1953, vol. I:92).

In order to gain an understanding of the manner in which foreign firms operate, grow, or contract in Bolivia, we shall return to the experiences of specific foreign entrepreneurs interviewed in 1981 and 1984. In many ways their experiences are no different from those of entrepreneurs in similar-sized indigenous firms. But as we shall see, there are distinctive aspects in the ways foreigners engage in business and particularly in their long-range family strategies.

One example deals with Mr. Gomez, a Chilean who set up a small furniture factory in La Paz in 1975. Like Mr. Salas's pasta and sweets firm described in the introduction, his was a family firm. He had entered into a partnership with his father and his brother. His parents later returned to Argentina because his mother could not stand the altitude, but his brother continues to run the store. Mr. Gomez's case also resembles that of Mr. Kim, the Korean, in that they both attempted to involve unrelated compatriots in their firms. In Mr. Gomez's firm, they were hired as skilled workers, whereas in Mr. Kim's firm, they were selected as partners.

Mr. Gomez originally arrived in Bolivia with three workers, but only one of them was still with the firm in 1984. Mr. Gomez was unsuccessful in obtaining visas for the others. The normalization of relationships between Bolivia and Chile after years of tension surrounding the Litoral, the deteriorating economic climate in Chile and, presumably, the period of economic prosperity Bolivia was enjoying at the time all contributed to Mr. Gomez's decision to set up his factory in Bolivia. Although he is not a carpenter, he had experience in the industry, for his father and his sister both own furniture stores in Chile. His father had moved into the furniture business when his farm was expropriated under Salvador Allende. He was following the example of kinsmen who had been active in this business for most of their lives. In addition to the three Argentinian workers, Mr. Gomez hired three more locally.

Beginning with upholstery, which requires little equipment, he soon purchased machinery for woodworking and later for the manufacture of polyurethane foam rubber. The space he has rented, which is in a house that is in constant danger of collapse because of the terrain on which it is built, is barely sufficient for the foam rubber plant and the carpenter workshop. The furniture is finished elsewhere in the city by carpenters working in their own workshops. He has salaried workers in his plant and puts out work to others. In 1981, he tried to keep even his out-workers engaged on a permanent basis. However, by 1984 this was no longer feasible, for consumption had fallen dramatically, and he had been forced to reduce his personnel from the 15 workers he had in 1981 to 9 workers.[3] Their severance was cushioned by the fact that he tended to lay off or reduce contracts with out-workers who had already set up their own workshops.

Indeed, Mr. Gomez's firm began to stagnate within two years of its inception. He found that sales barely covered costs and the family's subsistence and left little for reinvestment. He was never able to obtain any bank loans, for the banks required buildings rather than machinery as a collateral. Whereas in 1981 he was still very hopeful about being able to increase the production of polyurethane foam rubber, by 1984 he was forced to shut down this operation entirely, since the government had not acceded to his requests for hard currency. Perhaps his foreign nationality prevented him from establishing the necessary ties in the government hierarchy, for other manufacturers were not completely cut off from their supply of imported plastics. For the same reason, he has never had any government contracts. Another problem Mr. Gomez has had to contend with is the rapidly increasing price of lumber, especially for mahogany. Because of its high price and because mahogany is being exported in ever larger quantities, he has been forced to switch to other wood varieties. Also, there are no adequate drying kilns in La Paz, so lumber often cracks.

In 1984, Mr. Gomez's major problems, in addition to his difficulties in access to imported raw materials, were reduced demand and what he considered excessive competition. The latter was, in a sense, also related to the scarcity of hard currencies. Many stores dealing in imported goods were forced to carry national ones instead, and furniture was one of the few products with only a small proportion of imported raw materials. Because of these problems, he was forced to close two of his three retail outlets in the city. So even though wages had decreased substantially, when measured in U.S. dollars (from about $150 a month to $40 for a worker with lesser skills), the firm was far from prospering. Mr. Gomez has played with the idea of opening a chicken farm in the subtropical Yungas valleys, for he figured that although people could postpone buying furniture, they still had to eat. But in 1984 he was no longer too certain about the accuracy of this logic. Meat was suddenly abundant again on the market after a period of acute scarcity, for most workers could no longer afford to eat meat on any but an irregular basis. Meat had become a luxury item. Although Mr. Gomez and his cousin did, in fact, buy a chicken farm, they sold it (at a small profit) even before they had raised any chickens.

Clearly, Mr. Gomez felt extremely frustrated. The years were passing and he found that he was sliding backward rather than looking toward the future. Commenting that other countries have been able to limit inflation, he said that the opposite was occurring in Bolivia.

Everybody arrives here with an attitude that is detrimental to the interests of the country. Everybody tries to take advantage when business is on the upswing. They want to get rich and then leave. Even Bolivians think like this. The best professionals have only one desire, to leave the country. The wealthy do have money in Bolivia, but it only amounts to 20% of what they have. The rest they invest abroad. One talks with anyone, and all they want to do is squeeze out the juice and flee. But if one looks at it from a different angle, the country itself is at fault. Because if there was any real stability, things would be different.

Mr. Gomez thought that he would have to stay on, for liquidating under the present economic circumstances would entail an almost total loss of assets. Furthermore, conditions in Chile were probably not substantially better than in Bolivia. Nevertheless, at the end of our interview in 1984, he confided that he would like to open a small business in the United States, where a sister-in-law and her husband live, if he could only obtain a visa.

Between 1984 and 1988, when we interviewed him once more, Mr. Gomez's situation had again changed drastically. Despairing because hyperinflation made it impossible to earn money, and unable to obtain dollars for raw materials at the official rate, he returned to Chile at the end of 1984 to try his luck there once more. His brother had sold the furniture factory to their cousin (who had always directed the technical aspects of the factory) and had liquidated his stock of furniture and his foam rubber manufacturing equipment as well, a process that took the better part of 1985. Mr. Gomez remained in Chile for two years, attempting to open a foam rubber factory similar to the one he owned in La Paz. But he did not succeed. Small factories, he found, had difficulties competing with larger ones. He was forced to give substantial credit to his customers: "I had to work under a lot of difficulties for nothing." When he saw that economic conditions in Bolivia were improving, he decided to move his equipment to Bolivia and start anew, this time concentrating on foam rubber mattresses, a product that he had learned a lot about during his attempt to establish a factory in Chile. In addition to a mattress factory in La Paz, he has opened a second plant in Santa Cruz with a Chilean partner[4] who had been material in changing his mind about the renewed opportunities in Bolivia after Paz Estenssoro came into power.[5] With his cousin as a partner, he also has an interest in a small furniture factory. Finally, he is thinking of buying a farm near Santa Cruz.

In contrast to Mr. Salas's firm (see Chapter 1), the development of Mr. Kim's, textile manufacturing firm was more closely linked to the attraction and the development of partnerships with Koreans outside his immediate family. In the beginning, Mr. Kim worked with his family members and two outside workers. Mr. Kim purchased the thread, his children wound it onto the bobbins, and his wife sewed. As the firm expanded, he invited three other Koreans from their native city to participate in a partnership by providing capital and administrative skills. At present, six of Mr. Kim's daughters are married and live in Canada, having followed one of the sisters, who met her future husband (a Canadian-Korean) on a holiday trip to Canada. One son is studying computers in the United States and wants to become a professor, another is in Santa Cruz and a third is disabled. Friends in Korea acted as go-betweens on the marriage of the son we interviewed and his mail-order bride. The informant has, since then, set up his own firm, where he manufactures children's clothing on a putting-out basis to Bolivian seamstresses. He sells the goods in his own store. When the clothing field became overcrowded, he hoped to join other Koreans in the manufacture of iron construction materials, but those hopes were shattered by the devaluations of the last few years that have substantially reduced consumption.

Conclusion

The functioning of the foreign firms we studied is in many ways similar to that of their local counterparts. Like the latter, the foreign firms are often family run, or they are run with partners of the same nationality, which is another way of reducing the anonymity of work relationships. The only exceptions were the the Korean manufacturing families, who were willing to engage in physical labor in order to launch their enterprises, whereas Bolivians from similar social backgrounds would probably have shunned such labor. Relationships with workers are also similar, with the same gap appearing between management and workers. Wages are held artificially low by government decree and international pressure, even for regular employees who enjoy legal benefits. In slack times, the number of people engaged on a "putting-out" basis can be reduced at will.

Special skills brought in by foreigners have been transmitted to Bolivians. Workers who are retired early, or who retire on their own, often set up independent workshops with their retirement benefits. Competing on the same level as the foreigners, however, usually requires more capital than they enjoy. A carpenter who has worked for Mr. Gomez, the Chilean, for example, would still have to sell through an established furniture store at a considerable discount because it would be difficult for him to gain direct access to the same clientele. Alternatively, he might sell cheaper furniture, but then he would find himself in an even more competitive market. He could also work for a different furniture factory. Indeed, many of Mr. Gomez's workers originally worked in other furniture factories. Similarly, some of Mr. Salas's former workers compete in candy manufacture, which requires only simple, inexpensive machinery that can be acquired secondhand. In contrast, since pasta is more capital intensive, his other competitors are middle-class foreigners and Bolivians. Economic differences between owners and workers in more capital intensive industries offer the owners a greater degree of protection from creating their own competition than is seen in less capital-intensive industries.

Like their Bolivian counterparts, foreign firms are highly dependent on imported raw materials. The availability of these materials is
often dependent upon government subsidies. Since the 1930s such subsidies frequently have taken the form of variable exchange rates.
During periods in which variable exchange rates are in effect, the
government requires exporters (including its own nationalized mines)
to deposit a certain percentage of their hard currency revenues into
banks. For their deposits they receive bolivianos at a fixed exchange
rate that can be substantially lower than the street rate. It then charges
the importers rates that depend on the country's need (see Gomez
1976; Eder 1968:325,343,507). During such periods of variable exchange
rates (which have coincided with periods of high inflation), personal
ties in government circles can make a crucial difference in obtaining
needed foreign currencies and can enable importers and exporters to
illegally profit from currency manipulations. As a recent arrival, Mr.
Gomez, our Chilean furniture manufacturer, may not have been able
or willing to establish such connections. Yet it is possible for a
foreigner to manipulate ties in his home country, or among foreign
importers in Bolivia, to his advantage in order to secure a more
reliable supply of raw materials and more favorable credit terms.

The importance of such personalized international connections is
even greater in commerce than in manufacturing. In both sectors, they
are used for similar purposes. In commerce, some of the early import
firms established by foreigners in Bolivia maintained buyers in their
countries of origin. In manufacturing, Europeans used their contacts
with migrants whom they knew personally to engage in business in
countries where commercial transactions would otherwise have been
too risky or too complicated. Even today, personal international
contacts remain an important ingredient of business.

The Bolivian counterparts of foreign manufacturers and importers
were often forced to build such personal relationships from scratch.
A small lamp manufacturer we interviewed in 1981 was able to
convince potential part suppliers located in the United States to
provide him with smaller than their usual minimum shipments when
he paid them a personal visit. Such contacts are particularly important
during adverse economic conditions when suppliers might otherwise
lose confidence in the ability of their clients to honor contracts.

Perhaps the single most important difference between foreign
manufacturers and importers and their middle or upper-class Bolivian
counterparts is seen in the long-term strategies of the foreign
entrepreneurial families. The children in those families avail themselves
of their parents' worldwide contacts for education, training, internships
and jobs.

The longer-term decision on the part of both generations of whether
to remain in Bolivia depends on a number of factors. The more established migrants tend to stay because they cannot afford to sell out,
and many are well integrated into Bolivian society. Some of their

children opt to return to the country of origin, especially when they can claim that nationality and/or have been educated there. A second-generation German/Bolivian, the son of a German miner, with a highly capitalized, modern plastics factory in La Paz, expects none of his children to continue the operation of his firm. One son is in Germany, where he plans to remain; a daughter lives in Austria; and only the younger son, a veterinarian, expects to work in Bolivia.

The more recent migrants who have more shallow roots and who have not overextended themselves often consider moving on to greener pastures, although for some, as in the case of Mr. Gomez, the move may be only temporary. The Koreans we interviewed, for example, think about the possibilities of settling in Australia or Canada, where they have kin.

Again, we can find analogous situations to that in manufacturing in the mining industry and in some large-scale commercial establishments, with the difference that these firms developed indigenously and only later became multinationals. As we have already seen, only one of the three largest mining companies in Bolivia, Hochschild, was not founded by a Bolivian. The other two, Patiño and Aramayo, were national firms that later branched out to the United States, Europe and other Third World countries. These countries then became their major investment locations while re-investments in Bolivia were not even sufficient to maintain earlier levels of production.

Perhaps we can best assess the overall impact of the foreign manufacturers and their descendants on Bolivia by comparing their role with that of multinationals in other countries. Unlike the latter, who may gain special government concessions in return for a promise of higher employment, the foreigners we studied were not so favored. Consequently, they also shouldered more risk. The more recently established firms, in particular, did not enjoy the personal contacts necessary for obtaining official government contracts.

Yet the foreigners do not expect their factories to be entirely "modern" in terms of facilities, work relationships and distribution. Many of the factories are family firms with modest capital investments and small numbers of workers. They may put out work to even smaller Bolivian-owned workshops. Even though the owners uniformly expressed a sense of frustration in their inability to influence the government, they were not as alienated as the middle managers of the multinationals described by Nash (1979b). At the same time, they are less socially isolated. Ethnic cohorts are relatively small but important, and social contacts and intermarriage with Bolivians are frequent for most groups (with the possible exception of the Koreans). Similar to their Bolivian counterparts, the foreigners patronize and are condescending toward their workers. They often make invidious comparisons between local workers and those in their home countries. Like the multinationals, they are proponents of law and order even at the cost of dictatorships, and they fear "anarchy," i.e., worker unrest.

Multinational firms have often been criticized for removing profits made in Third World countries and investing them elsewhere. Indeed, although in some cases multinationals have generated subsidiary plants in those countries, in most cases there have been no such spinoffs. In contrast, in the small foreign firms we examined, new skills and arenas of work have been introduced that have had a multiplier effect. They have contributed to the generalized and specialized training of workers, not to "de-skilling."

Both kinds of firms suffer from the fact that their productive potential grows at a much faster rate than demand. This is especially true in Bolivia, where the consuming working-class base is normally relatively small and has eroded even more in the last few years. To alleviate this problem as well as others, the foreigners, like the multinationals are, to some degree spatially mobile. But the former are less capable of leaving than the multinationals are, since with such a move they would risk the total loss of their capital investments; unlike the multinationals, they can ill afford such a move. Further, contraction due to adverse conditions is more likely to take the form of a temporary reduction of output than relocation to another country. However, Bolivia does have a history of losing its technically trained national and foreign personnel.

At a recent symposium on migration to the United States, a group of anthropologists coined the term "transnational migration." According to their reasoning, migrants in an increasingly global economy no longer are required to assimilate into the cultural contexts characterizing the host society. Rather, they not only retain and even expand interests in their society of origin (and perhaps in other, additional societies as well), but they also establish economic and sociocultural niches in which ties in various countries figure prominently (see Basch et al. 1990). While the organizers of the symposium regarded this phenomenon as recent, one could argue that, at least in the Bolivian context, "transnational migration" of this sort is an old phenomenon and furthermore that many of its characteristics have not changed substantially over time. Swiss migrants to Bolivia, for example, carefully maintained social, economic and cultural ties with Switzerland even when corporate policy and the cost and distance of intercontinental travel did not allow them to return to their countries of origin more than once in a decade. Some migrants successfully maintained long-distance courtships over the many years before they were finally able to return to their home countries to marry their fiancees. Even those who married Bolivians often educated their children in their home countries so that they could increase their options. Perhaps because most Bolivian industrialization continues to be geared toward import substitution rather than export, the most striking characteristic of more recent migrant groups is the continuity of this form of adaptation. Apart from the greater frequency of travel to the home country and their greater interest in manufacturing, more recent immigrant groups to Bolivia, such as the Koreans, behave much as their Swiss, German and Middle Eastern predecessors did.

* * *

In conclusion, in order to answer our original question of whether foreigners contributed to the long-term well-being of a majority of the population in Bolivia, we must view their role in the context of all foreign involvement in the country's economy as well as in the context of alternate kinds of involvement in manufacturing that did not occur in Bolivia but are common elsewhere. At the same time, we must view the differential impact of foreign manufacturers on different social strata.

In her book, *Cities and the Wealth of Nations* (1984), Jane Jacobs argues that economic growth is more likely to occur when technologically similar kinds of cities interact and are protected from massive flows of unearned capital that tend to distort long-term development. In Bolivia, manufacturing enterprises run by foreigners and nationals interact in such a manner. Production has multiplied for firms of similar size and relatively similar technology. Low wages give the firms studied a competitive edge for some goods vis-à-vis legal imports and contraband with high transportation costs. If the manufacturing sector could be segregated from the rest of the economy, it would conform to Jacobs's ideal, to some extent. However, this is not the case.

For most of Bolivian history, industrial manufacturing was a mere afterthought in an economy based on agriculture, carried out by a self-sufficient peasantry who was forced to create a surplus on land whose control they had lost to the Bolivian elite, and on mining, which forced the country into debt because a handful of families took the mineral wealth out of the country and progressively internationalized the corporations they had founded. Fluctuations in the international demand for minerals, price manipulations by industrial countries and all attempts by the Bolivian government to increase its share of the mining revenues furthered the decapitalization of the mining industry by drawing investments elsewhere. Thereby, the industry perpetuated its dependence on low wages. When the large tin mines were finally nationalized in 1952-53, they could no longer provide the capital for development. Instead, the country became even more dependent on foreign grants and loans and hence forfeited control over the direction of its economy (see also Gomez 1976) to the U.S. government and international lending agencies.

As a result, while foreign entrepreneurs were successful in avoiding locations where they would have been forced to compete with multinational manufacturers, their mode of operation became permanently affected by another kind of multinational: the mining corporations that had Bolivian roots but later invested elsewhere. Small-scale capital could not generate petrochemical, steel or heavy industries that could produce the raw materials for these industries. They continued to be import-oriented. The short periods of time when they benefited from variable exchange rates upheld at the expense of mining merely created artificial conditions and widespread dislocation when the supports were suddenly dropped again. Bolivia has made a belated attempt to lessen its dependence on mining by investing oil revenues in larger industries and by obtaining new loans from international lending agencies as well as from private banks to finance both private and public industries (Irvin 1979). This effort has been successful in part, but at the cost of further decapitalizing mining and the oil industry and creating a short-term high-interest debt of totally unmanageable proportions. The result has been a default on both interest and amortization and the collapse of the national economy.

Under these circumstances it is entirely possible that the foreign entrepreneurs will use their ties with their countries of origin to leave Bolivia and return home if economic conditions in those countries make such moves attractive. At the very least, the foreign entrepreneurs will make certain, as many have already done, that their children develop alternative options elsewhere. The in-and-out strategy of the multinationals based in the more highly industrialized countries will then simply be repeated (with modifications and on a smaller scale) by the immigrant manufacturers. Should this occur, and the example of Mr. Gomez shows that it indeed can, even if it also shows that such decisions are reversible, the immigrant manufacturers will have left a contribution to at least a moderate degree of diversification of the Bolivian economy and to a slight lessening of the dependence on imports (albeit often at the cost of creating new dependencies on new raw materials and intermediate manufactures). The foreign firms have, however, made little or no change in the distribution of wealth, for the economy they have helped to create continues to enhance the position of the capitalist at the expense of the workers.

Notes

1. This estimate of the number of foreigners involved in Bolivian manufacturing firms was made by reviewing the surnames in the 1981 directory of firms of the Chamber of Commerce, *The Directorio Industrial Boliviano,* and determining which were neither Spanish, Catalán, nor Basque. Calculations based on a similar listing, the 1981 *Guía Directorio de la Industria Boliviana,* show that individuals with foreign, non-Hispanic names were involved in (i.e., were owners, or chief managers, or presidents of) 127 (40%) of the 317 private manufacturing firms listed, in almost half (94, or 48%, out of 193) of the firms with capital investments over $b. 1,000,000 (US $40,000), and in 31 (57%) of the firms with capital investments over $b. 10,000,000 (US $4,000).

2. Mr. Salas's case also exemplifies the effect of cyclical demand for gathered products. Cinchona bark production went through at least three boom periods, each followed by complete neglect. Only individuals with diversified investments could profit from these boom periods. A Bolivian might have owned an hacienda in addition to his cinchona business. For a foreigner, other forms of commerce or industry were the more likely choices. Another example of a foreigner who took advantage of a specialized market among an immigrant group is the owner of the bakery described in Chapter 8.

3. Of the fifteen workers in 1981. nine worked in the plant and six worked in their own workshops.

4. Mr. Gomez was unclear about the nationality of his partner in the Santa Cruz plant. Though at first he said he was from Chile, later in the interview he claimed that he was Bolivian. He said he had met his partner when the latter was working in a bank in Bolivia and later when he was working as a submanager of a foreign oil company in Chile. When they met in Chile, this man had expressed a desire to return to his home country, Bolivia, and start a business there, which resulted in their collaboration.

5. In 1988 he produced some six or seven tons of foam rubber a month and had a stock of some twenty tons of raw material.

5

Learning the Trade

In Chapters 1,3, and 4, we discussed, among other things, the manner in which the social, cultural, ethnic and national backgrounds of small-scale producers influence the activities they engage in, the ways in which those activities are combined, and even the degree of economic success resulting from those activities. In this chapter, we examine the specific processes involved in learning different trades and the manner in which these processes are dependent upon some of the same factors.

Modes of learning are often treated in isolation from the socio-economic and political matrix in which they manifest themselves. Social scientists and development agents alike frequently attempt to isolate such phenomena as "apprenticeship" (usually defined with reference to a specific archetype from preindustrial Europe) and plot their presence in, or evaluate their appropriateness to, particular societies. We argue for a more contextual approach in which ways of acquiring technical and related skills are examined in conjunction with alternative modes of transmission under particular conditions. We contend that models of learning should take into account the individual producer's position within kin and regional social networks as well as the wider national and international economic context.

The acquisition of skills (and, as we shall see later, tools and equipment) is undertaken by the would-be apprentice with the ultimate objective of becoming an independent producer. Given the fragmentation of production, this is indeed a reasonable goal. In a social anthropological study of a sample of 1417 first-generation migrants from rural areas of the department of La Paz to the city of La Paz, Albó et al. (1982) found that while only a third of the migrants who entered artisan occupations were able to establish their own firms within 6 years (and 36.4% within 7 to 12 years) of their arrival, three fourths of those who had lived in La Paz for over 26 years had their own enterprises.

We found that migrants and nonmigrants have the same average number of learning episodes (migrants, 1.62; nonmigrants, 1.61), but

differences exist in the degree to which they utilize kin ties to learn
a trade: The percentage of migrants who had learning episodes with
kin is significantly higher than for nonmigrants (58.3% vs. 42.4%).
However, nonmigrants more frequently learn from parents than
migrants do (24.2% vs. 16.7%). Interestingly, perhaps because they also
pursue more ambitious goals, fewer migrants than *Paceños* in turn
transmit their skills to their children. Among migrants, however, the
proportion of learning episodes with *affinal* kin is higher (20% of all
learning episodes with kin vs. 10.7% for nonmigrants).

As a corollary of the above, migrants had fewer learning episodes
with non-kin (28.4% vs. 40.9% for nonmigrants). Interestingly, 15.2% of
the nonmigrants learned from foreigners. This was true for only 2
migrants (5.4%).

Finally, nonmigrants have at least a somewhat better chance than
migrants of receiving formal training (6.1% vs. 1.7%).

The Transmission of Generalized Skills

One of the major variables that influence the acquisition of skills
is the extent to which they are related to skills learned
within the average household. Some of these skills are universal; thus,
such skills as sewing and cooking are acquired, albeit in different
forms, by both rural and urban women. Peasants probably learn a
greater range of skills in the course of their lifetimes than do their
urban counterparts. Many skills are universal only in rural communities. These include productive skills (usually sex-specific), such as
floor-loom weaving, adobe making, etc., and skills that are important
adjuncts to artisan trades, such as marketing (predominantly female).
Finally, many are widely disseminated in rural households, such as
weaving on European-type looms (male), various construction skills
(preponderantly male), urban marketing (preponderantly female), etc.
As Albó et al. (1982) point out, migrants often choose occupations
related to these skills. Their occupations are, however, not necessarily
of purely rural origin; many have been subjected to varying degrees of
urban influence.

Migrants are particularly likely to engage in economic activities
based on more generalized skills either in production or commercialization or a combination of both, that they acquired in their communities of origin. This pattern is particularly salient in the case of
traditional woven and knitted goods and those woven and knitted for
tourists. All types of weaving, especially the Spanish-loom version done
by men, have been transferred to La Paz. Women spin and men weave
tourist ponchos and *bayeta*. The *bayeta*, or Indian homespun cloth, is
now made into bags, wall hangings and pillow cases that are decorated
with appliquéd Tiahuanaco designs.

Eugenio is an artisan who benefited from his family's artisan tradition in this generalized manner. His grandfather had woven white *bayeta* that he dyed in bright colors for women's skirts. It was from him that Eugenio and his brothers learned this skill. One has applied his knowledge of traditional weaving to make ponchos out of synthetic fibers. Another buys women's shawls *(mantas)* that his wife and he sell on the market. They too weave. Eugenio eventually established himself as an artisan who makes woolen appliqué wall hangings for the tourist trade. He first helped one of his uncles in his custom dispatching office. Then, he went to Cochabamba and worked as a candle maker with other kinsmen. Finally, after completing his military service in La Paz, he began making wall hangings quite by accident. As it turned out, his aunt, an egg merchant, was ill and looking for a less arduous occupation. A tourist-store owner in the Calle Sagarnaga (Sagarnaga Street) gave her a sample that was appliquéd, and both Eugenio and his aunt made a copy of it. His actually came out better.[1] They purchased a book with Tiahuanaco motifs and set to work. When he married, he started his own workshop but continued to assist his aunt on the side. He already owned a sewing machine with which he had made skirts and trousers, a skill he had learned from his father, who frequently made clothing for the family and for sale.

The origin and dissemination of the appliqué technique constitute an example of how more generalized rural skills have been harnessed to new ends. Aymara and Quechua Indians have long embroidered scenes on cloth and, in one region, have made beautiful ceremonial belts out of feathers glued to pieces of wood. The application of pieces of colored *bayeta* onto a *bayeta* background by either sewing or gluing was introduced independently by two Americans to enable artisans to produce tourist goods on a larger scale than if they embroidered each piece.. The earlier, sewed appliqué technique was apparently taught by a Peace Corps volunteer to a disabled migrant from the rural community of Huatajata. The panels that he and his family made found a wide acceptance, first in La Paz tourist stores and later by exporters. The technique soon spread to the disabled migrant's other kinsmen and *paisanos* and from there, often through kin links, to migrants from nearby communities. In addition, as we saw in the previous example, the tourist-shop owners had individuals outside the original networks copy the technique.[2] Ultimately, individuals in the communities of origin also began making the panels. The technique is now so widespread that profit margins have dropped because of competition, and many of the early producers have been forced to abandon the trade.

Some of these skills are practiced in specialized communities or by individual specialists who gear their production mainly toward the market, but the skills are also practiced more generally by peasant families exclusively for home consumption. Thus, some women engage in spinning and floor-loom weaving commercially, but most peasant women do so only for their families. Knitting, which was traditional-

ly limited to finely knitted woolen caps, or *gorros*, and purses with
elaborate designs, made mainly by men all over the highlands, has
now become one of the major crafts engaged in by migrant women in
La Paz who make sweaters and ponchos for the tourist trade. Exporters
have further transformed the craft by introducing new designs and
establishing more stringent quality control. Knitting cooperatives located
both in the city and in certain rural communities make the cheaper
sweaters sold in crafts markets and the denser, more expensive ones
sold in specialty stores in the center of the city. They can compete
favorably with artisans who manufacture woolen sweaters on hand-
operated machines. The latter are, as we shall see, largely dependent
on a state monopoly for obtaining machine-spun alpaca wool, for
which they must pay extremely high prices. The knitter can reduce
costs by inviting rural kinsmen to come to the city to spin or by
putting out spinning and other piece work locally to recent migrants
(see Chapter 6). Machine knitting requires more initial capital and is
therefore more likely to be engaged in by more established urbanites.
Most use synthetic yarns to produce goods for national consumption.

Migrants who enter such trades as construction work and carpentry
are also able to fall back on generalized skills learned in the rural
community, although in many instances rural craftsmen, such as
carpenters, have themselves had earlier urban experience through
which they learned non-traditional skills, such as making window
frames and elaborate doors. The same holds true for tailors (usually
men) and skirt makers (usually women).

The commercial application of generalized skills in La Paz often
requires a process of further adaptation. Urban customers demand
goods made to different specifications, and even clients who are
themselves migrants from the same community of origin or are visitors,
the latter often being among the migrant artisan's principal customers,
seek products of higher quality or possessing special features that are
unavailable back home. Thus, a peasant might order a special skirt
(*pollera*) for a fiesta.

The application of generalized skills in La Paz thus often follows
complex trajectories. A typical sequence might begin with sewing for
family needs in the locality of origin and continue with part-time
tailoring for members of the same community, followed by
employment as a tailor in La Paz and finally by setting up one's own
shop there. The possession of generalized skills, then, does not obviate
a process of learning and often entails apprenticeship.

The most valuable skills transferred from the rural communities of
origin are not always directly related to a small-scale producer's
particular trade. Commercial skills may be equally or more important.
As we shall see in Chapter 9, commercial skills are part of the
repertoire of most rural women as well as some of the men.

There are situations where the link to the original rural activity is
more complex. A group of migrants from Achacachi, for example, sell

cloth in permanent stalls on a street corner situated in the center of the major lower-class market area. As a spin-off of this activity, some Achacachi women are making *mantas* for *cholas*. They purchase the cloth from local factories, make the braided borders with the help of other family members and sell the *mantas* in the same area as well as in rural fairs. In this case, the connection with the rural activity comes from both a tradition of costume making, which required links with the textile industry, and a tradition of selling or renting costumes and selling onions.

The most successful case that we encountered of an entrepreneurial migrant who employed his commercial skills to new ends was that of Celestino. Celestino's beginnings were humble. His father was an hacienda overseer without access to land. So Celestino became interested in selling jerked meat and onions in the subtropical Yungas valleys. When he had saved enough money, he and his brother purchased a truck. The truck was involved in an accident, and the motor of the truck they bought to replace it broke down. So Celestino went back to Compi, where he farmed land he had purchased from the former landlord.

Celestino's kinsman in the Yungas advised him to open a lumber-yard, which he did on a plot he had managed to acquire in El Alto and with equipment he purchased. While he was on a trip and his son was in charge, the equipment was stolen. But thanks to his kinsman, who acted as a guarantor, he was able to replace it. Celestino does none of the actual labor; he hires others. But he does purchase the wood in Santa Cruz. He can neither read nor write and relies on his sons, whom he has been able to give an education, to do the accounting. But he can make all necessary calculations in his head. As we saw earlier, he plans to build a hotel in Compi and retire there. At least until the mid-1980s his wife still engaged in the same activities as before their economic ascent. She sold onions on the market in La Paz and made frequent trips to Compi to cultivate their land. By 1988, however, he had set her up in a store he built that was adjacent to the lumberyard, where she sells plywood.[3]

Occupations related to generalized skills are especially amenable to the involvement of kin. Close relatives, particularly siblings and immediate cognatic kin, are frequently hired on short notice on a piece-rate basis for specific tasks to complete orders. A 22-year old second-generation male migrant helps his older sister make *polleras* by sewing the folds into the skirts. On occasion he also helps his mother, who is engaged in the same trade, but since she pays him less, he prefers to work for his sister. He also appreciates the extra gifts of money the latter gives him when business is good. Additional money comes from helping in his brother's restaurant. His younger brother also knows how to sew folds, but the sister sends him away when he comes around, as he refuses to work for his own mother and spends his time on the street.

Transmitting Specialized Skills

The more-specialized skills can be transmitted in similar ways to generalized ones, but since the learning process is usually longer, it can take place informally only within the same household as people who know the skill or between members of households with intensive, long-term associations. Apprenticeship represents the principal alternative option.

Long-Term Informal Learning

Major differences exist between migrants and La Paz-born artisans with respect to opportunities for long-term, informal learning. Migrants have access to well-defined networks, centered in their communities of origin but extending to migrants from these communities. In contrast, the network links of urbanites are more diffuse in terms of the background of the individuals involved, but at the same time are more strongly anchored in the urban productive traditions. As a result, they often permit more rapid economic advancement.

The Transfer of Specialized Rural Skills to the City. The activities engaged in by migrants are influenced by the specialties present in the community of origin, by common rural skills and by the trades embarked upon by early pioneers. The specialties that originate in rural communities include costume, silver-object, drum, flute, rug and rubber-sandal making. These artisans establish diaspora communities in the city. Such communities often compete with the home base, but the migrants may also become intermediaries for their *paisanos* (countrymen) back home.

A good example of this process is illustrated by the flute makers from two former haciendas on the northern altiplano, Walatha Grande and K'oani. Members of these communities have traditionally specialized, and continue to do so to this day, in making two kinds of flutes: reed flutes, including panpipes manufactured out of a climbing vine which grows in the tropical forest region around Mapiri, and thick flutes, called *tarkas*, made out of wood from the Yungas valleys. The former are characterized by a distinctive ligature, or manner of tying the tubes together. For generations, men from these communities have made the arduous 15-mile trip to Mapiri on foot and on mule-back to obtain the vine for reed flutes. Or they have gone to the Yungas for wood to make *tarkas*. They served all the communities over a wide area of the northern and central altiplano. Even though the two communities had been absorbed by an hacienda, the flute makers continued to ply their trade during the three to four days a week they did not have to work for the *patrón*.

However, the agrarian reform stimulated these activities. Some Walatheños migrated to La Paz before the land reform, and others migrated afterward. These persons continued to make flutes, which they sold in one particular area of the city, the Garita de Lima. One old woman interviewed in 1967 had migrated to the city long before the reform. She sold instruments made by her nephew at a site where she, like other old-timers, did not have to pay a fee since they used to sweep the area for the privilege of selling there. While they sold instruments manufactured in situ, either in standard sizes or following models brought by customers, other producer/vendors who migrated to the city after 1952 also sold flutes manufactured by family members. Some of them offered their wares only in La Paz, but others continued to travel the same circuit as their rural counterparts, who used to travel to fiestas where they would play instruments such as the *muceña* in fiestas on contract. But by the 1960s they merely made flutes which were sought by eager fiesta sponsors. These flute vendors migrated to La Paz, which became the major distribution center for instruments since the city was much more accessible geographically to their assured clientele. In 1967 they continued to enjoy this advantageous position. By 1981, however, they had moved away from their traditional market site, and there appeared to be fewer flute makers selling in their new locations. The popularity of traditional instruments has greatly diminished in the rural areas, while increasing tourist and export demand has probably not compensated for the shift in popularity to brass instruments. At the same time, the new demand for electronically tuned instruments for professional folklore groups is being met by a middle-class producer. Nevertheless the flute vendors were still active in promoting their wares in 1981, even in such outlets as elite art galleries.

A similar phenomenon can be observed among the rug makers from communities near Warisata, an altiplano village near Lake Titicaca. As an example, Emeterio comes from a community near Warisata, where many persons have specialized in rug making, an activity that may have been introduced by the teachers college there. His father produces rugs in the home community, and he and other members of the extended family, together with unrelated workers from other localities produce rugs in two locations on El Alto. He travels to and from La Paz, where he offers rugs for sale on the street corners. This assures him a better price and payment at delivery, neither of which is true for selling through stores. Emeterio has a pied-à-terre in the city, which he shares with kinsmen from El Alto.

Some of the migrants are from more urban communities that specialize in a number of activities for which there is regional demand. For example, the town of Achacachi, which, with its 4,000 inhabitants, is one of the largest towns on the northern altiplano, traditionally specialized in tailoring, shoemaking, carpentry and blacksmithery (Albó 1979:34, 136-144). Most of the fifty or so families engaged in these

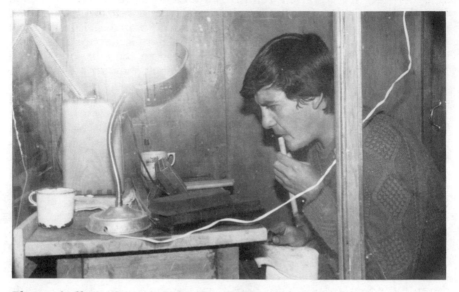

Electronically tuning a panpipe for professional musicians

occupations moved to La Paz after the agrarian reform, which changed the town from a community inhabited principally by hacienda owners into a town of peasants and merchants. These artisans were replaced in Achacachi by new migrants from nearby communities, many of whom eventually also moved to La Paz.

The most salient Achacachi artisans are the costume manufacturers. They had experienced a remarkable florescence with the increasing demand for urban style, sequined costumes modeled after those worn in the Oruro carnival and La Paz fiestas. Dance group leaders came from miles around to rent sets of costumes for a fiesta or made arrangements to use costumes that had been leased to other dance groups in more conveniently located communities. Many of these costume manufacturers have also moved to La Paz, where dancers generally spend more money on their costumes whether they intend to dance in urban fiestas or in their communities of origin.

In the city, they form a fairly cohesive unit. As we shall see in Chapter 10, they are the principal promoters of the Fiesta of Gran Poder, where their dance groups exhibit the most magnificent costumes. In some instances, family traditions in manufacturing costumes go back several generations, and there is considerable endogamy among craftsmen. However, spouses (both husbands and wives) may also be enculturated into the trade. The close cooperation of husband-wife teams was given expression by a costume maker whose wife had recently died. He had learned the trade from his wife, who in turn had learned it from her parents, and they, from their parents. When the wife was alive, the couple made elaborate *morenada* (a dance imitating descendants of black slaves) costumes, which they sold in Peru. When she died, he no longer went on these trips. "Alone, one can't do it. It always has to be with one's wife. That way, the business is well managed. In the places we went, for example, there are no authorities whom one can ask for assistance. One could be left to sleep on the street and no one would care." He also switched to simpler costumes. Now he was teaching the trade to the woman he was living with. In another family, a woman, her father, husband and father-in-law are all costume makers who make the same type of lighter costumes (i.e., with fewer beads and sequins). They frequently collaborate.

Achacachi is also known as a center for the manufacture and distribution of sandals made out of old truck and automobile tires. Although wearing such sandals is considered a sign of peasant status, migrants from Achacachi and elsewhere have found a ready market for them in La Paz as well, probably mainly among peasants who visit the city. Some sandal makers are based in their home town, others in La Paz. In 1967, we interviewed a 48-year-old man in La Paz who made and sold this type of sandal and were not surprised to find that he was originally from Achacachi, although he had lived in the city for fifteen years. He sold the sandals in Achacachi on Sundays, in Umala on Fridays and in Palcoco on Tuesdays. His wife sold sandals on a street near a market in La Paz all week long. Another man in his seventies, who originally came from Viacha, the other large town on the northern altiplano, learned the trade from his Achacachi-born wife, who in turn had worked with her brother even before she married. Since his wife's death seven years before we met him, he has been living with his grandson, who works for the municipal government and whose wife also makes sandals. His children have been upwardly mobile. His sons went to school until they were 17 and became taxi drivers. His daughters married white-collar workers (*"ingenieros"*). His children have invited him to come live with them in Cochabamba or Santa Cruz, but although he traveled as far as Buenos Aires when he was young, he dislikes the heat and plans to continue with his trade until he dies. However, he has stopped traveling to fairs some twenty years ago because of the high risk of being involved in an accident. He had been in an accident in which he hurt his hand, and from then on he was afraid to travel.

Most of the artisan trades experienced considerable transformations upon their transfer to the city. José, for example, lives in La Paz but comes from a community that specializes in weaving woolen cloth. His parents and four of his seven siblings are artisans. Originally, artisans from that community sold scarves on the streets of La Paz. Since the 1950s, middle-class and tourist demand for ponchos made out of handspun and handwoven woolen cloth has increased. In La Paz, José made ponchos with stripes similar to those of bags carried by llamas, except that he made them out of thinner alpaca instead of thick llama cloth. His ponchos are well known for their interesting natural-color combinations. While the scarves were made by women on floor looms, he works with a European-style loom that Aymara peasants have long used to make pant, skirt and jacket cloth (*bayeta* and *jerga*). Some of his co-villagers used to travel to the temperate and tropical valleys and even to neighboring Peru on mule-back to sell such goods. When he has large orders, he employs a number of female kin all of whom still have land in the community of origin. They also have founded a cooperative to improve their chances of finding large-scale clients. Like the carpet makers, some travel back and forth between the home community and La Paz.

One female weaver whose father sometimes works in the country and sometimes in the city finds life in the country uncomfortable: "The villagers are jealous of me, and so I prefer to work in La Paz." In contrast, another highly articulate weaver, who is the daughter of a *paceña* merchant and was married to a carpenter from Escoma travels to rural fairs and likes visiting her deceased husband's home. "I am from the country [she happened to be born when her mother was traveling to a rural fair]. I deal with people from there. We chat and understand one another." One of her daughters weaves too, and another still goes to school. "My siblings' husbands are Cambas [from Santa Cruz]. My nephews and nieces are teachers and "*ingenieros*." One of them is married to an Italian physician and lives in Santiago, Chile. I have distanced myself from them. They are white [*gente blanca*], so I don't deal with them."

Urban-Based Economic Activities

In general, however, for most skilled occupations, the La Paz-born artisans are at a considerable advantage, since many crafts are associated exclusively or almost exclusively with larger cities. For skilled occupations, as we have already seen, *Paceños* are more likely than migrants to have the opportunity to learn their trade progressively in the family workshop or from other skilled workers who have ready access to the family workshop. For example, Mr. Vizcarra, who learned to make dance masks out of plaster from his grandfather, has in turn taught his children and grandchildren the trade. The case of Mr. Vizcarra, one of the most famous artisans in La Paz, is particularly interesting because he is one of the oldest artisans we interviewed and because he has been the subject of another study as well (McFarren 1985). He practiced his trade until his recent death. "Orphaned when he was fourteen years old he was adopted by his grandfather, José Maria Morales, a mask maker who in turn had learned the trade from his father and from an Italian migrant who had been contracted to restore the Cathedral of the Virgin of Copacabana. While the father of Morales taught him the art of molding the masks, the Italian taught him how to polish and give the finishing touches to his work" (McFarren 1985). The following is from his interview with us.

My grandfather taught me the art since I was twelve years old. When I was thirteen, I was already working on my own. When I was fourteen, I knew a lot more, and when I was fifteen, I was fully trained. In fact, when I was sixteen, in 1925, when Bautista Saavedra was president, the director of [the Ministry of] Culture had me come and had me prepare the masks for the Tiahuanaco Theater Company. So I prepared masks for a *diablada* [devil's dance], *waca thokori* [a dance imitating Spanish bullfighting], *kusillo* [the dance of the buffoons or tricksters], *auqui auqui* [the dance of the ancient men] and *laquita* [a dance with men wearing tall feathered head gear playing panpipes]. So I had my first triumph at age sixteen! At that time, La Paz was much smaller, and much of what is now part of the city was occupied by haciendas with 200 to 1,000 Indians. They formed dance groups in each of these haciendas and came to see me to order masks.

As the growing city swallowed up the haciendas, he geared his production more and more toward the tastes of artisans who danced in increasingly more elaborate costumes. However, Mr. Vizcarra did not work continuously as an artisan for all of his life. When he was 22 he switched to work as a painter in a textile factory.

At that time, there was a president who strictly forbade dance groups in the entire city. "The *cholos* and the Indians dance these kinds of [costumed] dances," he said. "It's a shame that there are such dances in Bolivia." You see, there were a lot of foreigners living here at the time. So he forbade all such dances. What could I do? There no longer was any work, and so I sought work in the Said factory. I told the owner, Antonio Said, that I knew how to paint and prepare the surface to be painted. After a trial period, he took a lot of interest in me and paid me six bolivianos a week. That was a lot of money then, like 600,000 pesos today. Later, when [the owner] saw that I was a serious person who did not drink, he put me in charge of an enclosure where materials were stored, and I kept track of the materials. That's where I got to know Juan Lechín [who later became one of Bolivia's most famous labor leaders]. He worked with the dying vats and earned only three bolivianos. He had been working there for a long time already. Later he went to work in the mines, and I lost track of him until he suddenly emerged as the leader of the Catavi mines. Finally another president came into power who apparently liked popular dances. The fiesta of Trinidad was held once more, and the people who had the custom of dancing began to dance again. They came to visit me at my home in the Calle Los Andes and asked me to prepare sixty devils masks.

So Mr. Vizcarra gave up his job as a painter at the factory and returned to working as an artisan. Until his children were old enough to help him, he worked alone or with his wife. She is well versed in the entire manufacturing process and helped him when she was not selling clothing in an open market. She also helped him with sales. The children have all learned the trade but none of them engages in it on a full-time basis. The oldest son did at first paint masks for his father, but he decided to become a car-engine mechanic when he was seventeen. He even went as far as Panama for eight months to receive further training and is working for the army, where he teaches mechanics. One daughter studied to be a nurse, while the other two have not had any specialized formal training. Two daughters are raising their families in their parents' compound. The third daughter, who is married to a driver/mechanic, does not live at home. Like her mother, she sells clothing in street markets. In 1981, both of the daughters who remained at home were helping their father, for they too have been trained to make masks and other plaster objects. They worked during the entire week, usually in the afternoon after finishing the housework. By that time, Mr. Vizcarra had also taught his sons-in-law—one of whom works for a bank and the other for a soap factory—the trade. They frequently worked for him on weekends. By 1984 the two daughters had stopped working for their father on a regular basis. One was baking birthday cakes, and the other made wigs. But by then, one of the sons of his oldest daughter, who was still going to school, had taken up the trade as well.

Mr. Vizcarra paid his daughters, sons-in-law and grandson by the piece. There was little division of labor: Each member of the family both molded and painted the items allotted to them. He felt that he was too old to work on his own and was pleased that he could provide work for the extended family.

> This is my life, and all because my grandfather gave me that advice when I was a small child: 'One day you will grow up and you will have many responsibilities, so you have to prepare yourself.' And I obeyed and followed his word to this day. Now I am already an old man.

Similarly, the printer's trade is often passed down from father to son over many generations. Thus the grandfathers of two of our printer informants were also printers. One started working for his father in typography when he was very young. His grandfather owned a printing press: He was the founder of a newspaper in Cochabamba. And his grandfather's brother owned a press in Santiago, Chile. "I have a large number of kin involved in the business." After our informant worked for his father for two or three years, the latter helped him set up shop by giving him type fonts, paper, etc., and allowing him to use his equipment when he had large orders to fill. His father also acts as a guarantor for his loans.

Even the job of producing a specific item may be passed on from one generation to the next. The other printer informant mentioned above owned a small printing firm which has produced the same calendar (with all movable holidays) since the turn of the century. The original firm has spawned several offshoots, operated by the siblings of the present owner. Although the siblings compete with one another, they also cooperate in the acquisition of raw materials during periodic shortages.

The skills learned by family members may be put to uses that are different from those they had originally. As we have seen, the daughter of Mr. Vizcarra, the mask maker, manufactures wigs. The occupations of the family of Mr. Gutierrez, a tinsmith, discussed in Chapter 11, also exemplify both direct and indirect influences from the tinsmith trade.

Such institutions as Alasita, the fair at which miniature objects are purchased by *Paceños* of all social backgrounds to bring good fortune during the year, further the maintenance of urban crafts traditions. A large number of individuals, including many who do not engage in artisan crafts during the rest of the year or who are specialized in crafts other than the production of miniature objects, produce goods for this fair. Gypsum-mask makers mold animals, houses, market-vendor scenes complete with produce, and, most important of all, the grinning, open-armed figure representing Ekeko. Ekeko, if well attended to (i.e., decorated with paper streamers, sprinkled with alcohol, and offered a cigarette to smoke), will provide his owners with money and all the staples, household goods, represented by the miniatures, etc., tied to his body. Printers print large amounts of paper money in the name of the "Bank of Alasita" and print the wrappers for the myriad staple containers that are laboriously made and filled with the actual staples (sugar, flour, ground coffee, etc.) by honest artisans and with substitutes by the less scrupulous. Wood-carvers produce entire sets of dishes that fit into wooden boxes the shape and size of an egg. Instrument makers produce toy guitars, potters make tiny clay pots, and tinsmiths fashion miniature wheelbarrows, sewing machines, milk cans, etc., in addition to their largest selling items: cars, trucks and buses for would-be owners of full-sized vehicles. These too, like their more traditional counterpart, the Ekeko, must be filled with miniature goods and honored with paper streamers and alcohol.

Considerable time and effort is invested in preparation for Alasita. One particular tinsmith, for example, whose principal product is masks for dancers, sets aside several weeks each January to make miniature masks, trucks and buses. Similarly, a confectioner begins packaging staples some six weeks before the fair, where she rents her own stand. She first became engaged in this activity only three years before we interviewed her; but her mother, who roasts peanuts to sell in the market, had long engaged in this activity, and her grandmother used to make gypsum houses for the fair.

Although most of the objects produced are quite standardized, some are very elaborate. A prize is traditionally given by the munici-pality for the most artistic examples of each craft, and many crafts-men vie to have their masterpieces selected by the judges. Even some artisans who exhibit and sell only full-sized items may participate in the annual miniatures competition. Thus, a producer of woven willow furniture regularly presents miniature living-room sets, screens, etc. His father, who engaged in the same trade, participated in the competition in past years.

Lesser, seasonal efforts are expended to produce goods for a Christmas fair and to pleat palm leaf objects for Palm Sunday. The fiesta system also furthers craft traditions, such as elaborate sequin and bead embroidery, mask making, etc. The goods that are made are used exclusively for ritual purposes, and there are no factory-made substitutes. Production for fiestas involves thousands of individuals who produce everything from hats, masks, costumes, festive velvet skirts, gloves, rattles and other musical instruments to candles, wax flowers and crepe paper piñatas. Even more than Alasita, fiestas hone the skills of craftsmen who are called upon to invent new designs every year. The fiesta system in Bolivia thus involves the ultimate in specialty production, which is geared toward working-class consumers rather than elite consumers and producers, as in industrial countries.[4]

Apprenticeship

Apprenticeship with kin, acquaintances or strangers is by far the most common form of acquiring skills. Such apprenticeships may be undertaken either in fields that families have specialized in over many years or in new occupations. The former include tinsmithery and jewelry, mask and candle making. Family traditions may influence new activities as well. For instance, the son of a skilled smith, famous for ornamental gates in Sucre, manufactures car bodies with just a simple metal-folding device.

Apprenticeships vary widely according to the trade and the nature of the relationship between master craftsman and apprentice. Their duration ranges from a period of several months to several years. Apprenticeships may be quite informal or involve a more or less formal agreement. Some entail payments by the apprentice or his parents to the master, while in other instances the apprentice may receive food or a small salary from the start. These arrangements do not appear to be subject to any governmental control since small businesses are at least de facto not regulated by the same labor laws as larger, formally constituted ones.

A few examples will serve to show the vicissitudes and hardships involved in apprenticeships. Julio, a 30-year-old *Paceño*, has a tiny silversmith workshop in a patio on a working-class neighborhood. His wife is a bread vendor. Because he could no longer count on his father's financial support, he abandoned his high-school studies when he was 12 years old, and it was then that he learned from his father how to make toy cooking vessels out of aluminum. Julio's father was a migrant from a rural community, and had learned the trade in a large, German-owned aluminum vessel factory, where he had worked for 20 to 25 years before setting up his own workshop.

When Julio was 20, he apprenticed himself to a silversmith friend. In the beginning, he received neither salary nor food and had to be supported by his parents, with whom he continued to live. After three years he began to work in another workshop and began purchasing tools of his own. These permitted him to make some of his own silver objects in his spare time. He used some of his friend's more expensive equipment when he required it. Finally, after six years, he was able to purchase additional equipment, especially a laminating machine, and set up his own shop. He presently works alone most of the time, but the younger brother of his former master uses his shop from time to time and occasionally lends him a hand, for this helper does not get along with his brother and therefore prefers not to use his workshop. Some other fledgling silversmiths also use Julio's equipment on occasion.

Julio's career illustrates the important direct and indirect role of foreigners in the acquisition of skills, which we alluded to earlier.[5] It also illustrates differences in the problems faced by apprentices who enter formal contracts with non-kin and the usually more casual arrangements with close kin. While the former face the initial hardship of having to forgo an income for an extended period of time, the latter may face constraints in their relationship to their kin teachers. Thus, Julio's former master's younger brother obviously learned his skills from his brother, but he may have required other contacts to become independent. Perhaps significantly, he used a contact that had been established by his brother.

Those artisans who began their careers in the 1940s found their work life even more difficult in the beginning. Nicanor was orphaned and lived with an older kinswoman. When he was eight years old, he began working in a shoemaker's shop. Then he assisted a hatmaker, after which he was employed in a shoe factory for three years. When the factory closed after the workers attempted to unionize, he was forced to find a new occupation. So, at age 14, he became a tailor's apprentice. "In those days, things were different," he explained. "Some tailors not only paid no wages to apprentices at all, but they even had them serving their households as domestics. In order to learn how to sew, they had to wash diapers, sweep the floor, and even then the maestros would begrudge them a cup of tea. I received no food, nothing; and since my parents had died, I had to live on bananas and bread." After a month of this, Nicanor found work with another tailor, pretending that he was a *pantalonero*, a pant maker. Although it soon became evident that Nicanor in fact had few skills and had to be taught, the maestro paid him from the start. Despite the greater hold a master had over his apprentices at that time, the apprentices did have some options for changing their situation even then. In a society in which price was, and still is, more important than quality to the majority of the consumers, a lower skill level may suffice to produce acceptable products. Early termination of an apprenticeship thus becomes a viable option, albeit at the risk of limiting or slowing one's future advancement.

The fragility of the master-apprentice relationship in turn exacerbates the ambiguity inherent in this relationship. Apprenticeship involves an intrinsically asymmetrical relationship between two individuals that has the potential of being transformed into a progressively more symmetrical one. This transformation entails a paradox. The apprentice becomes increasingly valuable to his master as his skills improve. At the same time, however, it is to the master's advantage to maintain the asymmetry of the relationship as long as possible. Extending the duration of the asymmetry is, of course, exploitative. Yet the apprentice's resistance to this form of exploitation is mitigated to the extent that he can expect to benefit from the extended training once he has finally overcome the asymmetry (cf. Cooper 1980).

The nature of both the process of learning and the negotiation of the relationship itself varies according to factors intrinsic to a particular craft, such as the difficulty of learning the skill and the extent of competition. A master may attempt to extend the duration of dependency and limit potential competition by refusing to reveal trade secrets that might enable his apprentices to compete with him once they set up their own shops. Such a strategy is particularly appropriate in the rarer trades. Thus Mr. Chok'e, a jeweler who also trades in gilded trinkets in other cities, cloisters himself in his workshop every time he gilds the silver objects brought to him by the silversmiths he has trained. By doing so, he keeps the gilding process a secret, thereby forcing those he trained to continue to rely on his services. Recently he divorced himself from the whole lot because they took advantage of his absence and used his workshop to work for his clients directly.

A maestro may also perpetuate dependency by refusing to permit a worker to engage in certain parts of the labor process.[6] For example, the owner of a tailor shop is likely to draw and cut the suits but leave the rest of the work to his assistants. Although his reason may be to prevent wasting material, the result is the same: Most of the learning takes place through observation and imitation, but an apprentice cannot perfect his skills without being given the opportunity to practice them.

The more formalized division of labor that exists in some industries may also promote dependency. In the shoe manufacturing industry, for example, stores order specific models of shoes from contractors, who in turn subcontract uppers, soles and assemblage to different individuals. Nevertheless, such arrangements need not always lead to permanent dependency. Sometimes they are conducive to multiplex symbiotic relationships. Thus, although car repairmen who specialize in different kinds of repairs may first work in one or in several garages on a contract basis, they are the owners of their tools and hire their own assistants. They may also have clients of their own. Later, if they are able to amass enough capital, they may become the owners of their own garages and enter into similar agreements with other specialists.

The dependency between shop owners and workers can also be perpetuated for reasons other than the lack of access to skills. As discussed earlier, elite ownership of the more sophisticated means of production was the rule in the past and is still very prevalent today. Although the problem of upward mobility is less pronounced at lower levels of technical complexity, it is also very difficult there. Craftsmen attempt to acquire their own tools and equipment gradually while working for others. They may, however, be frustrated in their plans. Many switch into other crafts that require lower capital investment. But this means that they further add to the crowding in these occupations. Mr. Mamani, for example, first learned carpentry and tailoring but was not able to accumulate sufficient capital for stock and equipment to open his own shop. He thus became a hatter because the trade required relatively little capital to become independent. Although his father made hats in his community of origin, he had abandoned his trade and become a merchant. So Mr. Mamani learned the art of hatmaking from a friend. Much later, when he married a young woman from a family that considers itself socially superior, he learned how to operate a metal lathe and presently has a booming business in reboring truck engines.

Finally, a craftsman may find it difficult to replicate his master's network of clients or essential contacts with suppliers of raw materials. Thus Mr. Loayza, the middle-class lamp maker mentioned earlier, had to visit the factories of U.S. parts manufacturers to persuade them to supply him with small lots of parts. It is unlikely that his female assistant will ever be able to replicate these connections, even in the implausible event that she could come up with the rather substantial amount of capital required to buy an adequate assortment of parts. Similarly, as we have shown earlier, foreigners may have an advantage over locals in certain areas of production because they have access to their fellow countrymen and to the foreign community in general and are also more familiar with its special needs.

It is not always in the maestros' interest to perpetuate dependency. Because of economic circumstances, maestros often find it advantageous or unavoidable to establish more flexible ties with their workers. When there is little work, they cannot afford to keep all of their workers, and it is in their interest to allow them to find work elsewhere. If a maestro has a more capitalized firm, he may even help his workers set up their own workshops, where they can engage in work for him when he needs it. The economic conditions and the maestro's superior contacts may assure their loyalty to him. A Chilean furniture manufacturer has chosen this solution. He came to La Paz during a period of relative prosperity and established a large workshop for high quality furniture and a foam rubber manufacturing plant. He employed craftsmen he brought with him from Chile. All but one of them returned to Chile when they ran into difficulties in obtaining residency permits, so he continued with Bolivian workers. When economic conditions deteriorated between 1980 and 1984, forcing him to close all but one of the retail outlets for his furniture and idle his foam rubber manufacturing equipment, he encouraged some of his workers to establish their own workshops, where they continued to work for him on a part-time basis. When he sold the firm to his cousin, the latter continued this flexible arrangement (see Chapter 4 for details).

Migrants and *Paceños* differed with respect to the apprenticeship situations they chose. Migrants seemed to prefer kin. Eleven out of 48 migrant owner-operators had taken apprenticeships with kin, while only four out of 53 *Paceños* did so. In contrast, *Paceños* more frequently sought apprenticeships with relative strangers, often looking for those with particularly good crafts reputations. As we have already seen, perhaps because of a desire to learn certain specialized trades, far more *Paceños* worked for foreigners at one point or other in their careers.

Factories are an additional source of skills. Factory workers frequently open their own shops in related activities where, besides the skills they learned in the factory, they invest their social security benefits accrued during their period of factory employment.

The development and perfection of artisan skills are subject to serious limitations. Many of the goods produced by artisans can barely compete with manufactured goods. Those artisans who are particularly successful tend to diversify into other activities, such as owning a bus or investing in real estate, rather than taking the risks involved in putting all their eggs in one basket. This strategy enables them to temporarily abandon an activity during an economic crisis or reduce work in that activity to a minimum while pursuing other ones (see Long and Roberts 1984 for a discussion of a similar phenomenon in Peru). Finally, the owner of a large workshop may become more and more involved in management and in the endless bureaucratic red tape which is an integral part of doing business in Bolivia.

Career-Paths of Individuals Who Underwent Apprenticeships. Jesus, a migrant from a Titicaca lakeshore community, began his urban career at the age of 14, when he apprenticed himself to his brother-in-law (his sister's husband). This brother-in-law, after working for a large foreign-owned aluminum factory, invested his earnings and knowledge in his own plant for aluminum vessels. Upon marriage, after eleven years of dependent work, Jesus established his own workshop. At present, he engages seven workers led by a maestro, a skilled metal worker, who is paid at a piece rate on a long-term contract. A niece, one of his major clients, travels to Cochabamba and Santa Cruz, two large Bolivian cities in the valleys and lowlands, to sell his wares. Jesus and five other small-scale producers, including some Koreans, have formed a purchasing cooperative to purchase raw materials from a foreign importer. He claims that the Koreans are secretive about their manufacturing techniques and that they have no time to drink, in contrast to his Bolivian cronies, characteristics he seems to both resent and admire. His wife and friends maintain that he drinks excessively and that he has relegated most of the production to his workers and supervision to his wife, who also cooks for the crew. Jesus's response is that sometimes there *are* slack periods, but when an order must be filled he works for more than 12 hours a day. His income was well above that of a skilled worker employed in a large factory.

Career patterns similar to that of Jesus are exceptional among migrants. They are far more characteristic of *Paceños*. Alcides' career path is a good example of the careers of many *Paceños* who have undergone apprenticeships.

Alcides' work history began in 1949, when he was twelve and his father died. His mother, who sold jewelry, landed him an apprenticeship with one of her clients. The deal was that he would not get paid for his work until he had mastered the trade. Alcides learned rapidly. He loved his new work. After a week he was already able to etch metal, and after a month he could set stones. A month later he had reached the skill level of a journeyman. At this point, he also started to take evening courses in typing, so his day began at the jewelry workshop at 8 a.m. and ended at 10 p.m. However, after four months, he still did not receive any compensation for his work, so he joined the workshop of a Peruvian who had arrived recently. At the beginning, the workshop had practically no tools (see Chapter 7), but as earnings accumulated, the shop was better equipped and finally expanded to include seven journeymen. At the age of 15, Alcides became the shop foreman, and when the owner was away he managed everything alone. Since things were going well without him, the owner began to drink and left the shop in Alcides' hands without ever increasing his wages. Alcides' compensation continued to be limited to a share of 50% of the work he personally performed. This led Alcides to join the shop of another Peruvian, an elderly gentleman whose work he very much admired and who promised him a 70% share.

After a while, Alcides' life took a different turn. He began to work as a typist in an office where he could earn more. Then, in 1955, he obtained a scholarship to study at a police academy. Because of politics his scholarship was rescinded after only one year. His sister, who engaged in contraband, suggested that he join her. He opened a shop in a room provided by his mother-in-law to sell jewelry he purchased in Arica, a Chilean free port. His wife, whom he had recently married, worked as an auxiliary nurse, and because she earned enough for household needs, all of his income could be invested in tools and equipment. Again, he was forced to return to the primitive methods with which he had learned to cope in the beginning of his career. But eventually he earned enough to furnish the workshop and later to enlarge it.

At present, Alcides works in a well-equipped workshop. At times he has employed as many as 15 workers and, as we shall see in Chapter 9, has gained an international clientele. He has no further plans to enlarge his shop. "I have no love of money," he professes. "We all have goals, and I have reached mine. Economically I am well off. Two of my children are going to school, and one is already married." In 1984 his eldest son, age 23, was working in New York in an office, which, in turn, awakened his 18-year-old daughter's interest in learning English. In 1988 she was continuing her studies of the English language and was planning to learn computing. Although both she and her brother were married, Alcides continued to assist her. "I do not wish to leave wealth behind. When children see that their parents are rich, they cease to study and become nobodies. Rather, I would like to take a trip around the world with my wife to celebrate our 25th wedding anniversary." He was recently involved in an exchange program in Ecuador, but he felt that he had more techniques to teach the young instructor there than he could learn from her. He is proud of Bolivian workmanship.

"I would like to serve my country," he professes. "As president of the Association of Goldsmiths and Watchmakers, I have represented Bolivian artisans in Venezuela." He would also like to act as a teacher abroad. Indeed, he is actively involved with a group of Bolivians who are attempting to further Bolivian artisanry and was teaching a course in new techniques to a group of jewelers when we visited him.

Perhaps his artisanry will be continued in the family in the next generation. His older son is well versed in the trade, and in 1984 Alcides hoped to land him a job in an American factory through a Peruvian jeweler contact. In 1988, the son was still working as a mechanic in New York. "It would be nice if I could pass on the shop to one of my children," he confided wistfully in 1984, "but since my younger son wishes to study medicine, I cannot refuse him." Yet in 1988 this son was working in La Paz as a mechanic in a garage owned by a Swiss immigrant.

Skill Acquistion in Factories

As mentioned earlier, another source of skills is work in factories. One artisan began working in a small workshop when he was fifteen, after his second year of high school, because his father had died and his mother did not have the means to allow him to study. He worked in La Paz for ten years and then went to Argentina for four years, where he worked in a larger factory owned by a German. He feels that it is there that he acquired most of his more specialized skills in upholstery and furniture design. Upon his return to La Paz he worked in a larger furniture factory. At that time he already had an automobile upholstery workshop of his own in Miraflores. He then moved to Obrajes, a middle-class and elite suburb, because there was too much competition in Miraflores and because he felt he could better take advantage of his skills in making and re-upholstering fine furniture with an upper-class clientele. For example, he might be asked to adapt a design made by an architect. He also continued reupholstering car seats. There he worked with artisans who also had their own workshops and worked for him on a temporary basis. The disadvantage of this system is that he could never be sure that they would appear on a given day (particularly if it was a Monday), even when he had a lot of work for them. Finally, by 1988 he had moved once more, this time to a location close to the center of the city, near a place where people offer used cars for sale.

Skill Acquisition Through Formal Education

Many occupations like carpentry, plumbing, mechanics, electronics, and business require a considerable degree of formal training in trade schools or through correspondence courses. Formal education is seen as a major avenue of upward mobility for all Bolivians. Parents sacrifice to educate particularly their male children to a level that exceeds their own. Only graduates from a local trade school, Pedro Domingo Murillo, are employed by the factory repair shop of a highly capitalized plastic-container factory owned by a German immigrant. A man with a more modest metal shop applies a range of skills learned both informally from kinsmen and skills, like mathematics, acquired formally in the same trade school. Similarly, a mechanic learned his job at Pedro Domingo Murillo, where he attended night classes for four years while working in his father's workshop. He feels that the teachers were more rounded then than they are now. They taught him mechanics as well as electronics, welding, etc. "Now everything is more specialized and one has to take one-and-a-half-year courses in each occupation." He ascribes the change to the fact that this would be more lucrative for the school. He says that education became accessible to everyone because of Paz Estenssoro. Nevertheless this school was not free.[7] In Chapter 10 we will describe another attempt by the government to increase the level of skills in the work force.

Correspondence courses are often taken in order to attain additional skills and thereby improve employment flexibility, i.e., to be able to take a number of different jobs, consecutively or simultaneously. Courses in radio and television repair appeared to be particularly popular.

Conclusion

When viewed in isolation, the processes by which artisans acquire skills in Bolivia appear rather haphazard and disjointed. However, when viewed in the context of the place of artisanry in an under-developed nation (in which there is stratified access to the means of production, a high rate of rural-urban migration and the concomitant transfer of rural skills to cities, long-term urban crafts traditions, and poverty that often forces individuals to provide for their own subsistence at a very early age), certain patterns begin to emerge.

Because of the interpenetration of larger and smaller firms, individuals can learn craft-production skills in the factory and then put them to use in independent production.[8] For instance, a boot manufacturer had great difficulty in keeping workers because they would set up their own shops as soon as they achieved a degree of competence in their trade.

In a dependent economy, flexibility through diversification or the reduction of operations must take precedence over economies of scale. During the colonial period, access to craft skills was open to all; but the limitations that craftsmen were subjected to in their attempt to ascend the economic ladder were strongly influenced by ethnicity. Ethnic discrimination began to decrease in the middle of the twentieth century, but elite status, however defined, still entails privileges in terms of access to raw materials, bank credit, liberation from customs duties, etc., giving elite enterprises (usually the larger ones) an advantage over those (usually smaller ones) established by the upwardly mobile. As we shall see in Chapter 7, international agencies often reinforce such privileges by favoring larger over smaller concerns in their lending practices. Now, as before, excellence in a craft leads to only limited upward mobility. To get ahead, the family of a craftsman must move into more elite professions and from there perhaps back to industry. Only the foreigner who has the necessary start-up capital can generally establish the elite connections needed to parlay technical skills directly into ownership or management of an industry in his field of expertise.

In addition to the advantage of having few elite connections, the skilled worker-entrepreneur faces limitations inherent in the economic system. Because of these limitations, narrow specialization in one's field of expertise is not necessarily considered the best strategy. Unless an entrepreneur can establish a monopoly, he is dangerously exposed to the vagaries of politics as well as national and international economic fluctuations. Instead, an entrepreneur frequently prefers to diversify either by vertical integration or by branching into unrelated economic activities.

The skilled worker is placed in a curious position. Economic and political uncertainty lead to strategies of diversification, low specialization and a relatively undeveloped division of labor, thereby creating opportunities for individuals with wide-ranging skills. Yet the same conditions coupled with elite privilege limit the full development of any particular skill. The formally trained technician is often confronted by an analogous situation. Unless he finds a position in the important but shrinking public sector, he is better off becoming an owner-manager of multiple enterprises than continuing as a specialist with widening responsibilities. Alternatively, he may leave the country during an economic downturn. Beyond a certain point, in both the case of the skilled worker-entrepreneur and that of the technician, the importance of specific skills is diluted or lost altogether.

The processes mentioned above also provide a partial explanation for the prevalence of skill transmission along family lines and the frequent choice of kin and fellow countrymen as masters among migrants seeking apprenticeships. The transmission of skills along family lines adds to the household budget and contributes to maintaining rarer skills within contexts defined as cooperative. Hiring kin creates mutual obligations that may go beyond the immediate contract. In addition, more information can be obtained about the availability, qualifications and reliability of a prospective apprentice, who, in turn, finds it easier to hear about openings. For the same reasons, kinsmen are likely to be hired for part-time assistance, particularly on short notice. This is true, in a more attentuated way, for fellow migrants from the same locality of origin. But even among migrants, kin-based recruitment of apprentices, although prevalent, is not the norm.

Finally, the nature of the dependency between master, journeyman and apprentice is affected by these same limitations as well as by the opportunities created by an economic system with a simple division of labor. Masters often treat apprentices and younger workers in general in the authoritarian and paternalistic manner the elite adopt toward their workers, but the enterprising apprentice is not entirely at the mercy of his master as he may be able to improve his position by moving elsewhere. In contrast, the relationship between the owners of the enterprises and master journeymen is more egalitarian, since the latter may already have become partly independent or could decide to accelerate the process if treated as inferiors. Both master/apprentice and owner/journeyman relationships, then, are fraught with tension, for both are potentially competitive.

In conclusion, a focus on the contexts of learning rather than simply on the processes of transmitting technical knowledge is essential for understanding the rationale behind the idiosyncrasies of each mode of learning.

Notes

1. The archaeological Tiahuanaco motifs had long been popular in tourist crafts in La Paz.

2. It is interesting to note, however, that even in that example, the artisan's mother is from Huatajata and still has "her sheep there."

3. We did not inquire whether she still cultivated land in the community of origin.

4. Obviously, custom production of other goods (e.g., in construction and carpentry) is geared primarily toward the middle class and the elite.

5. A parallel example can be found in the case of Mr. Gutierrez, the tinsmith (cf Chapter 11). His father learned new metalworking techniques from his European employer, while the kinsman who taught him the art of manufacturing fireworks had in turn acquired his knowledge from "Japanese and German" specialists.

6. The extreme solution to avoid the problem of generating one's own competition is to work alone. Mr. Gutierrez, for example, has followed this path. He complains that every time he worked on projects with others, they would copy his techniques or designs and steal away his clients by under-cutting his prices. This is one of the reasons why he has been working alone for a long time (see Chapter 11).

7. For a further example of a person who received training at the Pedro Domingo Murillo school see Mr. Gutierrez's life history in Chapter 11.

8. Although we did record some instances of the inverse process, we could not ascertain its extent since we interviewed only a few factory workers.

6

The Social Relations
of Production

As we have argued earlier, the process of industrialization does not necessarily entail an inexorable progression toward greater concentration of productive capacity, increasing division of labor and mechanization. Rather, it entails flexible accommodation to local, national and international circumstances. The path taken by industrial development also depends upon previous adaptations that continue to shape its course.

Nowhere is the flexibility of this process more apparent than in the social relations of production. We will argue that the social relations of production (and distribution, which we will broach superficially in this chapter but discuss in more detail in Chapter 9) involve the creation of extensive networks of variegated ties, some of which are specific to the type of transaction involved and some with a broader range of applications. Since the nature of these ties varies to some extent according to the type of manufacturing activity and the social class position of the producer, our analysis will take as its points of departure concrete cases of firms that illustrate the diversity of these relationships. We shall then analyze the range of variation for each type of relationship discovered.

Before we move to the analysis of specific cases, we will first examine the size and social characteristics of the work force in small-scale industries in La Paz from the vantage point of our aggregate sample.

A salient feature of small enterprises in La Paz is the high involvement of kin in the work force. Some 70% of all firms included kin in the work force. Of these, almost three quarters (72.7%) included members of the owner's nuclear family, and about half (53.3%) included kin outside the nuclear family, and 14.3% worked exclusively with members of the nuclear family. Spouses worked together in 41.6%

of these firms, and children were included in 46.8% (or 29.4% and 33%, respectively, of all firms).

The kind of kin who are most likely to be involved in an enterprise depends on the kind of activity. Both sexes are more likely to be involved in activities that are less sex-typed, such as the garment industry, the fur and jewelry trades, tinsmithery, mask making, baking, and printing, and hence wives are frequently employed in these trades, while women are excluded from mechanics shops. As we shall see later, the degree of capitalization of the firm also plays a role.

Despite the salient role of kin, a large number of workers in firms of all levels of capitalization are not related to the owners. This is true even in those instances where sufficient numbers of workers could potentially be recruited from within the nuclear or extended family. As the case studies will demonstrate, upward mobility in the younger generations is one of the reasons for not hiring close kin. Another reason is the need for extended families to diversify their sources of income in the face of the prevailing economic uncertainty.

Less and more capitalized firms are remarkably similar with respect to the degree to which they include kin: The percentage including kin in the work force is practically identical as is the likelihood of working with kin outside the nuclear family.

Some of the differences between less and more capitalized enterprises, such as the fact that the more capitalized firms never employ only members of the nuclear family, can be ascribed to differences in size. Differences in size may explain the fact that the average percentage of kin workers in less capitalized firms in which more than one person works (55.3% overall and 41.3% in firms with both kin and non-kin involved) is far higher than in more capitalized firms (where the corresponding figures are 8% and 9.3%). The somewhat higher average number of kin workers in more capitalized firms (1.67 vs. 1.56 in less capitalized ones) may also be related to firm size.

There are, however, some salient differences that are not related to differences in size. For example, almost twice as many of the more capitalized firms employed no blue-collar workers who were related to the owners, which in turn may be due to the lesser involvement of members of the nuclear family in these firms (45% vs. 53%). This may be explained by fact that in the more highly capitalized firms kin are mostly employed as white-collar workers, in managerial roles, or as partners. Although kin, including members of the immediate family of the owners, do, on occasion, perform skilled work in the firm, most blue-collar workers do not belong to the same socioeconomic stratum as the owners and managers.[1] In contrast, in less capitalized firms they play a wider variety of roles.

The same factor may explain the types of kin most likely to be found in smaller and larger firms. Siblings are more likely to be involved in larger firms, where they are often co-owners; in less capitalized firms, the kin are often nephews, who take apprenticeships in their uncles' workshops.

The Enterprise of Doña Flora

We begin our analysis with the firm of Doña Flora, who in 1981 was an upwardly mobile, forty-five-year-old, second-generation, rural-urban migrant who produced in her workshop in La Paz woven and knitted woolen apparel that she exported and sold to foreign tourists in La Paz and to Bolivian clients in the city of Cochabamba. Like many other producers of tourist items, Doña Flora was engaged in a wide range of economic activities. At the time of our first visit, she was involved in a combination of manufacturing, whole-sale and retail activities—concerns that entailed manifold commercial ties and labor relations. Since such relationships were among our major interests, one of the first questions we asked was who her workers were. Doña Flora introduced the workers in the room as her children, in-laws and nephew. However, subsequent observations and information gleaned from interviews with other members of the family cast doubt on the veracity of her claim that she worked only with members of her kin group. During a later visit, our Bolivian assistant obtained a more probable version from an older woman who was helping Doña Flora repair defective sweaters. She told her that the workers were her own children and that her family was not related to Doña Flora.

Why did Doña Flora try to hide the true identity of her workers? The most probable answer sheds light on the precarious relationship between master and worker in Bolivian industries and on the cutthroat competition in small-scale production. On our first visit, Doña Flora may have suspected that we were foreign buyers in disguise and that we were using our avowed scientific interest as a subterfuge to obtain direct contacts with artisans. Such buyers would have been hesitant to attempt to lure away close kin, who could be expected to have long-term interest in the firm. In fact, when Doña Flora branched out into the manufacture of jackets, the extended family to whom she had put out the sewing was able to make direct contact with her major foreign client, a buyer from London, and began working for him directly. The experience had been particularly galling, since it was the very same client who in 1973 had encouraged her to diversify from sweaters and ponchos into tailored garments.

Doña Flora's trouble with these workers led her to make changes that illustrate a pattern many employers followed of shifting between work arrangements that entailed different degrees of dependence and intensity. The workers she lost sewed in their own homes. She would bring the work to them and pick it up when it was ready. In 1978, Doña Flora expanded her workshop and hired workers to work there permanently.

Preparing the warp for woolen cloth

Doña Flora's seamstresses were just one part of an enterprise whose great complexity became more and more apparent to us as we observed her at work and interviewed various members of her work force. For example, Doña Flora generally purchased alpaca wool from altiplano producer-vendors who came to the city to sell it. However, when she had large orders, this source often proved insufficient, forcing her to travel to distant fairs to buy wool directly from the alpaca herders. She then paid elderly women who worked at home in El Alto to spin the wool with wooden spindles. She herself also engaged in this activity when she had the time. In addition, Doña Flora purchased machine-spun wool from the would-be state monopoly, and later, when the price the monopoly charged became prohibitive, she bought the yarn from a factory that produced it clandestinely.

To prepare the warp, Doña Flora combined different natural colors of both hand- and factory-spun yarn. This was a laborious task done with the assistance of anyone who happened to be available: her youngest teenage son, her mother on her periodic visits from the Lake Titicaca community where she and her husband had returned after he retired from his job as a porter in the La Paz beer factory, and sometimes an additional worker or two. Her preferred spot for this activity, which requires an area as long as the cloth to be woven, was a plot she owns on the flat El Alto. On the day we accompanied her, her neighbors, two young women who had recently migrated from the altiplano, came out to watch and help her disentangle the yarn in the hopes of learning an aspect of a new trade. With but a few iron pegs and two metal basins, it took four persons six hours to prepare the 200-vara (180-yard) warp, not counting the hour spent by the two neighbors unraveling the unruly ball of yarn and the hour travel time to El Alto. That day, Doña Flora took advantage of our presence (and our jeep) to take the warps to a rural community located 15 kilometers away; otherwise she would have had to go by bus or prevail on her younger brother to take her there in his ancient pickup truck. The community enjoys bus service twice a week from La Paz. One of the dairy-farm families in the rural community--a widower, his two daughters and four sons--weaves for Doña Flora. The family was introduced to her by a former weaver and *compadre* (ritual kinsman) who gave up his trade for a factory job. On occasion, the family has worked with as many as four looms at a time, some provided by Doña Flora, but during our visit, only one was in operation. Although the family could have also prepared the warp, they preferred to handle only the actual weaving. Doña Flora had her own ideas about the pattern of stripes, and besides (according to Doña Flora), the weavers were afraid that she might suspect them of cheating by using less yarn or substituting yarn of inferior quality.

In addition, Doña Flora engaged a weaver to work full time on her own patio. A peasant from Lake Titicaca, this man (with whom Doña Flora has established ties of ritual kinship) had, in the past, furnished her with cloth when she was selling goods to tourists in a street market.

After the cloth was woven, Doña Flora and her two daughters washed it in a river that was half an hour away by bus and carded it to give it a smoother appearance. Then they handed it over to the four workers we have already encountered, who cut it, sewed jackets and made appliqué designs on pillow cases and wall hangings with the shop's two sewing machines.

Doña Flora's second major line of craft goods (in addition to those made from woven woolen cloth) was alpaca sweaters and ponchos. Her principal source of sweaters was a kin group in Huarina, while ponchos were knitted for her by women in the Cochabamba area with alpaca wool she provided. She, her daughter and the mother (mentioned earlier) of the permanent workers spent a great deal of time mending small imperfections in the alpaca sweaters. When a large shipment had to be prepared, Arturo, her cousin's son, would come after school to help. Often he stayed overnight repairing ponchos and sweaters and packing them for export. Indeed, during one year when Doña Flora's sons were in the military service, he joined the household altogether. Doña Flora also had machine-knitted alpaca sweaters made in her own shop, and she traveled regularly to Cochabamba to sell them and other goods made out of artificial fibers that she purchased in La Paz. The two-way nature of this productive and commercial venture made the expense and time involved in the 500-kilometer trip well worth her while. On these trips, Doña Flora was accompanied by her younger brother (who was sometimes also sent on business trips to cities as far away as Lima) or by Arturo.

Although Doña Flora made most of the crucial decisions regarding her enterprise herself, she also obtained managerial advice and help from various others. Assistance with the paperwork was particularly important, since Doña Flora is illiterate. Her son-in-law, Indalecio, was in charge of the paperwork involved in exporting and shipping. Indalecio--who lived with his former wife Ricarda and their children in a separate part of Doña Flora's compound and generally shared meals with Doña Flora--had learned these aspects of the business when he was working for a major dispatching firm. He and Ricarda entered into a partnership with Doña Flora. In addition to Indalecio's managerial assistance, Doña Flora received advice from buyers and hired an outside accountant to go over the accounts with her.

Besides these two major lines of business, Doña Flora (as well as Ricarda) engaged in other, subsidiary ones whose relative importance waxed and waned according to the health of their manufacturing enterprise. Both had market stalls in a biweekly street market, where, among other things, they sold clothing purchased in El Alto and "Laura Ingals bonnets" (of the kind Bolivians see on television in the dubbed *Little House on the Prairie* series) made by Doña Flora's other daughter, who was seventeen in 1981. The two daughters-in-law who lived in La Paz engaged in similar marketing activities. A final source of income was transportation. At one time or another, both Doña Flora and her older daughter owned buses. In 1981, this was true only of Indalecio and Ricarda, who operated their bus on one of the regular city bus lines. When he had the time (and the bus was in working condition), Indalecio drove the bus himself. At other times, Doña Flora's younger brother took over.

Analysis

The work relationships in Doña Flora's firm are representative of both the range of ties required in the day-to-day operation of an artisan firm and the mutability of the work relationships over time necessary for the survival of both owners and workers.

Work Relationships with Kin. Work relationships with kin in Doña Flora's firm included the unremunerated collaboration of household members, partnerships with close kin living in semidependent households, the companionship and/or collaboration of siblings and more distantly related kin, and various other transactions. The latter included the sale of products made by kinsmen and the contracting of a kinsman to transport goods to distant localities in return for the payment of his bus fare and a small variable bonus.

One of the major advantages of kin ties lies in their potential multiplexity. Individuals are tied to their kinsmen through other kin in a variety of ways, creating a system with considerable feedback. As a result, a firm owner rapidly learns if a kinsman or kinswoman is available to undertake some urgent task or to fill a more permanent position. A kinsman may thus become a part-time or even full-time collaborator at one time, a companion at another.

On the negative side, a kinsman who is available and nearby may not be equally suited for all the roles he is called upon to play by a more successful member of his kin network. Doña Flora's brother was probably a good companion on her trips to Cochabamba, but when it came to collecting a debt in Lima, he did not have the necessary clout to settle the matter. It later took the more astute Doña Flora and Indalecio only a day or two to do so. Similarly, this brother did not make an ideal driver. But he was available and needed the work. Also his limitations, unlike those of a stranger, were known. As the saying goes: *"Mejor es el mal conocido que el bien por conocer"* (Known evil is better than unknown good).

Attaching close kin to a firm has its limitations. During an economic downturn, an overreliance on a single major source of income by all members of an extended household may, in fact, be detrimental to their economic well-being. The need for economic diversification was among the reasons why Doña Flora encouraged one of her sons to emigrate to Australia, encouraged her bachelor brother to work as a porter in Washington, D.C., and encouraged her younger son to obtain a job in the U.S. Embassy in La Paz. The occasional order for goods from Australia as well as the possible option of following her son there, the generous remittances from Washington, D.C., and the regular income from the Embassy were more important to Doña Flora--at least during the economic crisis of the mid-1980s--than the direct involvement of these kinsmen in her firm.

Conversely, Doña Flora may not have acted in her long-term interest when she insisted that her son-in-law Indalecio join the firm rather than using his talents as a shipping agent in a more indirect or intermittent manner. To be sure, Indalecio could always have spent more of his time driving his bus when export orders dwindled after 1981, but he would not thereby have fulfilled his potential.

Work Relationships with Non-Kin. Arrangements with non-kin are equally variable. At the lowest level of intensity are one-time sales to customers in the market. But producers/middlemen attempt to cultivate and consolidate ties that could potentially develop into longer term relationships involving repetitive transactions. By looking at Doña Flora's activities, we can see some of the ways these ties were cultivated. For example, she invited a German buyer who bought from her regularly to dinner when he came to discuss a new shipment. She purchased sweaters from the same altiplano producer for many years, thereby assuring a relatively stable source of good-quality products, and she established *casera* (preferred-customer) relationships with knitters and stall owners in Cochabamba. Particularly valuable ties were consolidated through bonds of ritual kinship. Both the mother of Doña Flora's in-house workers and the weaver from Huarina became her *compadres*. So did the in-house weaver mentioned earlier who, upon his entry into a factory, introduced Doña Flora to the family of altiplano weavers to whom she put out work and from whom she, on occasion, bought knitted gloves. We, too, became her *compadres*.

These relationships with non-kin may be intensified over time as confidence builds and/or the need arises. The Latin American who took one of Doña Flora's sons along to Australia was a long-time client. At present, Doña Flora's son carries this man's surname, an indication that he has become fully integrated into the family.

Conversely, such long-term ties may become deactivated or even severed. The latter frequently occurs when one party disappoints the other and sometimes occurs when a worker becomes independent or is no longer needed. In the latter case, however, the relationship may simply become dormant or it may be downgraded and only one of its components continued.

Doña Flora seems to have relied quite heavily on chance encounters to establish her network of work relations with non-kin, although in at least one instance--the weaver family near El Alto--she was aided by an outgoing worker. In addition, she re-engaged at least one person with whom she had a previous work relationship in a new capacity. Chance also played an important role in many other small firms we investigated. For example, it played a part in whether an apprentice would be hired. Thus, prospective apprentices often went from workshop to workshop in search of openings. But often the initial contact was less the result of chance than the fact that the prospective apprentice came from a family the owner knew in the neighborhood or, in the case of first- and second-generation migrants, from the same community of origin. In addition, already-established workers often recommended their own kinsmen or fellow townsmen.

Spatial Dimensions of Work Relationships. The ties necessary to succeed in craft production of the kind that Doña Flora engages in cut across local, regional and national boundaries. Within the city, she had ties with her urban kin, clients, shipping agents and sundry officials. Her spinners lived in El Alto, where she herself also owned a parcel of land and where she purchased goods from middlemen to sell in La Paz proper. But for many reasons, her ties had to extend beyond the city. Rural artisans can charge less for their labor because they have additional income--often their principal source--from their land. Migrants, like Doña Flora's weaver, with strong ties to their communities of origin, are not forced to switch to another economic activity when business is slack but can return to their home communities to farm while continuing the relationship with crafts firms on a part-time basis. Cochabambinas, with their special skills and lower wage demands, also constituted an essential component of Doña Flora's network, as did the market vendors in the city of Cochabamba who opened a new market for alpaca sweaters and goods coming into La Paz from abroad.

The most important ties of all were those with foreign buyers, for only they could open up practically unlimited (albeit very fickle) markets. Participation in international fairs in cities as distant as Caracas and Bogotá served the same purpose. Finally, encouraging kinsmen to emigrate to Washington and Australia opened new sources of remittances and potential economic alternative sources whose value increases as Bolivia's economy deteriorates.

The spatial expansion of small-scale enterprises is, of course, not a universal phenomenon. Many enterprises operate on a strictly local basis. Although interregional expansion of the kind exhibited by Doña Flora's firm tends to be associated with somewhat larger firms, the operation of even small workshops may entail frequent travels that may include remote locations. For example, a lamp maker who invested several thousand dollars invested in imported chandelier parts also has wooden parts made to order in Santa Cruz and sells lamps on consignment in a store there. In a way, such firms act no differently from much larger multinational firms, such as the comestible oil firm that has headquarters in La Paz and factories in Cochabamba and Santa Cruz.

Social Class Interaction. The network of individuals on whom Doña Flora relied to produce and distribute her goods cuts across class boundaries. At a social level well beneath her own, Doña Flora had ties with herders/market vendors who provided her with wool and with the elderly women on El Alto who spin for her. These ties were clearly of long duration. They were also multiplex; for example, the women who spin for her had previously sold her *mantas* when she had a stall in a tourist market. The women had requested the change. Even though spinning is one of the lowliest and least paid occupations, the spinners may have preferred a stable relationship with a successful producer to a less certain one involving the sale of *mantas* on consignment to a stall or shop owner. From Doña Flora's vantage point, a *casera* relationship with spinners was equally important. To give someone wool to spin entails a degree of trust. Besides, she needed to ensure that her spinners would be available when their services were required. In sum, personal relationships must be established with all workers regardless of wage levels.

There are fewer differences between Doña Flora and her network contacts on the next higher social class level. Sewing ponchos entails a higher level of skill than spinning and is commensurately better remunerated. Skills at this class level are also rarer than those at lower class levels, and it is easier for a dependent worker to become self-employed and hence a competitor. Assuring a worker's loyalty to the firm thus becomes both very important and, at the same time, difficult. However, even when a worker leaves a firm, the tie may not be broken entirely; for in small-scale industries, competition and collaboration are not mutually exclusive (see e.g., Piore and Sabel 1984). Thus, a craft firm that has successfully lured away a customer from a competitor may turn around and subcontract part of the work to the very same rival. This relative openness of artisan production, which permits master craftsmen to become proprietors, results in a system with progressive rather than abruptly graded social rankings. However, social rankings *are* rigidly structured in a few, highly capitalized state and private craft exporting firms.

Ties that cut across social class boundaries are facilitated by the fact that owners of small enterprises personally engage in many aspects of the productive process. These tasks are not necessarily those for which the owner would have to pay the highest wages. Indeed, the opposite may frequently be the case.

Like the social mobility of the workers, the willingness of many owners of small industries to engage in many aspects of the trade may also help to decrease the social distance between owner and worker. However, the work may still remain quite hierarchically organized. In fact, perhaps in order to maintain a dominant position, bosses even of small workshops often treat apprentices quite harshly. In addition, men in particular may progressively dissociate themselves from productive tasks and become mainly managers. Concomitantly, in the larger, more highly capitalized firms, the social distance between owner and worker is more pronounced than in Doña Flora's firm. However, even in those cases, relationships, especially between owners and senior workers, often continue to be couched in personalistic terms.

Doña Flora's ties with individuals whom she would consider her social superiors were associated principally with her role as an exporter. We shall deal with that type of relationship later.

Variants

Work Relationships Seen from the Vantage Point of the Dependent Worker

Using examples from the same production activities we described earlier, or from related activities, we now reexamine major types of work relationships from the vantage point of the dependent artisan.

Dependent Kin. First let us focus on the role and position of the dependent family and kin workers. As we saw earlier, the son of Doña Flora's cousin, Arturo, who like Doña Flora is a second- generation migrant from a rural community, has enjoyed a close personal and work association with his aunt, that has spanned a long period of time. In 1976, when he first began working for her, he was studying literature at the university. He helped his aunt count, check, and pack sweaters and other goods in preparation for shipping. On weekdays, he worked evenings, while on weekends he and Doña Flora would sometimes prepare shipments until late at night and he would sleep over. Also, when Doña Flora had errands to run, he could be relied upon to answer the telephone and even to do the housework. Some years later, when the university closed under the military regime of General Luís García Mesa, the work relationship evolved naturally to include Arturo's traveling to Cochabamba, sometimes with Doña Flora and sometimes alone. Doña Flora would pay the bus fare and an additional amount at the end of each trip. This amount varied according to what Doña Flora felt the services were worth at the time they were rendered. The main advantage for Arturo appears to have been the fact that he could take goods of his own along without incurring extra costs. Some of the goods he sold in Cochabamba were made to order in El Alto. In addition, he sold some sweaters and woven goods with appliqué designs that he himself made. However, taken alone, his production would have been insufficient, for he could not complete more than one or two items between his weekly trips.

Arturo's relationship with his aunt also must have contributed to his technical knowledge, providing him with skills that have, on occasion, come in handy. He proudly showed us an appliqué poncho he had made for himself as well as drawings for future work.

At one time, Arturo lived with Doña Flora for a protracted period. Her sons were away doing military service and she wanted a companion. Nevertheless, Arturo regarded his work as an artisan-merchant as only a temporary job. If the university did not reopen soon, he planned to attend a rural teachers college and become a rural schoolteacher.

Arturo's economic relationship with his aunt is thus flexible in terms of the time schedule involved and adaptable to changing circumstances and personal needs. Although, as in any asymmetrical economic relationship, there is a potential for exploitation by the person in the stronger position, kinship may often limit such abuse. Indeed, some artisans prefer to hire non-kin because they can demand more from them.

Dependent Poor Artisans. As we saw earlier, the knitters are among the most poorly paid artisans. Possessing skills that are widely disseminated and popular among women because they can be undertaken at home and without too much interference with regular household duties, they are at the mercy of unscrupulous and aggressive middlewomen and store owners, who often pay them little more than their costs and, at least in the case of the latter, take their goods only on consignment. Long delays in securing payment are all too common; knitters often have to make several visits to the store owner before they are finally paid.

In order to protect the interests of these artisans, development agencies and religious organizations on the one hand and kin groups on the other have been attempting to develop cooperatives (whose evolution and functioning are the subject of Chapter 10) designed to assist the knitters in the acquisition of raw materials as well as the sale of sweaters and similar goods. However, these cooperatives have rarely been able to overcome the asymmetry in the relationship of the knitters with intra-urban middlemen and exporters.

Skilled Artisans

The case of Alejandro, a second-generation *Paceño* in his mid-twenties, represents an analogue to the work experiences of Doña Flora's more skilled workers (or, more accurately, those with rarer skills). Alejandro spent several years in Argentina as a teenager, where he learned tailoring from his aunt and uncle. Later he worked in an electronics store in La Paz and then as a factory worker in the garment industry. But when the underwear factory where he was working closed, he purchased several industrial sewing machines and began to sew pre-cut women's clothing for an Argentinean schoolteacher and her husband (also a teacher) who engaged in this business on the side. The latter did the cutting themselves and put out the rest of the work to as many as ten workshops during good times and as few as four or five when business was slow. Until a few months before we interviewed him in 1981, he employed three assistants on fixed salaries. He had secured their services through an advertisement he placed in the newspaper. At times, when he had a lot of work, he also hired kinsmen (brothers and a brother-in-law), but he generally preferred strangers because he felt that he could place more stringent demands on them. However, orders had fallen, and so in 1981 he was working alone or sometimes with his wife. Since they had two young children, she helped him only sporadically, and her help was with those facets of the work that she had had time to master. Meanwhile, Alejandro's workers set up their own independent shops, where they took in work from the same Argentinean couple. Alejandro felt cheated: "When we study a trade at the academy, we have to pay for it." His workers had gotten a free ride and were now competing with him! Alejandro was becoming wary of employing workers, even if orders were to pick up again.

To fill the gap in orders, Alejandro was sewing padded men's wind jackets for export for a locally based Korean firm. However, the piece rate was low for the skill and time involved. Alejandro dreamed of opening his own retail store, but the location of his workshop was too distant from the center of La Paz, and he lacked the necessary capital. (He figured he would need a minimum of $b. 50,000 or US $2,000 to build his own stock.)

Alejandro's case illustrates the dilemmas faced by the semidependent worker under conditions of extreme economic uncertainty, such as those prevailing in Bolivia. In better times, there were at least two viable options for a young man with his skills: entering a factory job and establishing an enterprise. But by 1981, new factory jobs were becoming increasingly rare. Alejandro had lost his job when the underwear factory where he was employed was forced to close. Other factories were not faring much better. He felt that he did not have the necessary capital to launch an entirely independent enterprise. Yet semidependence did not provide the steady work or the returns he may have hoped for. Having already lived in Argentina, he decided to seek the security of permanent employment there. Interestingly, his kin network remained a major component of the solution he chose. And he, like others, felt that a mixture of strategies was necessary to reduce the risks.

Alejandro's preference for the stability of a factory job was a rather unusual reaction among the craftsmen and small-scale industrialists we interviewed, who more commonly expressed an appreciation for the freedom that could be gained from being one's own boss. For example, a worker in a well-established paper goods and printing firm expected to retire early and use his severance pay to buy a taxi. Conversely, Estes (1984) notes that women workers in a bread and pasta factory in La Paz tended to stay as long as they could. Similarly, Kirsch (1977) found that workers in the Peruvian textile industry usually did not leave their jobs voluntarily.

Work Relations in More Highly Capitalized Small Industries

Work relations in more highly capitalized small firms show considerable similarity to those in less capitalized ones. However, their larger scale and the greater social distance of the owners to at least their lower-paid workers do have an impact on the social relations of production and distribution. These firms are also more likely to be unionized, and a higher proportion of the workers enjoy effective protection through labor laws.

Cafe San Isidro, a coffee processing and export firm, serves as a point of departure for our analysis. Mr. Gonzalez, the owner, has worked with coffee in one way or another during most of his productive life. He was born in the city of Tarija, the eldest son of a pharmacist. The latter's death when Mr. Gonzalez was only nine years old resulted in the family's impoverishment and forced the youngster to seek work with a carpenter. Subsequently, he apprenticed himself to a mechanic and continued in this occupation until he was nineteen. Then he worked for a short while as a government employee, but he lost his job in 1952 when the Movimiento Nacional Revolucionario came to power. At that point, an Italian entrepreneur hired him to work as the supervisor of a coffee plantation in a newly colonized area, and he was later promoted to the position of treasurer of the same firm's noodle factory and coffee-processing plant in La Paz. Soon after, the Italian's partner left the firm, taking along most of its liquid assets and the firm was closed. In compensation for his years of service, Mr. Gonzalez received a coffee-processing machine and a large enough cash settlement to purchase a factory site. Making use of his considerable knowledge about coffee—for example he is able to judge the quality and water content of the beans offered to him by producers and middlemen by eye, without resorting to the usual time-consuming testing—he began processing coffee and selling it to exporters, first as one of many other economic activities and then as his principal venture. Finally, in 1979, at the insistence of his son-in-law, an economist working toward a university degree who had joined the firm that year as an administrator, Mr. Gonzalez took advantage of a period when credit was available to expand production by obtaining first a loan of $b. 1,000,000 (US $50,000) and then an additional loan for $b. 4,000,000 (US $160,000) the following year.

Mr. Gonzalez's son-in-law was not the only one of his kinsmen who worked in the firm. A variable number of other kin have found employment there as well. Work in the firm has enabled his children (Mr. Gonzalez has four sons and two daughters) and his wife's nephews and nieces (whom he has raised subsequent to his brother-in-law's death) to finance their studies. When Mr. Gonzalez has been absent from the firm, his eldest married son, who studied industrial engineering, has weighed the coffee and analyzed its quality. Since he knows English, he also translated incoming telex orders from abroad. For his assistance, he has received a salary, part of which went toward the education of the younger siblings. The other children also helped. When we interviewed him, Mr. Gonzalez expressed his hopes that one of them would eventually take over the firm. The nephews and nieces that he has helped to raise also worked in the factory.

According to Mr. Gonzalez, hiring kin not only helped them earn a living but generated savings in overhead costs as well. While he paid the mandatory accident and health insurance premiums and made contributions to FOMO (Fomento de Mano de Obra, or Development of Manpower, a state run vocational training program) and several other institutions for those workers who were not his relatives, he saved these expenses when hiring kin. When the latter became ill, he simply paid for their medical costs out of his own pocket. Hiring kin when they were needed also helped prevent overstaffing during lean periods. By law, one could not readily lay off permanent workers without paying one month's salary as severance pay for every year worked.

The factor of production that has allowed Mr. Gonzalez to compete on the world market is the accuracy he achieves by and the low cost involved in the hand sorting of coffee beans.[2] He hires some fifty women on the average to select the beans by hand, but on occasion he has hired as many as seventy-four. These women were paid on a piece-rate basis and are employed seasonally. Since they are also engaged in other economic pursuits, including petty commerce in the local markets (and have few other options), they accept low wages.

Social Class Differentiation

The firms of Doña Flora and Mr. Gonzalez exhibit both remarkable similarities and major differences. Their owners' social backgrounds are very different. Doña Flora is illiterate and comes from an Aymara peasant background. She still retains strong rural ties. Mr. Gonzalez, although he is also a migrant, has a Hispanic, middle-class, urban background. His rural ties--he even learned Tacana, a lowland

Women sorting coffee

Indian language, when he was administering his Italian boss's coffee plantation—are of a secondary, derived nature. Both had once been downwardly mobile: Doña Flora, when she was first widowed, and Mr. Gonzalez, as a child. Doña Flora's husband and Mr. Gonzalez both engaged in similar trades, the former permanently, the latter during one period in his life. Both reached their present position in part as a result of their entrepreneurship. And, although both retain ultimate control over decisions for their firms, both rely heavily on upwardly mobile kinsmen. Both give considerable responsibility to their sons-in-law, taking advantage of the technical expertise they gained through specialized education. In both cases, the sons-in-law were used as mediators with the outside. Indalecio mediated between social strata, while Mr. Gonzalez's son-in-law mediated between more traditional and self-reliant ways of doing business and those practices that relied more heavily on international finance.

It should be noted that since education is not the only criterion of social class standing—family connections and wealth are often more important—the educated manager, whether kinsman or not, does not necessarily enjoy a higher social standing than the less-educated owner. Rather, this career pattern is just one of a number of parallel paths to upward mobility and one which, without the benefit of other ingredients, such as marriage into a moneyed or well-connected family, may enable only limited ascent on the social ladder.

Owner-Worker Relations

Perhaps more significant differences between highly capitalized firms and smaller firms lie in the relative positions of the owners and (at least) the lowest paid workers. In Doña Flora's firm, there was a relatively continuous progression from spinners, homeworkers, in-plant weavers and knitters to her own role or place in the firm. In contrast, the fifty to seventy-five women who sort Mr. Gonzalez's coffee beans and who are at the heart of his enterprise are highly unlikely to aspire to his position. Similar to the situation in Doña Flora's firm, his relationship to his workers is often long and personalized, but in Mr. Gonzalez's firm the ethnic and class gap is much more pronounced and unlikely to be bridged in a single generation or even in two generations.

It would be a mistake, however, to entirely dismiss the potential for workers in the more highly capitalized firms to become competitors of those firms. It might be possible, for example, for a coffee sorter to open a small coffee-roasting and retailing outlet and compete with that aspect of a larger enterprise. For an example of such competition, we must expand our analysis to include other case studies, such as the sweet and noodle factory of the Salas family described in Chapters 1 and 4. This family has few grounds to fear competition from former workers as far as its capital-intensive, automated noodle production is concerned. In contrast, half a dozen former workers have engaged in their own production of sweets, an activity that until the mid-1960s was done with very simple machinery. Interestingly, these workers have not broken all their ties with the parent firm. They purchase its products in the retail outlets to increase their assortments of goods.

Conversely, as we saw in Chapter 5, many dependent craftsmen employed in workshops also find it difficult to amass sufficient capital to set up their own shops, and so they must content themselves with dependent positions.

Union activity is more characteristic of more formally organized factories, where wages and working conditions are subject to collective bargaining, than of smaller shops. Perhaps because there is relatively little possibility for internal mobility within factory employment, including even purely lateral movement between factories, the demand for better wages becomes even more important. Also, larger groups have greater bargaining power. Smaller factories that are large enough to have their own unions also benefit from the superior political and economic clout of unions in larger private- and public-sector industries. In contrast, artisans are more mobile than factory workers--both horizontally and vertically--enabling them to improve their situations by finding other jobs. At the same time, fragmentation and owner domination of artisan syndicates impedes collective bargaining.

Factory workers have, at least in theory, made important gains, beginning with a relatively progressive labor code enacted in the mid-1930s. In fact, however, their position as a group has fluctuated considerably with the country's economic situation, the sporadic moves toward "rationalization" of production, the pressures by external lending agencies on the government to introduce "economic stabilization measures," and the varying political philosophies of the groups in power. In addition, there is considerable variation both between and within industries and among different categories of workers within individual factories.

In order to provide a better understanding of owner-worker relations, let us turn once more to the Salas family's sweet and noodle factory (introduced in Chapters 1 and 4) and look at labor relations from the vantage point of Ignacio, the man who has worked for the company as a chauffeur for many years. In 1981, the factory had twenty-eight workers. Half of them had been with the firm for a very long time. When we interviewed him in 1981, Ignacio estimated that four of the workers were around seventy years old and presumably had worked for the factory for more than 20 years. An additional ten had worked there between one-and-a- half and two years, and three for less than three months.

While the Bolivian labor code provides certain benefits and a degree of job security for more senior workers, it gives little protection to those who have worked in a factory for less than ninety days. So, in order to reduce costs, owners often find some excuse to fire their junior workers at the end of their first three months of employment. "It is not that these people don't do their jobs well," says Ignacio. "After they have served in the army, they have to find work. And because they have never held a job before, they have to hold on to it even if the work is very taxing."

Labor demands and complaints in the Salas firm are handled by the union (see Chapter 10), and in times when union meetings are banned, mediation is handled by the five workers with most seniority. In the absence of specialized supervisors, the more senior workers have considerable responsibilities directing the work and training those with less experience. Once the training period is over, every one knows what to do.

In 1981, the official minimum base wage for factory work was $b. 3,400 a month (US $136). According to Sr. Salas, he was paying a minimum of $b. 4,000 (US $160) up to a maximum of $b. 8,000 (US $320) for skilled mechanics (one of the latter is a schoolmate of one of his brothers). In addition, he pays bonuses in April, July and at the end of the year as well as retirement benefits/severance pay. Workers also receive certain benefits in kind. For example, Ignacio can buy his lunch at the factory cafeteria at half price, so that five hot meals cost him only $b. 40 (US $1.60).

Ignacio's workday begins at 7:30 a.m.. He is given half an hour off for lunch and then continues working until 4:00 p.m.. After a break of two hours, he returns to put the trucks away. By 7:00 p.m. he is ready to leave for home. On Saturdays, he works until noon. Since the official work week is 40 hours, he works overtime each week. Although, legally, overtime should be paid at twice the regular rate, the extra hours appear to be paid at the same rate in this firm.

Workers and their families are insured through the obligatory state accident and health insurance system and have free access to services in the workers' hospital (Hospital Obrero). But like many other workers, Ignacio prefers to use private clinics and doctors even if it means paying for the treatment out of his own pocket. "If one has an operation done in the Hospital Obrero, one leaves the hospital dead. There is no guarantee. Any doctor is allowed to operate. So when my wife became ill, I took her to another clinic. Of course, they take $b. 400 [*sic*, more likely 40] out of our paycheck each month, but I prefer to go to a private doctor, so that I can get well quickly."

The Salas family also sponsors the traditional New Year's and carnival celebrations, for which they provide beer and pork from their farm in Viacha, where the pigs are fed waste products from the factory. The entire family joins the workers on these occasions.

Interaction between workers and management outside of the work context also includes sports. On Saturday afternoons, the older Salas brother and some of the workers skip lunch and play *fulbito* (a version of soccer with teams of six players designed for a small playing field) on the fields of the Banco Minero against workers, employees and owners of other sweet and noodle factories, and stores, as well as salesmen. After the games soft drinks are enjoyed by all.

In 1981, there were major changes in the air. It was still unclear how the factory's major expansion project in El Alto would affect the workers. Capacity was to be increased by 70%, and there were plans to hire nine more workers, including a caretaker and a porter. The sales division was to continue at the present site near downtown La Paz, while all the existing machinery would slowly be moved to the new facility in El Alto. Thus the factory was--as we saw earlier--following a general trend. For many workers who did not wish to relocate to El Alto (or who did not already live there), the move would mean a long and wearing commute.

If the move has, indeed, occurred, the problem was most likely compounded for those workers whose wives sold goods in the La Paz markets or who owned stores there. In 1981, Ignacio told us he himself expected to retire from his job in another five years or so to open a grocery store, so the move was not likely to affect him personally.

Job Permanence. Ignacio's description of the Salases' sweet and noodle factory suggests that a worker's degree of job permanence undergoes several transformations in the course of the worker's career. The youngest workers are rotated every few months, while those who succeed in establishing themselves in the factory tend to remain for long periods of time. Finally, a worker may retire (or be retired) early and set up a small enterprise: a store, taxi, bus or small-scale industry with his/her savings and severance pay.

Although our other interviews with factory owners and workers do not provide a clear confirmation of such a sequence, the first two steps are corroborated by Albo's study of first-generation rural-urban migrants in La Paz (Albo et al.,Vol. II, 1982). The study shows that young male migrants (first-generation female migrants were rarely employed in factories) experienced a high rate of turnover when they first entered factory employment. When they lost their jobs, most appear to have become discouraged and sought other forms of employment (p. 160).[3] However, those who managed to gain a foothold in factories enjoyed an average tenure of 8.3 years in the same employment. They were often older workers (factory workers were generally over 30 [p. 122]) and had come from other kinds of employment (p. 160). (Only 35.8% of Albo's sample of 53 workers had worked in a factory as their first job [p. 124]). This average tenure for factory workers was considerably longer than the 5.6-year average in artisanry and the 6.2-year average in public employment. It was, in fact, exceeded only in certain commercial activities (particularly store ownership). These findings find further confirmation in a study of a La Paz food-processing factory (Estes 1984), where the average period of employment was 16 years for women and 19 for men.

Established factory workers in Albo's sample tended to remain in factory work (presumably until they retired). However, as we shall see later, our own interviews with independent artisans and owners of small factories indicate that Ignacio's plans to become independent exemplify a career path that is quite common.

The low level of permanence for entry-level workers appears to result from a combination of factors. One is that because factory employment is considered desirable, factory owners can systematically weed out workers who do not work up to standards. They can always find other candidates.

The extent to which employers make use of this tactic varies considerably. At one extreme are factories like the plant that produces acrylic yarn; most of its 16 workers had worked there for only a few months. The work conditions were particularly harsh, with long hours and strict rules concerning absences and tardiness. As a result, although there was always a crowd of candidates waiting at the gate early in the morning, few who were hired were employed for very long. In our informant's shift, only he and one other worker had worked for the factory for more than a few months.

A somewhat different situation characterizes factories where work is more highly skilled and established workers have undergone a lengthy period of apprenticeship. In one such case, a medium-sized boot factory, workers set up their own shops as soon as they acquired the necessary skills. Similarly, a furniture factory kept only half of its workers upon the completion of their apprenticeship period. Again there were indications that many opened their own workshops. At the other end of the continuum are factories like the Salases' sweet and noodle plant, where only a few workers are rotated and most are permanently employed.

Rotating workers before they can gain seniority is not the only means that factories use to reduce a large work force. As we saw earlier, in his coffee firm Mr. Gonzalez prevents such a situation and at the same time reduces his costs by employing close kin and by hiring workers seasonally. Similarly, Camisas Estrella, a shirt factory with a permanent labor force of 35 workers (mainly women), also engages 10 to 15 additional workers on a putting-out basis. These workers make the cheaper shirts sold by the factory with their own, less-sophisticated machines and receive no benefits. By using these workers, the factory can increase its capacity substantially in periods of high demand without incurring additional fixed costs.

Once workers have succeeded in gaining seniority, it is difficult and expensive to fire them legally. When firms find themselves in a situation where they have an excessively large labor force that they cannot reduce by legal means, they employ a variety of illegal and other strategies. Some factory owners quite flagrantly disregard the labor laws altogether (see Estes 1984). Others find solutions that are more consonant with the spirit of the law. Thus, whenever orders at Camisas Estrella drop below the production level that can be maintained without cottage labor, the owner of the firm urges his workers to take vacations a year in advance; when that situation occurs at Cafe San Isidro, some of the permanent workers are moved into subsidiary sidelines, such as coffee roasting.

Remuneration Systems. As Ignacio's case shows, the pay scale in Bolivian industries is extremely complex. It consists of a minimum base wage to which several obligatory (and sometimes also voluntary) bonuses are added. Eder (1968:174) lists the obligatory bonuses paid after the stabilization decree of 1956 as follows: "bonus based on length of service (average) 15%; profit sharing . . . 8 1/2%; Christmas bonus 8 1/3%; "Sunday pay" (paid but not worked) 16 2/3% [a type of bonus that seems to have been discontinued and replaced with overtime rate schedules]; paid vacation 2 weeks to one month (average cost) 6%; severance pay (average cost) 8 1/3%; lay-off pay (average cost) 2%; hospital and medical care--this varied from a simple first aid clinic to relatively costly hospital facilities, such as those at major mines."

Subsequent remuneration systems were variations of this scale. Thus Irvin (1979:209) describes wages in 1977 as follows:

Minimum wages are extremely low. The average non-qualified worker has a basic monthly wage of about $b. 300 [the exchange rate at the time was $b. 20 to the dollar], to which is added various subsidies. For a married worker with two children, these subsidies are $b. 144. Three times a year, workers received fixed bonuses, which average to be $b. 55 monthly. Some workers receive varying levels of additional monthly fees, the small bonuses they achieved through political channels: for commerce and industry, $b. 250 ; in construction, $b. 50, for example. Working extra hours receives double wage, working Sunday triple, working evenings 25% to 50% extra. Minimum wage taxes sum to about 9.5% plus a small general income tax. Percentage increases over the basic wage are given for longevity, ranging from about 3% to about 40% over 20 years. Indemnization is paid on dismissal at a rate about one month's salary for each year of service.

Although these figures seem low to us, they do show the complexity of wage computations. When workers are paid at a piece rate, remuneration levels become even more complicated. For example, at Camisas Estrella, some of the 35 permanent workers (all but three of whom were women) were paid a fixed wage, while others were paid by the piece. Nevertheless, because both categories of workers received the same fixed bonuses, differences in individual productivity did not result in marked differences in pay. Thus a worker who ironed or sewed might earn $b. 50 per dozen shirts, but during the time it took her to finish the work she could earn an additional $b. 150 in the form of bonuses.

Remuneration sometimes also includes certain payments in kind. A number of factories provide food at half price, and some even make payments in the form of goods they manufacture. The city's major brewery, for example, gives its workers an allowance of up to two dozen 750-gram bottles of beer every week, depending on seniority.

Total wages in factories are substantially higher than in artisan workshops; they compare favorably with the median income of those artisans who head their own shops. A successful artisan can, however, reach much higher wage levels than his factory counterpart. In addition, the work rhythm in artisan shops is often (but not invariably) much less hectic.[4]

In addition to the various bonuses, a factory owner is obligated to pay a variety of indirect social benefits to the National Security Administration. Eder (1968:174) lists the following: "sickness and maternity 5 1/2%; professional risks (accident, etc.) 7%; old age and death pensions 8 1/2%; family subsidy [which Irvin lists as a direct payment] 8 1/2%; cheap housing 5 1/2%." Some of our informants were indeed able to obtain cheap housing by applying to the housing authorities. Thus a worker in a paper factory was able to purchase an airy two-bedroom house for between $b. 500,000 and 600,000 (US $20,000 to 24,000) with a 25-year mortgage in an area originally planned primarily for residents whose houses had been destroyed by the construction of a turnpike to the La Paz airport. However, the fringe benefits are often more theoretical than real. For example, like Ignacio, most of our informants preferred to use private clinics and doctors instead of the workers' hospital, which has a bad reputation.

Finally, perks also may include access to a soccer (or *fulbito*) field, free shorts and sweat shirts for the company team, and food and drinks for one or two fiestas.

Work Organization

The organization of work in the Salases' factory is also representative of firms of its size. More-senior workers train and supervise those who are less experienced and mediate directly between them and the owner/managers, from whom the senior workers take orders directly. In larger factories, a section manager may give orders to the senior workers. In a large paper and plastics factory, for example, one technician was in charge of both the injected plastics and polyethylene film sections. As Estes (1981:3) notes for the food-processing factory she studied, decision making is thus highly centralized: "All decisions, however minor, are made by [the owner], from determining wages--there are no standardized wage or promotion criteria[5]--to deciding if a worker may leave for a medical appointment." On the other hand, the fact that there are few formalized links in the chain of command provides considerable latitude to the individual senior worker.

While, at the extreme, the owners' involvement in running a factory may entail the constant meddling described by Estes, it may also take more benign forms, such as the active participation in soccer games. Again the Salases' firm is not exceptional in this regard, although in larger factories the custom of owners and workers participating in soccer games may be on the wane. A worker in a plastics and paper factory explained that in his factory the section manager was still playing soccer with the workers but the owners no longer participated because of the fights that sometimes break out on the field.

In the factory she studied, Estes (1981) found that despite the direct involvement of the owners in production management, a "modern" style of interaction, i.e., one with impersonal, universalistic and contractual qualities, slowly began to displace a more "traditional," i.e., personalistic, affective and particularistic, style in the 1970s. The owners resorted to the tradition, personal style only in those instances where they could still draw some immediate benefit from it. We would argue that the presence of seemingly contradictory styles of interaction dates at least to the inception of an effective union movement--as early as the 1920s in some industries. In fact, an impersonal, albeit not contractual, style seems to have characterized the relationship between owners and forced laborers in the colonial *obrajes* (factories). As the example of the Salases' factory clearly shows, one category of workers may be treated differently from another even in a predominantly personalistic system. The change from "traditional" to "modern" may thus not be part of an inexorable evolutionary progression, instead, the adaptations that occur may be piecemeal and often reversible responses to particular economic and political circumstances. When seen in this light, such phenomena as the ruthless exploitation of workers and the existence of unions characterized by personal relationships will no longer appear as aberrations or transitional forms but as aspects of both short- and long-term calculations on the part of both owners and workers.

Relationships Among Owners and Managers

To complete our analysis of work relationships in small factories, let us turn to the relationships among owners and between owners and managers. Most of the small factories that we studied either were individually owned and operated or were family firms in terms of ownership, management or both.

Cafe San Isidro and Camisas Estrella are individually owned. In the latter, none of the owner's family members were involved; in the former, close kin were involved as salaried employees. Ownership and management of such firms may become more complex in subsequent generations. Sometimes, the firm remains intact after the original owner leaves and is run jointly by those members of the family and/or their spouses who have the skills and interest. That was the situation in the Salas case, where the father, who had retired to the warmer Yungas valleys, put his eldest son in charge of the factory. When the father died a year before we interviewed this son, the firm was inherited by his wife, three sons and two daughters, who all hold equal shares in the enterprise, now organized as a limited liability company (*sociedad de responsabilidad limitada*).

Family corporations have inherent drawbacks, however. Particularly enterprising family members may find that they do not benefit from their extra efforts. Therefore, they frequently prefer to establish their own private firms. Muebles Robles, a firm that was established in the mid-1950s by the senior Robles, illustrates these problems. The firm was reorganized and enlarged in 1974, when Robles's sons joined as partners. While the founder continues to work in the firm, his nephew, who is not a shareholder, has been hired as its administrator. One son's wife also works in the factory, while the other son is in charge of the store. The latter, however, has hired an employee to run the store in his stead. In addition to these kinsmen, a brother of the founder works in the firm as a carpenter. Like the administrator, he does not have a share in the factory. At the time that we interviewed this family, the two sons were in the process of establishing competing factories (which may lead to the dissolution of the firm).

Conclusion

The three firms dealt with in detail in this chapter share a number of similarities. Their founders are all migrants: Doña Flora came from the altiplano; Sr. Gonzalez, from Tarija; and Sr. Salas's father, from a pueblo near Burgos, Spain. The principal members of each firm are kinsmen, and many of the workers come from the same village or urban barrio and are also related. The owners all attempt to establish long-term relationships of trust with persons who provide material, special services, machinery or credit or who might become clients (*caseras* or *caseros*). Doña Flora nurtured her contacts with spinners and foreigners, Sr. Gonzalez personally visited the peasants and intermediaries who grew and sold coffee, and Sr. Salas maintained close ties to persons who had worked for him. He played *fulbito* with them, and they continued to sell his wares.

The owners not only tried to intensify their relationships, but they attempted to broaden their scope as well. Ties to other areas of Bolivia and abroad were essential. Doña Flora regularly visited Cochabamba and sought foreign buyers; Sr. Gonzalez gained his entry into coffee production through an Italian and continued to bring coffee samples to the foreign embassies in Bolivia in order to establish new clients; and Sr. Salas had to make extensive ties with Europeans for his ingredients (sweeteners, color and paper) and for machinery (some of which he obtained from Germany and Italy, where a brother and a sister have studied and worked).

The owners depend on educated members of their families, often in-laws, to establish contacts with government officials that will help to gain access to government-subsidized materials, such as sugar and wheat; to facilitate export (e.g., translate orders and decipher regulations); and to establish credit with banks. But in order for these firms to survive, they all also depend on their poorer dependent workers whom they can dismiss at will: Doña Flora's knitters; Sr. Gonzalez's coffee selectors; and Sr. Salas's entry-level factory employees. More capitalized firms and those that, like Sr. Salas's, deal with staples (like noodles) can and do enjoy greater security. By the same token, to the extent that they are not displaced by machines, the workers themselves in these firms—at least the longer-term employees— enjoy somewhat greater job security and better working conditions.

Notes

1. On the other hand, even lowly paid secretarial work is not considered demeaning for members of the middle class. The stigma is attached to manual work.

2. The coffee that he himself had classified as first grade was recently recategorized as "superior" by his German clients, and his second-grade coffee was recategorized as first grade. Many of the women who sort the coffee beans have worked for him season after season for long periods of time. Indeed, some were on the payroll of his predecessor. When the coffee season begins, they arrive without being asked. Despite their seasonal status, he gives them the government-decreed extra bonuses. In this case, the use of manual labor does not result from low capitalization, for the firm also owns an expensive mechanical sorter; sorting by hand is simply more refined and selective. Mr. Gonzalez is not sure whether some of the more modern optical sorters might provide results that are equal to those achieved through hand sorting, but for the time being he claims that his level of production does not warrant the additional investment.

3. This conclusion is derived from the fact that the average number of factory jobs held since their arrival in La Paz by individuals who were so employed was only 1.15 at the time of the study (p. 124). Many workers also become discouraged by the hard work expected from them. But perhaps more important is the fact that owners can reduce their expenses by limiting the number of workers eligible for full benefits and at the same time maintain flexibility in their ability to fire workers.

4. Exceptions are, for example, bakeries, where assistants are paid by the quantity of the flour processed and where the work pace is fast and furious during short periods each day.

5. This observation goes counter to the labor regulations described earlier and underlines the degree to which theory and practice may diverge in Bolivian industry.

7

Financing Production

Treating capital as "congealed labor" rather than as a *Ding an Sich*, i.e., as an object with its own laws and dynamics, forces us to consider the manner in which capital is accumulated. This includes analyzing the social relations of production that have led to accumulation.

We are used to dealing with capital in terms of ideally fixed values, and as a corollary, we assume full convertibility between different forms of capital. This means that we consider the source of capital as irrelevant. Further, we take it for granted that future economic performances may be converted (at a cost in the form of interest payments) into present assets (capital equipment, raw materials, etc.). The very term "congealed labor" alerts us to the fact that capital is produced by means of a historical process that may vary from situation to situation. This fact, in turn, leaves open the possibility that different forms of capital may not necessarily be interchangeable. Unfortunately, the foregoing implications have rarely been recognized by Marxist social scientists. Rather, the term has been used mainly to underline the difference between what a worker receives and the price that his employer obtains on the market for a worker's effort.

In this chapter, we argue that small-scale producers in Bolivia find it exceedingly difficult to convert one form of capital into another or to borrow capital on the strength of future labor prestations. In Bolivia, perhaps to a greater extent than in more industrialized countries, the source of capital does indeed matter. Bank loans, for example, are available, in practice, only to those with substantial fixed assets (more specifically real estate). Commercial credit is restricted in similar ways. Often, it is available only to those who have developed long-term relationships with specific suppliers. Loans from money lenders presuppose assets in the form of jewelry and other valuables that can be used as collateral or require personal ties with the moneylender.

An approach that questions the interchangeability of different forms of capital highlights the fact that the sources of capital that come into play at different times in the history of an enterprise and at different stages in a producer's career vary. A producer in the process of establishing a firm does not have the same needs and possibilities than at other stages in the firm's life. Similarly, the founder of a new firm who has engaged in other activities previously or concomitantly is not in the same position as one who has not had such experiences.

The Capitalization of Firms of Different Size

Like labor relations, capitalization is in many ways similar in small and large firms. With regard to labor, we saw in earlier chapters that in both large and small firms kinsmen play an important role. Similarly, both small and large firms make use of different forms of labor, either simultaneously or consecutively. Finally, both factories and artisan workshops distinguish between permanent and temporary workers and also sometimes put out work.

Some of the similarities in labor relations between smaller and larger firms have parallels in terms of capitalization. Starting capital in all firms, regardless of their size, is often provided by the extended family, especially parents. And both small and large firms employ multiple strategies to reduce catastrophic capital loss. These strategies include, for example, decapitalizing the firm by diversifying into transportation and real estate.[1] Other similarities between firms of different sizes include the fact that both smaller and larger firms are often launched with money earned in formal salaried employment. In addition, firms of all sizes use both capital goods and raw materials as hedges against inflation or as a means to speculate.

However, there are also major differences. Artisans find it much more difficult to gain access to bank loans than do larger industries, forcing them to spend many years saving money while working as dependent workers. Lending agents, whether private banks or international development banks, continue to be biased against lending to the smaller-scale producers. The very criteria employed by the banks to measure credit-worthiness are not necessarily the best indicators of the health of a firm. For example, banks often look at current business strategies, but hyperinflation, prevalent in many Latin American countries, may dictate different strategies than those present under more normal circumstances. Rather than looking at present strategies that may merely represent short-term adaptation to current conditions, banks could obtain a good measure of the future potential of a workshop by looking at its past overall performance. Such a criterion would, for example, enable some small producers to borrow money for raw materials. Under present criteria, such borrowing is particularly difficult, since, unlike capital goods, stocks of raw materials cannot normally be used as collateral for loans. While this affects all industries, artisans, who often work with only rudimentary tools or machinery, are at a particular disadvantage.

Self-Financing

Most artisans and the founders of at least the smaller industries must rely principally on their own and their spouses' capacity to save in order to accumulate the capital necessary to launch an enterprise. Many begin purchasing basic tools during their apprenticeship period. This strategy makes sense even if an artisan does not expect to become independent for many years because he or she may, while working for someone else, produce goods for some customers directly. Some of our informants saved more than half of their wages to invest in tools and other equipment. Thus, one carpenter earned some $b. 70 (US $2.80) a week, of which he spent only $b. 30 (US $1.20). Once, when he received a Christmas bonus of $b. 200 (US $8), he was able to purchase a machine worth $b. 500 (US $20).

The career history of a jeweler who works in a small workshop tucked away on a patio far from the commercial center of the city and who therefore produces mainly for stores, provides a good example of the progressive acquisition of tools in order to become independent. Mr. Aliaga, who was thirty years old in 1981, began his career at the age of twelve, when he helped his father make aluminum toys. The aluminum dust was highly toxic, especially when one worked without a mask; so, eight years later, after completing military service,[2] Mr. Aliaga decided to switch to jewelry making. For three years he worked for a friend. At first, he did not earn anything, and so he lived with his mother. He reciprocated by helping her in her small restaurant and giving her $b. 30 a week. For an additional two years he worked for a second jeweler. Both of these employers refused to let him use their equipment for repair work and other small jobs on the side, so Mr. Aliaga began to acquire tools of his own. With only two pairs of pliers and a pair of scissors to his name, he first made silver chains at a small table in his mother's house. When he finally became independent, in 1977, he first used his friends' equipment and then, one year later, acquired his own small, second-hand laminating machine. Finally, he purchased a small electric polishing machine.

Mr. Aliaga's wife does not help him with his trade. She attempted to learn the craft but could not get the knack of it. Instead, she sells bread twice a week in a nearby market. He would like to open his own store, but this would require an initial capital of $b. 100,000 to 150,000 (US $4,000 to $6,000), which he does not have and which, as we shall see later, he has no way of securing from other sources in the foreseeable future.

While artisans tend to invest their savings in activities similar to those in which they were apprenticed, some invest in different activities instead. Doña Flora, for example, sold her knitting machines in 1984 and purchased leather-working equipment. Another informant, who worked as a hatmaker for four years and for shorter periods as a tailor, carpenter and taxi owner-operator, finally was able to open a workshop to rebore vehicle engines in partnership with his brother-in-law. As we showed in Chapter 3, Celestino, who owns a lumberyard, obtained his starting capital from his marketing and trucking activities, and when misfortune befell his lumber business, he worked his land to make the money he needed to replace the stolen equipment. And the owner of Café Mamita first ran a dry-goods store.[3]

On a more capital-intensive level, the elder Salas invested money earned from the sale of cinchona bark and the manufacture of quinine in a candy, pasta and bread factory (see Chapters 1, 4, and 6). However, as we explained in Chapter 4, such transfers of capital from commerce to manufacturing are relatively rare, since commerce is regarded as providing more flexibility than industry during major economic and political crises.

An important source of start-up capital is earnings from current employment in larger, formally constituted firms and in the public sector. The start-up capital may take the form of savings invested in a secondary activity, often in anticipation of an eventual lay-off or retirement from wage employment. Mr. Aguilar, for example, invested in a secondary activity when he established his lumberyard and carpentry enterprise on land he inherited and with machinery he purchased with earnings from his employment as a carpenter in a large textile factory. Since a son also works in the family enterprise, Mr. Aguilar has been able to continue his formal employment while running his own business. Mr. Loayza, the lamp maker, established an enterprise that is only marginally related to his original profession. He invested his savings from his work as a government economist in a large stock of lamp parts. Once his business was established, he gave up his government position and dedicated himself to lamp making. One of the smaller soft-drink manufacturers initiated his business with money earned as a plumber for the municipal government. His decision to found the firm was influenced by his wife's wholesale soft-drink dealership. He began with a pedal-operated machine, progressed to a machine with a production capacity of eighteen bottles a minute and finally to automated equipment that operates five times as fast.

Severance pay is a another common source of capital for establishing an enterprise. When severance payments are actually made, which is, in practice, far from universal even in formally constituted firms, such-lump sum payments may constitute sizable amounts. For example, a metal-lathe operator, who was laid off from his job in the workshop of the same factory where Mr. Aguilar is employed, used his severance pay as a down payment for a lathe. At present, he runs a successful business repairing and custom manufacturing car parts. Similarly, the bankruptcy of a larger printing shop led to the establishment of several small presses by the former employees, who were given equipment in lieu of severance pay. And we have already encountered the example of Mr. Gonzalez, who received a coffee-processing machine as well as cash as severance pay from his Italian employer and thereupon established a coffee export firm worth over three million dollars in 1981, when we first interviewed him.

Two final sources of savings capital are, as we saw in an earlier chapter, earnings from previous employment and the proceeds of the sale of a firm in a foreign country.

Spouses may coordinate savings strategies to enable one or both to acquire capital goods. Thus, Alcides was able to equip his goldsmith shop with all the necessary tools within a single year because his wife's salary as a nurse was sufficient to run the household. He was able to reinvest all of his own earnings in his workshop. The common practices of hiring only family members and enlisting the assistance of one's children serve a similar purpose.

Renting Equipment and Doing Without

Often, to accumulate capital, if that is at all possible, an artisan must spend many years coping with inadequate or improvised tools and machinery or borrowing and renting equipment. The use of borrowed and rented equipment and facilities is particularly common among carpenters, bakers, jewelers, and mechanics. Thus, at the beginning of his career, Mr. Aguilar, who makes furniture and doors, prepared his work in several large, machine-equipped workshops that rented out space and machine time. Subsequently, he did most of his work with improvised machine tools that he built himself while he continued to rely on the better-equipped workshops for doing precision work. When we interviewed him in 1981, shortly after he had moved his workshop to a new location, he had finally been able to purchase more elaborate equipment on credit. He now rented out his equipment to one worker who came daily and to five to ten additional carpenters who rented his equipment by the hour--usually to make doors and windows.

Although the rental charges for machinery are generally not excessive, the logistics of working in this manner are often extremely complicated. For example, at the start of his career, an artisan who makes upholstered furniture would buy lumber he needed in El Alto and have it trucked down to a shop that rented machine tools in the barrio of Munaypata, a drop in altitude of almost a thousand feet and a distance of between ten and fifteen kilometers. There he would cut the lumber, and then he would carry the boards on his back up to his own workshop, located some five hundred feet higher. At this point, his travails were still not over. When he finished the furniture, he had to bring each piece down to the market, located nearer the center of the city.

Many, if not most, carpenters never succeed in acquiring their own machine tools. One of our informants, an elderly carpenter who originally worked in a glass factory making wooden molds, owns only a few hand tools. After he was laid off from the factory for political reasons, he worked with rented machinery for thirty years. He and his wife, both first-generation migrants from a Lake Titicaca community, lived in extremely humble lodgings. Similarly, all three of the smaller-scale bakers we interviewed rented their ovens on a long-term basis—one of them, as we saw earlier, shared it with a kinsman. In addition, many producers of cookies, *empanadas* (cheese turnovers) and *salteñas* (elaborate turnovers made with meat and vegetables)—mostly women—pay the owners of bakeries by the tray for the use of their ovens.[4]

In some trades that do not require much expensive equipment, renting and borrowing appear to be common only at the beginning of an independent producer's career. When Mr. Aliaga (who—as we saw earlier—produced some jewelry on his own while still working for another craftsman) became independent in 1977, he had to beg his friends to let him use a laminating press. Although his friends did not charge him anything, he often had to join them for a few beers, "wasting" time in the process. Now that he has his own equipment, the brother of the jeweler for whom he worked before becoming independent comes to use *his* equipment. Since he also helps him out from time to time, Mr. Aliaga does not mind the imposition. However, he does avoid letting others use his delicate laminating press with any frequency. "I know that I have to use it slowly," he explains, "while my friends use it any old way. One must be careful." He still depends on other artisans to gild his silver objects.

Another jeweler described similar experiences. Early in his career, if he used other artisans' equipment, he would have to invite them out for food or drinks. Otherwise, they would pretend that they were out when he came. By the time that we interviewed him, others were coming to use his equipment. He lets them use it only half a dozen times or so. The gifts he receives in return are scarcely worth it. He told us about a friend who came to work with his equipment and gave him in return fifteen pesos to buy a *thimpu*, a cooked dish for which street vendors actually charged twenty five pesos.

On occasion, elaborate symbiotic relationships develop between owners of equipment and other artisans who seek access to it. Thus, Mr. Guachalla, a graphic artist who works for a printer and also runs a small printing operation at home with his wife (see Chapter 3), has an informal arrangement with the owner of an offset printing machine whereby he is charged a very low rate for its use in return for free repairs.

The major alternative to borrowing and renting for a small-scale producer who cannot afford to purchase equipment is improvisation. Many cabinetmakers use only hand tools, and even these may be of an improvised nature. Similarly, a creative car-body mechanic made an entire body for a Toyota four-wheel-drive vehicle with only a handmade sheet-metal folding tool. In spite of the primitive equipment used, the car is indistinguishable from factory-made versions. Other artisans buy improvised machine tools or build them themselves. For example, before Mr. Aguilar purchased powerful, imported carpentry machine tools, he worked with machines he assembled himself. He built his own sawing table, having bought only the motor and a few other parts. Similarly, Alcides, the goldsmith, employed a primitive system of smelting gold that had learned from a Peruvian artisan who was attempting to establish himself in La Paz. Instead of using a blowtorch, he used a powdered-milk can with a protruding wick. He was able to regulate the smelting temperature by blowing into an attached tube that was directed against the flame. One of the most remarkable examples of innovativeness is seen in the case of Don Alfonso, the blind peanut-butter manufacturer (described in detail in Chapter 2). Disappointed with the poor fuel efficiency of conventional roasting techniques, Don Alfonso designed a rotating peanut-roasting drum and a grinding mill and had the parts he needed custom made and assembled by various mechanics. As we shall see in the next chapter, some of the improvised techniques and working conditions are highly dangerous.

Finally, insufficient access to capital may also result in the continued employment of labor-intensive techniques (described in Chapter 6) in lieu of mechanization.

The Family as a Source of Capital

As we saw in Chapter 5, the family plays an important role in providing children with the opportunity to learn a skill within the context of the family enterprise or enabling them to continue living at home during a period of unpaid or lowly remunerated apprenticeship in another establishment. More rarely, the family also contributes cash, equipment and/or other forms of aid to set up a son or daughter in his or her first enterprise.

Such direct assistance is very common among market vendors. We will deal with that in Chapter 9. Giving start-up capital to children appears to be less prevalent in small-scale manufacturing than it is in marketing. Perhaps this is because parents feel they have fulfilled their obligations by permitting their children to live at home while learning a trade. Moreover, a young artisan usually works for a time as a dependent worker before setting up an independent enterprise. An additional factor limiting the frequency of parents providing start-up capital is the fact that small-scale producers may be loathe to encourage their sons or daughters to cut their contribution to the family enterprise and at the same time become competitors. We did, however, record many instances where individuals obtained substantial aid from close kin to set themselves up in business.

Parents and parents-in-law are the most likely source of start-up
capital. It may range widely in nature from cash to materials, equipment or real estate and from outright gifts to loans. Doña Flora, the
woolen-goods manufacturer, assisted each of her children in different
ways. She gave $b. 60,000 (US $2,400) to her oldest son who went to
Australia; $b. 110,000 (US $4,400) to her second son to enable him to
open a mechanic's workshop; $b. 50,000 (US $2,000) to her third son;
and enough capital to purchase a small bus to her daughter. Similarly,
Alcides, a successful jeweler with an extensive elite and middle-class
clientele, obtained his workshop from his in-laws. Mr. Blanes, who
engages in automobile and bus bodywork, uses a shop and adjacent lot
owned by his father, an army officer in charge of cargo shipping. In
addition, when he happens to be out of work, Mr. Blanes drives his
father's bus. Since he is the only person who operates the bus, this
arrangement provides a reliable additional source of income. Finally,
Celestino, the migrant sawmill owner, gave his son a small field in his
home community so that he could plant onions as an extra source of
cash. In 1981, Celestino was toying with the idea of returning to his
rural home and leaving his business to his sons in return for a fixed
rent.[5]

Providing direct financial assistance to children (or helping them
to obtain an education) may constitute a form of social security. For
example, the jeweler whose case we described in Chapter 1 received
start-up capital in the form of an interest-free loan of jewelry from
her mother-in-law. In return, her husband often took care of his
parents' store, and as we indicated before, they jointly planned to
establish a small clinic. And Doña Flora now receives remittances from
her sons who live abroad.

Parents do not always treat each of their children equally. For
example, Doña Flora's daughter felt that she had been shortchanged
when her mother gave each of her children a roughly equivalent sum.
She had assisted her mother with the manufacture and sale of sweaters
and other goods all along and had never received more than food and
clothing in return. In contrast, her brothers did not have to help much
at home while they were attending school or learning trades as
apprentices.

Siblings and even more distant kinsmen as well as friends are often
also called upon to provide assistance, although they are asked to do
so less frequently than parents and parents-in-law. For example, a man
who makes knitwear gave a small knitting machine to his brother and
sold him a second one. He himself had purchased his first machine
from his father-in-law. By 1981, several members of the large, extended
family were in the business of making jumpsuits and other knit goods,
some with simple machines and others with expensive circular
machines that are capable of making knits with elaborate multicolored
patterns.

Sometimes such loans supplement larger loans given by parents or parents-in-law. For example, a mechanic who specialized in welding and in rebending vehicle springs received loans totaling half of his start-up capital--some $b. 25,000 (US $1,000)--from his father, his father-in-law and his uncles. He invested the money in an anvil, wrenches and other tools.

Friends and kin other than parents and parents-in-law are more likely to charge interest. Thus, neither the father nor the father-in-law of the mechanic just mentioned (from whom he borrowed $b. 3,800 and $b. 3,600, respectively) charged him any interest. In contrast, his godfather (who presumably was also an uncle) charged him $b. 400 per month for a loan of $b. 5,000.

Loans from more distant relatives tend to be shorter-term loans; they typically expect to be paid back within a few days or a few weeks. However, loan periods of one year are not uncommon. One artisan we interviewed repaid the loan he had received from his godfather after a year. Another paid his father-in-law back after a year, but he continued to owe money to his father. None of these relatives had stipulated when the loan was due.

In addition, loans to kin other than children tend to be based on reciprocity: The person receiving the loan knows that the donor may request a similar loan when she or he is short on cash. One mechanic, who owns a tire repair shop, sometimes borrows $b. 2,000 or so for two to three weeks from close kinsmen to buy tools or tires. He reciprocates in kind. Lending specialized tools such as welding or paint-spraying equipment to kin and friends is another form of reciprocity.

Finally, kinsmen often establish partnerships. Two brothers-in-law we interviewed began their careers by jointly renting a bakery. They used the oven at different times during the day. The partnership lasted for a year and a half, until the production volume and scheduling requirements forced them to make separate arrangements.

Commercial Credit and Bank Loans

Sources of funds other than those already described (as well as high-interest loans from moneylenders and pawnshops) are, with rare exceptions, available only to those producers who have already accumulated substantial capital in other ways. The discussion that follows therefore applies mainly to producers of middle- or upper-class origin and to those with working-class backgrounds who are already well established.

Well-established firms, especially those that are more highly capitalized, usually find it quite easy to acquire machinery on credit. Credit periods vary from six months to two years. Few producers calculate the effective interest rates. We figured, however, that interest rates have run two percent or more per month, and they are calculated in dollars, a fact which, during periods of rapid devaluation, can present major difficulties.[6] However, in 1981, none of our informants reported running into serious problems in keeping up with their payments.

Credit for raw materials is more difficult to obtain and, when available, may be for periods as short as three days or so. Often, such loans are conceded only to regular clients who purchase large quantities. For example, a knitwear factory usually received credit for three days for raw materials. However, in 1981, the factory from which the firm's owner obtained yarn insisted on cash terms, probably for fear of another devaluation of the peso boliviano. In contrast, when the inflation rate was lower, the same factory gave its preferred customers seven days to settle their accounts. Mr. Loayza purchased his lamp parts from U.S. factories on credit, with payment due three to four months after the actual shipping date and calculated at an annual interest rate of 10-7/8%. Usually shipments arrived within two to three months.

Some suppliers concede credit only upon deposit of some form of collateral. Thus, the lumbering company in Santa Cruz from which Celestino buys his lumber concedes credit upon deposit of titles to real estate. However, Celestino prefers to pay cash because he is afraid that his family might not be able to get the titles back if something should happen to him.

Most Bolivian small-scale producers do not view bank loans as a viable alternative source of capital. Bank loans require collateral, almost always in the form of land and buildings belonging either to the person requesting the loan or to someone willing to act as a guarantor. In addition, borrowers must often be able to demonstrate a certain level of cash flow through a bank account. Such requirements are too stringent for most would-be borrowers.

Some of the artisans we interviewed felt that they had no possibility whatsoever of obtaining a bank loan. For example, Mr. Estrada, a shoemaker who makes flats for *cholas* figured that he would need $b. 30,000 for a machine to make soles. But even after ten years as a dependent worker (three years as an apprentice tailor and seven as a journeyman), he did not have the financial means of acquiring the machine, and so he continued to hammer the soles on his knees with only a leather apron to protect them. While Mr. Estrada has not even attempted to secure a bank loan, a jeweler we interviewed attempted to obtain a bank loan in vain. He was told that he would have to prove that he was paying taxes for his workshop. But when he investigated the matter at the municipal revenue service, he was told that since he makes jewelry for a shop, he was in effect a dependent worker and was therefore not subject to direct taxation. Conversely, however, some of the artisans who deal with consumers directly are reluctant to forsake their semi-clandestine status and expose themselves to being taxed. In addition, the municipal authorities' valuation of a workshop may have only the vaguest relationship to its actual value. In 1984, for example, inflation had long since made the original valuation categories obsolete,[7] but the banks still used them to set lending limits.

More highly capitalized firms may have difficulties securing bank loans too. Thus Mr. Gomez, the immigrant from Chile (described in Chapter 4) who makes high quality furniture as well as foam rubber, has not been able to secure a bank loan because he cannot offer real estate as collateral.

Even when a small-scale producer owns land or a house, he may not always have clear title to it. Also, as we saw in the case of Celestino, who refuses to relinquish his house titles in order to secure commercial credit, Bolivians are reluctant to jeopardize the only kind of asset they consider relatively secure. Another example of a Bolivian who was reluctant to jeopardize his assets in order to secure a loan was Mr. Gonzalez, the coffee exporter. His son-in-law found it difficult to convince him to request a bank loan that would enable the company to export coffee. Mr. Gonzalez would have preferred to work only with his own capital and not face the risk involved in becoming indebted. A carpenter expressed a similar apprehensiveness of becoming indebted, even though he and his three partners had been able to secure a five-year loan to purchase machine tools at the advantageous rate of 8% per annum from a fund for artisans and small industries, which will be discussed later.[8] He felt that the interest payments were too high and would have preferred to amortize the debt more rapidly.

Just as in the case of commercial credit, the difficulty of obtaining bank credit is compounded when the borrower requests working capital rather than credit for capital goods. Some kinds of loans from international development banks are specifically earmarked for capital goods. The equipment purchased may, in some instances, count as part of the collateral, while raw materials and intermediate goods generally do not. In addition, the length of time it usually takes to secure a loan and the absence of lines of credit render bank loans impractical for uses that require short-term flexibility. The experience of a successful furrier illustrates the difficulty both of obtaining large enough loans and of finishing the paperwork in a timely manner:

> Financing production is one of the big problems we face. We have clients who buy US $3,000 to $5,000 worth of merchandise. At present, we have instituted the system whereby they pay 50% in advance and send us the rest upon delivery because it is impossible to work with the banks.
>
> The first time I wanted to make a foreign shipment, I went to a bank where I knew someone who had been a client of mine and where I had an account. I showed them the letter of credit for US $4,000 that the client who had ordered the goods had made out to me. They replied that I would have to present the transport documents. At this point, I requested that they at least advance 25% of the amount so that I could begin working on the order. Their response was that the letter of credit had not

been properly confirmed. So I borrowed money left and right as best I could and sent the merchandise off. Then I returned to the bank with the customs documents showing that I had filled the order. The bank's response was that I would need a letter confirming that the order could not be revoked. When that letter finally arrived and I presented it to the bank, they claimed that it should have been sealed with a red seal. I told them that I had studied economics but had never thought that something like that would be necessary. So I got in contact with my client yet once more and obtained the document as specified. This time, they looked up the cash flow in my account, which was not much, and they told me that the average balance on my account had been more or less $b. 10,000 (US $400). They also found that my net worth was some US $40,000. Therefore they would be willing to lend me $b. 20,000.

Two days later, I went to the bank expecting to be able to collect the money. I was wrong. They told me to present a request and come back in two to three days, for they would first have to investigate the guarantor. When I returned, they told me that everything was fine with the guarantor, but that I would have to wait for the board of directors to meet, for they would deal with the matter. When the board had finally decided the case, they were willing to give me only $b. 10,000. An entire month had elapsed since I had made the request. Disgusted, I told them that I had by now received payment for the shipment and no longer needed the loan. Of course, I have never gone back to that bank. I now go to another one, but its the same thing. I haven't received a cent. It is all to no avail.

Personal contacts are clearly an asset for obtaining bank credit expeditiously. For example, Mr. Loayza claims that he has had no problems in obtaining loans from a bank to import chandelier parts from the United States. As a student of economics and a former government employee, he is friendly with the bank president, the chief executive officer and the treasurer. Another producer who uses personal contacts to obtain loans is one of the partners of the cabinetmaking workshop mentioned earlier who works for the military and has access to loans given by the army.

The general perception among artisans that bank loans are impossible to come by is borne out by bank statistics. In 1981, loans to artisans amounted to only 1.42% of the total bank financing of the private sector, which was the second highest figure in the five-year period between 1978 and 1982. In the three-month period between October and December 1980, artisans in the department of La Paz (located mostly in the city) received a total of $b. 10 million (US $407,664), or 0.54% of the credit made available to the private sector in the department. In contrast, private industries received 35.1% of all bank credit in 1981, and industries in La Paz secured $b. 944.4 million (US $38.5 million), or 51.1% of the private sector loans.

Ironically, lines of credit earmarked specifically for artisans do exist. Financed by the World Bank, such credit is channeled through regular private banks. The loans are intended mainly for the acquisition of capital goods and have been used by wood-carvers, carpenters and cabinetmakers. In 1981, interest rates for these loans amounted to 18%

(13% plus 5% for a fund to absorb bad debts), up from 14% when the World Bank loan programs for artisans were started a year or two earlier. In 1981, one of the two programs offered credit of up to $b. 180,000 (US $7,200), and the other offered credit up to $b. 300,000 (US $12,000), both for a period of six years for capital goods and two years for raw materials. A private agency (CESEP) aided potential borrowers with the assessment of their needs and with the required paperwork and provided short courses in goldsmithery, weaving and pyroengraving. The director of this agency, Mrs. Villalaba, has attempted to create cooperatives in rural areas and to assist them in gaining access to credit. Her hope is that banks will regard such cooperatives as more credit-worthy than individual small-scale artisans.

In 1984, two cooperatives were in the process of formation. One consisted of a group of furriers in a village in the department of Oruro, the other of a group of sheepherders near Lake Titicaca who wished to improve herding techniques and eventually establish wool industries. An artisan who had attended a course in Italy in techniques in the furrier trade, for which he had received a grant, was scheduled to teach a similar course to the furriers, and a young woman was working with new designs for the rugs the furriers produce. But other than that, the deepening economic crisis had halted progress on these programs.

As of 1984, the only bank credit given to a group was a loan administered by the union of sidewalk shoemakers in 1980. Thanks to this loan, twenty-two shoe menders were able to buy sturdy hand-driven sewing machines. Although most or all the shoemakers repaid their loans and the experience was cited by a liaison officer for the U.S. Embassy as a model case, the rural cooperatives mentioned earlier were the only new candidates for group loans. All other loans were made to individuals, few if any of whom were likely to have come from the poorest segments of the artisan population.

By 1988, the possibilities for small-scale firms to obtain credit had improved somewhat with the establishment of PRODEM. PRODEM (Fundación para la Promoción y Deasarrollo de la Microempresa, a nongovernmental organization established in 1986 with the support of a grant from USAID) is one of the very few organizations of any kind that provides credit specifically to small-scale enterprises. Initially, it gave credit to small groups of 4 to 7 market vendors from the same neighborhood who were selling national products; later it extended its scope to small-scale producers as well. Although credit is extended to the individual members, the group is jointly responsible for payments. In 1987-88, the average loan to small-scale producers was $b. 550 (US $234), with an average loan period of 4-1/2 months and an interest rate of 2% per month. In 1987, 816 small-scale producers obtained loans amounting to a total of $b. 377,330 (US $160,566). The principal beneficiaries were tailors, followed by shoemakers, carpenters, hatmakers and jewelers. Finally in August 1991, PRODEM helped

Sidewalk shoe repairmen working with machines purchased with a loan from the World Bank

found Banco Sol, an independent commercial banking venture that lends exclusively to microenterprises (Rhyne 1991). A second organization that provides credit to small-scale enterprises is FENACRE (Federación Nacional de Cooperativas de Ahorro y Crédito de Bolivia). Since 1975 the organization has obtained US $4.5 million from BID (Bank for International Development), and since 1980 it has obtained an additional $4 million from USAID. Statistics of how many small-scale producers have benefited from this program were unavailable. In both instances, the rate of repayment has been excellent, with PRODEM figuring a rate of delinquency of only 0.21% and FENACRE reporting a rate of 2.5%, which demonstrates the lack of foundation of the notion that small-scale firms are too risky to finance.

Larger, long-established firms, with considerable assets, including real estate, have fewer difficulties in obtaining loans, although they too are plagued by the lengthy procedures involved. Thus, the owners of the sweet and noodle factory described in Chapter 1 purchased their first machinery for cash but were later able to secure loans on the basis of buildings, machinery and land. Nevertheless, they had to wait for four or five months for the mortgage to come through. By 1981, interest on regular loans in pesos bolivianos amounted to 32%; as a result, the factory preferred to obtain loans from Argentina and Brazil, where interest rates were lower.[9] Similarly, commercial credit was more reasonable in East Germany, which compensated for the fact that the quality of some of the East German machinery did not equal that of its Italian and German counterparts.

In contrast, the owners of a well-established shoe factory specializing in boots for the military found it more difficult to secure loans. They were able to obtain only one fourth of the amount they originally asked for and then only in U.S. dollars. Finally, an aluminum-pot manufacturer got together with four or five colleagues and obtained a bank loan for 30 to 60 days at an interest rate of one and a half percent per month using real estate as collateral. This enabled them to purchase raw material through small importers at lower prices than those charged by the major import firms. The interest on the bank loan was 3-1/2% per month, less than rates charged by kinsmen and other local moneylenders on whom the pot manufacturer was forced to rely during the early years of his enterprise.

Some producers combine commercial credit and bank loans. For example, a producer of knitted sportswear attempted to secure a bank loan when he fell behind on his payments for a circular knitting machine that he had imported from West Germany.

The Acquisition of Real Estate, Capital Goods, and Raw Materials as an Investment Strategy

The impossibility of securing a loan without substantial collateral; the uncertainty of being able to obtain an import license for raw materials in a timely manner; the unpredictable scarcities of raw materials and intermediate goods purchased from local importers; and the insecurity of savings accounts[10] all call for unorthodox savings and investment strategies. In 1981, even small-scale market women immediately converted excess capital into tangible assets (such as blankets and jewelry), which would be readily reconvertible into cash at a later time, in order to beat inflation.

Small producers are more likely to stock up on raw materials beyond their immediate needs or even purchase equipment that they may not be able to place into service for a while. Thus Alcides, the jeweler, accumulated a stock of a special wax to make molds (for lost wax casting) and 300 pounds of materials for the molds themselves, enough to last many years and even to bail out a friend in need. Materials that had cost him $b. 2,500 in 1977 would have cost him $b. 140,000 in 1984. In addition, there were many times when the material would have been entirely unavailable in the city. Similarly, Mr. Loayza accumulated a six to eight month supply of chandelier parts worth US $60,000 to $70,000, a substantial figure for an operation run from a garage by the owner and one part-time worker. Shipments by surface from the U.S. take six to seven months and air shipments cost much more and take a month and a half. Yet, with inflation high and the value of the peso boliviano sinking every day, he felt that the parts were a good investment. At least he was able to maintain the value of his capital. Nevertheless, he did not automatically adjust the price of his lamps to the rate of inflation because to do so would have lessened his competitive edge. On a larger scale, a medium-sized shirt factory had enough stock of cloth and other raw materials to last six months.

Sometimes small producers invest in machinery years before they are actually able to make use of it. A carpenter we interviewed had been working in a smaller workshop in a neighborhood where high-voltage electric current was not available. By working with simple equipment and also saving part of his wages from formal employment in a large factory, he was able to invest in powerful bench tools. Only later did he set up a new shop in another neighborhood, where he was eventually able to obtain current of the appropriate voltage for the machinery he purchased earlier. Some of the more intricate financial machinations for purchasing equipment were dealt with in Chapter 2.

In conclusion, the financing of small-scale industries is subject to the same pressures to maintain flexibility as are labor relations. A firm caught with large debts in times of economic crisis is unlikely to survive. And producers who invest in a single enterprise rather than holding some of their assets in real estate or in foreign accounts may suffer disproportionately when demand drops. These considerations explain why elite Bolivians often engage in diverse activities even at the risk of spreading themselves too thin and why even very small enterprises often invest in more than one venture.[11] There are, of course, factors that counterbalance the tendency toward diversification, the most important of which is perhaps the fact that firms engaging in activities that require a higher degree of capitalization face less competition. Indeed, those firms that hold a virtual monopoly in their specialty may be able to withstand even severe economic depressions. However, few Bolivian producers are so fortunate; for most, diversification provides one of the few possible safeguards against business failure.

Notes

1. Note, however, that real estate is also a *condition* for obtaining loans.
2. Military service is regarded as a rite of passage to adulthood. Changes in careers and migratory moves are often made upon its completion.
3. She established Café Mamita, a coffee-roasting business, when the Movimiento Nacional Revolucionario government began to ration staples and control their sale.
4. Some oven owners discourage renters from in turn providing their goods to third persons, but we know at least one baker working in rented facilities who also bakes goods by the tray for other producers.
5. In 1984, however, he no longer mentioned this plan.
6. In 1981, local banks were charging interest rates of 32%-35% per annum for loans in pesos bolivianos and foreign (e.g., Brazilian and Argentinean) banks were charging 11%-15% (presumably for loans calculated in U.S. dollars).

7. Low valuations were further encouraged through bribes given to assessors to lower tax rates. The trend was reversed only in the mid-1980s, when taxes were increased dramatically.

8. In addition, one of the partners, who works for the military, has taken out a three-year loan from the military insurance corporation (COSMIL).

9. Actually, the subsequent drop in the value of the peso boliviano would have more than compensated for the high interest rate.

10. Inflation rates often exceed interest obtained on savings accounts. In addition, in 1980, dollar accounts were suddenly declared illegal and all dollar holdings were converted into pesos bolivianos at the disadvantageous official exchange rate.

11. A study of PRODEM, the nongovernmental organization mentioned earlier, showed that 12% of the market vendors who received loans through the program used their loans to finance "other business." Interestingly, only one such individual failed to make payments on loans on time, an indication that the strategy of diversification is indeed viable.

8

Production

In the last chapter, we discussed the ways in which small-scale producers acquire equipment, improvise equipment when they do not have enough capital to buy it locally or import it, and use both equipment and stocks of raw materials as a hedge against inflation. In this chapter, we take a closer look at the production process itself, including the procurement of raw materials as well as other factors affecting the kinds and quantities of goods produced.

Procuring Raw Materials

One might expect that one of the major distinctions between different kinds of producing firms is whether they use raw materials available within the country or whether they must import materials from abroad. The scarcity of foreign currency in a country where the balance of trade has suffered from the collapse of the traditional sources of foreign income in mining and the sale of natural gas should favor industries based on materials that are locally available. While this is indeed the case in some industries in Bolivia, we shall see that a number of factors related to the availability, quality and price of primary and intermediate goods impede the most effective use of local resources. These factors, in turn, are dependent on the adequacy of the infrastructure to exploit the resources, the cost-effectiveness of producers of intermediate goods, and the degree of competition with outside markets for primary goods and intermediate products. Among other things, these conditions are influenced by governmental policies, the degree of dependence on imported means of production, and the creation of monopolies.

National Raw Materials

Small-scale enterprises must increasingly compete with the direct export of unprocessed and semiprocessed raw materials. Thus, leather has become expensive because much of it is exported in the form of semiprocessed hides.[1] High-quality lumber, such as high-grade mahogany, has become all but unaffordable and unavailable to Bolivians, who are now employing types of wood that were shunned in the past (see the example of Mr. Gomez in Chapter 4). Similarly, coffee exporters are willing and able to pay much higher prices for coffee beans, forcing local coffee-roasting enterprises to scramble for second-grade coffee at ever higher prices. As we shall see later, to ensure a steady supply at reasonable prices, some artisans are contemplating the creation of a "bank" for raw materials. While many of the materials mentioned above have become unavailable because of Bolivia's integration into the wider economy, some materials are, ironically, still available because of the country's isolation from modern productive practices. Thus, the fur industry relies almost entirely on the extremely high mortality rate of infant alpacas for its furs.[2]

In some instances, consumers regard local materials as inferior or too common. For example, artificial gemstones imported from Switzerland are regarded as much more fashionable in La Paz than are semiprecious stones from the altiplano. In contrast, the latter do find a market in other Bolivian cities. Therefore, as in the case of intermediate goods, a producer may import some of his materials even when local ones are available.

Some materials are legally available only from government sources. In 1981, all gold had to be purchased from the Banco Minero. This led to a booming black market for gold brought in directly by gold miners and sold at half of the official price. In contrast, nationally mined precious stones cost about the same as stones imported from Brazil because of *their* thriving illegal export. Gold was also smuggled abroad. In order to prevent the illegal export of gold, the government restricted the export of gold jewelry. A consultant from HIID (the Harvard Institute for International Development) working with UDAPE (Unidad de Análisis de Políticas Económicas), of the Bolivian Planning Ministry, found that a jeweler he visited in 1988, who was equipped with the latest equipment, was not allowed to produce golden chains for export. Thus he was forced to produce only silver chains, which meant that he could take advantage of only 10% of his productive capacity.

Another alternative to imported materials is recycled ones. Bottles are reused until they break. Tires are retreaded and, after they are beyond their original use, cut up and used to make engine bushings or sold to sandal manufacturers, who carefully separate the plies and use the inner layers to make sandal uppers and the treaded layer to make soles. Similarly, consumers reuse most paper as wrapping or toilet paper; the remainder is recycled commercially to manufacture toilet paper. Most metal is also recycled. (We know of no used-car dump, for example.) Used tin cans, particularly the larger lard and alcohol containers, find a ready market among tinsmiths, who make everything from water containers to kerosene lamps and masks out of them. Finally, one of the major sources of silver for jewelry is old silver coins, and *cholas* have new gold jewelry made out of old pieces that are no longer fashionable.

Nationally Produced Intermediate Goods

Similar problems are associated with national intermediate goods. Bolivian goods in general and--of particular relevance to our discussion--intermediate manufactures still suffer from a reputation of poor quality. In earlier decades, purchasing nationally made goods was usually an option of last resort. And even today, a Bolivian who can afford to do so is likely to buy a foreign-made product instead of an equivalent nationally made one, even if he or she has to pay a premium for it.[3] In many instances, national factories do, indeed, produce cheap goods because only by pricing goods low can they be assured of a large enough market. In other instances, a monopoly position and/or protective import duties make it possible for a firm to continue producing inferior goods. For example, Bolivian automobile paint is much cheaper than imported paint, but it is more difficult to apply and is less durable. Also, it is not always available in the desired colors.

Some Bolivian firms that produce intermediate goods are state owned, so their existence and continued survival may be only tangentially related to their competitiveness. The only reason one textile factory that went bankrupt continued to operate was because of a state takeover to safeguard employment. Some such firms operate with antiquated equipment, while others are overequipped because some functionary obtained kickbacks for importing more expensive machinery. The cost-effectiveness of intermediate goods is also influenced by the fact that, in addition to practically all of the capital goods, many of the raw materials must also be imported. As a result, some goods that compare favorably in quality with imports, such as windowpanes for vehicles, have little or no cost advantage over equivalent imports.

Even when local intermediate materials are available, producers of finished goods often alternate between using them and importing such materials. For example, a car-body painter uses Bolivian or imported paint according to the client's ability to pay. A shirt manufacturer makes cheap shirts out of local cloth and finer ones out of imported cloth. And candle makers buy paraffin from the national petroleum industry, but since its production is insufficient, they must also request permission to import.

Sometimes there are no alternative sources to nationally produced intermediate goods, leading to periodic speculation and scarcity. Thus, strikes in the sugar industry may force candy manufacturers to close their factories or to drastically reduce production.

Some firms seek to temper the effect of these periodic shortages, price fluctuations and problems with the quality of intermediate goods by finding more reliable sources. Thus Don Alfonso, the peanut-butter manufacturer (see Chapter 2), was able to purchase peanuts even when they were scarce because he had established a reliable long-term relationship with an intermediary who reserved peanuts for him at all times. Similarly a Korean producer of children's knitwear stopped producing his own cloth and began to purchase it from a fellow Korean whose higher volume enabled him to equip his firm with better machinery.

Other firms have moved toward vertical integration. A foreign sausage manufacturer (mentioned earlier) was contemplating raising pigs and opening a slaughterhouse of his own in order to assure a steady supply of pork.[4]

Special problems arise when an industry is dependent on a government monopoly for intermediate goods. The state has a virtual monopoly on the production of alpaca yarn, which is essential for making sweaters with knitting machines. For a time, the yarn was inexpensive; but then the factory jacked up prices and began exporting most of its production. The price increase was (in addition to the decline of tourism during politically unstable periods) a major factor in the declining sales of such producers as Mrs. Salinas, who was forced to lay off two of her five workers when the price of factory-spun wool rose from $b. 28,000 to $b. 80,000 or 90,000 in a period of four months in 1984. Only producers of hand-knitted sweaters were unaffected, since they could use the much cheaper hand-spun wool. Many knitters were also substituting cheaper blends of sheep and alpaca wool and even llama and alpaca wool as well as blends with artificial fibers, often imported from Peru.

Trade barriers to protect national industries also make raw materials more expensive. Thus, if those industries were not protected by high import duties, certain imported synthetic textiles, for example, would cost 25% less than national ones.

Imported Materials

By far the largest proportion of all raw materials and intermediate manufactures, from flour to metals and plastics, as well as equipment, and from hand tools to machine tools, is imported. For most such goods and materials, the internal market would be too small to make national production profitable, while transportation costs would render export impractical. Not surprisingly, many industries are involved only in the final stages of production. For example, the bus manufacturers we interviewed import the motor and chassis (the *torpedos*) and manufacture only the bodies themselves. Even producers who rely heavily on local raw materials may import semiprocessed materials to tide them over a period of scarcity. A cooking-oil producer, for example, processes Bolivian soybeans but also imports unrefined vegetable oils from abroad.

Importing goods usually involves long delays and uncertain arrival dates. So, in order to assure adequate supplies, a factory must maintain large stocks. While, as we have already seen, such stocks can also be a safeguard against inflation, the firm requires more capital than its counterparts elsewhere to maintain such supplies--capital which, given the difficulties of financing described earlier, is often lacking.

As a result of these problems with direct importation, small-scale producers generally purchase materials from import firms despite their higher prices. Some, like the aluminum-pot manufacturers, have found an intermediate solution. They make their purchases through individuals who have import licenses, but they place their orders jointly. Thereby, they are able to bypass the more specialized, expensive dealers and avoid taxes charged to first-time importers. At the same time, they can more readily escape the value-added tax. In addition, a number of producer syndicates, such as the candle makers and machine-knit sweater manufacturers have imported--or were in the process of requesting government permission to import--raw materials. Such syndicates also organize the distribution of government-sub-sidized staples, particularly flour.

Inputs that cannot be imported legally or are subject to high import duties can usually be acquired through the thriving contraband market. Our informants obtained everything from precious stones to essences, vehicle tires and textiles in this manner.

Although securing adequate supplies of imported raw materials and intermediate goods is difficult in Bolivia even during normal times, doing so in times of economic and/or political crises constitutes a test even for producers who are veterans of many previous crises. A mere rumor of a new devaluation may send prices skyrocketing, and hyperinflation of the kind Bolivia experienced in the early and mid-1980s may lead, as it did then, to price increases of raw materials that outpace even the increases in street exchange rates. At the same time, lower consumption makes it difficult for producers to pass on their costs to the consumer, who may choose to forgo a purchase altogether. This problem is compounded by the fact that the cost of imported raw materials can vary considerably, depending on whether the producer has access to dollars at the official exchange rate or must obtain them at the usually much higher street rate. Political connections or bribes to the right official can have a considerable impact on such matters (see Chapter 2 for details).

Production in Smaller and Larger Firms

With the following examples, we wish to show the level of earn-ings and the standard of living of small-scale producers and illustrate both the complex manner in which the factors described above manifest themselves concretely and the way in which they are influenced by seemingly "non-economic" variables associated with the running of a household as well as by gender and marital relationships. In addition, we wish to examine the production problems inherent in specific activities at different levels of capitalization.

Reliable production figures are extraordinarily difficult to come by in Bolivia. Unless individuals receive fixed wages, they are usually reluctant to divulge income figures for fear that tax authorities might obtain the information, and they are often incapable of doing so because few keep written accounts. In addition, income figures in pesos bolivianos are difficult to translate into dollar figures. Official exchange rates change rapidly and may differ markedly from the street rate. Price levels of controlled staples further complicate comparisons of the standard of living at different times. The income statistics and estimates given below must therefore be treated with caution.

According to a study undertaken by the Bolivian Labor Ministry in 1978 on employment in La Paz (Bolivia 1980b), the average weekly income of a person engaged in a registered small-scale manufacturing enterprise (fewer than five workers) was $b. 368 (US $18.40), while the corresponding figure for larger enterprises was $b. 622 (US $31.10). For all types of activities,[5] heads of small-scale enterprises earned 61% less than those of larger ones. While the former earned 50% more than blue-collar workers in the "formal sector," they earned less than white-collar workers in that sector (pp. 42-45, 71-72).

On the basis of a small number of cases where we deem the information given to be reliable, we estimate that an unskilled worker earned some $b. 2,000 a month in 1981 (US $80); a semiskilled worker, between $b. 2,500 and 3,000 (US $100 to $120); a skilled worker in a small industry, between $b. 3,000 and 3,500 (US $120 to $140); and a skilled worker in a larger factory, $b. 5,000 (US $200). The owner of a small workshop would often have a very uncertain income with the amount ranging from $b. 1,000 in some months to 5,000 in others (US $40 to $200). The owner of a somewhat more capitalized firm typically earned between $b. 5,000 and 8,000 a month (US $200 to $320) and the owner of a small factory earned $b. 30,000 (US $1,200) and up.

The serious economic crisis Bolivia suffered throughout the 1980s and the sometimes erratic economic policies of a succession of military and democratic regimes have led to an inexorable decline of production, only partially mitigated by adaptive strategies. As we saw in Chapter 1, sales began to decline in 1979-1980 and fell precipitously in the mid-1980s. Between 1980 and 1985 industrial production dropped an average of 9.4% annually, and the decrease was 15% in 1984 alone (I. Taller de Política Económica, 1985, Table 1). The remaining clientele changed constantly, with everyone on the lookout for cheaper goods regardless of quality. Few producers had the option of cutting costs by substituting local raw materials for imports; most were simply not available. In fact, some national staples such as rice and sugar also became scarce because agro-businesses and larger farmers were keeping them off the market in protest against government-decreed prices. Subsidized imported goods became scarce too, making it impossible to produce such items as cookies and cakes, which depended on them. Finally, a strong currency since stabilization in 1986 combined with the liberalization of imports and price differentials with neighboring Peru, where basic staples continued to be subsidized until 1990, has led to a further decline of many industries that could no longer compete with imports.

Earnings have decreased commensurately. Casanovas et al. (1985:64) figured that a self-employed, small-scale producer earned an average of $b. 4.663 (US $9.33) a week in 1983. Escobar de Pabón and Maletta (1981, quoted in Casanovas 1985:69) calculated that the average weekly income in 1980 was $b. 523 (US $21). The figures represent a 25% decrease in real income in the three-year period. The erosion of income was lower than in services, transportation and construction but almost three times that in commerce, where it was 9% (Casanovas 1985:64).

Competition

Another major problem in a small and highly uncertain market is competition. As we indicated in Chapter 5, competition in Bolivia comes about mainly in two ways: from the proliferation of low-technology activities where entry is not unduly hindered by capital requirements and from imported goods. Competition from the latter occurs at all production levels, from low-technology activities to the more capital-intensive ones.

The case of the clothing industry illustrates the mushrooming competition that can arise even in specialties that were once monopolized by a few firms. As a Korean immigrant to La Paz put it:

> The times for producing ready-to-wear clothing in Bolivia have passed. The Bolivians have learned to make clothing themselves. They can do it in their homes at low cost. They don't pay taxes or rent. And they do not have to worry about the cost of labor. They also already have good equipment to work with. Eighty percent of the Bolivian population appears to be so poor that they cannot buy better quality clothing. So you have to produce low-cost items. But that is where the competition is most severe. So things have become more and more difficult.

A Bolivian producer of knitwear blames the Koreans for spoiling the market. While the Koreans used to sell only clothing, around 1979 they also began selling cloth, leading to increased competition. He figured that there must be 100 producers with machines in Bolivia and

500 that sew clothing. While these producers had access to cloth before, they did not have the contacts to obtain high-quality knits:

> There are only some ten persons who make high-quality cloth; the rest only make ordinary material. If the Koreans didn't sell material, we would be well off. I used to sell T-shirts for $b. 1,600 (US $64) per dozen. Now I can only charge $b. 1,000 (US $40). We only earn $b. 200 (US $8) per dozen. They [the homeworkers] don't count their own work, while we have to include the workers, the wear on the equipment, and electricity. In contrast, they work with manual equipment. Also we have to pay taxes.

Other activities where competition is particularly severe include *chola* skirtmaking, because, as we have already seen, capital costs are low, and the rebending of motor-vehicle springs. The latter activity requires few tools. The workshops are located on sunny streets, and the sun's heat is used to bend the springs. The sun heats them enough to give them sufficient flexibility for bending but does not heat them enough for the metal to loose its temper. In one street alone there are dozens of these workshops, spreading the work very thin.

In some activities, some producers with dependent workers have been forced to abandon their craft altogether because of competition from their own workers. A migrant couple from the Lake Titicaca area who made pillowcases and other tourist items out of colored woolen cloth or *bayeta* sewn onto white cloth used to have as many as fifty men and women working for them. Many of them began selling directly to the stores. Now, the husband drives an ancient taxi (after losing his truck in an accident), while the wife knits sweaters and sells in her sister's grocery store. They also have some land in the husband's community of origin.[6]

In addition to competition from firms on the same level and from individual workers, competition can also come from above, from factory-made goods produced out of different materials. The tinsmith trade, for example, is languishing because plastic pails are slowly edging out coated metal containers.

The government itself sometimes generates what private firms consider unfair competition. Thus, some branches of government have their own printing facilities, where they not only print materials related to government but take in orders from private individuals as well.

Producers are best able to compete if they can afford equipment that will produce types of goods that artisans with simpler machines are incapable of producing, if they are specialized in making goods that others don't have the skill to make (see Chapters 4 and 5) or, as we shall see in Chapter 9, if they produce for special markets. In addition, handmade goods may have a quality advantage over factory-made ones. As one shoemaker put it: "People buy shoes made by the Manaco factory when they have money; otherwise they buy them from smaller producers on the street. But you cannot repair shoes from Manaco. They have cardboard insoles that cannot be nailed back in place like mine." Others compete by keeping costs lower than those of their competitors through self-exploitation and by administering their own enterprises. The head of a bakers' syndicate suggested cooperativism as one means of reducing competition. He argued that there were far too many bakeries for all to be able to make a decent living: 1,200 in 1981, employing some 4,300 persons in La Paz alone.

Bolivian producers also suffer from competition from contraband goods and from legal imports, a phenomenon that has been exacerbated by the economic measures taken by the Paz Estenssoro regime to strengthen the peso boliviano. All but the most bulky goods that are expensive to transport and those based mostly on local or heavily subsidized raw materials have been affected by contraband.

Work Hazards and the Risk of Theft

In addition to competition, small-scale producers face a number of risks whose severity is compounded by the lack of even the most simple precautions and the impossibility of obtaining insurance. Among these risks are work-related accidents and toxic chemicals. As we saw in Chapter 3, artisans often work under very adverse conditions. Their workshops lack ventilation, and because many workers must use inadequate equipment they often take extraordinary risks. Thus, Mario spray painted signs for movie houses (covering over lettering in other languages and inserting Spanish titles on printed posters) in a tiny room whose only ventilation was from a door that opened on a narrow, walled compound. He also slept there, and his wife made cookies there while he worked. He used leaded gasoline and dry-cleaning fluid to thin his paint, which he sprayed on paper and metal objects. He had already been told by a *gringo* (foreigner) that he was endangering his health. Someone else had told him to drink milk in order to counter the toxic effects (presumably of the lead), and he has followed this advice. He has to stop working every so often to breathe some fresh air. He has thought about buying a fan to extract the air but claims that he cannot find a small one. Although he did own a mask, he did not use it because he had difficulty breathing through it. Instead, he sometimes stuffed cotton wads in his nose to filter the air. He wished he could switch to a less dangerous activity, like making neon lights, where the only painting involved would be to paint the hoods of the lights, but he lacked the required capital.

Automobile-body painters also often paint without ventilation and masks:

When one is painting, one breathes in much of the spray. Without realizing it, one becomes addicted. Many painters become alcoholics. Since we are constantly painting with the smell that is akin to alcohol around us, we come to like alcohol. I myself have passed through this. One gets used to it after a while. It's just the smell. . . .

A sign painter and a confectioner working in a poorly ventilated room

> Welding harms the eyesight. Of course, one always uses a shield when welding, but an apprentice does not use one until he has learned because otherwise he might not weld a seam properly. Also, glasses cost money.

Rudimentary equipment is another potential source of accidents. For an entire year, Mr. Blanes, who does car bodywork, used welding equipment that did not have valves to regulate the fuel and oxygen mixture. Thereby he—quite consciously—exposed himself to the ever present risk of an explosion.

Sometimes accidents involving toxic chemicals result from the mislabeling of a bottle. Thus, one jeweler's wife died when she mistook the contents of a bottle containing acid for a soft drink. In sorrow, the jeweler then committed suicide by drinking some himself. Another jeweler complained about the damage the acids he used in gilding jewelry were doing to his eyes. This was one of the reasons why he was planning to get out of production and only sell jewelry. In the meantime he hoped that eating a lot of onions—a tip he had learned from his *paisanos*, who are preponderantly curers—would prevent his eyesight from deteriorating any further. Similarly, another jeweler complained that the fumes were attacking her pancreas and said that she was therefore doing the work that creates fumes outdoors.

Another perpetual concern of small-scale producers is theft. In the absence of any viable possibility of obtaining insurance, they are under constant risk of losing much of their capital overnight. While larger producers can afford night watchmen, the owners of smaller enterprises whose workshops are not in the same location as their residences must either send a member of the household to sleep in the workshop or take a chance.

Artisans are sometimes reluctant to report a burglary to the police. "If I go to the police and bring the detectives here," claimed one carpenter, who had been robbed several times and had recently lost valuable equipment in this manner, "they will tell me that I first have to pay them a given sum and only then will they catch the thief."

Sometimes the burglaries are inside jobs. Artisans often mistrust their own workers, who they feel might run off with tools or materials, which is another reason for their preference to work with close kin, over whom they feel they have more control. They are also wary of other persons with whom they are in daily contact. A shoemaker, for example, caught a tenant opening his workshop with a key he had found. At other times, the suspect is a former spouse acting to seek revenge. Silvia, the cookie baker claimed:

> My [former] husband had my kiosk robbed of everything through some-one else. So, during all this time [since the robbery], I have had no capital and no means to make a living. Once, because of the anger I felt [against him] I stayed at home for several days. And when I went back to work, everything was gone. The people around there told me: "Your husband has been around. He came and went. He did this harm to you." I even consulted sorcerers. Lucía told me to have them read the coca leaves. And that too pointed to him as the culprit. So it is he who did it, without any compassion, not even for my children. One needs luck for everything in life. So, since then I don't have the capital to start over again. On top of this, there was the devaluation. . . . I am ruined. And so I began to work [as a cook in El Alto], and the work was very hard.

Similarly, the kiosk owned by Doña Flora's daughter was robbed three times. She too suspects her former husband.

In addition to the material loss incurred, a burglary often deals a severe psychological blow. The carpenter mentioned above, who was robbed of valuable equipment, is reluctant to purchase new equipment. "I thought about starting anew, but I can't forget what happened to me. Sooner or later the same thing might happen again." Similarly, Mr. Mena, a baker, considered himself a workaholic before his bakery was robbed. As we shall see later, he was working in two places at the time he married, but the robbery made him change his lifestyle.

> We had money to spend then [at the time that we married]. But we didn't know how to spend it well. There was no one to teach us. I had, by that time, become estranged from my father. We did have the desire to save, but a thief stole all our belongings one night, even our blankets—when we had just married. We said to ourselves: "Why are we getting all these things for the thieves? Let's eat and drink." That is why we don't have much now; otherwise we would be well off. We have the house in Villa Pabón. That's the only thing we did for ourselves. But we don't even have the money to improve it. If one has a lot of children, one spends a lot.

Case Studies of Production

Clothing Manufacturers

The first two case studies that we will present illustrate the fact that households often depend on a multiplicity of incomes from different sources. They also demonstrate the influence of location and the associated problems of transportation on production. Both are cases of households in which clothing production, an activity that (at least at the lower levels) requires relatively little capital, plays a major role.

Our first example is of a very small-scale enterprise: sewing *chola*, skirts or *polleras*. Doña Nilda, a 32-year-old married woman, had sewn skirts ever since she was 12, having learned to sew from her mother, who was also a *pollerera*. After having lived in Santa Cruz for eight years, Doña Nilda and her family they were living in cramped and poor quarters in La Paz. The room that they rented from her wedding godmother for $b. 200 (US $8) a month was barely large enough for a bunk bed and a manual sewing machine. Nilda, her husband and their six children all managed to sleep in this tiny abode--five of them in a single bed. Nevertheless, it was relatively close to the center of La Paz, near enough to good schools for the children[7] and to the major shopping areas. When she needed to buy materials for her *polleras*, she could leave the smaller children locked in the room, promising them sweets when she returned. She hoped that eventually she would be able to rent an additional room in the same compound, buy a house in Obrajes, where her husband had just set up shop as a vehicle body painter, or move back to Santa Cruz, where they owned a small house.

Nilda's husband earned between $b. 2,000 and 2,500 (US $80 to $100) a week. She claimed that in Santa Cruz her husband had been able to command much higher prices for his work. Their oldest son, who was 13 and did not like to go to school, helped his father. In addition, he had two other workers. Nilda herself charged $b. 600 (US $24) for making a *pollera*. This amount did not include the cloth, which was provided by the customer, but included the lining and other materials, which cost her $b. 380 (US $15.20).[8] She had left her sewing machine in Santa Cruz, so she bought a used one from her cousin on credit for $b. 3,000 (US $120). However, at the time of the interview, it was broken, and she was unable to fix it for lack of spare parts, which forced her to sew by hand. She was hoping to purchase a new machine on credit.

Nilda could sew as many as four or five *polleras* a week. On the rare occasions when she had no orders for new *polleras*, she went to the Avenida Buenos Aires, where she knew people who gave her *polleras* to mend or to turn inside out. For those services she received between $b. 100 and 150 (US $4 to $6).

She seemed to be contributing more than her share to the support of her children. She was spending some $b. 100 to 180 (US $4 to $7.20) a day for their food and other needs.

> Sometimes my husband gives me $b. 50 [US $2]. What can I buy with that, if half a kilo of meat alone costs almost $b. 30 [US $1.20] and a pound of noodles $b. 11 [US $0.44]? I give the two children [who go to school] $b. 7.50 [US $0.30] or, when I don't have enough, $b. 5 [US $0.20] each to buy a snack during recess. My husband scolds me and tells me that I should only give them $b. 3 [US $0.20]. But how could I do this? The bus alone costs $b. 4 [US $0.16]. And how can I let them watch the other children eat while they themselves go hungry? He has no answer to that.

Nilda's expenditures also included the enrollment fee of $b. 74 (US $2.96) for her two school-aged children. In addition, she had to spend almost $b. 800 (US $32) for their school materials and had to contribute $b. 15 (US $0.60) to $b. 20 (US $0.80) every time the school celebrated a school fiesta, including the Day of the Teacher, Mother's Day and the school's anniversary. But school is important to Nilda. She herself completed school only through sixth grade. Her father had subsequently enrolled her in an academy, but since he was poor, he could not pay for the school materials the teachers requested. So, in the belief that as a woman she did not need to be educated, she had decided to quit school. "At that time, people weren't interested in studying. Now they learn quickly and are interested [es rápido e interesado]."

Nilda buys more than one set of clothing at a time. "This way they last longer. I brought a lot of clothing from Santa Cruz, and they are using them up now, handing them down from the older to the younger ones. For the older ones, we buy more. When they are older, they will demand more clothing. That's why—I'm telling you--even before that I will have gray hair."

One of the reasons Nilda did not like it when her children left the compound is that they came home dirty, which meant more washing. She washed the clothes at the tap on the patio. Alternatively she would let the wash accumulate, and getting up at four in the morning, she would travel to Calacoto and wash it in the river. However, since the bus charged $b. 2.50 (US $0.10) for a bundle of clothes, a round trip cost her $b. 10 (US $0.40) every time she went. She took the children and their lunch along. She herself claimed not to get hungry when she worked.

> I only drink a soft drink when I am finished. I used to chew coca and get [even less] hungry. But I recently gave it up after I had two teeth extracted. They say that chewing coca shortens one's life by a day [every time it is chewed]. When I chewed coca, I used to be able to sew and sew, and I did not become sleepy or hungry. I was able to sew up to two days without sleeping at all. But it weakens us.

Also the habit is expensive. Her father, who still chewed coca at the time, was spending 20 pesos a day.

Doña Nilda suffered from a terrible marriage. Her husband came home drunk two or three times a week and beat her. He rarely gave her enough money to run the household. And yet, he was forever suspicious; when they lived in Santa Cruz, he did not like the fact that she worked, for he feared that she might meet another man. When she came to La Paz to bear her youngest child in her parents' house, he followed her, leading to their present situation. The house in Santa Cruz is in the name of her husband, which could mean additional difficulties should the couple separate. Her marriage was arranged by her father, whom she now accuses of pushing her into an untenable situation.

Our second example is of a male counterpart of Nilda, a more elderly tailor. Raúl, who was born in 1928, is a migrant from Compi who has practiced his trade in La Paz since 1946. Today he works alone, but at one point he had a joint workshop with some cousins. Difficulties with the wife of one of his partners forced him to set up his own workshop in a building owned by another relative. There he had as many as five or six workers, some of whom were his kin. Later he married, but the relationship soured and his wife left with all his equipment. Since 1977, he has worked in a small shop tucked away on a side street. For fear of having to pay taxes, he does not even have a sign over the door.

Raúl feels that he is slowing down with age. Today it takes him a week to finish a new suit, if he hurries, and four days to make a coat. When he was younger, he had been able to complete a coat in a single day.

In 1981, he still had as much work as he could handle. He charged $b. 1,500 to 1,600 (US $60 to $64) for a suit, which included approximately $b. 800 (US $32) for material, $b. 600 to 700 (US $24 to $28) for his labor, and $b. 100 (US $4) for having the trousers sewn by an outworker. His other expenses included $b. 200 (US $8) for rent, $b. 25 (US $10) for water and $b. 80 to 90 (US $3.20 to $3.60) for electricity each month. The outworker he used took the cut material to his home community and sewed the trousers there. For remaking a suit (turning the material inside out) Raúl charged between $b. 200 and 400 (US $8 to $16). Although he asked for an advance of 50%, one of his major problems was that customers sometimes failed to pick up the clothing they had made or redone. One suit had been hanging in his shop for two years!

Raúl's wife runs a store in his home community and travels between the community and La Paz with potatoes, and he himself returns there on occasion to work the fields. Crops from these fields contribute substantially toward feeding the four of their six children who still live at home.

In May 1984, when inflation had already accelerated to unprece-
dented levels (but had not yet reached its maximum rate), Raúl was
charging $b. 80,000 (US $40 at the official exchange rate and US $23.50
at the street rate) to make a suit and was earning barely enough to eat.
For, instead of the $b. 45 to 60 (US $1.80 to $2.40) that a kilo of meat
cost in 1981, the cost in 1984 was $b. 6,000 to 7,000 (US $3 to US $3.50
[official]; US $1.75 to $2 [street]), and a small loaf of subsidized bread
(weighing 70 grams) cost $b. 70 (US $0.035 [official]; $0.02 [street]), up
from $b. 1.50 (US $0.06) in 1981. While he had been able to afford half
a kilo of meat or so before, he was buying a quarter kilo now. By
scrimping and complementing purchased food with produce from his
land, including some milk from cows, and with the contribution of his
wife's economic activities (she was also raising pigs, lambs and
chickens for sale), he could feed four persons for $b. 5,000 to $b. 6,000
(US $2.50 to US $3.00 [official]; US $1.50 to $1.75 [street]) a day, but
he could easily have spent $b. 10,000 (US $5 [official]; US $3 [street]).

Analysis. Both of the above cases exemplify the uncertain nature
of family incomes that wax and wane with competition, the health of
the national economy and factors related to family dynamics. In both
Raúl's and Nilda's case, there has been a considerable decrease in
economic activities and in earning power. In Nilda's case, this appears
to be due to the move to La Paz, where competition was higher and
where the economy was on a downslide. The latter factor clearly
played a major role in Raúl's productivity; he not only earned less in
adjusted terms in 1984 than he did in 1981, but he also produced less.
His age and probably his wife's dynamic economic activities also
contributed to his decrease in productivity.

In both cases, considerations related to production influenced the
location of the enterprises and--since members of both households
worked in their homes--the family residences. Raúl lives in La Paz
rather than in Compi to be closer to potential clients (indeed, when
he lived in Compi at one point, he did little more than take care of
the children while his wife traveled to the city). Nilda has chosen to
live close to the center of La Paz in order to have access to input
sources. In the absence of day-care facilities, just leaving the house to
shop for materials was already a major endeavor. That problem would
have been compounded had she lived farther away from shops. Her
ability to return home quickly outweighed the problems she endured
with inadequate housing.

Working in their place of residence enables members of the households in both of our examples to take care of their children. In this
respect, Raúl's example presents an interesting parallel to that of Nilda.
Since some of Raúl's children are going to school in La Paz, he--and
not his wife--takes care of them. We found similar arrangements in at
least two other cases, where the wife was active in commerce and the
husband's more sedentary activity led him to play a more active part

in child care than is usual in Bolivia. Potentially, Nilda could take advantage of the same solution if she and her husband buy a house in Obrajes--if she felt that she could trust him. Presumably her husband could take care of the children when she had to go to the center of town.[9]

Even though women make substantial contributions to the economy of both households, the two cases offer contrasting perceptions of women's roles. Nilda's case is a study in contradictions. On the one hand, her husband tried to impede her work because he was threatened by the contact with the outside world it permitted and required. As we saw in the case of the cookie maker, Silvia, in Chapter 3, upwardly mobile men (whether husbands or sons) often take pride in the fact that their wives (or mothers) do not work. In particular, selling in the market is viewed as demeaning by such men. On the other hand, while Nilda could not have raised her family on her income alone, it was crucial for her to reduce her dependency on a drunken and unreliable husband. Raúl's view of women's roles appears to be diametrically opposed to that of Nilda's husband and more in line with lower-class perceptions. In Raúl's case, the wife may well be the principal source of the household's subsistence. In fact, as mentioned above, Raúl was--at times--content to take care of the children. And, at present, his wife's income has reduced his worries regarding the declining demand for men's clothing.

Sewing *polleras*, a predominantly female activity, requires little capital. Indeed, *polleras* made out of expensive, heavy material are sewn entirely by hand. More typically, however, at least a pedal-driven sewing machine is needed. Even very poor women are able to prevail upon some relative to lend them or sell them a second-hand machine, although the dearth of spare parts, usually at its worse during periods of economic crisis, when extra income is most needed, often slows down production. Women often sew in rooms that also serve as living quarters, thereby saving on rent for a workshop. Casanovas and Pabón found that 54% of the independent workers in their sample (i.e., workers who owned their means of production, worked only with members of their families, apprentices and/or temporary help, and who, according to the authors' estimates, represent 40% of all small scale producers) worked in this manner (1988:20-29). Only 13% had workshops outside the home. Obviously this practice aggravates crowding, all the more so since, according to the 1976 census, 47% of the families in La Paz lived in single-room homes (Casanovas and Pabón 1988:90).

Capital requirements are somewhat higher for tailors, who need more space for cutting. However, for them, too, some aspects of trade, particularly sewing trousers, can readily be done in a corner of a room. Tailors often put out trousers to independent workers.

As we saw in the example of Maria in Chapter 1 and will see again in Chapter 10, tailors and *polereras* are highly dependent on fiestas to sell their products. The timing of their work and their strategies for gaining access to clients are therefore tightly linked to the fiesta system.

Bakers

Our next two examples are of bakeries, enterprises that entail higher production costs and are very dependent upon state policies regarding subsidized flour, pricing and hygiene. In the first case, the owner has a slightly higher income than Raúl; the second case is of a middle-class individual who owns and runs a medium-sized bakery.

Manuel Mena, who was born in 1925, has been working as an independent baker since 1957. Initially, he shared an oven with his brother-in-law and started out with one hundredweight (quintal) of flour a day. Soon, he increased his production to 2 to 3 quintals, and within a year, he was converting 10 quintals of flour into bread on weekdays and 12 on Sundays and was not taking a single day off. At that time he employed 4 workers. Because he found that his work schedule conflicted too much with that of his brother-in-law, he decided to rent an oven by himself. In fact, he worked in two locations, the place where the oven was located and a place where he prepared the dough.

In the late 1970s, he was converting 3-4 quintals of flour a day. In 1981, he made much less bread, converting only 2 quintals a day. But he and his wife made cookies and *empanadas* (cheese turnovers) in addition to bread. His wife sold the cookies for $b. 1.50 (US $0.60) and the turnovers for $b. 1 (US $0.40) in nearby schools. A year or two earlier, they processed 50 pounds of flour a day for cookies and *empanadas*, from which they earned $b. 50 (US $2), but in 1981 sales were no longer what they used to be, so they were baking only half as much. He believed that schoolchildren were buying more soft drinks and fewer cookies and *empanadas* because of the prizes they could win if they were lucky enough to select the right soft drink bottle. With a progressively deteriorating economy, they did not have enough money for both. Nevertheless, he earned as much from making cookies as from baking bread the weight and price of which are subject to government control. Infractions could cost him a fine of $b. 500 to 1,000 (US $20 to $40). As he put it: "From our earnings from making bread, we used to be able to buy the basic things like food and rent. Earnings from cookies went into entertainment and things like that. Now we are poor." At least he could count on regular orders for 300 to 600 *marraquetas* (hard bread rolls) a day from the nearby army barracks, which constituted a regular source of income, even if the army only paid after two days.

His costs included a monthly rent of $b. 3,000 (US $120). With flour no longer rationed, he preferred to buy his supply in a store rather than in the cooperative run by the bakers' syndicate. Even though it cost 10 pesos less in the cooperative, he could avoid paying taxes (that are based on working capital) to the state if he bought from the stores, and the quality of the store-bought flour was better.[10] In 1981, he no longer employed any workers, although one of his two sons and his daughter helped out when they had time.

Mr. Mena was incapable of figuring his exact earnings. We shall therefore quote the detailed calculations we obtained from a Mr. Ortíz, a larger-scale baker who explained to us why making price-controlled bread was a losing proposition:

> We make *marraquetas*, but at a loss. I will give you the figures: A hundredweight of flour has 46 kilograms. To this one adds 9 kilos of salt and sugar. That is a total of 55 kilograms. That should result in 785 $b. 1.50 (US $0.06) *marraquetas*. But since the *marraquetas* lose weight when they dry, we can only make 550 per quintal. We have to give 50 *marraquetas* to the store, which is their profit margin, so we receive $b. 750 (US $30). From this sum we have to deduct the cost of the flour, which amounts to $b. 620 (US $24.80) including transportation, which leaves $b. 130 (US $5.20). But then one has to pay for the water, the rent of the oven and the labor of three workers: one who makes the dough, an assistant and a baker, at a cost of some $b. 190 (US $7.60) a day. So it doesn't work out. The only way to make a real profit would be to cheat on the weight. The small baker absorbs this loss by employing family members. If four persons work in a family, they should be earning four day wages. However, in actuality they only earn two. Bakers thus prefer to make special breads, whose weight is not controlled. [However, bakers were not allowed to make only special breads].

In the case of Mr. Mena, this would have meant a family income of $b. 4,800 (US $72) a month for bread alone after deducting rental fees for the oven and before subtracting energy and other costs.
The head of the national baker's union concurred with Mr. Ortíz:

> Wages are figured according to the amount of flour processed, between $b. 30 and 40 [US $1.20 and $1.60 per bag of flour]. In addition, one pays a bonus of $b. 1,000 [US $40]. But if you processed two bags a day you would only earn $b. 70 [US $2.80]. Bakeries generally process some four or five quintals. With 3 persons helping [the owner] they would earn, say, $b. 175 [US $15] in all [which] they have to divide among themselves, resulting in only $b. 43 [US $1.80] for each person working. That is why we have problems. At the same time that they freeze bread prices, the authorities demand that we improve our bakeries with wall tiles, good paint, cement floor and many other things. If we don't comply, they force us to close. They don't care if four families have nothing to eat as a result. They shut their eyes to the harsh realities. That is the policy of the government.

The government's pricing policy was particularly galling to the bakers because the cost of flour had risen much more than that of bread. In February 1981, a bag of flour cost $b. 310 (US $12.40); in

March of the same year, it cost $b. 610 (US $24.40), and yet the bread price had been allowed to rise only from $b. 1.50 (US $0.06) for two buns of 60 grams each the same amount for one bun weighing 70 grams.

Like Raúl, the tailor, Mr. Mena was once much more productive than he is at present. Nevertheless, unlike Raúl, who owns only rural property, he has been able to build his own house in the city. He has also been more successful in providing his children with an education beyond the elementary level. The family's income in 1981 was at about the level of a semiskilled factory worker in a larger firm or perhaps somewhat higher. However, in view of the fact that husband and wife worked full time and had the assistance of their children as well, they may have been relatively worse off than the factory workers, especially if one considers the fact that they worked seven days a week. In addition, there was always the threat of flour shortages and an uncertain market.

A description of Mr. Ortíz's bakery will give an idea of the economics of one of the three "industrial" bakeries in La Paz (the smallest). Established by a foreigner in 1939, this bakery was, until recently, the only bakery in La Paz to produce German style-bread. The present manager/co-owner worked as manager since around 1961. He and his partner purchased the firm a few months before its founder's death.

In 1981, they were processing 10 to 12 quintals of flour a day, mostly on contract, with a peak production rate of 16-18 quintals.[11] Unlike most Bolivian bakeries, the plant was equipped with electric kneading machines (imported from Germany) and modern ovens. In 1981, the bakery employed 14 workers. Most of them had worked for the firm for twelve to fifteen years, and one had been there for twenty-three years. However, five years earlier, Mr. Ortíz decided to pay the workers the severance-pay benefits they had accumulated. Their wages were calculated according to a complex scheme. Each received $b. 37 (US $1.48) per hundredweight of flour he or she processed, but since Bolivian law established a minimum wage plus bonuses worth $b. 1,800 (US $72) per month, each worker actually received the equivalent of $b. 110 (US $4.40) per quintal. During a month when there was little production, a quintal could cost as much as $b. 300 (US $12).

Mr. Ortíz complained that although his workers did excellent work, they were very reluctant to learn new techniques, such as diversifying the product by mixing different kinds of flour, employing additives to improve quality, or changing the product's appearance.

When the bakery opened, 90% of the customers were foreigners. They liked their bread with cumin. Now, they are mostly Bolivians who prefer even the German-type bread without cumin. Since this type of bread has a long shelf life, it can be shipped to Oruro and even to Cochabamba and Santa Cruz.

The rye the bakery requires for its German bread is not a traditional crop in Bolivia, so for a time it had to be imported from Germany. Later, Mr. Ortíz gave some seeds to a group of German volunteers providing technical assistance in rural areas, and they grew the crop with good results. However, the Germans left after a few years and production ceased. In 1981, the firm began importing rye from Argentina. In addition, Mr. Ortíz was providing seed directly to a few peasants who produced solely for him. Each brought him some 10 to 15 quintals of rye per year. The poppy seed that is used in some of the breads must also be imported, which is a difficult proposition; because it is a potential raw material for opium, its distribution is highly controlled. In 1981 Mr. Ortíz was still drawing on stock from the previous year. Cumin too is imported because the local variety is not suitable for use in bread.

When we visited him again in 1984, Mr. Ortíz was distraught. The crisis had deepened to the extent that flour had become scarce and rationed. The bakery had been forced to reduce its output to 35% of its capacity. In fact, in March production was limited to only 12 days, and in April, 5 days, in part because of workers' strikes and in part because of the lack of flour. Even the demand for rye bread, consumed by a clientele less affected by the crisis, had decreased substantially. However, the bakery still had a workforce of 12.[12] Flour, of which there were two qualities, had to be procured with coupons given by the government. One type of flour was made from imported grain but was milled locally and cost $b. 28,000 (US $14 at the official or US $8.25 at the street rate) per quintal. The other type was milled abroad and cost $b. 39,000 (US $19.50 [official]; US $11.50 [street]). The firm made 20% special breads, whose price was not controlled, and 80% regular bread, whose price and distribution were controlled by the government. In 1983, the Siles government had established a rationing system controlled by neighborhood councils, which checked the weight of the bread and the ration cards of each customer. Each family was allotted a daily ration of 10 to 15 small loaves. The few remaining loaves were then sold without restrictions. According to Mr. Ortíz, the system worked to the detriment of those who had to work during the few hours when the neighborhood council heads were present and to the advantage of those with time to stand on line in front of more than one bakery, having managed to obtain ration cards in more than one neighborhood. The latter could then sell their surpluses at speculative prices.

Analysis. Bakers differ from tailors in the high capital costs their profession entails. In order to become independent, they must accumulate substantial sums or money or they must rent an oven. Those who choose to do the latter frequently share the oven with others, either by time-sharing or by baking cookies, *empanadas* and other baked goods prepared by individuals working on a smaller scale. Baking is one of the few activities in which production cooperatives have been relatively successful (Zapata 1978). However, bakers tend to view cooperatives as a transitional solution, just as Mr. Mena viewed his sharing arrangement with his brother-in-law, which he ended as soon as his level of production increased. Production tends to be on either a very large scale (there are two bakeries in La Paz that employ several hundred workers, one of which produces bread, other baked goods and noodles, and had annual sales totaling US $2,823,425 in 1978 [Estes 1984:37]) or a very small scale. The intermediate size of Mr. Ortíz's firm--probably related to the nature of its specialization--appears to be exceptional.

In contrast to work in the garment industry, baking requires only a low level of skills for most aspects of production, which may be one reason why baking is often a family operation.

Both Mr. Mena's case and Mr. Ortíz's case, like that of Raúl, the tailor, have demonstrated decreasing productivity as the economic crisis has progressed. In the case of Mr. Mena, the market for cookies decreased, while in the case of Mr. Ortíz, Europeans and wealthier Bolivians began to purchase less fancy breads, at least in part because of the rapid increase in prices, so Mr. Ortíz's competitive edge resulting from his specialization has deteriorated.

However, bakers do have the advantage of a product with relatively inelastic demand. Crises affect them in other ways. The constant strikes and the scarcity of flour make it more lucrative for some merchants and bakers to hoard flour and sell it at high prices or to smuggle it abroad. Since the price controls on bread did not allow for an adequate return, bakers found it necessary to resort to both legal and illegal devices to circumvent them.

Two Furriers

The next two examples deal with furriers, one male and one female, one located in the old market district near the center of La Paz and one in El Alto. Both would be classified as *clase media* in Bolivia, corresponding roughly to lower middle class in the United States.

Mr. Antelo, a man who was 30 years old when we interviewed him in 1981, comes from a family of furriers. His maternal grandfather immigrated from Peru and taught Mr. Antelo's mother how to make blankets, slippers and other items out of vicuña pelts. She in turn taught his father. In the mid-1950s, when Peru prohibited the export of vicuña furs and Bolivian vicuña wool was being exported to England, where it fetched high prices, the family shifted to alpaca furs. This entailed a change in techniques. Vicuña furs were cut up into rectangles, and sections from the same part of the animal--neck, back or legs--were laboriously sewn together by hand. Thus, blankets made out of *patitas* (feet) consisted of hundreds of pieces. Due to the unequal coloration of alpacas and the small size of the baby alpacas, which, as we have already seen, furnish the bulk of alpaca furs, the same system could not be applied. Instead, the furriers invented an interlocking pattern that makes maximum use of the furs.

Mr. Antelo himself began working as a furrier when he was only 14 years old, and by the time he was 20, he had already become independent.[13] After six years, during which he worked with two workers without any machinery, he was able to purchase an overlock sewing machine that greatly speeded up the manufacturing process.

In 1981, Mr. Antelo and his wife worked with nine workers: four who washed and tanned the furs; two cutters/seamstresses; two apprentices; and a vendor, who sold in the artisan market near San Francisco. The couple controlled the work, prepared the furs and did the paperwork, including that for shipping. Sales were in the wife's hands.

One of the main problems these furriers had was lack of space. The workshop had an area of only 120 square meters. The furs were washed and dried outside. When it rained, work was slowed down considerably, since the heat of the sun was needed for the hides to dry properly. As of 1981, they had not been able to afford electric dryers.

In that year, a skilled worker in the fur trade who was paid by the piece could earn some $b. 1,500 (US $60) a week, or $b. 6,000 (US $240) per month, plus the government-mandated bonus of almost $b. 1,000 (US $40) a month, a wage that compared favorably with that of a highly skilled factory worker or the owner of a mechanic's workshop. Mr. Antelo told his workers to keep their salaries a secret. He was afraid of being criticized for paying too much. According to Mr. Antelo, more usual salaries were $b. 1,000 (US $40) per week for a skilled worker and $b. 500 (US $20) for an apprentice. His total labor costs for an alpaca blanket came to $b. 220 (US $8.80). He figured a profit of $b. 300 to 500 (US $12 to $20) per blanket (after materials and labor costs other than his and his wife's labor and without amortization of equipment). He calculated that he could produce 25 to 30 blankets a week and that his own monthly income was somewhere between $b. 8,000 and 10,000 (US $320 and $400), with his wife earning somewhat less. While he had to pay a value-added tax of 5% to the state and another 2-1/2 % to the city on all local sales, he received a subsidy of 10% on all exports.

Mr. Antelo attributes part of his relative success to the fact that he studied at the university for several years. The fur trade demands considerable planning and capital invested in hides. The hides are least available during the months when demand is highest (September to December) and most abundant when demand is lowest (January to May). Mr. Antelo accumulated stock worth between $b. 30,000 and 50,000 (US $1,200 to $2,000).

While there are a few furriers with a similar output to Mr. Antelo's, none of the enterprises have succeeded in becoming substantially larger than his. Those with the expertise do not have the capital, while those with sufficient capital do not have the expertise. Thus, one attempt at establishing a large-scale fur industry failed miserably because the owner was cheated by her workers. In contrast, there are a host of much smaller producers. With no labor costs other than their own time, they can make a profit even when they sell blankets at $b. 2,000, a price at which Mr. Antelo would only break even. At any rate, Mr. Antelo felt that the industry was an anachronism, doomed to disappear when alpaca husbandry improves and mortality decreases. At that point, he plans to produce some other item, such as lamb-fleece linings for jackets.

Mrs. Romero's enterprise was in many ways similar to that of Mr. Antelo. Like Mr. Antelo, Mrs. Romero learned the trade from her parents, and she, too, had been active in the profession for many years. Both of their enterprises exported a large percentage of their production or had done so in the past' and both also had their own retail outlets. But unlike Mr. Antelo, who concentrated on a single type of product, Mrs. Romero produced rugs, dolls, woven wall hangings, leather jackets and--lately--cartoon-like ceramic figurines. In addition, she sold a variety of tourist items that she did not produce herself.

In 1981, Mrs. Romero had 6 permanent workers, five of whom she claimed were her siblings and in-laws.[14] Like Mr. Antelo, she had purchased a sewing machine which enabled her to produce two or three rugs a day rather than one a week. Her firm was selling some 35 to 40 rugs a month, half the amount they had been selling a year earlier.

In 1988, she employed 80 persons including homeworkers. However, in her firm's best year, she had some 300 people working for her in one form or another. In 1987 (a year which was far better than 1988, when she had not received a single order from abroad by July), she exported some US $30,000 worth of merchandise. She figured that her profit from these exports amounted to some US $1,000 to $1,500. In addition, she sold some fifty rugs or so per month, earning anywhere from a dollar to five dollars per rug, depending on whether or not she knew the customer. In 1988, her fourteen in-house workers, who, like Mr. Antelo's workers, were paid by the piece, earned some Bs. 300 (US $150)[15] per month and received a free meal each day. Their earnings were substantially above the minimum wage of $b. 60 but were far less in real terms than Mr. Antelo claimed he was paying his workers in 1981.

Analysis. On a general level, the two cases above are examples of the transmission of trades along family lines and of the expansion of an activity as non-kin (who may eventually become independent competitors) are hired.

On a more specific level, these examples of the furrier trade show a typical progression of an economic activity in a Third World country whose role in the world market, like that of other Third World countries, was and continues to be a provider of raw materials, both abundant and scarce—raw materials that have often been exploited, with little regard to continuity and ecological cost. The vicuña blanket and vicuña wool trade clearly shows this progression. The trade was sustainable when wild vicuñas were abundant, and it profited briefly from foreign demand. But that demand led to the destruction of entire herds of animals. The trade collapsed as the herds vanished, and international trade in vicuña products was finally banned. Its successor, which depends on the high mortality rate of infant alpacas, may be equally evanescent, for an increase in the world demand for alpaca wool may bring pressure on alpaca herders to reduce mortality rates. If the industry then shifts to lamb fleeces, it will have to face much greater competition from producers in other countries that also raise sheep.

Like *pollereras* and tailors, furriers face seasonal variations in demand for their products. For the former artisans, fiestas create a seasonal demand, while for the latter, the seasonal variable is the supply of pelts. As for tailors and bakers, there is an elaborate division of labor in the fur trade, and as for tailors but unlike bakers, most steps require skilled labor. Additional problems of production include inadequate washing facilities, which means that producers must make trips to distant rivers, and lack the space to dry the pelts. The trade requires less capital than bread baking but more than tailoring. Without a relatively expensive overlock sewing machine, piecing the pelts together takes an inordinate amount of time.

Automobile Mechanics

In Bolivia, as in many Third World countries, the separation between manufacturing and the service industries is more fluid than in the more industrialized countries. Repair often entails the manufacture, or at least the adaptation, of parts, and quite frequently, old products are remanufactured to serve the same or new ends. Automobile parts are adapted from available used parts or made to specifications by lathe operators; tires are retreaded; bus bodies are mounted on new or used truck chassis; dance masks are repainted; hats reblocked; and men's jackets turned inside out. As a result, although our focus was on manufacturing rather than service industries, we have not excluded the latter entirely from our study. The automobile industry provides a good example of the overlap between these sectors. The examples that follow will give an idea of the range activities and levels of capitalization of firms engaged in this industry.

One mechanic had a workshop located on a major highway, where he repaired springs, reinforced chassis and engaged in other, similar work. In 1981, he earned between $b. 500 and 800 (US $20 and $32) a week "when there [was] work." He lamented that his repair shop was not located on the other major highway, which leads to major cities; work on the heavier trucks and buses that used that highway paid better. He owned his own tools but had to pay a monthly rent of $b. 500 (US $20) for the building, where he also lived. In addition, he paid the city $b. 300 (US $12) a year for the permission to work on vehicles in front of his shop. He also paid a flat $b. 380 (US $15.20) in federal, and $b. 400 (US $16) in city, taxes. Disillusioned, he hoped to eventually land a job as a policeman, but this would have required paying a bribe of some $b. 3,000 (US $120).

In contrast, another mechanic, who runs a metal-lathe shop, never lacks work. Since spare parts for automobiles and trucks are often expensive and difficult to obtain, most of his work consists of reconstructing broken parts. In 1981, he earned between $b. 500 and 800 (US $20 to $32) a day after expenses. He paid one of his workers $b. 500 (US $20) a week and the other $b. 900 (US $36) a week, which was more than Mr. Lozada, in our previous example, earned.

Mr. Blanes repairs bus bodies and then spray-paints them. He possesses his own tools and equipment--worth some $b. 60,000 (US $2400). He works in a walled compound owned by his father--who doesn't charge him for its use--and on the street in front of it. For the right to paint vehicles on the street--a dirt road with very little traffic--he must obtain and periodically renew a permit from the traffic police. One of his major worries is the weather. Since he works outdoors, he must wait for a sunny day without much wind. From July to September the wind is often too strong to paint.

In 1981, Mr. Blanes charged $b. 5,000 (US $200) for painting a car with imported paint. For painting a small bus with locally manufactured paint, he charged between $b. 2,000 (US $80) and $b. 2,500 (US $100) for materials and $b. 3,500 (US $140) for labor. Half of the total sum was paid when the contract was made and half upon completion of the job. Mr. Blanes usually does not release the vehicle until he is paid. However, on occasion, he takes pity on owners who do not have the necessary cash in hand. In those cases, he rarely gets paid. The vehicle owners usually disappear into thin air.

It takes Mr. Blanes and his two assistants a week to complete painting a bus. This means that they can complete four paint jobs per month. However, in August 1981, they painted only two small buses. As a result of the deepening economic depression, bus owners were postponing paint jobs. During that month Mr. Blanes earned $b. 6,000 (US $240). Business tends to pick up just before fiestas. For Carnival, for example, on August 5, the day of Our Lady of the Snow, vehicle owners often have their vehicles blessed in the pilgrimage center of Copacabana. In 1981, Mr. Blanes painted two large buses and two small ones in time for Carnival.

Finally, a fourth mechanic built bus bodies. He employed 4 persons, all of whom worked on a contract basis. His clients imported *torpedos*–trucks with chassis and cabins but no cargo area–and he removed the cabins and built new bodies with both national and imported parts. Clients who could not afford new *torpedos* gave him old trucks to convert. In times of economic crisis, when the government restricts imports, business consisted entirely of transforming old vehicles. When we visited him, he was working on four buses. Clients gave him an advance for the materials and paid some 20% of the labor cost up front. They paid the rest as work advanced. However, on occasion, he provided credit at an interest rate which for one client amounted to some 100%. This client, who had not yet paid for the *torpedo*, was ultimately forced to sell the bus upon its completion in order to cancel the debts.

Analysis. In addition to illustrating the overlap in manufacturing and service, these examples of automobile mechanics and painters underscore the flexibility the craftsmen must have with regard to the physical space they use for engaging in their trade. Most automobile mechanics, like bakers, require a considerable amount of space for their trade. The equipment they are able to afford determines not only the types of repairs they can engage in but also their degree of dependency on more highly capitalized shops. For some, like the mechanics who rebend springs (encountered earlier in this chapter), a sunny sidewalk becomes part of the workshop, which leads to severe overcrowding of the trade. Many other automobile mechanics work on vehicles on the street, although this often means paying the city for the right.

Inadequate facilities often delay work. Rain may make it impossible for a body shop to paint a car for days, and the dust in the streets and in the open, dirt-floor courtyards can also cause delays. A number of mechanics who are engaged in different specialties, each with his own apprentice or journeyman, may enter into an agreement with the owner of a courtyard (who may himself be a mechanic) to use the space for practicing their trade. Rent usually amounts to 10% of the proceeds. In this manner, a client can have a number of different repairs made simultaneously. The concentration of automobile mechanics in the same city block has the same effect. The client may make separate deals with different specialists working on the same street, often with one of the mechanics (who receives a commission) doing the mediating.

The more capital-intensive enterprises, like those of the bus body builders, also show both the problems of dealing with customers' financial difficulties and the potential for usury in the relationships with consumers. The automobile mechanics' workshops are predominantly in male hands, whereas some other trades requiring similar skills are not as gender specific.

A Plastics Manufacturer

A final example of what, for Bolivian standards, is considered a medium to large firm is a factory for polyethylene film and plastic containers established around 1964--the first factory of this kind in La Paz.[16] The owner, born in Bolivia of German descent, worked for a pharmaceutical company before setting up the factory. In 1977, the factory employed its greatest number of workers (140), but since then, with deteriorating economic conditions, the firm had to reduce its work force, and by 1981, there were only 100 workers left. They were mainly skilled or semiskilled, trained in the industrial school, Pedro Domingo Murillo. Ordinary workers earned US $200 a month. Only those who had been particularly productive received annual bonuses of 50% of a monthly wage; in 1981, 40% of the workers obtained bonuses. According to the *Guía Directorio de la Industria Boliviana 1981* (Cámara Nacional de Industrias 1981), the firm had capital assets in the amount of $b. 18,800,000 (US $750,000) in 1981.[17] The firm imported the resins it used from Germany and from the United States.

The owner regarded the low volume of each order as his major problem. Whereas in the United States a single run would consist of one million units, he makes only 10,000-30,000 units at a time. In addition, although the bulkiness of plastic goods does provide a degree of protection from competition from contraband goods, the latter do make considerable inroads into the local market.

This factory is one of the few firms we studied in which higher mechanization resulted in economies of scale that in turn have resulted in the elimination of many smaller producers. Unlike the related foam-rubber industry, where advanced technology is not essential, the plastics industry appears to have become increasingly dominated by a few larger firms. While the small size of the market makes it unlikely that these firms will further consolidate, firms with access to relatively large amounts of capital do, in this instance, have a competitive edge.

Notes

1. According to a producer of leather handbags, so much semiprocessed leather was exported in 1979 that some tanneries closed altogether and the artisans had great difficulties in obtaining leather. In 1981 leather prices were not much lower than in Colombia and the quality of the leather was not as good.

2. Conversely, pork is expensive because human consumption of corn competes with its use as a fodder.

3. Not surprisingly, some local producers label their products, particularly clothing, as though they were made abroad.

4. He ultimately decided that raising his own pigs would not be cost-effective but that slaughtering them in his own facilities would be beneficial.

5. Unfortunately the figures are not broken down by sector.

6. For other examples of this budding-off process, see Chapters 5 and 9.

7. Doña Nilda prefers to send her children to a school close to the center of La Paz than to the neighborhood school. She claims that she does not like the atmosphere in the nearby school. It is dirty, disorganized and the children do not wear uniforms. In contrast, the more centrally located schools have large patios, there is order, and the children wear clean uniforms. Also, the children are of a higher social class. Doña Nilda went to a similar school until sixth grade, when her parents (she has five siblings) could no longer afford to send her to school. It was she who suggested to her parents that as a woman she did not need more education.

8. Another informant said that she charges between $b. 500 and $b. 600 and figures $b. 250 for materials. Since she is already old, it takes her two to three days to sew a *pollera* by hand, but she charges the same amount whether she does it by machine or by hand. She claims that the machine flattens the cloth too much.

9. Whether she would have sufficient access to clients for *polleras* in a heavily middle-class neighborhood is another matter.

10. In actual fact, his savings from buying from the cooperative would have far surpassed the amount he would have had to pay in taxes.

11. Mr. Ortíz ascribed their low sales to the fact that people had run out of cash because of the week-long carnival celebrations.

12. The figure of 18 workers Mr. Ortíz gave in 1984 for the size of the workforce in 1981 does not correspond to the figure he gave during the earlier interview; perhaps he had an earlier year in mind.

13. Several other members of Mr Antelo's kin network are also furriers. They assist one another with loans of small sums of money between $b. 10,000 and $b. 20,000 as well as materials.

14. We have some doubts about the veracity of this claim.

15. In January 1987, the government issued a new currency, the boliviano, to replace the peso boliviano. One boliviano is worth one million pesos bolivianos.

16. The owner figured that there were some 30 plastics factories in Bolivia in 1981.

17. The owner figured that a minimum of US $20,000 is required to open a plastics factory.

9

Commerce

Selling One's Own Goods

The degree to which producers are involved in the commercialization of the goods they produce varies from activity to activity. Some producers have a highly specialized clientele and spend little time looking for new clients. Thus, Doña Silvia sells all the cookies she produces to three or four stores that cater to upper-middle-class to elite clientele. Others, as we saw earlier, work for one or two stores or intermediaries who put out work to them under a variety of arrangements. For many more, production and sales are temporally and spatially highly intertwined. A costume manufacturer must discuss with a client the design of a costume or of a metal rattle, a cabinet or lamp manufacturer the design of a piece of furniture or candelabra, and a printer a page layout. And, more generally, for a large number of independent artisans the place of production and the place of sales are one and the same or are adjacent, enabling them to move constantly between production or at least the management of production and sales.

Many small factories achieve a similar result by dealing mostly or exclusively with intermediaries and retailers who buy at the factory. However, many small producers have been forced to resort to much more elaborate mechanisms of distributing their products.

The Personnel: The Importance of Kin

Kin play a major role in sales. In an earlier study on marketing activities (J.-M. Buechler 1972), one of us pointed to the importance of kin in the choice of a commodity in sales and exchange among market women in general, and, more significantly for the present purpose, among vendors whose activities were largely confined to one location. The latter category included a high proportion of individuals born in La Paz and, more specifically, many vendors selling locally manufactured goods. Ninety percent of the vendors in this category "cited some kin influence, while only 4% denied such contacts as being important and 6% presented incomplete or inconclusive evidence. More specifically, 60% mentioned the influence of kin on the commodity sold; in 37% of the cases kin were the actual source of produce" (pp. 178-179).

A frequent device is to entrust sales to a member (often female) of a nuclear or extended family. Often, the wife takes over distribution. This was the case in at least 22 of the 112 cases from which we gathered information regarding sales.[1] In some instances, this takes the form of a strict division of labor (9 cases). The wife is in charge of a store, or a market or street stall, while the husband is engaged almost exclusively in production. One man, for example, makes pails, toys and other tin objects that his wife sells at their fixed market stall. She leaves the house at 7 a.m. and returns only at night. The children stay at home with her husband, who, as a result, rarely leaves the house. In addition, she sells at the annual fair on Palm Sunday in El Alto. A woman sometimes sells goods manufactured by others as well as those of her family. The wives of two candy producers sell candy produced by their husbands as well as imported sweets. In other cases the division of labor is less clear-cut. One woman makes the covers for the wicker furniture that her husband produces at home and attends the store located in the home as well as their more centrally located one. And jewelers may work in areas adjacent to the stores in which their wives sell their jewelry so that they can also attend to the needs of clients. In turn, their wives may also be involved in certain aspects of *production*, such as stone setting. Finally, production and sales may be totally integrated, as is often the case with costume makers, where husband and wife sew and sell in their storefront workshop.

The integration of the couples' commercial activities may take other forms too. In one case, the husband would go to the stores in the tourist area on the Calle Sagarnaga to offer his popular ponchos on consignment, while his wife collected the money later. Her familiarity with all aspects of the family concern enabled her to take charge of the business upon her husband's sudden death.

By 1988, there were indications that a trend was under way toward greater involvement of middle-class wives in the businesses in which their husbands were involved. The wives of at least three of the middle-class producers we re-interviewed in 1988, who had not been active in 1981, were involved in what had become the family business or in a secondary activity in which the husband was also involved. Perhaps the proliferation of more elegant boutiques and tourist shops also has something to do with this phenomenon.

At other times, a child (8 instances out of 112), a parent (5 cases), a sibling (4 cases), or other kin (4 instances) take over or assist in selling. Daughters (7 cases) are frequently recruited. Such daughters are likely to be single and live at home, like Adela, who lives with her father Victor and sells all the chairs he produces, which he carries on his back for the one-mile stretch to the market in the Calle Ochoa. She took over the sales site at the market from her brother, who switched to salaried employment in a furniture factory. The latter, in turn, had received the site from their father, who was the founder of what later became a street market specialized in furniture. Adela's sister, who is married to a carpenter, also sells furniture in the same market. Only Adela's mother has apparently never been involved in selling furniture. She lives in her rural community of origin most of the time, where she raises pigs for the market and provides the household with agricultural produce. Selling chairs is not the only economic activity that Adela engages in. She also makes *polleras* that she originally sold to stores and now sells directly to consumers in smaller quantities. Protracted illness has forced her to slow down.

Unlike Adela, Albertina, who sells wooden trunks made by her father as well as closets made by other carpenters, is married. She, her husband, who is a musician, and two older brothers all live with her parents.

In 1967, one of us (J.-M. Buechler, field notes) recorded similar cases. One person interviewed was Julia, who sold shoes made by both her father and two brothers. Like Adela, Julia, who was 40, was unmarried, and like Adela and Albertina, she lived at home.

The single case we recorded where a son was in charge of selling goods produced by his parents involved a carpet vendor. In contrast to most street and market commerce, which is dominated by women, carpet selling is predominantly, if not exclusively, a male activity. The carpets are made in El Alto and in certain altiplano communities, especially around Warisata, near Lake Titicaca, and the carpets are sold, or special orders taken, by men, while women, often young girls, do the actual knotting. The young man we interviewed was born in La Paz, but his parents were born in Warisata, where they have returned to make carpets. In addition to selling their carpets, the son sells those made by several young girls who live in that same area in El Alto whom he hired, and also those made by his sisters, who are engaged in the same activity in a workshop in El Alto. He hawks his wares from door to door in the wealthier areas of La Paz, taking special orders as he goes. He has also traveled to Oruro and Cochabamba.[2] Other carpet vendors offer their wares in a prominent location in a middle-class neighborhood of La Paz on weekends.

Although the numbers are too small to discern a distinctive pattern, the involvement of mothers of producers in the commercialization of their children's output may be related to the mothers' long-term involvement in commerce, which has enabled them to establish strong footholds in the La Paz markets. This was the case with one woman who had succeeded in obtaining one of the most coveted sites for selling tourist goods. She sells woolen hats she makes herself, sweaters and ponchos she purchases from other women, and wooden handicrafts made by her son and--on a smaller scale--by her husband. Another woman has a site in the major clothing market where she sells machine-knit sweaters made in her son's small factory. And a widow, who originally sold shoes produced by her husband in a street market, now sells shoes made by a son.

In the cases we studied, more distant relatives recruited to sell goods included a producer's cousin's son who travels to Cochabamba alone or with his aunt to sell wares (see Chapter 6); nephews who travel to Cochabamba with machine-knit goods obtained from their uncle; and the niece of an aluminum-pot manufacturer who also travels to the same city. Sometimes arrangements between more distant kin can be traced to an earlier division of labor within the household. Thus, Natividad, whom one of us interviewed in 1967, first sold candles produced by her husband and then, upon the latter's death, sold candles produced by her nephew.[3]

Non-kin placed in charge of sales at factories often had close preexisting links to the owners. In large factories, such as the largest beer factory in La Paz and the major producer of cooking oil, employees are given bonuses in kind or access to commodities produced by the factory under advantageous conditions. Often, the wives or other kin of the workers then resell these goods.[4] In other instances, former employees become preferred clients. We have already described the process of budding-off of new enterprises from parent firms (see Chapter 5) and how the working arrangements may change from wage or piecework employment to a system of putting-out work (Chapter 6). The fledgling firms may, in addition to these production ties, also maintain commercial ties with the parent firm. This is true for the sweet producers who are former employees of the sweet and pasta factory of Mr. Salas. Although they have created competition for the parent factory, some who are involved in commerce as well as production also have become loyal customers of their erstwhile employer, from whom they buy those products they do not manufacture themselves. Since the daughter firms invariably have access only to simple technologies, the parent factory may stand to gain more from the new situation than they lose.

Salespersons hired by small-scale producers sometimes also have close previous ties to their bosses. Thus, a man who makes miniature hats hired a young woman whom the family had known since she was a child to sell in the San Francisco tourist-goods market.

Enculturation into Selling

Small-scale producers are often enculturated into selling techniques as part and parcel of becoming artisans or other producers (see J.-M. Buechler 1972:180,198,204,208-210,216 and 274). A fledgling vendor who helps her family in marketing may receive a small amount of cash to purchase goods wholesale, with the understanding that the proceeds from the sale of these goods will be hers to spend and reinvest. Alternatively, a mother may provide capital in the form of the goods themselves. Perhaps even more important, mothers and other close kin, including sisters, aunts (mothers' sisters), first cousins and mothers-in-law, may pass on a stall or sidewalk location to a young vendor or share its use with her. Already-established vendors often borrow cash from their parents and other close relatives when they have not yet been able to establish a credit relationship with a wholesale supplier. Such loans are sometimes interest-free, sometimes not (J.-M. Buechler 1972:274-276). Market vendors often begin their careers by assisting their mothers or other close kin, but other than that they are almost invariably self-employed.

Some producers gained their expertise in selling from commercial activities they engaged in before they became producers. Most peasant women have had extensive experience trading or bartering at rural fairs. Many have also sold produce grown by their families or kinsfolk in urban street markets. Such skills come in handy when they establish themselves as small-scale producers in the city, for they very frequently sell their goods directly to the consumer.

Men are more likely than women to be engaged in long-distance trading, for example, between the highlands and the semitropical Yungas valleys (see J.-M. Buechler 1972, 1978). The informants we talked to who had been craftsmen in the specialized rural communities had also traded their goods at rural fairs within and beyond their region. But the goods they traded while living in the rural communities are not necessarily related to the crafts they later produced in La Paz. Thus, migrants from Chajaya, a community near Charazani, in an area that has a tradition of trade in medicines, now employ their commercial skills in the sale of jewelry. For example, Nicacio used to travel with jewelry for a La Paz merchant. Now he continues to travel widely with gilded earrings and other jewelry he manufactures himself or puts out to others and then gilds. His wife sells jewelry in an open market. Since his profit margin has decreased because of the general deterioration of the Bolivian economy, he plans to give up his workshop and dedicate himself entirely to wholesaling jewelry in major Bolivian cities. Thus, commerce can provide not only an opening to enter small-scale production but also a two-way door enabling an artisan to escape an activity that has ceased to be lucrative. This phenomenon is common among second-generation migrants as well.

An earlier study on market women (J.-M. Buechler 1972) under-lines the importance of kinsmen in the process of enculturation into selling. In particular, women who were born in rural areas and later migrated to the city in connection with their market activities were highly dependent upon kinsmen:

Kinsmen contributed to the initial decision to migrate in 37 out of 60 cases where such information was recorded. They also provided the migrant vendors with lodgings in 47 out of 80 cases.

Not only did kinsmen affect migration and residence, but they were also directly influential in the newcomers' selling activities in some way. Thus, in 22 out of 30 cases they initiated the vendor into selling and taught her the basic skills involved. Frequently, they were the source of capital and/or credit to begin their marketing venture. In almost half, or 49 cases of the total sub-sample of 102, both rural and urban kin, mostly rural, influenced the commodity sold. Sometimes kinsmen were the direct source of the commodity sold; while in other instances they provided the channels for the marketing of particular wares. . . . Kin may also aid in obtaining a permanent daily sales site. A permanent migrant may buy or "inherit" a stall from a real or fictive relative (or obtain it from a local market syndicate), friend, countryman or neighbor. Interviews with 25 vendors in the markets about other women who had left the market and their own retirement plans specifically revealed that 30% of the stalls vacated had been given or sold to relatives or obtained as a result of kin ties. . . . Most of these had received their stalls from their mothers or from their mothers-in-law, mother's sisters, sisters, first cousins or husband. (pp. 204-205, 208-209)

The case of Lucía provides a good example of enculturation into selling. Lucía's mother migrated to La Paz as a teenager with an illegitimate child. There she met and married a migrant from another area. After a time, she and her husband began making candles from a mixture of beef drippings and candle stubs from churches. Lucía assisted her parents in making the candles from a tender age, as did her brother and later his wife. Lucía's and her brother's role was to straighten the wicks before their father dipped them repeatedly into the hot tallow and wax mixture and then again when the candle had hardened. Lucía also helped cut up the tallow before her mother melted it in a large copper cauldron. When she was finished with her homework, she would help her mother for at least an hour, and on weekends they all worked together as well.

But Lucía also assisted her mother in selling the candles, beginning at an even earlier age—when she was only four or five years old.[5] Before she started to go to school, she carried candles for her mother while her mother was doing her rounds distributing them to her clients.

She remembers that sales were particularly good on Tuesdays and Fridays, propitious days for black magic, when people lit candles to harm their enemies. The family made special small candles for this purpose. Business was even more brisk during times of political turmoil, when all who wished to topple the government would burn candles. Politics brought more regular clients as well. Lucía and her mother would regularly stop at the home of Doña Espinosa, a former hacienda owner whose land was expropriated during the agrarian reform. There, before an altar of skulls (see H. Buechler 1981:360-363), she kept a number of candles turned upside down burning constantly in the hopes of vanquishing her nemesis, the MNR party. While Doña Espinosa was unsuccessful in overturning the agrarian reform and getting her land back, the ten or twelve dozen candles she bought every time Lucía and her mother visited her certainly did no harm to their business. In addition, Doña Espinosa could be counted on to give Lucía gifts of cast-off clothing and, later, weekend employment doing the grocery shopping for her.

While selling had its fascinating and rewarding side, it was also hard work for the young Lucía. To her death, Lucía's mother would lament the fact that her daughter was forced to work so hard when she was so small and ascribed her short stature to the heavy burdens she had to carry.

Lucía stopped accompanying her mother on her rounds when she began going to school but continued delivering candles to some of her mother's regular clients at the Church of Gran Poder. Much later, when she was fifteen and attending classes to become a seamstress, her childhood friend Yola, who by this time was selling peas on her own in the market, told her that she was being stupid to help her mother without getting anything out of it for herself. "You should tell your mother to give you some capital so that you can sell for yourself," she told her. When Lucía approached her mother with the request, her mother told her that she would not have the time to sell in the market and go to school. Instead, she gave her some church candle wax and 40 pesos so that she could buy an arroba (25 pounds) of tallow and string for wicks and start making candles herself. With materials of her own, Lucía was able to make candles once a week. Then she accompanied her mother on her rounds once more. They would pool their candles, and her mother would tell her how many of the candles they had sold belonged to each one. Only then did Lucía realize what a lucrative business candle making really was: The profit was double the amount of the initial capital.

> My mother had no fear of spending money. She even maintained her married son and his family until she finally got tired of it and told my brother to establish his own household. Now I too was earning money hand over fist [*como si nada*] that I could spend on the clothing I liked, for I didn't like the clothing mother bought me. I bought a little red skirt, a jacket, a special lunch pail, a radio. . . . And then I continued studying to become a seamstress.

Although her parents' trade ultimately declined and the family decided to return to her mother's community of origin and set up a grocery store, Lucía made good use of the marketing skills she had acquired. She first traveled to La Paz to sell onions grown by her parents and other community members and later traveled there to sell pork purchased in a neighboring rural market.

Commerce as an Entry into Production

Other small-scale producers were involved in marketing *before* they became involved in production. Not surprisingly, it was often the goods that they sold that they eventually came to produce. For example, Mr. Parra became a printer after a long period of traveling to Peru and bringing back printed wedding and fiesta announcements. He entered the printing business quite by accident. He had brought back a manual printing machine but, as a novice in this particular market, was unable to sell it. Rather than having his capital sit idle, he decided to use the machine himself. Like another, more established printer we interviewed who was also a retailer and wholesaler of materials he purchased in Lima, Mr. Parra continued traveling to Peru, both for materials for his printing business and for additional items to sell in his shop. By 1984, he had given up production and returned to his former commercial activities.

Retailing

For small-scale independent producers, the most common form of selling their output is through direct sales or through a combination of direct and indirect sales. As we saw earlier, producers often sell directly from their workshops or from adjacent stores. Sometimes the shops are not even marked by signs. In such cases, the producers must rely entirely on advertising by word of mouth. Putting up a sign could attract the attention of tax authorities, so the added sales could be offset by higher costs. Others, who for obvious reasons are better represented in our sample, advertise the location of their workshops with signs, sell on the street, sell at market sites, or sell from strategically located stores.

At the bottom of the commercial pecking order are the *ambulantes*, or itinerant vendors, who sell their goods on street corners or in parks and/or peddle their wares from house to house. Although an *ambulante*'s claim to a particular sales site may be tenuous, the site may, in time, acquire a degree of permanency. As we showed earlier, some carpet makers from the altiplano and El Alto walk the streets in middle-class La Paz neighborhoods, carrying a carpet or two on their backs, while others spread their wares on the low walls encircling the Plaza Isabel la Católica in front of one of the tourist hotels every Saturday. At the same time, the more adventurous go from house to house selling carpets and taking special orders, often paying annual visits to their clients, who may in turn direct them to their friends. A woman who roasts and sugarcoats peanuts sells to stores but also peddles her wares at the entrances of movie theaters. Another woman sells rings, earrings and other adornments made out of palm leaves next to a church before and on Palm Sunday.

At the next level of the market hierarchy are the vendors who sell in fixed locations that are open to commerce only during certain weekdays or certain times of the day. The use of these sites requires the payment of a fee to the municipal government. Thus, one woman sells machine-knit goods manufactured by her son on Saturdays in the *supermercado*, a street market for contraband goods and some local manufactures at the edge of the lower-class commercial center of La Paz.[6] Although the market is open on Wednesdays as well, the family sells most of its output to intermediaries, so selling on the principal market day is enough.

Other producers are limited in their selling activities because the locations where they sell their goods are open to commerce only before and/or after hours of peak traffic. At other sites, selling hours are limited for other reasons. Thus, a cookie maker who inherited from her mother a *puesto* (market site) that faces the entrance of a school, has hired someone to sell to school children during recess and after school at that site. She herself sells at another site, where potential clients pass by all day.

Even the temporary locations have become coveted assets. Doña Flora's daughter recounted how her *puesto* in the *supermercado* had risen in value since she acquired it in 1973.

> In the beginning, we were only allowed to sit on the street until 10 a.m. When the authorities first distributed the sites, they told us to wait all day. My mother was expecting me at 11 a.m., at the latest, and I arrived at 6 p.m. When I explained why I was so late she wouldn't listen to me but gave me a slap in the face because she thought I had shortchanged her by the 5 pesos [her mother had given her to pay to the city officials]. Much later, when my husband and I went to live in Santa Cruz and she wanted to sell the *puesto*, someone offered $b. 8,000 for it. I told her, "Don't sell it. It costs 5 pesos." Later she bought another site next to mine and we made a single stall out of it, but we both continue to sell there.

Finally, at the highest level of the market hierarchy, many artisans have access to market sites where they can sell throughout the week. Often, all the vendors in a walled marketplace, an entire street, or a section of a street sell the same type of good. Locally manufactured goods sold in such specialized markets include cheap furniture, sandals made out of discarded automobile tires, handicrafts for tourists, pottery, and aluminum ware. For producers of handicrafts, for example, the most prestigious location is the *mercado artesanal* of San Francisco, the crafts market located next to the Church of San Francisco in the center of La Paz. Many of the more prosperous producers of alpaca sweaters, wood-carvings, copper goods, etc., have *puestos* there. The artisans sell either only goods they produce themselves or, more frequently, a mix of their own goods and goods purchased from other artisans through close kinsmen or hired personnel.[7] Specialized markets facilitate shopping for customers looking for a particular item, and, although such markets generate a highly competitive atmosphere, they also promote cooperation among neighboring vendors. If a vendor must be absent, she can entrust sales to her neighbor. When Adela was ill, her neighbors sold her chairs for her. She asked for a fixed price, and the neighbors were allowed to keep whatever they could obtain above this price. In addition, street vendors often store their larger items overnight for a fee of one or two pesos (in 1981) in the stores of neighbors who have expanded their operations.

Some producer households also sell in weekly rural fairs. Thus, one producer who buys shawls (*mantas*) and adds braided fringes to them has a permanent *puesto* in La Paz but also travels to fairs on the altiplano. Similarly, as we saw in Chapter 3, a number of migrants from altiplano communities that specialize in particular productive activities continue to travel to rural fairs with their goods.

While there is a wide range of capital investment in market sites and stalls—which include everything from a bare spot on a side-walk to stalls in enclosed markets rented from the municipality and wooden structures in walled-in areas owned cooperatively by the vendors—and in the goods sold by a *puesto* vendor, the range is much wider in stores. At the upper limit are the elegant stores in the center of the city. Some factories, forgoing wholesaling entirely, operate as many as three such stores, where they make all of their sales. At the lowest level are stores and workshops located in tiny, windowless rooms partitioned to various degrees between sales and work areas.

For many artisans, selling in the open markets is impractical. To be sure, shoemakers repair shoes on the sidewalk, but those who make shoes, as well as tailors, hatmakers and costume manufacturers, are far better off if they sell and produce in a single location. For, unless they can engage their wives in selling, producers who cannot sell where they produce must rely entirely on intermediaries to sell their output. Mr. Zapata's progression is typical. At first, although he worked independently, he made *chola* shoes for a factory that sold to intermediaries. Then, he obtained a *puesto* in the Garita de Lima, where his wife did the selling. Women liked the good quality of his shoes and his use of shiny patent leather. Because they liked his shoes so much, a dance group that dances during the Fiesta of Trinidad "Diamantes" asked him to make shoes for all the women in the group. They and others came back the next year and the following year, and he became well known. Gradually, he became specialized in fiesta production. At first, he made only fancy *chola* shoes, but some dance groups require sandals, so he made these as well. Once he became known for this kind of work, his customers urged him to open a store, and so he now has a storefront and a small work area behind it. For the dance group sales, he makes a contract with the dance group organizer, and then each member comes to have her shoes fitted. Since his workshop is in the back of the store, he can oversee sales, which makes it possible for his wife to engage in other activities. By 1984, when fiesta attendance had dropped considerably because of the increasing economic crisis, she began engaging in smuggling from Peru.

Mr. Calle, who also makes *chola* shoes, used to sell to intermediaries as well. But he had trouble with a *cacera* and stopped making shoes. After a period of traveling to fairs to sell potatoes with his wife, the couple decided to make a major effort and open a shoe store. Mrs. Calle continues to sell potatoes (in one week alone she made 3 trips to fairs on the altiplano), and Mr. Calle sometimes goes along. Recently he has stayed in La Paz, however, because they cannot leave the children alone, and so the Calles, like the Zapatas, now engage in separate activities.

Although many products are sold in stores dispersed throughout the city, others are sold in stores that--like the markets--concentrated on certain streets. Fiesta goods are a salient example of this pattern; in fact, in this case there is a further lumping of subspecialties. Another area is geared almost entirely toward the tourist trade (as well as magic and herbal medicine). Often, vendors sell on the sidewalk in front of stores selling similar goods or carry their wares in baskets or bundles and offer to show them to prospective customers in an entrance to a nearby patio.

Fairs and Exhibitions

In addition to permanent selling sites and to locations where vendors can sell on certain weekdays or particular hours of the day, small-scale producers take advantage of a number of more sporadic sales opportunities, including annual fairs, fairs organized on an ad hoc basis by the municipality, and exhibitions in government-owned locales. By far the most important of these opportunities is the Feria de Alasita mentioned in Chapter 5--a fair of miniature objects that is held in a number of Bolivian cities (and, in a different form, in rural communities as well). Depending on the location, the fair has a different schedule and has different characteristics. In Cochabamba, Alasita coincides with All Saints' Day; in Santa Cruz, it takes place in September; and in Sucre, it is in July; while in Potosí, Alasita lasts for four consecutive Sundays in June. Finally, in La Paz, where the largest fair is held, it is a week-long affair that begins on January 23, the eve of the day of the Virgin of Peace, the patron saint of the city. The most ambitious producers obtain stalls for the entire week from the organization that runs the fair. This is not easy, and choice locations are few; vendors must remain around the town hall all the time for the two weeks before the fair starts in order to be sure they will be there when the city gives out the *puestos*. At the fair, they set up their own standardized stalls out of wooden poles and corrugated metal sheets and sell both their own miniatures and those of other persons who

A stall at the Feria de Alasita

cannot afford to pay for their own *puestos.* The latter also have the option of selling on the street on one day during the fiesta when sales are not limited to vendors renting *puestos.*

For some producers, Alasita has helped open up markets beyond the sales at the fair itself. A major attraction for Bolivians and tourists alike, Alasita provides maximum public exposure. Thus, a manufacturer of leather goods made his first contact with some Germans during the fair, which ultimately resulted in the founding of a larger leather-goods factory in which the foreigners had a financial stake.

One producer, who specialized in miniature hats representing all hat styles worn in Bolivia, regularly traveled to the other Alasita fairs as well; but he was an exception. Often, he received prizes for his work. In 1980, he received three first prizes in the Alasita fair in Cochabamba alone.

Another smaller and less varied fair takes place during the Christmas season. Vendors sell crêches, Christmas decorations and toys. Some producers set up stalls during both Alasita and the Christmas fair. Two artisans, one who makes both large and miniature milk containers and one who specializes in the production of rattles and other fiesta paraphernalia, make miniature kitchen ranges complete with pots and pans that they sell at their own *puestos* during both fairs.

Finally, a few producers sell at the Feria de Ramos, an annual fair geared toward the needs of peasants that takes place on El Alto during the week of Palm Sunday. Among the items sold there by small-scale producers are hand-forged tools and locks; spinning wheels[8]; and sheet-metal goods, including pails, storm lanterns and oil lamps.

In recent years, the municipal government has organized a series of fairs, including a highly popular book fair that are held on the Prado, the wide promenade in the center of the city, and rotating artisan fairs in various city plazas. Other fairs have been organized by a project sponsored by the Mothers' Clubs (also conduits for the distribution of food by Caritas), which were set up under church auspices. The municipality has also sponsored a series of temporary crafts exhibits in the Casa de la Cultura, while the cultural branches of foreign embassies occasionally open their doors to artisans as well. But between 1980 and 1984, a series of attempted coups during the Meza regime as well as its international reputation for direct involvement in drug trafficking scared away tourism. Subsequently, the numerous strikes that blocked traffic in the center of the city and immobilized public transportation during the Siles government further undermined the industry. Moreover, a number of artisan fairs, such as the one that was scheduled to take place in Calacoto (an elite suburb of La Paz) in 1981, were canceled because of political turmoil.

On a more positive note, various projects have been planned to create new centers where artisans can sell and exhibit their wares, give live demonstrations of their skills and learn new ones. On a small scale, one such venture has already been initiated privately by Mr. Murillo, a wood-carver/architect. He runs a locale where he shows his own work and allows other artisans to give demonstrations and sell their products for short periods. In return they only have to pay him 5% of what they sell to cover costs.

Consumer Credit

Most small-scale producers in Bolivia produce inexpensive goods that are retailed on a cash basis. Payment for larger items is more problematic. Workshop owners rarely give credit for repair work. Many ask for advance payments of 50% with the rest paid on delivery. As we saw in the previous chapter, some require additional payments as the job progresses. Those who do, on occasion, permit a customer to pay later very frequently find it difficult, if not impossible, to collect the outstanding sums. At the same time, some manufacturers find it impossible to rely entirely on cash retailing. In particular, cabinetmakers often have to give credit in order to be able to compete at all. A Chilean furniture maker, whose customers are mainly middle class and upper class, figures that he sells 30% for cash, 30% on short-term credit installments of two to three months, and 40% on longer-term installments of six months or even longer. A larger firm makes 40% of their sales to private individuals on a cash basis and the rest on credit of between eight and ten months at an interest rate of 2% per month, with an initial down payment of 40%. Although these more-established, larger firms have had problems with delinquent payments, they do end up collecting outstanding debts. The Chilean furniture maker found that although clients do pay eventually, they may extend a six-month credit period to ten months. The second, larger firm mentioned figures that over half of the payments for its installment-plan sales are delinquent. The company regularly hires lawyers to deal with its delinquent customers, for "people are very irresponsible."

Not surprisingly, smaller firms, which often find the legal system expensive and confusing, typically do not sell on credit. The owner of one small firm learned the hard way. He used to sell on credit frequently, but he soon found that a number of customers simply refused to pay.

> I guess I made a mistake. Maybe I should have worked with someone who collects debts. When one goes to their homes, they hide. They pay half of the furniture and the rest on credit, and then they leave telephone numbers but never answer. Some of the outstanding amounts are $bs 5,000 [US $200], others $bs 8,000 and 10,000 [US $320 and $400]. My capital is no longer growing. In fact, it is shrinking. Some ten persons owe me a total of some $bs 50,000 [US $2,000]. The credit was for three months, but they haven't paid it since last May [almost a year]. They say that they don't have the money or "tomorrow I will bring it," or they have someone say that they are away on a trip. I went to see a lawyer, but he would charge me up to $bs 5,000 [US $200] and maybe I will still not succeed. I might be throwing good money after bad. I prefer to go myself. Half of them are in the military. The others are civilians. One Mr. Pinto, who owes me $bs 6,000 [US $240], told me that I could go and complain wherever I wanted to or shoot him when I told him to give me the furniture back in return for what he had already paid for it. Now I only sell for cash. I prefer the furniture to remain stored or even to fall apart. But I won't sell on credit any longer. I lost a lot of money. I worked day and night to accumulate some capital, but now I have nothing left.

The Seasonal Nature of Retailing

The seasonality of sales in Bolivia is perhaps even more marked than it is in countries like the United States. Not only must the producer contend with such variables as temperature (which in the case of La Paz is actually less important than in northern climates) that affect particular products but not necessarily entire industries, but entire industries may come to an almost complete standstill during the off-season, because there are few fiestas then. With the exception of Carnival, almost all major fiestas, both rural and urban, take place during the dry season between May and October. The high point is the Fiesta of Gran Poder (around the middle of May), where sixty or more dance groups participate in festivities that culminate in a parade from the Garita de Lima to the Prado. The fiesta season determines not only the production of dance costumes but also that of more formal clothing in general, for members of dance groups dress in matching street clothing during certain parts of the fiesta. As one informant claimed, even weddings and the production of goods associated with weddings are influenced by the fiesta cycle. Carnival is an ideal time for eloping, the prevalent form of initiating cohabitation among lower-class and lower-middle-class Bolivians. Unless the couple decides not to formalize the relationship, weddings follow soon after. In addition, at least in rural areas, fiestas influence the sale of goods that are not related to fiestas per se. Frequently fairs are associated with fiestas, which enables participants in the festivities and other visitors to stock up on such items as pottery and metal containers.

At least during economically more stable times, the fiesta season is therefore a period of frenzied activity, when artisans hire temporary help and often work through the night. For example, in 1980 one tailor made sixty suits for the Fiesta of Trinidad alone. The men of an entire dance group had their clothing made by him to ensure uniformity of color and quality. Similarly, Mr. Parra, a printer whose shop is located in a lower-middle-class neighborhood, sells invitation cards and *colitas* (tiny booklets or cards elaborately decorated with ribbons with the name of the fiesta sponsor printed on them that are pinned on each guest at a fiesta as a memento) principally from April to June, when most weddings are celebrated.

At least one informant, who specializes in the production of masks and rattles, extends the season by going to Puno, Peru, where a major fiesta is celebrated in January, and from there to Oruro for its famous carnival (see also Albó and Preiswerk 1986:132). Others prepare for the Alasita and Christmas fairs, but after their preparations are complete they switch from sewing new clothing to mending or renewing old clothing by turning pieces inside out or engage in a completely unrelated activity. A shoemaker who specializes in *chola* dance flats makes these shoes from June to September. Once the season has ended, he turns to producing ready-made suits for others. At the extreme, some individuals make a brief, temporary switch into fiesta-related activities that may be quite different from their normal occupations. A woman from the Cochabamba valley, for example, arrives in La Paz each year just before carnival with a number of workers to make and sell a special type of sweet consumed only during this time. Following an ancient tradition, she and others from the same community set themselves up in an empty building lot and produce the sweets in large iron cauldrons that swing from hooks over an open fire. During the rest of the year she runs a store in her home town of Punata. And, two weeks before Palm Sunday, another woman switches from her usual activity of sewing *polleras* to making palm frond adornments.

Other industries, while less influenced by seasonal variation than those affected by the fiestas, nevertheless experience a substantial increase in sales at certain times of the year: Sweets sell best before the citrus fruit season begins in May and during the school year, when children buy candy during recess; furniture, in December and in June when employees and workers in larger factories receive their extra pay (*aguinaldo* and *sueldo extraordinario*); and jewelry, during the Christmas season. Finally, a shoemaker who specializes in soccer shoes increases his sales during soccer championships.

Wholesaling

Selling to Intermediaries

A number of small-scale producers do not sell their wares themselves. They sell their products through intermediaries for two quite different, but not always mutually exclusive, reasons: lack of time to engage in sales personally and lack of access to direct outlets.

Obviously, it would be impossible for most larger-scale producers to sell their entire production directly to the consumer or even directly to retailers, even though many do control retail outlets and, in fact, often seek to eliminate intermediaries whenever possible. Conversely, unless they can hawk their product directly on the street, many very small-scale producers do not have easy direct access to consumers. Their scale of production may not warrant obtaining a permanent sales site; or transportation costs may outweigh the benefits of direct sales. Finally, producers situated somewhere between these two extremes may not have the personnel available in their households to engage in direct sales and, at the same time, may find it more lucrative to have those family members who are available spend as much time as possible in production.

Intermediaries as Outlets

In some trades it is common practice to sell to merchants, who accumulate merchandise (called *juntar*) from a number of producers, for resale to retailers and exporters. Shoe stores, for example, often make contracts with individuals who either purchase finished shoes from individual shoe-makers or, as we shall discuss later, put out different tasks (making uppers, cutting soles, assemblage) to different producers. Similarly, women who knit alpaca sweaters for the tourist market and for export often sell to intermediaries and stall owners who seek them out in El Alto. Sweater-producer cooperatives often sell to such persons, too; but *juntar* practices create fierce competition among intermediaries. They often grab the bundles of goods to assert a prior claim, leaving the producers little choice but to sell the goods to them at the prevailing rate. Producers who had themselves engaged in this kind of activity did not consider it very lucrative. "Your work only benefits others," explained a shoemaker. "I used to *juntar* for resale in the market, but one only earns 20 or 30 pesos, which is nothing. My clients would tell me that they didn't have the money to pay me [for the goods I had brought to them earlier on credit] when in fact they had already sold them and were using the proceeds as their working capital." Similarly, Doña Flora complained that buying sweaters on El Alto was less lucrative than producing them in one's own workshop, and the quality was far inferior.

Sales to distant markets are often handled by intermediaries, who may purchase from one or two producers or from many. Medium-sized factories that do not have their own outlets in other cities often employ this system. Thus, the sweet and noodle factory sells on commission to a number of intermediaries who travel to different Bolivian cities. Since the factory is interested in opening new markets, it sells the goods to them at a special discount. Although the factory prefers cash sales, it does concede a 30- to 45-day interest-free grace period to its major clients. A Korean producer of children's clothing hired salespersons of his own and opened an agency in Cochabamba, but for some time he also sold to a number of merchants who traveled to all parts of Bolivia. However, the middlemen did not have the success he had hoped for, and selling to intermediaries cut too much into his profit margin, so he ultimately decided to cut back production and retail all his output in his La Paz store/workshop. On a smaller scale, a maker of miniature hats in La Paz sells many of his hats to intermediaries from Cochabamba and Tarija. Likewise, a man who produces aluminum pots sells most of his ware to two intermediaries: a wholesaler, whom he got to know when he was working as a dependent worker, and a niece, who travels to Cochabamba and Santa Cruz. She buys as many as 100 sets of pots from him each week. For these she sometimes pays cash, she sometimes pays half of the total in cash and the rest when she returns from one of her trips, and she sometimes obtains the entire purchase on credit. "For example, she traveled for Carnival and came back only yesterday [several weeks later]. My business suffered, but what could I do?"

Some of these intermediaries engage in complex, two-way trans-actions. As we saw in Chapter 6, Doña Flora bought alpaca sweaters on El Alto for resale in Cochabamba, where she purchased high-quality sheep's-wool sweaters for resale in La Paz. By 1984, her daughter had added wood-carvings and jewelry to the stocks of woolen goods she took to Cochabamba, both articles that, unlike woolen goods, her family has never produced.

Selling to Retailers

While many producers must resort to intermediaries to gain access to both the wider national and the international markets, local sales generally are handled through more direct channels. We have already seen how producers prefer to enter into sales agreements with kinsmen and other individuals with whom they have previous ties than with strangers. Here we shall deal with the producers' relationship to retailers who are strangers.

As in the case of middlemen, the relationship between retailers and the more privileged producers is less problematic than their relationship with the poorer ones. Some of the larger producers have wholesale outlets in other Bolivian cities. Larger factories generally sell goods to retailers for cash, reserving short-term credit of 30-45 days for their larger, preferred customers. More frequently, they give no credit at all or at least insist on being paid on the same day. One man has his mother deliver orders in the city at seven a.m. and insists that the clients pay before noon when she returns to El Alto.

Some producers encounter special problems in selling to retailers. One of these is that retailers must charge government-controlled prices for some goods. One of the producers we talked to, a large sausage manufacturer, experimented with selling special cuts of beef through the only large food retailer in La Paz. Beef prices are government-controlled, and at least in theory, all cuts of beef except innards and tongue cost the same. In practice, this means that in order to acquire a prime cut such as a filet, a consumer must purchase a large amount of bones together with the desired cut and must deal with a *cacera*, a vendor with whom the client has established a special, long-term relationship or the client must buy from an upscale store that caters only to elite customers. The retailer with whom the sausage factory worked was finally allowed to price cuts differentially, as long as the average price conformed with the price fixed by the government.[9] Similarly, as we saw in Chapter 8, bakers often must deal with stringent government controls on bread production. During periods of scarcity, they must not only sell bread at a fixed price—which sometimes does not make allowances for their usual profit margin—in order to obtain highly subsidized flour, but they must also reduce the production of the more lucrative specialty breads, whose prices are not controlled.

Although larger producers sometimes suffer from such problems as the inability to fill retailer demands, their problems pale beside the plight of many of the poorer artisans who are dependent upon stores or market vendors as outlets for their products. Their constant struggle to collect payments for goods left on consignment is illustrated by one furrier who eventually was able to set up his own outlet:

> The artisan has to sell his goods each Saturday because on Sunday the family has to buy food [to cook a good Sunday meal]. So he brings goods worth [say] 20,000 pesos and they [the stores] pay him 200 or 300 and tell him to return on Wednesday for the balance. On Wednesday, they inform him that his merchandise still hasn't sold. So it goes. Each time he comes, they give him 200 or 300 until he has finally received what they owed him. But by then the money has been spent and could not be reinvested. He can not capitalize. [So much time is wasted], that the producer can't go out to

buy furs and process them. That is why my colleagues aren't getting anywhere. The arrangement is entirely in the favor of the merchant. I myself had to suffer in this manner when I established my own workshop. I was finally able to improve my situation when I was able to purchase a small overlock sewing machine after six years of working under this kind of arrangement.

As we saw earlier, small-scale producers who live and work in El Alto often have no choice but to sell to middlemen, for it would take far too much of their time to travel constantly to the business center of La Paz to collect debts owed to them by store owners. Despite such tensions, relationships between small-scale producers and particular stores can become quite stable. In a way, they become similar to putting-out systems, with the exception that the artisan provides both the labor and the materials.

Production/Commerce of Goods with Low Added Value

Commercial relationships blend imperceptibly into putting-out systems. Thus, one technique for commercializing a product can also be considered an extreme form of a putting-out system. A producer adds some value to an intermediate product, but his or her main concern is to accumulate larger quantities of goods at reasonable rates for wholesaling. This special case of a production system merits a mention in the context of commercialization because producers engaging in this type of production move easily into full-time selling and back again.

Again, Doña Flora's enterprise may serve as an example. As we have already seen, throughout the years of this study, both Doña Flora and her daughter purchased alpaca sweaters in El Alto for sale in Cochabamba and for export. The value they added to these sweaters was limited to quality control and the repair of defective merchandise. In 1988, both Doña Flora and her daughter had at least temporarily given up their earlier more intensive involvement in production and were limiting their activities to this aspect of the family enterprise.

In Doña Flora's example, the value added was related more to a superior understanding of the market than to the possession of particular technical skills. In contrast, in other instances—even though the producer's principal role continues to be in marketing—skills play a more important role. For example, Mr. Chok'e, a jeweler, moved from commerce into production and, when we interviewed him, was in the process of progressively moving back into his original role as a full-time merchant. Originally, Mr. Chok'e was an itinerant jewelry vendor who traveled to the Yungas valleys and other areas with an older man to sell jewelry. Subsequently, he opened his own workshop and hired a number of workers. But within a few years he sent them all home and worked with them on a putting-out basis; he provided them with silver, they made the jewelry pieces, and he gilded them. With the finished jewelry, all destined for *chola* clients, he traveled to the cities of Cochabamba, Oruro and Potosí. Mr. Chok'e's mastery of gilding techniques and possession of the necessary equipment gave him some hold over the people who worked for him, for, as we saw in Chapter 5, he was very careful to keep this skill a secret. Nevertheless, in 1981 he was planning to give up even this aspect of production and dedicate himself to selling full time.

Mixed Strategies of Indirect Sales

Although small-scale producers regard the above modalities of commercializing their products as distinct, this does not mean that they do not engage (or at least attempt to engage) in more than one modality simultaneously or in rapid succession. Larger factories may simultaneously sell goods to stores, to intermediaries, directly to customers through their own outlets, through bonuses in kind, or by giving their workers the option of buying limited quantities of their products at cost. Individuals who primarily work under a putting-out system for one or two firms may simultaneously also engage in direct sales of their own goods. Thus, one jeweler works mainly for a single store but, on occasion, also makes or repairs jewelry for individual clients. Another, with comparable arrangements, has gone a step further by also opening a small jewelry store on El Alto. Similarly, few producers of handicrafts rely on a single market. Those who produce primarily for export also usually own stalls where they can sell to tourists.

Attracting Clients

Role of Social Class

The social-class background of a producer, including his or her economic situation and associated social connections, has an effect on who the producer's clientele will be. It would be incorrect to say that producers with elite or middle-class backgrounds produce only goods consumed by members of the middle and upper class and that lower-class producers make only goods for lower-class consumption. But when transactions between individuals with widely divergent class positions take place they are often mediated by intermediaries who are frequently of intermediate status. While this is by no means a hard and fast rule, and there are many examples of low-status individuals selling directly to high-status ones and vice versa, the tendency is nevertheless there.

In part, the tendency of firms with high status owners to use intermediaries is the result of the scale of the enterprise: The higher the standing of an owner or manager of a firm, the more likely that the firm's volume will be high, which, in turn, is obviously correlated with the presence of intermediaries on the one hand and the employment of systems of putting out work to lower-status individuals on the other. However, there are other factors at work that are not correlated with high volume. Producers with middle-class backgrounds are more likely to have access to middle-class and elite clientele than are producers with similar volumes of production but with lower-class backgrounds. We have already explored some of the mechanisms at work in our analysis of financing production; in the commercial sphere these mechanisms are even more salient. For example, even with the same initial capital as Mr. Loayza, the lamp maker, a lower-class individual would have had difficulty duplicating the commercial connections underlying Mr. Loayza's enterprise. Not only did he need to make contacts in the U.S., but to sell chandeliers to middle-class and elite Pazeños he also needed to set up a store in a middle-class neighborhood. It is obviously helpful if one's father owns a house in a strategic location, as Mr. Loayza's did. Similarly Alcides, the goldsmith, had an edge over other jewelers in building an elite clientele because his parents-in-law set him up in a middle-class neighborhood. This does not mean that upward mobility is impossible, but it does take time to achieve the connections necessary to build a clientele in a higher social class. In fact, upwardly mobile individuals may be more successful in catering to some of the more costly needs of their class equals than to the needs of higher placed individuals. An example of this is Celestino's lumberyard discussed in Chapter 3.

There are, of course, exceptions to this phenomenon. Certain goods for which there is a middle-class and elite demand are still largely associated with rural producers and producers of recent rural origin. Knotted alpaca rugs are an example. As we have already noted, the producers or their relatives often sell these rugs directly to higher-status consumers. However, wealthier merchants usually interpose themselves between the producer and the consumer of other traditional goods sold mainly to tourists, such as sweaters and other handicrafts. The trend has increased in recent years, and there are now fewer producer/vendors selling in the tourist-goods market of San Francisco than there were fifteen years ago.

One of the major ways in which poorer producers--often women--are exploited, however, is through this imposition of intermediaries--often men--between lower-status producers and higher-status consumers. As we shall see, the exploitation has led to a number of attempts, mostly embryonic and sometimes exploitative in their own right, to enable small-scale producers to gain more direct access to the consumer. Middle-class mentors, such as foreign missionaries and embassies, may serve as an alternate or complementary route of developing a wealthier clientele. Individuals may improve their social position considerably in a relatively short time if they are exceptionally successful economically, which, particularly if they have had some education, may accelerate their ability to establish the connections necessary to gain a high-status clientele.

Advertising and Wooing Clients

Small-scale producers advertise their businesses by means of signs over the doors to their enterprises or at the entrance of their patios; by leaving business cards at the firms or homes of likely customers; through newspaper, radio, or much more rarely, television advertising; and, most importantly, by word of mouth. Unless its location alone advertises a business sufficiently, or a producer is able to rely on a neighborhood clientele or on a network of friends, fellow migrants, and/or relatives for business, the producer must rely on some of the other forms of advertising. The *chola* skirt makers (*pollereras*) whom we got to know through our assistant from Llamacachi were able to rely on word of mouth advertising alone. The core of their clientele is made up of fellow migrants from their community of origin and from neighboring communities as well as residents of these communities who visit the city and order skirts for fiestas. Those producers whose business locations are more clearly marked also often rely heavily on word of mouth advertising. The reputation of a small-scale producer can be of crucial importance in activities like sewing fancy skirts or custom-made clothing, where skill levels and punctuality in filling orders may vary markedly and where competition is severe. Similarly, a lumberyard known for its honest dealings may attract clients away from competitors. A reputable producer may often build a clientele simply through references, the path followed by a young seamstress from the Beni department who was able to build a clientele in Potosí for her children's dresses entirely through word of mouth:

> I had to sew so that my husband could study. He earned very little. I borrowed a sewing machine and sewed children's clothing for the wife of a physician—some 400 little dresses. Since they were sold all over the city, word spread that "the Beniana" made nice things. Soon I had someone bring my machine to Potosí, and I sewed from dawn to night.

Often, however, more elaborate networking techniques are necessary to build a clientele. For example, close relatives may be recruited to advertise a business. Thus, two sisters who are couturieres in an advantageous suburban location advertise the third sister's butter cookies and party cakes. As we have already seen, Patricia's father, who works for the electric power company, helps her find clients for her printing enterprise through his work contacts. Moreover, former employers may also recommend erstwhile workers with whom they have remained friendly. One tailor we interviewed secures some of his clients through the recommendations of the owner of a large store for which he once worked, and the same man also helped him set up his own workshop. As a result, he has enjoyed the patronage of such distinguished individuals as the mayor of La Paz.

As we shall see in Chapter 10, costume makers who were originally from Achacachi commonly participate in and even sponsor fiestas in order to attract clients. For example, they dance regularly in the Fiesta del Gran Poder. Thereby, they have gained a national reputation for their fine morenada costumes. Their periodic inventions of new types of costumes and even new dances further help the producers to hone their skills and thereby maintain a competitive edge.

Some producers, both large and small, complement word of mouth advertising with advertising through the media. Newspaper ads are the most prevalent form, followed by radio announcements, the latter geared mostly to a lower-class clientele without access to television. Television advertisements have become too expensive even for middle-sized firms. Moreover, our informants felt that in a time of crisis no one was going to buy their products anyway, so it was useless to spend a lot for advertising.

For many small-scale producers, the telephone is a crucial adjunct to business. Many live in remote locations, and houses are often erratically numbered, if at all. However, in Bolivia, having a telephone entails a major investment, for one must first become a shareholder in the telephone company at a cost of some US $1,500 (in 1981). Few can afford such an outlay. But this is not all. One must also arrange for access to a telephone line, which, given the rarity of telephones in many outlying neighborhoods, can be a long and difficult process. The example of the seamstress who migrated to La Paz from the Beni illustrates the difficulties that can be involved in communicating with clients in Bolivia. Her landlord had recently lost access to a telephone, and the seamstress was distraught:

> It used to be that my friends with whom I had gone to school would send me clients. They would tell their friends to call me and set up a date. So people whom I did not know at all would call me. Now they just have to come [and hope that she is there]. When someone came the other night, she took me by surprise. How was I to know that she was planning to come?

Catering to Special Markets

Through product specialization and the manipulation of networks, a producer may eventually acquire a specialized clientele. Different jewelers, for example, cater to different segments of their widely divergent market. Thus, one jeweler makes jewelry only for *cholas*. He has chosen a location on the Plaza 16 de Julio in El Alto, which is appropriate for this clientele. There is less competition than in the center of La Paz, and less capital is required. In the center, one can sell more gold jewelry. Here he can sell only silver jewelry. In contrast, another jewelry shop, located at the edge of the main elite and middle-class shopping area, specializes in making jewelry for a middle-class clientele. The jewelers further differentiate between their La Paz clients and those in other Bolivian cities. For the La Paz market they use modern European designs adapted for Bolivian tastes with more color, more adornments and more material; for the markets in other Bolivian cities, they make jewelry that is more traditional. However, these jewelers maintain that since the early 1980s people have begun to appreciate workmanship more than the amount of gold used. Finally, Alcides caters to a foreign clientele. He moved his workshop and store to a high-rise in the center of town, where German and Japanese customers, directed there by their embassies, can find him more readily.

The history of Alcides' efforts to build a clientele is characteristic of the relationships between Bolivians and foreigners. As we saw in Chapters 4 and 6, contacts with foreigners are often employed by Bolivian small-scale producers for economic advancement. Such ties may enable them to gain access to particular skills. They may also lead to employment in a foreign agency—which is seen as providing security in times of economic uncertainty—or even abroad, as well as access to educational opportunities abroad for one's children. Such contacts can also open up specialized markets. Ties to foreign-based missionaries are one such channel. Thus, Protestant missionaries introduced Don Alfonso to the production of peanut butter and also bought his product. Similarly, Alcides first gained access to a foreign clientele for his gold jewelry through his studies with Jehovah's Witnesses. He describes his experience as follows:

> I began to study with the Jehovah's Witnesses to see whether they could provide me with an answer to some of the questions I had. At the time I had little hope of finding an answer, but soon I found that they had a calming influence on me. I liked this, and for some five years I spent a lot of time studying the Bible. It was through them that I became acquainted with a German man, Mr. Schwarz. He came to my home and saw my work. He was so thrilled by my workmanship that he would come to observe me at work at least once a week. He told me, "Alcides, I would like to introduce you to some of my compatriots. We Germans prefer to work with people we know. So I thought you would be the ideal person. These friends are honest, and you can rest assured that they are trustworthy." He came with one person and then another and another. The orders grew and grew, and I was earning more and more. They continue to pass on my name to their friends. Often, they arrive from Germany with a visiting card from an acquaintance who had something made here. Of course, they are very demanding. They like good quality, and I know that I cannot let them down.[10]

In order to increase the credibility of Bolivian goldsmiths on the world market, Alcides is pushing for a system of identifying craftsmen by means of numbered stamps. His efforts to cater to the needs of foreigners have not been at the expense of his wealthy *chola* customers. He continues to appraise their jewelry and resells old pieces he acquires from them. For, although they have to be more careful because of rising theft, *cholas* still like to wear a lot of jewelry.

As we saw in Chapter 4, the two foreign sausage manufacturers also cater to both foreigners and Bolivians by making specialty goods, which are purchased mainly by foreigners, as well as products that correspond to local tastes.

Selling to the State

Since La Paz is the seat of the national government, it is not surprising that many producers, including relatively small-scale firms, fill orders for various state agencies. For some producers, state contracts constitute a major market. In fact, some small factories cater almost exclusively to this market. One makes boots for the military, and another regularly sells furniture to various government agencies. Such work entails a lot of red tape, contacts, sometimes bribes, and above all a lot of patience. The paperwork alone regularly takes six months. A ministry makes a call for bids either through the press or--if it knows that a company is solvent--by invitation. According to the same furniture manufacturer, "One usually has to fulfill all sorts of legal requisites. Then they choose three companies and interview them through the Junta de Licitación [or purchasing committee]." The hurdles that must be overcome do not end at this point. All of our informants complained that only the decentralized agencies like SAMAPA, the agency that provides water to the city, paid within a short period. All of the other state agencies made them wait three to four and even six months. In contrast, if the producer delayed his delivery, he was fined. A carpenter described his experience with state agencies as follows:

> When they finally give you a contract and you deliver, they don't pay you. You wait for a month or a month and a half, and then they only pay you in part. It's discouraging; but that is the way things are here. It's different in other countries. For example, we worked for CONES a number of times. It's an institution that provides assistance to schools. We made benches for them. They asked us for a bid for 150 benches. Let us say that they normally would have cost $bs 60,000 [US $2,400]. But we had to make an invoice for $bs 80,000 [US $3,200] so that they could pocket the difference. And they created all sorts of problems even then. They would call us and say that they had given [the job] to someone with a lower offer. But we would already know what that offer had been because we knew the person. . . . Then they would promise us lumber. But the lumber would only arrive when we had already made the benches. They would tell us that the lumber had yet to be milled in Santa Cruz or come up with some other excuse. We couldn't wait, because we had to fill the order

within four months. Otherwise they would have fined us $bs 150 [US $6] a day, which would have lowered our profit.

While during normal times the state's bills do eventually get paid, it can be next to impossible to collect outstanding debts during an economic or political crisis.

Exporting

Bolivia has traditionally been and continues to be an exporter of raw materials rather than of finished products. Nevertheless, there have been some attempts to export a limited range of goods, including clothing and handicrafts. Export of the latter increased in the late 1970s, when a number of exporters and later producer/exporters dedicated themselves to this activity. An example of a producer/exporter is Doña Flora. She first established ties with foreign buyers when she had a permanent crafts stall in a street market. At that time, she also sold to Bolivian exporters. A Bolivian exporter married to a Californian showed her how her sweaters should look for a foreign market and how to wrap goods for shipping, while his wife taught her the importance of preparing shipments on time. From then on, she dealt with the foreign buyers directly.

Even during the best of times, exporting manufactured goods from Bolivia presents a host of problems. The small size of the internal market does not provide a sufficient market base for producers to attain competitive economies of scale, while high transportation costs from a landlocked country and the reliance on imported industrial inputs further increase production costs.

Even those producers whose goods could compete in price in a foreign market often must forgo exports because the stores importing their goods require high production volumes. The accumulation of large stocks or the coordination of production among large numbers of small producers is difficult. As Mr. Pereira, a manufacturer of leather goods, said, "We look for boutiques rather than 'Pier Imports' [an American chain store for imported crafts with which he has been in contact]." The same person showed us an album filled with the calling cards of dozens of large importers that he had picked up at an international trade fair in Frankfurt, Germany. "They are all useless," he said. "I would have any number of connections but no way of producing on such a scale." Similarly, a wood-carver told us about a carpenter friend who makes coffins. A visitor from abroad found the coffins and their price attractive, but he wanted 8,000 units per month, which was more than the carpenter could ever have been able to produce.

Exporting also requires a larger amount of capital for the same volume than production for the internal market. Small producers generally do not have the capital reserves that would enable them to provide the usual 90 to 160 days of credit to importers from abroad. They depend on the proceeds of the sale of one lot to purchase the raw materials for the next. Especially in the artisan industries, pure exporters are often at an advantage over producer/exporters with respect to access capital. However, as the example of the knitted-goods industry shows, there are major pitfalls for the exporter who is not thoroughly familiar with all aspects of production, and the producer/-exporter is sometimes at an advantage. Doña Flora's success with exporting knitted goods from both sources depended in part on her ability to accumulate sufficient quantities (up to several thousand sweaters at a time) but also depended on her ability to maintain strict quality control. Her clients were well aware that quality control was one of the major problems in the crafts trade. Some had learned the hard way. One client had amassed 10,000 sweaters through middlemen who purchased whatever they could find in El Alto, but he was forced to throw most of the sweaters away when they arrived at their destination because they were poorly made. In contrast, Doña Flora did not hesitate to reject sweaters that failed to meet her standards.

However, the export of artisan goods is cutthroat indeed. Shipping agents are frequently approached by producers with promises of money if they direct foreign buyers to their firms. Doña Flora was not immune to this tactic; she had benefited from it on earlier occasions when her son-in-law was still working as a dispatcher.

The export business requires a network of connections including links with government officials, bureaucrats, and other middle-class and/or upper-class individuals. For producers with lower-class backgrounds the establishment of such links can be particularly difficult, and hence they nourish the ones they already have with particular care. Some have been remarkably successful in this endeavor. The manner in which Doña Flora established ties with foreign buyers is ample proof that she could successfully defend her interests vis-à-vis her social superiors. In this, she is representative of the veteran La Paz *chola* market vendors who instill respect among the lower classes and the elite alike. However, she frequently sought brokers to assist her in this task. We saw her visit an agent of the Bolivian Institute for Small-Scale Industry and Artisanry (IMBOPIA) without the accompaniment of a broker. But she never traveled to international fairs by herself. In part, this may have been because she felt the need for a male companion, but it was also because the transactions at such fairs required literacy and she could neither read nor write.

Her son-in-law, Indalecio, became Doña Flora's principal broker. In 1981, she felt that her daughter Ricarda's marriage to Indalecio was one of the most important links she had to the middle class. Ricarda had met Indalecio when she dispatched goods to other countries. At first, the couple had moved to Santa Cruz, where Indalecio was put in charge of reorganizing the branch office of the shipping firm for which he had worked in La Paz. However, Doña Flora succeeded in persuading him to return to La Paz and join her firm. They shared the profits according to the amount of capital each had invested and labor each had contributed. She tried hard to keep the marriage together despite Indalecio's sexual escapades. His education--he was only a year away from obtaining a university degree in economics–and his experience with shipping could not fail to be an asset to the firm. In 1984, after the marriage had broken up, Doña Flora was less positive about Indalecio's contribution to the firm. Had he not mixed up two shipments to Spain and England, the firm might not have lost two good clients. Now, her most important upward link appeared to be with her accountant, who was assisting her in her attempt to switch into the leather industry. As with the Ecuadorian who took her son to Australia (see Chapter 6), she had succeeded in creating a multi-purpose link. Earlier, the accountant helped her with the arithmetic and kept an eye on her interests vis-à-vis her son-in-law. Now, as an experienced manager of a leather goods firm, he was able to assist her in an entirely new role.[11]

Additional problems arise from competition from neighboring countries. Thus, Peruvian handicrafts are generally cheaper than Bolivian ones, even though the Bolivians regard their goods as qualitatively superior. One of the reasons for this appears to be a greater reluctance in Bolivia to mechanize aspects of the production of handcrafted goods. For example, Mr. Pereira brought back from his travels to foreign fairs a prospectus of a gadget in use in Central America and in Ecuador that enables a person to make three drawings, such as the designs he embosses on his leather goods, simultaneously. He showed the prospectus to various artisans to no avail.

Neighboring countries are also beginning to copy Bolivian designs and to import Bolivian goods for re-export as locally made goods. They are even hiring Bolivian artisans to produce Bolivian-style handicrafts in their countries. Even Bolivian coffee, well liked by importers because of its better flavor, a result of its being grown at relatively high altitudes, cannot make a name for itself among foreign consumers because importers mix it with coffees from other countries and sell it under the name of these better-known countries of origin that have higher production rates.

Some neighboring countries, such as Peru, have (at least in the past) instituted special subsidies for nontraditional exports, including handicrafts. For a time, Bolivia instituted such subsidies as well, but they were lower than those in Peru (10% in the case of leather goods as opposed to rates purportedly as high as 40% in Peru). Nevertheless, in some instances, such subsidies made it possible for Bolivian products that would otherwise not have been exportable to compete abroad. Thus, a multinational factory producing vegetable fat and cooking oil was able to export its products in the early 1980s. By 1988, all export subsidies had been discontinued in Bolivia.

Finally, a small producer can easily misjudge the market for a product. It may be subject to fads, or a particular fair may not provide the appropriate forum for a specific item. Thus, the craftsman who makes exquisite miniature hats representing the styles of all the different regions of Bolivia had little success in a crafts fair in Los Angeles. Visitors and buyers preferred apparel and larger items, and the diversity of the Bolivian hat styles meant little to them. In fact, most of the sales he was able to make consisted of replicas of Mexican sombreros. Similarly, at least one of our informants lost a lot of money with exports because she failed to insist on secure forms of payment. Twice, German importers cheated her because she acceded to their request for two invoices, one for the amount agreed upon and one for a lower amount that they could show to customs officials in Germany. Initially they paid with a checks that, as it turned out, were not covered. When the payments finally were made, they were for the amounts on the fake invoices; because those invoices also carried her signature, it was impossible for her to collect the difference.

To be sure, there have been a number of formal or semiformal attempts at overcoming these difficulties, among them the formation of producer cooperatives and of government agencies whose stated purpose is the opening of new foreign markets. But, as we shall see in Chapter 10, these mechanisms have had mixed results, at best.

Exporting and Economic Crisis. If exporting is difficult in good times, it often becomes impossible during times of crisis. Political crises affect exports in several ways. Foreign buyers for such items as handicrafts are often reluctant to visit Bolivia during political turmoil because they are afraid of being caught in La Paz during a coup attempt or a strike and, probably more importantly, because they fear that their suppliers may find it difficult to fill orders in time under such conditions. While some of our informants felt that these fears were exaggerated, arguing that foreigners underestimate the resourcefulness of the producers, at least one producer confided that the uncertain political and economic climate in Bolivia made her reluctant to attempt to expand her operation[12]:

> The political and social problems have a strong influence [on export]. We are unable to do as one can in the United States, where, when someone says, "I would like to buy 10,000 bags," one is in the position of being able to tell the client, "Okay, I will make the 10,000 bags." Here, there could be a transportation strike tomorrow, another strike the next day and the next. . . . So, I prefer not to fool my clients, not because *I* or *my workers* would let them down but because of the kind of society we have here and the kinds of things that are happening in Bolivia.

A more direct effect of the political situation in Bolivia on exporting was seen in the economic sanctions imposed on Bolivia by foreign nations after the political coup of President Meza. The sanctions were in the form of high customs tariffs. As a result of the high tariffs, the producers who went to a fair in Frankfurt had to sell their products at a loss or pay the high cost of shipping them back home. Similarly, Bolivia's dispute with Chile over access to the ocean has affected artisans who attempt to trade in Chile. When a group of Bolivian artisans attended a producers' fair in Chile, they found to their dismay that Chile imposed an import tax of 30% on their products, while the artisans from other countries could bring in their goods duty free.

Having an equally important, if not greater, effect on export are the fluctuations in the exchange rate to the dollar and the governments' attendant economic measures (see Chapter 2). A few examples of the plight of small-scale producers throughout the 1980s will serve to illustrate both the hardship that economic crises have created and the extraordinary resilience with which the producers have faced these crises.

Café San Isidro, a coffee-producing and export firm, is our first example. It is a family firm with eight permanent workers and up to 74 seasonal workers. The job of the seasonal workers is to sort the coffee by hand. In 1981, the firm was operating normally, permitting it to make its payments on loans of US $200,000 incurred in 1980 and 1981 for new equipment. It had been able to amortize those loans by the time of our second visit, in 1984. But by 1983, it had ceased to export altogether and kept its permanent work force busy roasting coffee for local consumption. Worried about the high price of coffee resulting from a poor harvest, the owner, Mr. Gonzalez, had taken advantage of the seemingly high bank interest rate (14% per annum) and had placed much of his working capital in a bank account instead of investing it in more beans. As it turned out, the drop in the purchasing power of the peso far exceeded the interest Mr. Gonzalez received on his bank deposits, and so he decided to enter the export business once more. He was hoping that a new regulation would take effect that would permit him to import food staples for part of his foreign-currency receipts provided he sold them to his workers. He expected to sell the staples he would be allowed to import at a profit, for he could count on his workers, many of whom were themselves also market vendors, to acquire the goods for resale at further illegal markups. Ultimately, the proposed system of controlled imports appears to have been abandoned, because when we discussed the matter again in 1988, Mr. Gonzalez said he had been paid 40% of the proceeds of his exports in dollars which he could sell in the street and 60% in pesos bolivianos. He even believed that the larger exporters did quite well under this system. Whether it was because his hopes for more favorable regulations did not materialize; or because of the low world market prices in 1985, resulting from increasing competition from other exporters (according to one informant their number had increased from 4 to 19 between the late 1970s and 1984); or because hyperinflation combined with forced dollar deposits made exporting unattractive under any conditions; or for a combination of these factors, Mr. Gonzalez reduced his exports from 6,800 bags in 1981 and 1983 to 4,000 bags in 1985, 2,000 in 1986 and only 1,100 in 1987.

Mr. Gonzalez was not the only coffee processor to stop exporting during the period of hyperinflation, and as a result of the decreasing exports, the International Coffee Organization cut the Bolivian annual export quota from 150,000 bags to 102,000 bags. But now that the stabilization of the peso has made exports more feasible again (Mr. Gonzalez's exports were back up to 3,000 bags by mid-1988 despite the fact that world market prices were low), Bolivia may not be able to take advantage of its full export capacity,[13] at least not at world market prices. The country may have to sell its coffee at lower than market rates (e.g., US $112 to $115 rather than $128) to exporting countries that did not reach their quotas. Ironically, the latter include countries like Paraguay, which has no production of its own; it merely re-exports coffee imported from other countries.

The case of Café San Isidro illustrates a number of political and economic processes. The Siles government's (1982-1986) decrees were an attempt at creating a system resembling what Paul Bohannan, Frederik Barth and other economic anthropologists have called economic spheres, i.e., mutually exclusive cycles of exchange, in this case entailing the exchange of labor for imported staples and vice versa. The rationale behind this seemingly complex system was actually quite simple. It was one of many attempts on the part of the Siles government--under popular pressure--to mitigate the effects of the IMF-mandated wage freezes. Other such attempts included the use of periodically adjusted fixed exchange rates in lieu of allowing the peso to free-float. Combined with the obligatory deposits of foreign currencies earned through exports, the restrictions on the use of foreign currencies, and the fixed prices for both imported and nationally produced basic commodities, such an exchange rate policy was designed to make wage controls more palatable.

For some informants, the Siles years were even more difficult than for Mr. Gonzalez. In some instances, export ceased altogether or was drastically diminished as a result of the monetary policies we have discussed. Thus, the Pereiras, who had a thriving business making and exporting leather goods, reduced their exports by some 70% between 1981 and 1984, a loss that they were fortunately able to offset by expanding their sales to foreign tourists. Similarly, Mrs. Romero felt that she lost most of her capital during those years:

> On one day I would sell twenty fur rugs like hotcakes, and the following day I would go and buy materials and find that I had lost money. During the entire period of the UDP [the Unión Democrática Popular, President Siles's party], I was unable to export. I had some 28 clients who would call me from Japan, Denmark, Australia and the United States. I also had clients in Canada and Brazil. And in that period, I lost them all. The payments arrived at the bank, and the bank might give me 40 pesos for

a dollar when the street rate was already 1,300. I lost my capital, and I lost my clients. The UDP ruined us totally. It was the worse government we have ever had.

In order to escape her predicament, she chose a solution which was used by a number of artisans: temporary emigration. Others used a slightly modified form of this solution and transported their goods personally.

I went to the United States and worked there. I earned good money there. I no longer exported. For if I did . . . Well, I went there with some 17 other artisans, and we began to work there. We worked 14 to 18 hours a day. We imported the raw materials from here [Bolivia] and worked there. Often, we also brought goods from here[14]. The American Embassy invited us. We were there for six months. And once there, the Bolivian Embassy helped us a lot as well. Everybody helped bring us materials. We worked and worked and earned double or triple of what we earned at home. And we were happy. We worked without resting. My sister would prepare the materials--tan the hides and have the wool spun--and send them. Here in Bolivia one couldn't do a thing, not a single shipment. That's why I say that it's better to leave. For there one can work, bring along raw materials, make exhibitions of one's work, obtain orders, take along finished rugs, and have everything. It's better to go abroad. Also Bolivians don't like Bolivian goods. It's terrible. Let's see if I can go abroad and attend a fair. It's important because there are a lot of people who can no longer live [and for whom this would give work]. Sometimes even I am losing hope. At least now the situation is stable. Things have improved a lot because there is stability. One can invest without fear of losing everything. I only hope that the stability will last.

Mr. Araujo, who produces high-quality *charangos* (a stringed instrument) and other musical instruments, was similarly affected:

During the Siles regime, I had to cease exporting altogether. All payments from abroad were made in the form of letters of credit through the Banco Central, which paid me in pesos bolivianos at the rate of $bs 79,000 when the street rate was $bs 350,000. I had to pay for [many of my inputs], such as varnishes, at the black-market rate, and so I lost US $16,000 for two shipments alone. [There was no other way of exporting.] Letters of credit are paid by one bank to another bank, and when [the Central Bank] got hold of the dollars they wouldn't say, "Oh, this is a poor artisan." They would wish you good luck and good-bye. When I had to purchase imported materials, I had to pay in dollars I acquired on the street. At present we are still not exporting. Unable to get instruments from me, my clients have found suppliers in Peru and Ecuador. They write me that they are unhappy about the quality of these instruments but happy with the low prices. Now I will have to travel to Spain and to Germany to convince them that things have changed. They claim that they had put a lot of effort in promoting my instruments, and if I tell them that I am interrupting my shipments once more I will lose them for ever.

Like Mrs. Romero, Mr. Araujo has been able to recuperate financially as a result of his travels. He began to travel abroad, in part to engage in direct sales of high-quality instruments that he took with him and in part to perfect production techniques. Some of the artisan fairs he visited paid his travel expenses, which further increased his profits. In addition, he launched a more aggressive internal marketing effort, began working 16 hours a day, reduced the price of his instruments and, as we saw earlier, set up his wife in a up-scale shop in an area frequented by tourists.

In contrast with the Siles government, the Paz Estenssoro government (1986-1990) resorted to a radically different approach to the national economic situation, an approach that was predicated on stabilization at all costs and essentially followed IMF recipes. The major departure from orthodox economic theory (but one consonant with U.S. interests) was the government's liberalization of imports. The idea—and, to a degree, the actual effect—was to tap the large amount of hard currencies from the drug trade and possibly the holdings of Bolivians abroad.

While both Mr. Gonzalez and Mrs. Romero welcomed stabilization because it made trade more predictable, other informants were less pleased. The Paz Estenssoro austerity measures combined with trade liberalization made the peso boliviano a "hard currency," which merchants from neighboring countries like Peru accepted as a medium of exchange. While the strength of the peso may have represented the "health" of the drug economy, it was not related to the state of the rest of the economy. Small-scale producers could not compete with activities, including commerce, related in any way to the drug trade. Importers from other countries were buying handicrafts in Peru, where prices were lower because, unlike in Bolivia, basic staples continued to be heavily subsidized.[15] And, as we saw earlier, imported goods were now often cheaper in Bolivia than locally manufactured ones. Even the artisans themselves sometimes substituted Peruvian intermediate manufactures for local ones. Thus, Doña Flora bought dyed and spun Peruvian yarn to make some of her sweaters and brought back from Peru thin, synthetic sweaters that she resold in her street market site in La Paz.

Ultimately, the fate of the export of manufactured goods from Bolivia may have more to do with factors over which Bolivian producers have little control, such as restructuring of the economy in Peru (as was occurring in mid-1990) or a reduction in the cocaine trade, than with their entrepreneurial talents. Nevertheless, with their ingenuity honed through their experiences in facing innumerable crises, Bolivians will probably always find a way to engage in some export activity.

The Crisis in Pricing

The mood in 1984 was one of despair. Wages that did not keep pace with the rampant inflation cut demand even for basic necessities. The decreased purchasing power of the wage earner forced the artisans and at least those factories producing cheap consumer goods to lower their prices and content themselves with much lower profit margins than before if they were to make any sales at all.

Hyperinflation made it difficult for producers even to set a price their goods. Merchants were in constant contact with their sources of foreign currency for information on the exchange rates, which could change considerably from hour to hour. On some days, during which rumors of some new economic calamity circulated, many closed shop entirely and did not reopen until the situation had calmed down a bit. Particularly hard hit were businesses that sold goods on credit and those who produced goods whose price was fixed when they were ordered. By the time the goods were delivered at the predetermined price, or the final payment on goods sold for credit had been made, prices had often more than doubled. To deal with pricing, one firm was considering a total change in production from shoes to pastries, because the interval between the time pastries are ordered and the time they are delivered is too short to be unduly affected by price fluctuations. Other firms, with more capital at stake, hung on to the best of their abilities without making major changes. For example, one shirtmaker has always depended on selling shirts on credit through workers' unions. The factory delivers the shirts to the union for immediate distribution. The amount owed is then subtracted from the workers' pay at the beginning of the following two or three months. The factory sells to some twenty unions, including the Corporación Minera. During normal times, this system assured a reliable source of income. Sometimes it took a year to be paid, but that did not present a problem when the currency was stable. However, with hyperinflation, costs doubled by the time the factory was paid. The owner felt that he had to continue the system, however. He was incurring a risk, but he had to keep his workers occupied. Without this system, there would be no sales. Similarly, a shoemaker said that although some of his clients recognized the fact that a price adjustment was warranted when a pair of shoes contracted earlier was made at a later time, most of his clients just became angry.

There were, of course, exceptions. Some producers actually benefited from the crises in both legal and illegal ways. Thus, a producer of popped cereals ceased popping rice and noodles and concentrated instead on salted popcorn, for which demand had risen considerably because there was a scarcity of bread. Coffee roasters increased their production because more and more people were substituting a cup of coffee and, when available, a small loaf of bread made out of subsidized flour for one of their customary hot meals. There were also illegal ways to turn the crisis to one's benefit. Instead of selling bread at government-controlled prices, bakers often managed to smuggle part of their flour ration to Peru or sell the flour to consumers under the table at a multiple of its cost to them. Similarly, jewelers (and others) could make good money from the illegal purchase and sale of gold and by acting as intermediaries in the sale of jewelry. During our third visit to Bolivia, in 1988, Alcides, the jeweler, admitted that in some ways he earned more during the depth of the crisis than he did at present. As he put it: *"En río revuelto, ganancia de pescadores"* (Churned up waters make for good fishing).

Notes

1. In many additional cases, the wife also sold some other good on the market, which she may or may not have produced herself.

2. When we special ordered a small carpet from him, he asked us for an advance and left another carpet as a guarantee that he would fulfill the contract. One month later he brought the finished rug, as promised.

3. She continued to procure the raw materials herself.

4. One of us (Judith-Maria) first observed this pattern in 1967. Wives and daughters of factory workers in glass, textile, garment and aluminum-pot factories all sold goods procured by their husbands or fathers. In one instance, a young unmarried woman gained access to aluminum ware because her mother's cousin worked for an aluminum factory and could act as a guarantor (see J.-M. Buechler 1972:275).

5. Lucía would have been five years old in 1952, the year the Movimiento Nacional Revolucionario party came to power.

6. Once vendors manage to smuggle contraband goods across the border and across several checkpoints on the altiplano, they can sell the goods quite openly in La Paz.

7. Vendors earn very low wages. In 1981, a vendor typically earned $b. 1,500 a month with no free meals, less than what she would have earned as a domestic servant.

8. Spinning wheels are a novelty on the altiplano, where women customarily spin with wooden spinning whorls.

9. However, soon after the experiment was initiated the large supermarket in question closed.

10. By the time we interviewed him, he no longer appeared to be interested in Jehovah's Witnesses but professed to being a devout Catholic.

11. Just what benefit the accountant expected to derive from this latter role could not be determined.

12. The interview took place in 1984.

13. According to Mr. Gonzalez, Bolivia was in the position of exporting double its quota in 1988.

14. The large piles of finished rugs awaiting shipment to Mrs. Romero that we saw during our visit to her shop in 1984, while she was in the United States, seem to indicate that a large part of her transactions was in the form of goods manufactured entirely in Bolivia.

15. Some producers, like Mr. Pereira, who makes leather bags, have shifted their exports toward European markets, which appear to be less price sensitive than those in the United States.

10

Power and Empowerment

The collective efforts of small-scale producers in arenas traditionally defined as "political" and "ritual" provide us with a means to understand how persons are controlled by others and how they themselves become empowered. We begin with an analysis of the role of the state and continue with that of producers' organizations, which, in general, may be viewed as opposing the state. We will deal with the manner in which the control of small-scale production is manifested by reiterating the major ways in which the state and the artisans vie for access to materials, commercial sites, capital and markets and how each seeks to undermine the other. We will end with a description of the fiesta system and will discuss how interpersonal relationships, in general, and power relations, in particular, are reflected in it, and how it exercises a collective constraint on individuals but also enables them to gain power over others.

As shown in the preceding chapters, the government often impedes the artisans' production by monopolizing materials, such as gold and wool, or it distorts artisans' production by subsidizing others. The government (in this case, national) allows producers to import certain equipment, raw materials, and intermediate goods and imposes heavy import duties on others. It may or may not provide producers with foreign currency at official (usually more advantageous) exchange rates to import goods. And it fixes wages and prices and rations scarce subsidized goods. An extraordinarily unwieldy governmental bureaucracy overregulates many aspects of production and commerce and sometimes taxes certain goods and inputs doubly or triply while allowing labor conditions for apprentices and health/accident insurance for kin in small-scale operations to go unattended. The state is often a competitor, but it may also be a client. Government (in this case, municipal) allows producers to sell their products on certain streets and impedes them from doing so on others. Contacts with the government through previous employment and middle-class intermediaries help to grease the wheels of bureaucracy in order to avoid unfavorable actions and gain contracts.

Our informants spoke candidly of the passive and active strategies they felt they had to engage in to counteract governmental actions considered abusive, capricious, unfair or ill-conceived. They often claimed that no one could run a firm in Bolivia without, on occasion, acquiring goods through contraband, evading taxes, entering into informal labor relations with kin, and engaging in other avoidance tactics. They also demonstrated and organized labor and hunger strikes.

Most important, for the purpose of this chapter, the state assists and permits international organizations to further the association of producers into syndicates and cooperatives, yet at other times or sometimes even simultaneously it prohibits producers to congregate and/or thwarts the further development of grass-roots organizations. Government, then, is regarded as one of the principal antagonists of private producers and, at the same time, is a source of potential benefits--a recalcitrant patron and benefactor; an organizer and, at the same time, a dissolver of organizations.

The Role of the State in Development

One of the more successful attempts at promoting crafts in La Paz is the municipal government's program of rotating exhibits and conferences in the Casa de la Cultura, a museum dedicated principally to modern art. The director of the program in 1981 was herself a *chola*, bilingual in Spanish and Aymara. She appeared to have a good understanding of the problems of the artisans and at the same time was knowledgeable about sources of credit for artisans and other related matters.[1] She had traveled widely in the 18 provinces of the department of La Paz. During her travels, she met with peasant women with whom she discussed the participation of women in community development, and she instructed them about matters concerning artisanry. She had also attended an international conference on peasant women in Asunción where she won a prize because of her superior knowledge of women's issues. In the museum itself, she organized and prepared the exhibits, which began with displays of the clothing of each rural region and were followed by exhibits of particular trades. As we indicated earlier, she was involved in educational programs. She was also attempting, as yet unsuccessfully, to assist a group of artisans in the purchase of a building in the Sagarnaga tourist district from which they could sell their goods. In 1981, one of her projects was to organize a roundtable with all government agencies connected to artisanry in order to discuss "the state of artisanry in Bolivia, the political mechanisms associated with it and the kinds of interlinkages among the institutions." She was also interested in creating patent and other laws to protect artisans.

On the national level, the major agency that deals with small-scale industry in Bolivia is INBOPIA (Instituto Boliviano de la Pequeña Industria y Artesanía, or the Bolivian Institute for Small-Scale Industry and Artisanry), which was founded around 1973. The institute's functions are to produce and disseminate new designs for crafts (sweaters in particular), to facilitate access to credit and to open new markets for products produced by small-scale firms.

According to one of its founders, who resigned from the agency five years after its creation, the organization has failed to deliver on its promises, largely because of the frequent changes in government. Often, new directors have deviated from the original goals, making progress difficult. Indeed, the agency has often been criticized by small-scale producers, who claim that it has competed with private merchants on the internal market and has lured away foreign intermediaries from exporters rather than opening up new foreign markets. In addition, some of its erstwhile officials have opened their own private export firms, which has led to further competition. The same officials have been charged with underpaying craftsmen, thereby decreasing instead of promoting incentives to produce, and with undercutting producers who export their own crafts. Artisans have also complained of the agency's choice of delegates for artisans' conventions abroad. Frequently, the agency has sent its own officials or individuals with little background in production rather than true artisans.

The capricious manner adopted even by the very government institutions that were set up to assist the artisan is apparent in the following example. When we visited the president of Wara Wara, the cooperative of woolen sweater producers, in El Alto in 1981, she was disconsolate. In May, her own and a number of other cooperatives had received an order from Japan channeled through INBOPIA, the first order the sweater producers received since they had organized as a cooperative six months earlier. Each member was allotted two sweaters to knit. The cooperative's share of 60 sweaters was to be picked up in two months; it was to undergo a quality check and be paid for on the spot. Since the amount the cooperative was to be paid was some 30% higher than the going rate, the women were eager to comply. They finished their work on time to avoid the stiff penalty threatened for delays. But on the day of delivery, they were told that they would not be paid for two weeks. A month later, they had still not been paid. Endless trips to the city only resulted in more and more the excuses: too many sweaters had been made, etc., etc. Finally, they were told that "a contract was, after all, only a piece of paper." "Yes," the president of the cooperative said, "perhaps. But a piece of paper should be worth something too." At the time of the interview, two months after they had delivered the sweaters, the members of the cooperative had still not been paid. Since many of the members had very little capital, their production may well have come to grinding halt.

Another agency with a potential impact on small-scale industry is FOMO (Fomento de Mano de Obra). According to its planning director,

FOMO is a governmental organization whose purpose is to train workers and peasant producers. It was founded in 1973 and has regional centers in the different departments of the country. In 1980, the program trained 3,000 workers nationwide. The participants in the urban programs are usually sent by the factories they work for, but they may, at least in theory, also come from small workshops. The La Paz center offers morning, afternoon and evening classes. The courses offered by a regional center depend on the needs of the industries in that location in a given year. In La Paz, they include courses related to electricity, mechanics, automobile mechanics and agriculture. Courses last from one to two weeks for agriculture and for three to five months for courses relating to the industrial sector, and they may include up to 15 participants, selected by previous testing. The courses are highly specialized and do not provide general training.[2] They have reached mainly men, but one on dairy farming in Santa Cruz has also attracted a number of women.

Until the mid-1980s, the agency's programs were financed by a 1% tax on wages, levied on all private and semiprivate firms, and an additional inscription fee of $b. 100 (US $4). But the tax reform bill of 1987 eliminated the tax, and only the smaller-scale industries decided to continue their support voluntarily. As a result, the agency has become dependent upon the support of various countries. The agency has received funding for equipment from the Inter-American Development Bank. In addition, FOMO sometimes makes arrangements to use the facilities of private and other public institutions. The teachers are themselves active workers in the professions about which they teach and have either received training in other countries, funded by fellowships from such organizations as the ILO (International Labor Organization), or attended courses taught by visiting specialists.

Producers' Unions

Sindicatos, or unions (actually producers' and market vendors' associations, although the same term is employed for workers' unions), were created to protect their members from the abuses of state power; to bring pressure on the government to act in the interest of the unions; to engage in activities that are facilitated by membership in a group; and, at the same time, to exercise both internal and external control over producers and vendors.

Many *sindicatos* trace their origin to 1952, when the MNR party came into power and initiated a series of social and economic reforms. Others were founded later as the result of disputes within existing *sindicatos* or to facilitate the establishment of new markets, for obtaining the right to sell on a particular street may require considerable persistence and may entail hardships.

These hardships begin long before a union is formally established.

As an example, let us turn to the creation of a furniture market in the Calle Ochoa. As we saw in Chapter 9, Victor was the first person to sell furniture in the Calle Ochoa, a location he chose because there was little vehicular traffic. Although some food vendors were already selling there, they did not sell at the same time of the day that he did. At first, the municipal police arrested Victor, but he gave them chairs as presents and so they left him alone. Soon, five cabinetmakers were selling there. Later, the market expanded further to include an entire city block. By 1981, 200 cabinetmakers were selling in the Ochoa street market.

As the market grew, it established a union. The union facilitated the expansion of the market, for now the vendors had an effective channel to resist the attempts of the police to oust them from the Calle Ochoa. However, for the founders of the market, like Victor, the union was a mixed blessing. Since Victor is illiterate, he was bypassed for positions in the union directorate, although his son, who is literate, was called to serve. The residents of the street had predicted that Victor would become marginalized if he allowed other carpenters to sell there. Their prediction came true. As we shall see later, he wavered about sponsoring the fiesta honoring the patron saint of the market because he continued to feel that his founding role had not been sufficiently recognized.

Latecomers to markets face different problems. Once a market is well established, it forms its own market syndicate that, among other things, regulates entry. There is often considerable resistance from those already established to admit new members. One artisan carefully approached a number of *puesto* holders of the *mercado artesanal* at an artisans' congress in Potosí in order to gain admittance and invited them to visit his workshop. He gained the support of some when they saw that he was not wealthy and did not represent a serious threat. Even so, the vote was far from unanimous. Producer/vendors often have a difficult time obtaining choice sites for direct sales to customers. Some of the producers selling at the *mercado artesanal*, for example, feel that the market has become dominated by merchants who have given up their own production or engage in it only as a sideline. Choice sites like those in the *mercado artesanal* are rare, and the producer/vendors feel that they should have priority over the merchants in having access to them.

Existing unions sometimes also seek the establishment of new markets. Thus, before a meeting of the association of goldsmiths of El Alto, some of the members expressed to us their desire to open up two plazas in El Alto to the sale of jewelry. At the meeting, the association's members decided that their preferred solution was to purchase a site where they could set up small, glass display cases and sell jewelry on market days; their backup plan was to sell on the periphery of one of the new plazas.

The decision of whether or not to belong to a union depends on

Inaugurating a new street market

many factors. Vendors or producer/vendors selling on a particular street do not have much choice but to belong to its union. In contrast, artisans who work in dispersed workshops have more latitude. One tailor decided not to join a union because of the high initial inscription fee of $b. 5,000 (US $200) in 1981 plus the required contribution of $b. 500 or $b. 1,000 (US $20 or $40) toward the rental of a meeting hall; because of the obligation to attend meetings "twice a week" (a gross exaggeration); and because he did not see any clear benefits from joining. He would have liked the union to provide loans for materials for tailors who were starting out in business, but he said, "There is nothing like that. On the contrary, those who are already capitalists seem to need money most." He had been pressured by the Bureau of Revenue and Taxation to join the union, but he refused. Instead, he invited officials from the Bureau to eat and drink, and in this way he got the papers proving that he had met his tax obligations in order more rapidly. The penalty for not belonging to a union is a higher municipal and income tax, for the unions have negotiated a lower tax classification for their members in return for collecting taxes from the members. The unions' role as tax collector for the municipal government and for the state may be one of the reasons even military governments in Bolivia have allowed a minimum of union activity to continue.

As we saw in Chapter 8, one of the major functions of some of the producers' unions and of the generally smaller producers' cooperatives is to make joint purchases of raw materials for members or to distribute rationed staples. For instance, the candle makers are organized into purchasing groups whose main purpose is the joint purchase of paraffin wax. One group had twelve members who lived dispersed in several neighborhoods but who had known each other from childhood because their parents or other kin had worked in the same trade. These purchasing groups are registered at the Chamber of Commerce and also belong to one of the three producers' associations, two of which have fifty individual members and the largest with a hundred members. It is in the name of the producers' association that the subgroups purchased the paraffin from the state. Each member orders as much as he needs from the purchasing group's president, and in addition, the group keeps a reserve. When the group has run out of paraffin, those who still have some left sell to those who have run out. When no one has any stock left, a new order is placed. The association's sole additional function seems to be the collection of taxes. It meets twice a year or whenever the need arises.

Similarly, the furniture-makers' union, with a membership of some 200 persons, buys plywood directly in Santa Cruz and arranges for its shipment to La Paz. Plywood had been particularly difficult to obtain, which has made joint action important. The cabinetmakers continue to make individual arrangements for all their other needs.

Finally, the bakers' unions distribute flour to their memberships, an important function, especially in times when flour is rationed. The ten bakers' unions in La Paz include most of the city's 1,200 or so small-scale bakeries. The unions, in turn, belong to the Confederation of Bakers of Bolivia, which was founded in 1971. One of these unions is the Society of the Bakers of La Paz, which was established in 1952, when the MNR party came into power. Once 200 members strong and the city's only bakers' union, it had only 140 members in 1981. According to its president, its specific functions are, "to provide raw materials; take care of official matters involving the municipal government (for sometimes there are abnormal situations in the *intendencia*, [the city office in charge of markets and producers]); obtain the identification card each baker must carry; and defend the economic interests of its constituents, to enable them to live at the same level as other small-scale artisans." The president went on to say that "the society has its own office. With the money deposited there by the bakers, the association purchases some 400 quintals of flour per week [in 1981]. Individual bakers have quotas commensurate with their capital and the size of their bakeries. Generally each baker receives 5 quintals." The society carries several brands of flour. The representative of the confederation acts as a liaison person with the central government and urges it to import flour during times of scarcity. Sometimes the government imports the flour and sometimes the confederation does so directly from other countries. It has also attempted to influence bread pricing but apparently to no avail.

Particularly in the early years of unionization, the union leadership often abused its position. For example, the Association of Upholsterers, Carpenters and Cabinetmakers of La Paz was dissolved in 1960 following a scandal that erupted when its head, who had collected a large sum of money from the membership in order to import machinery from the United States, absconded with the money. The informant who told us this story was a union member at that time and lost money; he had not joined an association since then, for fear that something similar might happen to him again. In contrast, according to its president, the twelve-member candle-makers' group mentioned earlier had experienced no difficulties managing the purchase of wax. The small size of the group and the fact that everyone knew one another prevented dishonest dealings.

Additional union functions include the organization of fiestas and the organization of soccer or mini-soccer (*fulbito*) matches--functions that we shall discuss in the section on fiestas--and the acquisition of land for the union membership. Around 1958, the cabinetmakers' union acquired land in Rio Seco, a neighborhood at the edge of El Alto, so that each member could build a house (or resell his or her plot to someone else). This program has continued.

Finally, the unions often attend and contribute to the cost of their members' funerals. The costume-makers' union, for example, contributes three or four cases of beer (36 to 48 bottles of 750 centiliters at

$b. 280 [US $11.20] per case) and a cash gift of $b. 1,000 (US $40) to the bereaved family. This same union once also owned a section of the cemetery and provided burial niches for its members. But, according to our informant, the burial niches were distributed among the directorate, and soon there were none left for the rank and file.

In theory, the leadership of a union changes every year; but in practice, the same individuals are reelected year after year. We saw this firsthand at a meeting of the jewelers' association of El Alto. The meeting dealt with the president's decision to abdicate for lack of both personal and financial support. After a long discussion among the members in the flowery, formal language deemed appropriate for such occasions, the president was persuaded to remain in office.

Apart from the prestige union leaders gain, the perks of the office are usually few—perhaps a beer or two now and then, a meal, or a cash present when a member requests a plot of land. The position does require a lot of bureaucratic work, with frequent visits to the town - hall, as well as the collection of money for fiestas and so forth. While women frequently hold office in market unions, some producers' unions, such as the cabinetmakers union, elect only men, despite the fact that women do much of the selling. During military regimes, union functions were pared down to a minimum. *Relacionadores*, or public relations officers, who were often erstwhile union officials, were selected by the municipal government to act as liaison persons between the union and the government. During those times, neither elections nor union meetings were allowed.

In the mid-1980s, a number of new producers' unions and federations of unions were created. Like their older counterparts, these unions serve the purposes of facilitating tax collection by the municipal government, providing a forum for the expression of the concerns of the sector and a means for members of the sector to express and assert their identity, and, at the same time, providing for some of the recreational needs of the members. But some of them also have more ambitious aims. They strive for a complete reorganization of the sector and, in particular, of government involvement in small-scale production. An example is the Federación de Artesanos en Arte Popular de La Paz (Federation of Popular Art of La Paz), formed in 1982 by 36 unions and cooperatives representing both producers and merchants of artisan crafts. At that time, the military was still in power and did not allow people to associate freely, so the meetings were held in secret.[3] Each organization sends three delegates. Artisans not affiliated with a union or a cooperative also send representatives. At least in theory, meetings are held every month.

During its first general assembly, the officers to the federation suggested a series of laws to assist artisans, including the creation of a central government agency analogous to the national tourist office (the Instituto Boliviano de Cultura) to deal with matters concerning crafts production. According to Mr. Murillo, one of the founders of the federation, the original purpose of the federation was distorted by the leaders who came into power in 1983, who were more interested in using the federation as a forum for party politics. The federation also faced competition from rival groups, which ostensibly were also for craft producers but, as Mr. Murillo put it, actually included only artisans not engaged in popular art. In 1984, the federation was planning the Third Congress of Artisans in Popular Art of the City of La Paz, to be held at the Museum of Anthropology, with the purpose of bringing the federation's agenda back on track and putting into practice the lessons some of the members had learned while traveling to exhibitions, fairs and conferences on artisanry in other Latin American countries. The new goals of the federation were described by Mr. Murillo as follows:

> Fundamentally, the aim is to request the government to create a central agency, specifically for popular art, and to seek more direct ways of financing and commercializing our products. What is happening is that the crafts producer is being exploited in a criminal manner. He is paid according to the whim of the merchant. So we want to provide protection from a social perspective. In addition, we wish to have access to international exhibitions, [and] be able to obtain fellowships and a number of other benefits given by such agencies as the OAS [Organization of American States] and other international organizations. We would like active members of the trades to be able to participate personally [in workshops, conferences and the like] rather than, as is usually the case, persons who have little knowledge about crafts production. I had this experience in Spain, where I attended a course on planning and promoting crafts production. Those who attended the course knew nothing about the sector. They were all managers chosen for political reasons with no knowledge whatsoever about the problems of artisan production. I think that an Ecuadorian and I were the only true members of the trade. It will never be possible to give the sector the attention it deserves when those who represent it have no knowledge about it. I recommended that those who receive fellowships and technical assistance should be artisans themselves. Only they can benefit from the courses personally and at the same time make the sector more viable.

In addition, the problem of the copying of Bolivian crafts in neighboring countries (mentioned in Chapter 9) has also been taken up by the federation. This issue was debated hotly with the representatives of these countries during the 1984 general assembly. "If the Bolivian government doesn't give the problem serious attention," Mr. Murillo concluded, "I think that we will soon have major problems."

Mr. Murillo hoped that the Third Congress would also lead to some form of classification of producers according to skill levels. He was distressed by the fact that IMBOPIA did not make any distinctions between various quality levels of crafts and paid the same for an item regardless of whether it was produced by a master craftsman or by a novice.

The preparations for the Third Congress of Artisans in Popular Art of the City of La Paz were to consist of a series of discussion meetings and work by three committees. The first committee was to analyze the role of state agencies in the craft industry, the problems of exporting crafts, the problem of the "indiscriminate exploitation and export of raw materials that leaves the sector without raw materials," the duplication and dispersion of government functions related to crafts production, and the need for a census of artisans (which the federation members thought might be available from IMBOPIA).[4] A second committee was charged with the task of formulating certain objectives to be presented to the central government and state agencies, including legislation geared specifically to protect crafts production, the creation of an institute for artisanry and popular art, and the establishment of the Bank for Artisanry and Popular Art. The third committee was to prepare for federation elections for 1984-85; create an archival library for artisans, where all the materials obtained by members on their travels abroad could be made available; classify and make a catalog of all the organizations within the federation according the form of organization, type of product and manner of commercializing it; and "prepare an exhibition and a crafts competition with prizes and fellowships given by international organizations."

While the agenda of the federation sounded ambitious indeed, the actual accomplishments of the organization were more modest. The discussion at a meeting we attended consisted mainly of finding a source of funding for office supplies and fixing the level of a fee to be charged to all members for an identity card and a corresponding registry, with the main selling point being that a photograph of the artisan would be laminated on the card. The leadership hoped that such a registry could be used to direct prospective large customers to appropriate producers as well as to inform them about the types of crafts available and the number of artisans producing them. After a long discussion, the fee of $b. 1,000 (US $0.50 [official rate]) was agreed upon.

Four years later, in 1988, Mr. Murillo was complaining about the same issues:

> Export has diminished substantially--first because there are no incentives to produce, and second because Peru and Chile are trying to lure away Bolivian artisans as though they were their own workers. Peruvians are having work done here and selling it as Peruvian artisanry, so they have taken away the originality of our crafts and our own channels of com-mercialization. The Bolivian authorities have not instituted appropriate laws. I have been fighting for such legislation for years and nothing has happened. Today the artisans have to resign themselves to this state of affairs because there is no one to protect them. I believe that soon Bolivia is going to lose its traditional crafts. It will be like with the problem of [access to] the sea. In ten years from now, we will be saying that these crafts traditions once belonged to us. Bolivia will be copying neighboring countries. It will seem as though the country had never had customs of its

own. And all this because the authorities don't pay any attention. They don't defend the national cultural patrimony. I see this on my trips abroad. One doesn't see anything made in Bolivia. They don't advertise what we have and do. So Peru, Chile and Argentina are trying to make capital out of what is ours, and we will remain without anything. . . .

I have many friends who have moved to Peru and Chile and they are doing well, but they are leaving their knowledge there. They are teaching others when they could have engaged in the same activities at home if the authorities had only paid some attention. Instead, such organizations as INBOPIA are directing their attention more towards small-scale industrialized production, a field craftsmen will find difficult to enter because it requires capital beyond the means of artisans. The same thing is true for the Planning Ministry and the municipal government. They would like us to develop into small industries so that they can tax us accordingly. As a result, they are ignoring artisanal activities.

The federation has, in fact, disintegrated since 1984. A final attempt at reviving it in May 1988 failed. The constituents became disillusioned when the mayor of La Paz offered only a small hall for the organization's projected activities. "The artisans dispersed again because they have to find a means of subsistence [i.e., they have to go back to work]." However, Mr. Murillo had not given up the fight when we spoke to him in 1988. In addition to running his own exhibition hall, as we discussed in Chapter 9, he and other artisans representing three associations of crafts vendors were struggling to convince the municipal government to overturn its earlier decision to convert a historic, centrally located building into a museum of modern art and to establish instead a crafts center there, as promised by the Banzer government in 1977. The Banzer government's plans had included the creation of a school for artisans, as well as exhibition halls and workshops where artisans could demonstrate their skills to visitors. At the same time, the artisans were trying to convince the mayor to call for preparations for the Alasita fair, and announce a competition with prizes, much earlier than usual in order to provide a longer lead time for artisans to prepare goods for the fair. In addition, they were pushing for the reinstitution of an itinerant crafts fair to be held in a different plaza in the city every week.

Cooperatives

In the 1970s and 1980s, some artisans' cooperatives were created. The major stated purpose of these cooperatives was to provide a means of bypassing the intermediaries--the merchants in the local markets and shops and the exporters. The formation of such legal entities would also have subsidiary benefits. They would be able to borrow money for raw materials and machines; establish redistribution networks for donations, such as food from Caritas; act as purchasing agents for staples; and become lobbying groups for artisans and the neighborhoods where they live.

These groups have typically been formed around a number of persons related through kinship, residence in a neighborhood, or the fact that they came from the same community of origin and work in similar or connected tasks of a trade. From such informal groups of persons who occasionally lent each other money or helped each other buy materials, complete orders and/or bring merchandise to exporters or shops evolved larger, more organized legal units of around fifty to a hundred members with such officers as president, vice president, secretary and "vocal," or messenger, planned meetings, a license, dues and fiestas. Although the members stressed the need for well organized—that is, hierarchically structured—groups that were integrated into federations on the city and perhaps even the national levels, they also voiced the need for an open, democratic structure of decision making and participation.

Many of these groups were initially set up by international development organizations. They gave the groups gifts to purchase materials and, especially in the beginning, also served as outlets for the goods, particularly hand-knitted sweaters, they produced. This dual role as benefactor and intermediary sometimes led to difficulties. A former member of one such cooperative described her experience as follows:

> The director [of a development agency] was the son of one of the members [of our cooperative], a young man who used to be unemployed. He treated the women as though they were his servants. And since they are so humble, they never protested. I think that we are all equal and we should not let ourselves be treated however they want to. They [the development agency] had told us that they were our employees. "You can come to the office whenever you want and do what you want." But the reality was different. It was quite the opposite. In our group, we treat everyone the same regardless of how poor a person is.

In addition, the severance of a privileged relationship with a development agency may lead to considerable resentment. For instance, when one agency dropped a group of women from its roster in favor of a group of poorer women, the former felt betrayed. They had lost an important outlet and felt that they had not been compensated for the sweater designs they had created. Their group had shrunk from a maximum of one hundred members in 1974 to a mere ten in 1981. And by 1988, the group was no longer functioning.

Mothers' Clubs are a similar kind of group. As one of us described previously (J.-M. Buechler 1985a: 175),

> Mothers' Clubs are supported by United Nations funds, organized as barrio-based artisanal weaving and knitting cooperatives with an average of 38 members. Financed by the sale of UN-donated staples

to neighborhood families, the capital is invested in wool bought at wholesale prices and sold directly to the members who then knit and weave sweaters, scarves, ponchos and shawls for sale. The members learn the technical and financial aspects of weaving as well as exhibiting their wares. Perhaps the most important lesson learnt, according to the [United Nations'] technician in charge, is the "value of women's work." The class base for these clubs was broad but separate from the ones on El Alto, the new working-class neighborhood on the fringe of the city, involving primarily newly arrived migrant women and those in Sopocachi, a more central residential district associated with more middle-class members.

Most of the artisans' cooperatives were and continue to be in the process of formation. Members expressed to us high hopes of being able to pay for a telephone, a post-office box, a centrally located stall or shop and a person qualified to line up large foreign orders and to assure quality and timely shipment and payment. As they saw it, the major obstacle hindering the success of a group was the ability to secure large enough orders to make the organization worthwhile. Such orders were, of course, dependent on the group's ability to fill large orders reliably, in a timely manner and on assured quality and price. Those factors, in turn, depended on organizations and on events beyond their control: in particular, the economic and political crises. They hoped that local, regional, national and international agencies would recognize their potential contribution to the economy and would help secure new avenues for growth, but they saw no real evidence that the present obstacles would be cleared away in the foreseeable future. The leaders and members were fully convinced of the necessity to organize at the same time that they expressed their disillusionment and voted with their feet—by leaving the cooperatives.

The case of the leader of the knitting cooperative Wara Wara, mentioned earlier, a woman who has been active as an organizer since she was a teenager, will serve to illustrate the origins, problems and opportunities of artisan organizations as well as the dedication of their more active members.

Marta was born in a rural community in a distant province of the state of La Paz:

I attended primary school there, and then I came here to the city with my older brother, who worked as a shoemaker [and now owns a small bar and restaurant], when I was only ten years old and worked as a servant for some four years. The work was hard, but with my goodwill I gained the family's appreciation: I cooked, washed, ironed, took care of the children. But what they paid me was nothing. In the evenings from seven to nine I would go to night school. I went to school for two years until *segundo intermedio* [the second year of middle school, i.e., eighth grade].

The work load was no better in the other places I worked. In one of them, they wouldn't allow me to go to school. They told me, "You know how to read and write. You can sign your name. Why do you want to learn more than that? Do you want to become a secretary or a doctor? It's enough that you work. You have to earn to buy clothing." Yes, there are households that allow you to learn something, but others don't.

Then I returned to my community where I continued to go to school. I [also] founded a Center of Mothers. I taught the mothers to read and write. I was [only] fourteen or fifteen years old. Then I returned to the city once more for a year.

During that time I visited my community regularly. I liked to go to community development agencies and to Radio San Gabriel and to a Catholic agency that deals with rural development. Well, as a result, they hired me as a community promoter. After working for them for six months, I became well known in my province, and so, already in 1976, they named me to work as a coordinator of women's affairs in the province. I worked in this capacity for six or seven months. In the communities there are always organizations, Mothers' Clubs, that are engaged in community work. I would go with my tape recorder and tape plays, songs and poems at the events they organized. I would take the tapes to Radio San Gabriel [to be aired]. So I was already a leader. Then I stopped working as a promoter and worked for the Catholic organization recording [radio] novels.

I continued my studies in the city and working as a servant. My parents were poor, and I had to earn my own living. I had to work twice as hard to get everything done so that I could go to night school. After school I would come home and do my homework until eleven or twelve at night. I finished two grades but then quit.

Later, when I married, there was no longer any time. I met my husband when I brought tapes to Radio San Gabriel. He produced a one-hour program and would visit the organizations in the communities. I would bring tapes from my groups from the communities with songs, poems and protests to the radio station. We married and had three children. We were married for some eight years. Then he left me. He continues to work for the same organization.

I went to live with my husband when I was seventeen. He was ten years older than I, and I did absolutely everything he told me to do, just like a daughter. But then I woke up and spoke up. He became angry and no longer allowed me to participate in organizations. He wanted me to take care of the household at all times. But I had other ideas. So he left. Also there must have been other women around him. He started divorce procedures, and I gave in. He is living happily with another woman and has left me with three children.

Until now he hasn't given me a single cent. I went to the authorities to force him to pay alimony, but it didn't help. People simply pay the authorities here in Bolivia, and even if someone is guilty they don't do anything about it. I went to the human rights commission, and they told me to fight on, that they would get me a lawyer. They worked on the case for a bit, but soon I saw that there was no justice to be had even from the authorities, and so I left things as they were. I am a mother and have to take care of my children. On some days, all we have for lunch is a little tea and a small loaf of bread. In Bolivia there is really no justice. He works for the church, but not even the church supported me.

Sometimes I become very resentful. If I were alone, I could work for some agency as a promoter. But with children I can't do it. I have to take care of them. We have brought them to this world; it's not *their* fault. They have to eat. But I sometimes I have nothing to feed them. So I get very sad.

[She then told us how she really only worked as an organizer for several months at a time]. I came here for six months, then worked there [in her home community] for five. That's how the people came to know me there and elect me as their leader. If I hadn't married, I would have done more. I no longer had any time. Here I also formed a group with a few neighbors to be eligible for receiving help from Caritas. It had a membership of 80 mothers. It was a difficult undertaking because my husband didn't want me to leave the house. So I had to do it in secret when my husband was at work. But I felt that this was not enough, so I decided to organize another group, this time of artisans—of knitters. I went from house to house telling people that we could do all sorts of items, form an association and ask for assistance. As soon as we had the first meetings, they became convinced. They told others and they wanted to join too. We organized it formally [as the Wara Wara cooperative]. Officials from INBOPIA came to visit us and everything. That was in 1976. Now we have been in existence for almost eight years. Since I was alone [i.e., divorced], they [the members] sometimes believed me and sometimes not. And then, when there was no market for their sweaters, they lost heart.

In the beginning we sold to the intermediaries in the artisan markets I would contact. But I realized that they paid us little and sold for a lot. I thought that INBOPIA could help us to export directly, and they promised to help us. They came to give us courses in a hall we rented for the purpose. Then they also offered us loans through a program for artisans from the World Bank. For that we had to become legally incorporated. We succeeded in doing this, [but] only five or six of the more than 35 members obtained loans. The legal process took an entire year. Each person bought a [hand operated] knitting machine and we had a spinning wheel built. The loan [which is for six years] is in pesos and [because of the inflation] that suits us fine. Many [of the members] regret not having requested a loan too, but because it took so long, they thought that it was all a hoax and they became demoralized. We started with 85 persons, when INBOPIA gave the courses. Then we were only 40 and finally only 33.

As far as the group I organized to receive food is concerned, now people are pleading to join. But I think that Caritas doesn't want to give more food either. On the other hand, in a group of artisans that does not have access to [free] food and has not found its market [the situation is different]. If we had a secure market, people would come from all over the place [to become members]. Instead we continue to work through the intermediaries, and sometimes INBOPIA organizes exhibitions and fairs. The last one was held in the Casa de la Cultura in April. But in those exhibitions we sometimes sell and sometimes not. We make beautiful things, and then they don't sell and we have to store them away at home. That's why people lose heart. It's not reliable work. In contrast, in the Mothers' Clubs there are more people. Nevertheless our artisan group continues to meet on Tuesdays. Since we are legally incorporated we can take steps to obtain sugar, cooking oil and noodles. Sometimes we divide an arroba or five kilos of sugar among ourselves. And, since many want to dissolve the group, we are doing embroidery, sweaters and toys mainly for our own use. Some women make better things, so they can sell them at Christmas time. I am teaching some special knitting stitches, and we are also practicing reading and writing. So we continue to help one another. If I am not there, a friend and neighbor steps in. If we didn't assist one another, the group would fall apart. Now we are preparing an exhibit for the second of August (the Day of the Indian) with all the things we have done. We are also thinking of planting trees along the streets because it's very windy here. For this we want to request the town halls to provide the trees. So, while there is no market, we want to do things to benefit our neighborhood.

We always had meetings [even before the advent of a democratic government], but when there were military coups they would prohibit meetings altogether. Then the group's leaders would go from house to house to communicate. I believe in working in groups, help one another, cooperate. We also have exchanges of ideas between groups, even with groups all over the world.

At the same time, there are impediments to communicating among groups; so in the same breath that Marta talked about exchanges of ideas, she discussed the isolation of artisans in El Alto from their counterparts in the La Paz basin.

Now the artisans have a federation, but only in the city. In El Alto, we are isolated from the city. Let's say that some order is channeled through the federation. Well, the intermediaries themselves form part of the federation, so the producers sell to them. We don't like that. In order to impede that sort of thing, we have organized a federation in El Alto. We meet on the fifteenth of every month. On May 30, we had a congress of all the artisans of El Alto, and we had a representative from each association. They wanted to name me, but because I am a woman who stands alone I have too many other things to do. At that meeting we discussed ways of selling in our own markets directly to the consumer. We also invited the authorities to attend. The Minister of Industry and Commerce promised to help us find markets, but since the economic measures have not been firmly instituted yet, nothing is too sure. We couldn't get anything concrete out of him. But what we did achieve was that our organization would not only represent the artisans of El Alto but also those of the provinces. So they will belong to our federation and not to the one in the city that is composed merely of intermediaries. There are fifteen organizations in El Alto. The smallest have forty or fifty, others sixty or a hundred, and some even more, members.

Power, Empowerment, and Participation in the Fiesta System

Both rural and urban Bolivians, particularly of the lower strata, manifest their mutual relationships at fiestas (see H. Buechler 1980). The fiestas include those celebrating rites of passage and celebrations in honor of Catholic saints. The cost of these fiestas is met either by gathering quotas from the prospective participants or through a system of individual sponsorships complemented by gifts given to the sponsors and reciprocated when the giver acts as a sponsor. Individuals take pride in volunteering to participate in costume dances, to sponsor or cosponsor dance groups, or to act as *prestes* (overall sponsors) of fiestas in honor of particular saints. At the same time, they are often under considerable pressure to do so. This pressure is exerted both by individuals in their social network and place of employment and by the organized groups they belong to--their rural communities of origin; urban associations; and producer, market and factory unions.

As we saw in Chapter 3, migrants participate actively in the fiestas in their communities of origin. In part, this is a reflection of the continued importance of ties with members of the home community and with fellow migrants from the same locality. In part, it is the result of pressure brought to bear on migrants to validate continued access to land by acting as fiesta sponsors. In addition, active participation in such fiestas secures a clientele for costume makers, tailors, seamstresses and other individuals producing for and selling goods at fiestas. For example, the participation of Sebastián, a migrant from Compi, as a *cabeza* (dance group sponsor) at the Fiesta of San Pedro, the patron saint of his home community, for five consecutive years led him to obtain lucrative contracts to make suits for the fiesta's mixed migrant/nonmigrant dance groups. Similarly, the costume makers who originally migrated from Achacachi regularly dance in the town's major fiesta. Since the fiesta is widely attended by people from elsewhere in the area, the costume makers can thereby advertise new costume styles and dances and attract potential customers.

Attendance and participation in rural fiestas is not limited to those held in the community of origin. In addition to actively organizing dance groups, mask makers, dance-shoe producers, and other specialists associated with the production of items for fiestas all accept invitations to attend or participate actively in rural fiestas all over the altiplano. They even participate in the recently instituted large-scale festival at the pilgrimage center of Urcupiña, near Cochabamba. At these fiestas, they can capitalize on the acclaim of dance groups who are well received and who are their own clients. For the costume makers, who generally rent rather than sell their costumes, attendance at fiestas also makes it possible to keep an eye on the dancers to prevent excessive damage to their costumes. Perhaps in order to have someone at hand who can do repairs on the spot, dance groups even contract with the artisans who have made their tin masks and rattles to attend the rural fiestas.

In La Paz, both migrants and nonmigrants participate in fiestas held in the honor of private images of particular saints, patron saints of markets and of specific occupations, and patron saints of neighborhoods. They also dance in two large fiestas--Gran Poder and carnival--that have moved beyond local and institutional boundaries.

Fiestas in the honor of private saints are predominantly urban phenomena. A person initiates the process by sponsoring a fiesta for an image he or she inherited or acquired in some other way. He/she then passes on the image, and the obligation to sponsor the fiesta, to a person who has volunteered to sponsor (or has been pressured into sponsoring) the fiesta the following year. Often, *prestes* have already been named for that following year, in which case an image of the Christ child replaces that of the saint proper for the second prospective sponsor. In this type of fiesta, there are no dance groups. The sponsorship consists of a mass and a party or a series of parties where specified kinds of drinks and foods are served and where the sponsors for the following years are named. The acting *preste* pins a colored ribbon on the incoming one: pink, if the new sponsor is taking over the charge from the owner of the image; tricolored like the Bolivian flag in subsequent transfers; and blue if the image is returning to its owner. The next day, the incoming *preste*, marked this time with a white ribbon, gives a smaller party when he picks up the saint and sets it up in a place of honor in his home.

In order to give an idea of the range of sponsors, let us examine three fiestas attended by a meat vendor, Lucía. Lucía attended a number of fiestas in La Paz in order to pay back her debt to individuals who had given her gifts of beer when she cosponsored a dance group of migrants in Compi, her mother's community of origin. During a single week in July 1981, she honored three *prestes* by attending and contributing to the fiestas they sponsored, all of whom were sponsoring fiestas for private images of saints that rotate among kin, friends and neighbors. One of the *prestes* Lucía honored was a restaurant owner and her husband, a man from Oruro, who owns a bus. Their fiesta was particularly sumptuous, with a brass band brought specially from Oruro, a table laden with dried fruit, cake, and *salteñas* (a meat and vegetable turnover); a lunch, consisting of a hot fricassee in lieu of the more usual cold cuts; and, of course, the traditional *picante* in the evening. But Lucía's brother lamented the impersonality of the mass for Saint James. "This religion is no good. It used to be that each *preste* had a separate mass [in the Church of Saint Francis, one of the largest in the city]. Now they herd [the *prestes*] in there like cattle." In fact, on that occasion, seven *prestes* and their followings attended the same mass. Another large group was already waiting its turn. The incoming *preste*, for the fiesta Lucia was attending, was the owner of the image and was the sponsors' landlord.

The *preste* of the second fiesta Lucía attended was a black coca merchant from Coripata, a friend of the family, who had danced in the fiesta in Compi where Lucia cosponsored a dance group and had given Lucía a gift of a case of beer. Most of his guests were fellow Yungueños.

The *preste* of the third fiesta was a lawyer specializing in property matters. Lucía and all the market women from her street had been invited because the *preste* and his wife had promoted the widening of the street, thereby enabling the meat vendors to erect their stalls. Some of the other guests were lawyers who were well known in the neighborhood, while others worked in the Ministry of the Interior.

The image of Saint James, in whose honor this third fiesta was being celebrated, belonged to the *preste's* wife. During a funeral some years earlier, she had pledged to assume the sponsorship of a fiesta and had challenged her friends and kinsmen to follow suit. Her younger sister had volunteered, and so a new cycle of fiestas had been born, increasing in importance as the years passed. When there were no longer any volunteers and the fiesta was in danger of extinction, the woman's husband initiated a new round by assuming the charge once more (thus, the current fiesta) and convincing a close friend to succeed him. This *preste* designate, a man who had worked in several garment factories and had begun to independently manufacture sweat shirts, had recently run into financial difficulties. As a result of competition from contraband goods from Taiwan, he and his wife were forced to close the family operation and switch to selling contraband goods themselves. At the time we interviewed them, they were also secretly manufacturing fireworks. Lucía believed that the couple would be able to honor their pledge the following year despite their uncertain economic situation. If they did not have the necessary cash they could simply nominate a number of cosponsors—*madrinas* and *padrinos*—one for the rental of the fiesta hall, another for the orchestra, a third for the cake, a fourth for party hats, and so on. The couple might then have to pay only for the meals and drinks up front. If we follow the same reasoning, although the total expenses of the *preste* of the first fiesta Lucía had attended amounted to some $b. 50,000 (US $2,000), the *preste* may have spent only some $b. 30,000 of her own money. Of course, she would eventually have to reciprocate for the gifts she received, but she could do that over several years. Some guests brought inexpensive gifts. Lucía took a case of beer worth $b. 370 (US $14.80) and firecrackers worth $b. 20 (US $-.80) to each of the three fiestas.

Small-scale producers also participate in fiestas organized by producers' and market unions. As we saw earlier, some of the major activities of unions are ceremonial in nature. The unions celebrate the day of the patron saint of their trade with soccer matches and fiesta sponsorships. The former have both recreational and display functions. For example, at a meeting of the jewelers' union of El Alto, one of the major items on the agenda was the organization of a championship *fulbito* match. With teams composed of artisans from all over La Paz, such championships play an important role in these organizations. In this case, the National Federation of Goldsmiths (to which the El Alto jewelers' union belongs) was sponsoring the two-day soccer championship in honor of the patron saint of the jewelers, Saint Michael. In fact, there were far more jewelers who played on the teams than came to the meetings, and some did not even belong to any union at all. Soon the discussion at the meeting centered on the team uniform. The members proudly confirmed their choice, made at an earlier meeting, of yellow and white, representing gold and silver, as their color combination. The uniforms had to be new because, according to one informant, "It is ugly to represent the association with worn shirts. If we have a strengthened, more inspired team, they will be able to do something for us and most of all for the association." In marked contrast with the reluctance displayed for volunteering to accompany the president to the town hall on official business, it was easy for the assembly to find volunteers who would sponsor the shirts, shorts and socks to be worn by the players during the championship games.

Often, the union leaders are obligated to sponsor fiestas as well, providing the financing themselves or collecting quotas from the membership. For example, the furniture union celebrates the fiesta of Saint Joseph with a *presterío* (a fiesta sponsored by an individual) and soccer matches among the six different specialties, from chair makers to closet makers. Union members are drafted into sponsorship roles. The pressure is particularly effective among union members who sell their wares on the same street; each must take her/his turn in acting as a sponsor. In order to make sure that sponsors designate do not shirk their duties, they are given a little flag (sometimes baked into a cake) and are handed the figure of the Christ child, and the statue of Saint Joseph is placed upon their heads, during the festivities in the preceding year. Nevertheless, sometimes a producer/vendor can postpone or even bypass the onerous charge. Although Victor, a carpenter who manufactures chairs was scheduled to assume the charge of cosponsoring the Fiesta of Saint Joseph on March 19, 1983, his daughter hoped that her father would be able to bypass the obligation. Had he not suffered enough when the market was established? At that time, he had to bribe the police with money and food to let him sell chairs in that block, and he had to bear the ire of the neighbors who threw water at him. Let those sponsor the fiesta for whom he had paved the way!

Some unions participate in neighborhood fiestas rather than holding their own separate fiestas. The most elaborate and onerous sponsorships are those of the dance-costume producers who, as we saw in Chapter 9, play a prominent role in the Fiesta of Gran Poder. Indeed, they are largely responsible for the recent expansion of what was once a neighborhood fiesta into a citywide event (see Albó and Preiswerk 1986). All of the 150 members of their union are obligated to dance in the fiesta at a cost of at least $b. 12,000 (US $300) per person.

The Fiesta of Gran Poder has been celebrated for over sixty years and has long enjoyed the status of being one of the most important neighborhood fiestas in La Paz in which fifteen or more dance groups have participated.[5] However, in the 1970s the fiesta grew rapidly (our

Costume makers dancing the *morenada* in the *entrada* of the Fiesta of Gran Poder

informants claimed the growth was a result of a ban on celebrating
Carnival), and by 1984, 58 dance groups with some 10,000 direct
participants (including organizers and musicians) took part in the
recently introduced *entrada*, a parade reaching from the neighborhood
of Gran Poder to the Prado, in the center of the city. Groups of
neighbors from the barrio of Gran Poder and from neighboring barrios
make up the core of some of these dance groups. Others are made up
of migrants from particular localities—groups that often also dance in
the fiestas of their communities of origin. Among these are dance
groups formed by migrants from larger villages and towns, of which
the artisan town of Achacachi figures most prominently. Of more
recent origin are dance groups formed by migrants from rural areas
and even by residents of rural communities. In addition, there are
groups composed of professional or semiprofessional artisans and
groups with no discernible geographic or occupational core at all, such
as groups of students and even of elite, often politically prominent,
Paceños.

Most salient of all are the groups whose core, i.e., its organizers,
is constituted by individuals exercising a particular occupation, a
phenomenon that has characterized the fiesta ever since its inception,
"when the first two dance groups were a *diablada* of the costume
makers [which has continued to this day] and a *morenada* of the
stevedores. In 1984, occupation was the main organizational criterion
of at least ten dance groups" (Albó and Preiswerk 1986:79, our
translation). No fewer than four of these groups were associated with
the production of dance costumes. Indeed, 38% of the organizers of
dance groups were artisans associated with production for fiestas and
an additional 16% were other types of artisans, a proportion that is
much higher than their representation as ordinary dancers (10% and
4%, respectively) (Albó and Preiswerk 1986:91). Interviews with 95
direct participants revealed that the largest proportion (32% of the men
and 24% of the women) were artisans, predominantly those involved
in the production of clothing (Albó and Preiswerk 1986:88).

An experienced 62-year-old costume embroiderer and dancer, Pablo
Quisbert, summarized the relationship between fiesta, devotion and
business as follows:

> If we don't dance, there are no shoemakers, hatmakers, carpenters, master
> masons, nor any business for the beer factory, nothing. Everything would
> go bankrupt. Even the barbers. For the fiesta we fix up everything. Let's
> take this dirty, ugly room of mine: If I have a fiesta, I have to fix it up a
> bit. I buy things, I have things ironed, I go to the barber. . . . So it get
> things going. Shoes too: "This shoe is ugly"; so I have to ask the shoema-
> ker to make new ones. The same thing for a suit. Then the market: We
> buy potatoes and meat. We contract a cook, a waiter; we give them work
> for four days or three days. So the cash flows, we live. If there are no
> fiestas, good bye. There is no income. That's how it is." (Albó and
> Preiswerk 1986:131, our translation)

Pablo Quisbert could have added automobile bodyshops to his roster of businesses who benefit from fiestas. One of our informants who works in a bodyshop told us he is busiest during the dry season, when most rural fiestas take place:

> At the beginning of the year, most of my work consists of spot painting. Most respraying takes place for Carnival, when the vehicles are blessed [*challa*], for Christmas, and finally for Saints' fiestas, for example, for the fifth of August[1] to go to Copacabana. For that they want to have their vehicles in good shape.

By sponsoring major dance groups, some producers have been able to substantially reduce competition. This became apparent from our interviews with producers who were less well connected with the participants in the Fiesta of Gran Poder. As Sebastián, the tailor who originally migrated from a rural community, put it:

> Many tailors who are capitalists are themselves involved with a dance group. They are also organizers, and so they receive the orders to make suits for the group. As a result, those of us who do not have a lot of capital are without work.[2]

Even if Sebastián had amassed the financial means to act as a major sponsor of a La Paz dance group, he might not have had the necessary social backing. Costume making is heavily dominated by migrants from Achacachi. As a migrant from Compi, a community specialized in selling onions, Sebastián was at a distinct disadvantage.

A severe economic crisis can have disastrous effects on anyone whose business is affected by fiestas. As we noted in Chapters 1 and 2, people often must cut back substantially on expenditures for fiestas during periods of economic decline. In 1981, Sebastián, the tailor, was desperate about the lack of orders. He was paying the rent for his workshop from his savings and was afraid that he would have to close within months if business did not pick up. He was giving credit to his customers in order to have any business at all. Nonetheless, he still felt committed to act as a sponsor in the fiesta in his home community, although he would have to borrow the money for it.

We conclude our description of the involvement of small-scale producers in fiestas with an account of Federico Gutierrez's "ritual career." Federico, a tinsmith, does not remember the fiestas his parents sponsored. But his older siblings assure him that they were sumptuous indeed. Among them were fiestas in honor of the images they owned. These circulated to other devotees in the neighborhood. But when his father was getting older, he decided to redeem them for his children by holding three or four successive fiestas in their honor, returning them to their chapel in the house and then not allowing them to be the object of *presteríos* any longer.

All of us inherited images of saints from [my parents]. I received the 60 to 70 centimeter high statue of Saint Nicholas, the patron saint of the bakers. My younger sister got the figures of the Christ child with Joseph and Mary and a host of both locally made and imported toy animals and other small objects. This *nacimiento* (crêche) was beautiful. It filled half a room when it was set up [for Christmas]. My other brother received Our Lord of the Word until for some reason my uncle, my mother's brother, took it along with him to Iquile near Cochabamba. My other sister got a San Antonio and my sister Lola, a large image of the Holy Family. My mother had, in turn, inherited them from her parents, who were bakers too. All these saints were displayed in a small chapel, some two-by-three meters in size. People from the entire neighborhood would come to say a prayer or light a candle there.

Carnival was another festive occasion. Five to ten friends and/or neighbors would get together, decide on a costume, rent a truck for a float and a band. On Friday, dance halls were free, so that people could [go to different ones in order to] decide where they wanted to dance on Sunday. On Saturday, the dance groups would visit the houses of *padrinos*, or cosponsors they had chosen for the occasion, and receive food and drinks. On Sunday, a parade took place and prizes were given to the best floats or dance groups. On Monday, the group might nominate a *madrina* for a private party, and on Tuesday, *Paceños* blessed their homes, workshops, and vehicles and went off to a picnic near the cemetery or again visited sponsors. Wednesday was another day for picnics and for throwing water and flour at passersby [a Latin custom on Ash Wednesday]. Finally, on Friday after mass, groups of relatives would gather and go for an outing on foot to Obrajes, where they spent the day eating, drinking and dancing to the sound of a guitar or harmonica.

As we shall see in the next chapter, Federico's mother traveled to rural communities to barter bread for produce. Federico relates that family members often accompanied her, for she usually timed the trips to coincide with fiestas:

Often we went to these towns when there was a fiesta. We loved to go because there were special foods and hot chocolate for the children. There was nothing nicer than to sit on a long bench with a friend or a neighbor whom we met during fiestas. We would meet cousins--sometimes as many as eight or ten. We would arrive in Indian file and take all the sweets we wanted, sometimes entire basins full. We would be given food separately by the waiters, and we would shout or sing "down with the flag of the old sponsor," "death to the old *preste,* long live the new *preste.*" We did this when the next year's *preste* wooed us to accompany her during the fiesta the following year. It was an honor to accompany her. It wasn't like today when sponsors prefer fewer persons in attendance [in order not to have to spend so much]. Today [material] wealth reigns, while then, it was considered an honor [to have served as a sponsor]. My parents became *prestes* in 1925, in Copacabana. After my father's death, my mother no longer sponsored major fiestas. Her friends recognized the fact that as a widow she could be called upon to sponsor a mass but no longer a *presterío.* As you know, a couple must undertake such a sponsorship here.

When his daughter was one year old, Federico pledged to dance in the fiesta in Laja, on December 8 and 9, for three years. This was an expensive proposition, since in addition to renting a costume and paying for transportation, he had to contribute to the cost of wining and dining the musicians. Ten years later, when he came back from Chile, he represented the *preste*³ for the following year at the same fiesta, and when the latter backed out of the sponsorship of the dance group, he felt obligated to act in his stead. After all, the outgoing *preste* was a childhood friend and his older daughter's godfather. He had sponsored her first haircut, was the godfather of a new kitchen range Federico had purchased and had acted as *padrino* when Federico's brother-in-law graduated from school. On a number of occasions, he had provided Federico with work. In addition, "It was a question of honor. They gave us a gold medal that the son of one of the dancers had donated." Federico went on to describe the obligations of fiesta sponsors:

> During the fiesta, a dance group sponsor has to provide food and drink for the dancers, the musicians and invited guests. Dancing goes on for four or five days. One has to serve breakfast, lunch and dinner to all these people, who may also bring their wives and children. After mass, on the day of the fiesta proper, you have to host all the guests. Of course, people bring *aros*, or gifts, but one can't count on it. The quotas collected from the dancers were really only enough for the Napoleon-type hats worn for the *llamerada* [a dance representing llama herders]. In order to save, we even made some of them ourselves, with a sewing machine we had brought along from La Paz. The money wasn't even enough to pay for the brass band.
>
> It was an incredible fiesta! Some of the dance groups came to give us gifts and then accompany the Baby Jesus. Mr. Guido collaborated by paying the brass band to play during an entire day, and some came with crates of beer, but there still wasn't enough to go around. After mass, we had to serve beer and cocktails [cane alcohol mixed with fruit juice] as well as *salteñas*. We used up barrels of *chicha* [maize beer]. Everything disappeared. Sometimes we would surreptitiously request the dance group leaders to ask their dancers and musicians to move on to the house of a *padrino*. There wasn't enough room in the large patio to move around. Miraculously, there was enough food and drink after all. On the last day, the day of the servants, there was no food any longer. We had to lie to the servants, and say that we had had to give back the cooking utensils already. At least the *preste* of the village sent us some cake. On one day, when the food vendors acted as sponsors, they congratulated me. They said they had never seen as many people at the fiesta.

Even though Federico was assisted by a number of *padrinos* as well as by his predecessor, he was forced to spend the family's entire savings on the fiesta. He was unable to say how much the fiesta had cost at the time, but he figured that it would have cost some $b. 30,000 or well over US $1,000 in 1981. Rita found it difficult even to get back her sewing machine, because the owner of the place where the fiesta was held said that Federico owed him money for rent. At first, he wanted the gold medallion as a guarantee, but then he relented. To make matters worse, the family no longer had access to rent-free lodgings because Federico's father-in-law had evicted them when he learned that he was planning to sponsor the fiesta. That December, just after the fiesta, he was unable to work, because he had to attend numerous fiestas to reciprocate the gifts of beer given to him by friends. In addition, he had to reimburse the store for 6 cases of empty bottles that had disappeared. "During that time, my friends would serve me alcohol rather than give me money." For Christmas, he did not even have enough money to buy a cup of tea for his daughters. As we shall see in the next chapter, his marriage almost broke up because of his sponsorship.

After Federico, no one took on the sponsorship of the dance group. Federico had given the medal to one of the group's principal founders, who "owns two or three large houses, a large bus and two minibuses and a Volkswagen," but because he knew what had happened to Federico, he refused the sponsorship and could not find anyone else to do it. So, the dance group was disbanded ten to fifteen years after it was founded. Federico has been dancing in a *morenada* instead, while another of the dancers has become *preste* in Copacabana.

Long-term financial ruin is not a necessary consequence of fiesta sponsorship. Federico's predecessor, a man whose work has ranged from repairing vehicles in a mine to raising rabbits and auditing accounts, returned to Bolivia all the way from the United States, where both he and his brother had migrated, so that he could sponsor a mass.

Notes

1. The director was originally from a rural community, the silversmith village of Umala. Her husband, who knew English and designed jewelry, met an exporter of handicrafts in Umala and began producing silver objects for her. When he died in 1969, his wife moved with her children to La Paz and continued producing silver objects for the exporter. It was the exporter who later suggested her for the position of museum director.

2. Among the courses that have been given in the department of La Paz are courses on fruit trees; animal feed; cashiering, plumbing; plan interpretation; machinery assembly, operation and repair; carpentry; mechanics; mechanical drawing; soldering and welding; electricity; polyethylene; lathe operating; and automotive electricity.

3. After the fall of General García Meza, control over such activities was considerably relaxed.

4. Such a census had indeed been undertaken by the organization but both the results and the questionnaires had been lost.

5. The account that follows, except where otherwise indicated, is based on Albó and Preiswerk (1986), particularly Chapter 4.

6. On that day, the Fiesta of the Virgin of Copacabana, owners have their vehicles blessed by the priest after the street procession and mass in the pilgrimage center of Copacabana.

7. Perhaps such leverage is crucial only during times of severe crisis, because Sebastian did receive contracts from large dance groups for the Fiesta of Gran Poder in previous years.

8. Federico calls the sponsorship of all aspects of a large dance group *"preste."* The usual term is *cabeza*, while the term *preste* is reserved for sponsors who invite all dance groups at a fiesta to food and drinks and are not associated with any particular one. In this case, however, Federico also had to invite the other dance group for food and drinks, not just the one in which he participated.

11

The Family History of
an Artisan Couple

In order to give a better idea of the interplay of the multiple strands in the lives of small-scale producers, we will present a detailed family history of the tinsmith we encountered at the end of the preceding chapter, his seamstress wife and two daughters.

Federico Gutierrez

Childhood Memories

This is a history of my life. I was born on March 3, 1933. My parents were Bernardo Gutierrez Varela and Doña Rita Velazco de Gutierrez. But my father died in September 1935 and my mother on March 21, 1945, my father's birthday.

My life was rather sad and melancholic, for I don't even remember my father. He died when I was two. I do remember my mother. I used to accompany her to fiestas. As the years passed, while I was going to school, she became used to being a widow. She had to work very hard because we were so many. The oldest of my siblings was Pastor, the second Elvira, the third Jaime, who is still alive, then came I, and the youngest is Leticia. Only three of us are left. Before this, two [others] died whom I never got to know.

Time passed. My mother died, and my older brother became the head of the family. Then I had an accident with my left leg.

I remember that my mother took us to fiestas, because she was a baker. She inherited a bakery in the Calle Catacora from her parents. They had made the house larger, and I remember that even the president of the republic, who was a *compadre* of my parents, came to visit. He would come, and they would drink for days [and] there was no end to the dishes. They had a variety of ingredients from *picante*, *saici* [a hot dish with minced meat], tortillas, *ranga* [a spicy beef stomach stew], to potatoes: some eight to ten different things. During those fiestas some friends would stay for several days in the house because [my parents] owned the house and it was large. They lived the way people used to live in the olden days: They had no tenants. I myself never had to clean my shoes or iron a shirt. Servants did that.

We had three servants working in the bakery. Some called my mother, "Mother," but, in fact, they were never legally adopted. One of them, a woman named Manuela, is still alive. Now she has a store in the Calle Illampu, where she sells suckling pig, and she is well respected. She would grind the cheese for a flat bread named *llaucha*. At the time, there were many varieties of this bread: some with onions, others with hot peppers [*ullupica*]. Then there was the man who put the bread in the oven and took it out again. He became my parents' *compadre*. He was well known because he was the first man to sell pastries in the street. My parents also had a large number of vendors selling these *llauchas*. People used to eat them after fiestas to get rid of their hangover. Life was good when my parents were alive. But as they say in Bolivia: "When the parents die, not even the dogs look at you." Everybody is against you.

My parents had good relations with the elders in their neighborhood. When their brothers and in-laws came, they shared food. Beer was cheap. My parents were frequently called upon to sponsor fiestas.

So we learned a number of things helping my mother. Especially for All Saints' Day, November 1, we would have to work hard. Beginning a month in advance, we would make the customary bread dolls and horses [see H. Buechler 1980] and all sorts of sweet breads. Now when I try the things they make for Holy Week, I am disappointed. They are not half as good. Sometimes I feel like opening a snack bar and experimenting with old-style *llauchas*.

Nowadays, youths have only their own personal interest in mind. But at that time, things were different. The parents fulfilled their obligations towards their children, and we in turn were always respectful towards our parents. If they told us to make breakfast, we had the obligation to obey. Later, those of us who still had the strength would go off to play, but generally most of us were so tired that we would go right off to sleep [after a long night's work]. However, my older brother would get out his books and study while we were sleeping.

Customers came to our bakery from as far away as [the altiplano towns of] Tiahuanaco and Guaqui. We would barter the bread for cheese and eggs that we used in the bakery. In those days, barter was common in the countryside. We would go to a place called Moco Moco [some ten hours by truck from La Paz], and we would take matches and sweets along and exchange them for red-pepper seeds, potatoes and *chuño* [freeze-dried potatoes]. We would go with what was left over from All Saints'. The first time, we were invited to go there by a *padrino* who had haciendas there. A few years before my mother died, we also went to Copacabana for a vacation and to barter. We stayed with kinsmen: my mother's cousins, *comadres* and *compadres.*

Mr. Gutierrez played with other kids in the streets, including all sorts of people who later had important positions. He laments having lost contact with them later in life. He participated several times in the annual or semiannual race for homemade carts that went from La Paz to Obrajes, an institution that was still flourishing in the 1970s. He went on outings to Obrajes and Calacoto and hiked with a Boy Scout troop down to the temperate valley of Rio Abajo. The best time to go there was during Holy Week, when the fruit were ripe and the hacienda owners were away in the city. As the saying went, "On Good Friday and Good Saturday God was dead and could not see what was going on; stealing was therefore not considered to be a sin."

Later, he and the other members of the soccer teams from his barrio were invited to play soccer all over the altiplano, in nearby valleys and even in Cochabamba. Everywhere they would be given food and drink. Federico played soccer on teams since he was seven and has continued to this day. He figures that he must have played on at least thirty different teams, in Chile as well as in his home country. As children, they would play for anything they had around: T-shirts, a cake, even the bun they had received for breakfast in the boarding school. He is proud of the trophies his fulbito (mini soccer) teams have won. Most recently, he has played in the annual championships for the handicapped, and his team has won three years in a row.

Even the accident he had at the age of twelve, which left him permanently disabled, did not stop his involvement in the sport; he could still play as a goalkeeper, albeit only in the minor leagues:

I had the accident in 1945 and hurt my knee. My mother was having it treated, and then my older brother continued. *(However, due to medical negligence, the leg became stiff.)* I remember that on July 21, 1946, at 11:30 in the morning, my brother came to the hospital and brought me sweets and some medicine. That was the last time I saw him, because then the revolution broke out and he never came home. This brother, who was like a father to me, died during the revolution of July 21, 1946, when [President Gualberto] Villaroel was killed. It was a savage revolution, the likes Bolivia had never seen before. Even the history books say that it was barbarous. In the hospital, I saw many persons who had been shot to death.

Soccer has also furthered Mr. Gutierrez's business. Recently, I have been playing with the chicken farmers of Pampajasi. They give me money for the fare or pick me up themselves. I got to know them through my work. I make feeding troughs for them. We are still friends. I also sometimes meet chicken farmers from the Yungas at the matches. They have some sort of cooperative. They talk among themselves, and so, sometimes people come to place orders whom I have never met before. That's why I play with the chicken farmers. One could say that I went to get a piece of the action (*les sacaba una tajada para obtener trabajo).*

In addition to baking, Mr. Gutierrez learned other skills that became important in his adult life. At that time, we stored the cheese for the *llauchas* in a kind of cooler with water. A cousin, called Pablo, would come and help. We called him *"loquito,"* "the crazy one," because he knew everything. He was skilled in everything from baking to blacksmith work and welding. I learned some of his secrets, a few of which could still come in handy today. For example, one could make a kerosene stove with three burners. It's all physics. But if I tried to sell them, someone would steal the idea away. That's why we poor people have no way of demonstrating that we are intelligent. Otherwise, we could patent our ideas, and people would buy them. I once made an ashtray that one could put in one's pocket, with a place for matches on one side and a container for the ashes on the other. But someone came along and said that the idea was his, and from that day on, I no longer wanted to show anyone my inventions.

Mr. Gutierrez was able to practice his metalworking skills as early as in primary school: I entered the Mendez Arcos school [a boarding school for orphans] after my leg healed. I enrolled in third grade because I liked to study--even in the hospital. We all tried to be at the head of our class because those who were in first, second and third place had the privilege of being able to play with the director himself. I was even allowed to enter his room. The other kids were envious and called me an apple polisher. The director's wife was a teacher, and she would also invite me up for fruit or soft drinks. Sometimes I would help her sweep the floor or solder something, because even as a small child I soldered small jugs and pots. At that time [the school] only had workshops for tailoring, shoe-making, nursing, carpentry, bookbinding and cooking. Since they didn't have one for tinsmithery, I had to find some way to make do with what I had at home. But then the director told me that since there were so many jugs that needed fixing, he would set up a room for me. So I would repair their jugs, and all they had to do was buy the materials and some equipment. That way, I was able to earn something. People would ask me if I could do this or that and I would answer yes. . . .

Formal Education

When we entered the sixth grade, the director told us to choose a profession. We could either go on to the [technical school] Pedro Domingo Murillo or the Colegio Bolivar. At the end of the year, the director would recommend the best pupils. Private enterprises would also ask for people. I decided to work in the Ultima Hora [the publisher of an evening newspaper], where I ended up working for three years before I got married. First, they gave us very little, but then they paid us full wages. During that time, I also went to the trade school Pedro Domingo Murillo [in the evening]. I took courses in tinsmithery, but I soon got tired of it because they didn't teach me anything that I didn't already know. So I told my brother that I wanted to leave, and I did. At this point I also left the orphanage to live with my siblings.

Then, I studied to be a commercial secretary for two or three years. Although one of my girlfriends was head of a secretarial pool and wanted to give me a job, I soon saw that this type of work didn't suit me. It represented a different way of life. I liked working with metal pieces, dirty things. For me the office was something [too] clean-- something for ladies. At this point, I went to work for Ultima Hora. I worked at the printing press. At night, I took classes in the Sucre School until the fourth year [of high school] but it was difficult to work and study at the same time. I was now financially independent from my siblings: I had my clothes made, paid for my food like any adult. . . . Eventually I became a typesetter. Finally, I had to leave because I hurt my leg once more while playing soccer, and the doctor advised me not to lift heavy weights. They paid me my indemnity for the years I had worked there, and I had some suits made and bought things for the home.

Informal Learning

Let me tell you how I learned [tinsmithery] from my brother when I was five or six years old. This brother, the one who died in 1946, was a pharmaceutical chemist. He would have received his pharmacist's degree just a month after he died, and he was already working in a laboratory. He taught me the basics of metalwork when he came back from the Chaco War. He had had some experience because my father was a blacksmith and had a workshop. At first, he assisted my father and later became a full-fledged master craftsman.

A German blacksmith who was forced to return to his country when World War I broke out sold Mr. Gutierrez's father all of his equipment, which the family purchased with the money the mother had saved and a small inheritance she had received from her parents. The workshop was located in what is now the Calle Mercado, in the center of town. Later, the family moved to the Calle Oruro and, finally, to a street in the tourist district.

Well, during the Chaco War my brother had seen how some of the more educated soldiers made a good living and so, when he returned, [he began studying pharmacy,] studying in night school and then at the university. He continued even after my father died and he had to head the family.

I remember that in 1940 or 1942 I already handled metal rods and made fences by making points at one end, like one sharpens a pencil, drilling holes and riveting the pieces together. There was also another kinsman working [in the family's workshop]; I think that he was a cousin of some sort.[1] He was older than my brother and more skilled. I learned even more from him than I did from my brother. In those days, welding was unknown. We joined the metal with an acetylene torch. We did it on the forge with the iron red-hot. Or we had to splice the pieces and hammer them until they were permanently joined. I learned how to cut metal, how to use the press just by observing the others, and I learned how to pedal a drill that was so large that I had to hold on to it while I pedaled.

The years passed. I called my brother "Father" because I had never known my real father. He would give me coins from time to time, and I was grateful. Ultimately, he no longer had time for the forge. He left our kinsman Pablo in charge. Pablo came to us with his younger brother Pedro, who was also still learning although he was older than I. Pablo was the master, and I was the assistant to the assistant. I helped both of them. I would also have to go and buy charcoal. Nowadays, people would be ashamed of going to the dirty courtyards where the charcoal was sold. At that time, no one was ashamed to go there in patched clothing. Then, I had my accident; and later, my brother Pastor died while I was in the hospital.

I made things even in the hospital. I amused myself making all sorts of toys. I was bored because no one took care of us. And after Pastor's death, my other siblings came to see me only occasionally. The people who had been wounded during the revolution received all the attention. All sorts of people came to visit them, even from abroad. It happened that the wife of [the assassinated] President Villaroel came to visit, and I was able to give her some little boats powered by rubber bands that I had made. Some Dutch volunteers gave us milk and bread, taught us lessons and provided us with tin cans we could use to make toys as gifts and for sale. I would adapt designs for cardboard toys from magazines. Sometimes we would also make dolls out of plywood. . . .

When I left the school for secretaries, I continued to learn from Pablo. By that time, he had set up his own workshop at home. He had also learned the art of making fireworks. He would travel to the Yungas valleys for the fiestas, and I would assist him.

Pablo had an enormous number of quality tools: as many as eight to twelve pliers of the same type but of different sizes. But then he had a serious accident. He lost his eyesight in an explosion in his workshop [and he could no longer work]. Slowly, he had to sell his tools in order to subsist, and his mother took advantage of him and sold or gave away many of them too. Pedro, his younger brother, took over [but by then there were few tools left]. Pedro continued with metal work and tinsmithery. He had, as the saying goes, fourteen professions. If he didn't have work as a mechanic, he would do carpentry. He knew radioelectronics, car repair--a kilo of skills, as they say. And slowly he built up his own workshop. He had all sorts of ideas about how to do fireworks. I used to read the Argentinean magazine *Los Hobbies*, and I would get all sorts of ideas for firework designs from the illustrations. Since I was still small, it was Pedro who would often create them. I would [also] accompany him to [fiestas in] Viacha, Escoma and other places, where people used to applaud our work. We made special things: One firework would go off and then another. We even found a way to ignite them electrically from a distance, and people would be amazed that no one was nearby when they would go off. We had the *preste* [sponsor] himself set them off with a special control.

Making fireworks was challenging and dangerous. The sulfur, chlorate and carbon compounds purchased in pharmacies had to be ground gently so that the vibrations wouldn't cause them to explode. Whistling rockets were made out of beryllium. Pedro and Federico invented elaborate scaffolds out of cane with whirling wheels powered by rockets and with the names of the prestes written in fire. Some of the displays had live doves flying out of cages made out of wool that disintegrated when the fireworks ignited them. They even made robots, cars, trains, boats, and bicycles with riders, all propelled by rockets. Some of the figures were made out of painted, molded sheet metal and could be reused. They adapted ideas from Mexican films and from magazines and invented some of their own.

The danger was constant. Careless smoking, inept handling of the fireworks by a worker under the influence of liquor, or even a spark from other fireworks set off nearby could maim and kill the pyrotechnic. Federico gave up this line of work as soon as he married, and now he makes only hot air balloons. He taught his nephews how to make them too. But he has never taught them the art of making fireworks, first because of the dangers involved and second because he feels that they have been ungrateful and don't deserve to learn this trade. So he just tells them that he doesn't know how to do these things.

As for Pedro: I helped him for some ten years until I got married and had to find my own way of earning a living. He had a sad end. He had a bad wife who drank and made a drunkard out of him as well.[2] Sometimes, I would have to give him some money for liquor, because when he didn't have his alcohol his lips began to tremble. He died four or five years ago. His children have learned foundry, mechanics and forging too, and one of them became a tailor. They didn't go to school much. They had to earn a living early. Apparently, they too are drinking.

Mr. Gutierrez started to become involved with tinsmithery on a full-time basis after his stint working for the newspaper: When things didn't turn out, I would go and ask Pedro, and he would tell me how to do them. Sometimes we would share the work and the profits. He taught me everything about making and installing roof gutters. . . . Then I returned with more experience from Chile. I studied hard to become a plumber and purchased a lot of books on the topic. Most plumbers just stop learning when they know how to do things more or less well. But I perfected myself in the art. You can take me to any construction site and I will know what to do. I think of myself as a master craftsman because I know everything there is to know and can carry it out too. For example, I made and installed a ventilation system for a tannery. Usually, it takes a technician to do this kind of thing, but I have become a technician myself. They now address me as "technician" rather than as "master craftsman." Of course, there are many things like motors and radios that I repair on occasion but only when it is essential.

The Role of Formal Training

Mr. Gutierrez attaches a great deal of importance to the formal education he has acquired, although that he has always felt short-changed in this respect in comparison to his brothers. After the death of his pharmacist brother, he and his other brother cast lots to determine who would be allowed to study. Federico lost, so the available support went to his younger brother. The latter was attending a seminary to become a priest, but when the oldest brother died, he entered the university and studied humanities. At the same time, he became a topographer.[3]

In contrast, Federico went to grade school, then took night classes in a technical school and received training as a secretary. He also took courses in plumbing in Chile. He is nevertheless proud of his education and considers himself a formally trained técnico and not merely a empírico, or self-taught individual. Thus, he prides himself for knowing how to calculate the surfaces of the complex geometrical figures involved in making tin objects, plumbing and other activities. He is proud of his sobriquet "ingeniero en latas," or "tin can engineer."

However, Federico's experiences with formal education programs were not always positive. He confessed that he gave up going to the technical school because they did not teach well, and he simply did not wish to become a secretary, both because he likes working with his hands and because he considers secretarial work to be women's work (una oficina era limpio para señoritas). As we shall see later, his wife made special arrangements when they were in Chile so that she could complete two crash courses in hairdressing and dressmaking in a six-month period. She could have gotten a scholarship to study haute couture in Paris, but she decided against doing so for financial (and probably family) reasons.

Social-Network Influences on Learning a Trade

The history of the Gutierrez family shows the importance of the family in determining occupations in the next generation. All of the siblings, including the two sisters, learned technical trades that are in some way related to the father's blacksmith shop or the second cousin's fireworks business. The latter influence demonstrates the importance of more distant kin in a person's career. Federico's interest in the tinsmith trade was also related to his mother's tin-article business, which she ran in addition to supervising the blacksmith shop. At the time, tinsmithery was considered a female activity. Federico's principal trade was thus a female trade. Even the pharmacist brother's interest in chemistry may have been related to tinsmithery, since he used his formal training to make better fireworks. Entrepreneurial skills and skills in the baking and restaurant trades were also imparted by Federico's mother.

Other informal inputs in Federico's repertoire of skills include those of foreigners, such as the European for whom Federico's father worked and from whom he learned metalworking techniques and, indirectly, the "Japanese and German" fireworks specialists from whom his kinsmen learned their trade.

Mrs. Gutierrez, Federico's Wife

Her Parents

My father was a carpenter. We were eight siblings. I was the only daughter from that marriage. My mother was the daughter of the administrator of a museum in Potosí. . . . She went to a private school run by nuns. When she was sixteen, she was raped by a foreigner who owned a store. Her parents had the man deported. Before he left, he gave my mother enough money to buy a house, so that when the baby was born she would have something to live in. At the time the little girl was born, my mother got to know a thirty-year-old widower with a child he had from another woman. He had come to Potosí to forget his sorrow. When he asked for my mother's hand in marriage, her parents refused because his family was *de pollera*. "He must be the devil who has come to bother us," they said. So my mother eloped with my father. He adopted her daughter. They had 18 children, but only 8 are still alive, if one includes my mother's illegitimate daughter. My father worked as a carpenter, and my mother didn't do anything except embroider, sew and take care of the household. Then he had to go to the Chaco War, where he made camp cots for the soldiers. During that time, my mother crocheted clothing for miners' families. When my father returned, they moved to Tarija where [most of us] were born.

In Tarija, my father first worked as a carpenter, but he was earning very little because it is a small city. Then, one day he went to see a movie with my mother and my brothers. After the movie, they went to a restaurant for a cup of coffee and something to eat. The owner

told him: "Here we don't serve coffee or food; we only serve drinks."
My father felt offended and told my mother: "No one humiliates me.
I will show this man who I am." My mother was afraid that he would
hit the man. But he told her: "No, I don't fight with anyone. I will
show him how one can earn money." From that day on my father
couldn't sleep in peace. He was thinking and thinking how to earn
money. He made a counter, some five tables and [a lot of chairs] and
he opened a restaurant right across the street from the place where the
man had refused to serve him. He put up a large sign, "**WE SERVE
TEA, COFFEE AND CHOCOLATE AT ALL HOURS.**" In the evening,
he would turn the sign around [to show the words on the back:] "**WE
SERVE DINNER, BEEFSTEAK, FILET.**" He told my mother, "You can
serve in the evenings until midnight, and afterwards I will serve
liquor." Lots of people came, and my father earned a lot of money.

My parents returned to Potosí in 1946 because of my sister. She
had married and was living there with her husband, who was working
in the company store of the Pallaviri mine. She ran a store and taught
in the school. She wrote my parents, "Come to Potosí, I am doing well
here."

*The family stayed in Potosí--where Mrs. Gutierrez's father opened another
restaurant--for only two years. At the same time, Mrs. Gutierrez's father
wanted to get back into carpentry because he had turned into an alcoholic
working in the bar. He was already suffering from delirium tremens and
hallucinations. Since carpenters, particularly fine cabinet makers, were in
greater demand in La Paz than in Potosí, the family moved once more.*

*In La Paz, Mrs. Gutierrez attended a public school. She was a naive child.
She recalls that twice she was given goods by her friends only to discover that
they had been stolen. Her mother didn't like her to talk to people for fear that
she would get into trouble. So she played mostly at home with her brothers.*

Mrs. Gutierrez enjoyed a particularly close relationship with her father:
My father was a very responsible, hard-working, loving, charitable
man. He was a man who should not have married. He was born to
be a priest. He wasn't the way we are. Hatred was unknown to him.
He never quarreled with anybody. During my entire childhood, I don't
remember him ever shouting at my mother. He never hit her, never.
He was very good, very loving. Maybe that's why he is never far from
my mind. I remember him every day. The best thing I inherited from
my father is the fact that I am charitable towards fellow human beings.
My mother was good too, but she scolded a lot. Perhaps it was
because her mother was an egoist. My daughters are also the way I
am, and I am like my father was. When someone came to the house
and asked for shelter, he would tell him to come in. And yet, no one
took advantage of him. No one stole from him.

Mrs. Gutierrez's Siblings

Mrs. Gutierrez has eight siblings and half-siblings: two half-sisters and six brothers. In addition, her mother raised her oldest daughter's illegitimate child as her own. All except Mrs. Gutierrez herself have had at least a high school education and, in the case of her brothers, a higher education as well. One of her half-sisters finished high school. She left Tarija and her own illegitimate child when she married and her husband obtained a job in the company store of a mine near Potosí. She opened a grocery store and, at the same time, taught in the school there. When her husband decided to move to La Paz, they sold her grocery store, and her husband promptly absconded with the money. Ashamed to tell her parents, she made a meager living working for a printer in La Paz. When her parents finally learned about her predicament, she was able to persuade them to move to La Paz too. Much to the consternation of her father, she then met a tailor and lived with him for many years, raising his children from a previous marriage and sewing pants in his tailor shop. However, she learned that the tailor was also supporting another woman. Once, she fought with this woman cut her in the face, so she fled to a mining town. The tailor followed her, and they lived there for eight years. By that time, the other woman had left La Paz; so they returned to the city. But, after a while, she got tired of the children's constant demands and she urged Mrs. Gutierrez to leave for Chile with her. Again, the tailor followed her, and she agreed to live with him once more after he promised to marry her. They continue to live in Chile, while the children all managed to obtain a higher education in La Paz on their own.   Similarly,   Mrs. Gutierrez's brothers all succeeded in becoming educated. Her father had lost most of his money when the family moved to La Paz, and he was hospitalized for half a year after receiving a blow to his head when trying to stop a brawl in a bar, so the family had to start anew. The eldest brother, Freddy, finished high school and then studied at the university while working in a textile factory during the night as well as assisting his father with carpentry.

At the time, my father was laying parquet floors for an *ingeniero*. My father kept my brother [Freddy] well dressed, and when the *ingeniero* saw my brother, he told him: "Listen *fifi* [dandy] who are you? Why have you come here?" "I am the carpenter's son," answered my brother. Then the *ingeniero* looked my brother up and down and said: "We don't want any *fifis* here. We want workers." So my brother took his suit off and began wearing overalls. But whenever the *ingeniero* saw my brother, he continued to taunt him: "You are very *fifi*. You really think that you are somebody, don't you?" My brother would rail against our people: "In this country, we can never become anyone. People will always try to put us down. They will always try to humiliate us because our father is a worker. They will never allow us to occupy the place in society that we have merited. So I will leave this country." He was studying engineering at the university, and when he went to Chile he continued studying engineering there while working in a factory at night.

After he finished his studies, he opened a small factory, hiring an older woman--who later became his common-law wife--as his administrator. At first, they made the transparent corners used to mount photos in albums, but they soon branched into a wide array of products, including glues and reinforcement rings for perforated paper--all products that the two of them produced with manual equipment in two small rooms. Finally, after five or six years, they graduated to products requiring more sophisticated machinery, such as floor polish, tempera colors and plasticine. Freddy improvised the first of these machines. For example, he adapted a dough-mixing machine so that it could be used for making plasticine by changing the beater to a specially made one with more blades, and he took an ancient, ordinary sewing machine and adapted the foot so that it would stamp out rounds of watercolor paints. There were setbacks, however. When he began to make floor polishes, a competitor set his factory ablaze. As he didn't have any insurance, he had to start again from scratch. But he succeeded once more and is now the owner of a large plastics factory, where he makes a wide variety of containers and toys out of various types of recycled plastic.

Two other brothers joined him in Santiago and opened factories of their own. They make products that do not compete with one another. One of the brothers is also a traveling salesman, selling his brothers' products as well as those of others. They all lend one another money.

The family also has its share of black sheep. One is the good-for-nothing brother who attempted to secure wealth by making a pact with the devil, only to have an abnormal child. He "earned" a living by defrauding his associates by means of a variety of nefarious business deals but then studied to become a quality controller for industrial products. Among other ventures, he attempted to launch a variety of industries in Bolivia, but he was thwarted by his own lack of expertise and by larger companies that jealously guarded the sale of the goods he was attempting to manufacture. He ultimately settled down in Chile to produce machine parts on a lathe. Then, there is a brother who joined the Hare Krishnas and is manufacturing ritual paraphernalia for them, and finally, there is the brother who is an alcoholic and who has taken every opportunity to steal from the family, including a suitcase full of jewels from his dying mother and part of the inheritance of his impoverished sister, Mrs. Gutierrez. The latter, then, had plenty of role models but, as we shall see, little opportunity to advance as far as her successful brothers had.

Mrs. Gutierrez's Formal and Informal Education

I finished primary school and then went on to secondary school. But after a year and a half, my mother didn't want me to continue. "Why did I want to study," she asked. It was enough for a woman to know how to read and write. I was always very meek. I never rebelled against my mother. She said to me: "You cannot go to school because you don't have shoes." So I didn't go. My mother always favored the boys. My brothers never had to do without copy books, books, clothing or anything, but I was treated like a servant--poorly clothed. She wanted me to help in the household. I would have liked to continue. It's important to know something. If one doesn't have a good educational base, one can't make a good match. [If you don't have a good education] anybody can convince you that something they want you to do is a marvelous idea, even if it actually leads you to financial ruin. That's what I think, and that's why I want my daughters to study.

I washed, cooked and ironed at home. But I liked to sew ever since I was a small child. I learned how to sew because of a lie. I was in second grade in high school, and my father had a dress with bell sleeves made for me. When my friends told me how pretty it was, I told them that my mother had made it for me. "Oh, tell your mother to make me one too. I want one just like it!" they said. But my mother did not know how to sew. The seamstress had made it. Then they brought material to our house, and my mother told me, "Why did they bring this? I don't know how to sew. Go and tell them that you lied. I have no idea how to make this dress."

I was afraid to tell my friends that I had lied. "What am I going to do?" I asked myself. "Now everyone in school will say that I am a liar." I felt that being called a liar was a terrible sin. So I told them: "My mother told me to tell you to leave the material and she will sew the dress for you." Then I took my dress apart, placed the pieces on the table and cut the cloth in the same way, and I sewed the dress with my mother's manual sewing machine. It came out almost exactly like mine. When my friend paid me and I saw that I had actually earned some money, I wanted to earn more. That's how I decided to learn how to sew.

When my sister returned from Camiri, I told her about the dress and she put me in a school where they taught sewing. I went there for only a year. My mother didn't want me to go any longer because they asked us to buy material, thread, scissors, and other things, and my mother told me that she didn't have the money. So I only learned some sewing. I was making a few dresses, but they weren't well made. I helped my mother at home and made dresses for people in the neighborhood. But I was always anxious, even though they came out well. I gave my mother some of what I earned and kept some for material to make dresses for myself. That was the time when I got to know my husband.

Courtship

Enculturation into social roles took place early.

Federico: Since we had a large living room [as children], my siblings and I would sometimes organize a [pretend] fiesta. Sometimes, we would baptize dolls because that would attract attention. When people would ask us where we were going we would say, "To a baptism." This is how children learned how to baptize a child. Children were timid in those days; they were not as forward as they are now. . . . I would invite five kids and so would my brother and sisters. Some 30, all in all. They would bring gifts [like in a real fiesta]. Before going home, someone else would promise to give a fiesta. . . . Sometimes the president or organizer of a soccer team would also invite boys and girls for a dance in the soccer field after a match. [Then there were the spring fiestas in the honor of a beauty queen.] For these a group of people would rent a dance hall.

We got to know girls in a number of ways. Some were introduced by friends. Or, if one saw a girl on the street, one would ask if one could accompany her. But one had to be circumspect, not like today when a boy kisses a girl the moment he gets to know her. One had to behave as well as possible so that the girl wouldn't be frightened or annoyed. When I visited my wife at her home, I would sit facing her with her father next to her. We could only talk about our studies. . . . We would also get to know each other at the fiestas.

Federico and Rita got to know one another when she was looking for a place to hold a fiesta. As she recalls it: They were planning a class fiesta, and since I had never gone to one, I was afraid to ask my mother whether I could go. So my friends told me: "Why don't you find a place near your house with a large room where we can dance?" My husband lived just two blocks away. I was friends with his sister. When I told her, "They are planning a fiesta in my grade," she said, "I will lend you my house, but you will have to ask my brother." So I went to see her brother and told him: "I heard that you have a house with a room that you rent out for fiestas." He answered: "We don't rent it out, but you can use it if you like." I didn't tell my mother that I was going to a fiesta. She would have hit me. She didn't like this kind of thing. I told her that I was going to copy my homework.

In my husband's house, there was a niche with a virgin with large earrings. My husband's sister had agreed to act as a fiesta sponsor and had taken the image home. . . . The fiesta ended at six-thirty, but I left at five because I was afraid of my mother. The next day, the sister told me: "You know something? One of you must have stolen the earrings of the virgin." I said that I hadn't done it, I had come home early, but would ask in my class. "Well," she said, "you will have to pay for them because you asked my brother for the room." I cried, for I knew that my mother would kill me. My friends said: "The miserable old thief, she must be lying." So I went to my husband's shop, and he told me: "Don't cry. If the earrings really got lost, I will pay for them."

The fact was that my husband was already grown up. I was just a girl. I am five years younger than he is. But when he saw me in the street, he would follow me and ask me if he could accompany me. Since [I thought I had to] pay for the earrings, I listened to him. I told myself that if I didn't talk to him, they might tell my mother. . . . If it hadn't been for that, I would never have talked to him. Only later, when we were already married, I found out that it had all been a lie. The virgin had never had those golden earrings. So I married because of my husband's sister. I had talked to him only because I was afraid. That's why I tell my daughters to tell me everything. I don't want them to be afraid of me, as I was brought up to be of my mother. Perhaps my mother guessed what had happened. When I told her that I wanted to marry Federico, she sent me to Chile so I wouldn't marry him.

Federico claims that he was popular with girls and was frequently invited to parties. For a number of years, he went out with a young woman whom everybody thought he would marry. But since he didn't pay her much attention, she finally married someone else. There were others, but during the day he worked and in the evening he continued his education and studied, so he had little time for them.

I only thought about my studies. This was my opportunity. I asked myself: "If I marry, who will give me that opportunity?" In the evening, after getting out of my classes, I went home and did homework until twelve. In the morning, I had breakfast and went to work. For a while, my older sister made lunch for me, but when she married, her husband objected and so I had to eat in a pension. Since some girls would offer to cook for me, I had to be careful not to fall into a trap. I said to myself that if I married, I would marry a girl with money. I didn't want to suffer all my life. . . .

My first girlfriend didn't think about the future. I felt that she would only act like a servant in the home. I thought that I would have to work hard all my life and perhaps open a store for her and have her sell. She came from a family that sold herbs in the Calle Linares. People would make remarks about her Aymara surname. They would tell me: "If you want to marry, we will introduce you to a girl of your race [*de tu raza*]. It would be a shame if she [the girlfriend] didn't know how to talk and how to deal with us when you invite us." She herself was *de vestido* [i.e., she dressed European style], but she didn't have any social polish. Her mother was *de pollera*, and because they dealt in herbs and things for witchcraft, people told me that it was better not to become involved with such a family.

Rita remained in Chile for three years. She was supposed to study, but according to Federico, she was so lovesick that she couldn't. Her family was dead set against the marriage. "How can you marry a simple workman?" they would ask.

Married Life

During the first years of their marriage, the couple lived in Federico's paternal home, which they shared with his siblings. These early years of marriage were marked by major quarrels between Federico and his siblings. At the same time, he began to drink heavily and to beat his wife when he was drunk.

Federico: Ever since I married, my sisters were envious. I was earning more than they were and I had my profession, even though I was not formally trained in it. I made all sorts of molds [out of metal]. I earned more then than at any other time in my life. So they began to sabotage me by locking me out of my workshop. [They had no legitimate reason for doing so]. I always paid my share of the rent, and if my sister served me some food I always compensated her in one way or another. Her husband would always come and ask me to do this or that for him, and I always did it. But he never reciprocated. They would borrow money to travel to Oruro to sell things, but they never shared the profits. They hit my little daughter, so we had to make a separate kitchen and a high fence so that she wouldn't go out, and [we even had to] lock her up so that her cousins wouldn't hurt her.

One of the reasons for the sisters' hostile behavior may have been that they were jealous of Rita. As Mrs. Gutierrez explains: When [my husband] was a bachelor, he gave his sisters money and other things. He bought clothing for his nephews, everything. But when he married me, he no longer gave them things, and I think that's why they hated me. They seem to have taught him to drink and to beat me. He was terrible. He would come home drunk and take out a knife. When he was not drunk, he was very good. Even today he loses control of himself completely when he is drunk. He would take out a knife and threaten to kill me and my daughters. At the time, my brother told me to leave for Chile with my little three-year-old daughter. My mother also told me: "Go to Chile. You will slowly forget him. He is very mean." But my husband refused to let me go alone. "Let's go together" he said. "I will work there too."

But we suffered there too. My brothers gave him work, but they paid him very little and we couldn't make ends meet. They signed a contract that they would pay him wages and provide food and housing. But as soon as they had signed the contract, they chased us out of their house, and so we no longer had enough to live on. At least he didn't drink any longer--because he didn't have his friends around--but he blamed me for the whole thing. So I inscribed myself in Caritas, and the ladies gave me oil, flour, rolled oats, and wheat every month. The social worker would visit us and saw that we were living in poverty in a small room. We just had one bed, where the three of us slept. And then my other daughter was born, and all four of us slept in the same bed. The social worker would ask me whether I had any relatives in Chile, and I would answer that I didn't because I was ashamed to tell her that I had brothers who were millionaires. Also, if they weren't going to help me anyway, what good would it have done to tell them? So I told my husband: "We can't continue like this. I want to find work. I will go to the Bolivian Club." [The people at the club offered me work.] They told me to come with my two daughters and that I would not lack anything. We made *salteñas* and other Bolivian foods. I earned more than my husband--three times more. He earned 200 Chilean pesos per month and I earned 600, and on top of that they gave us food. I didn't have to buy anything. There was more than enough food. For instance, if we cooked chicken and we couldn't sell everything, the rest couldn't be kept for the next day. So we had food in abundance. And I saved the entire 800 [probably an exaggeration]. My husband would help me on Sundays and evenings too.

Finally my brother found out about it. He had gone to eat at the Club Boliviano and saw that I was cooking there. "How can you go out to work?" he scolded me. I answered that it was no sin to work. Then he went home and told his wife, "I am angry. This man forces my sister to work as a cook." His wife answered him: "Your sister can't do anything else than cook. She doesn't have any professional title. She has no skills. She can be no more than a poor cook." I was really hurt. How could they say things like that? I didn't have a profession because my mother wouldn't let me study. I could have studied at the university. I told myself that I would show them that I could be something and didn't have to remain a poor cook. Perhaps because my pride was hurt, I told my husband that I was going to study. My husband told me: "You won't be able to do it. Here one has to study hard." "No, no," I answered. "I have saved money, and I want to study haute couture and hairdressing."

I got degrees in both. My sister-in-law was left with her mouth open. I had accomplished in one year what normally takes three years. Instead of going once or twice a week, I went every evening. And they gave me a grade of "excellent." When I showed her my titles, I told my sister-in-law: "You spoke disparagingly about me. Well, I didn't have a profession before because my mother made me cook, wash and help in the household for my brothers. That's why my brothers have professions and I don't. I had no one to help me. Now I have a profession, even if it is not an intellectual one. But I do have a blue-collar profession." My sister-in-law didn't say a thing.

Then we returned here [to La Paz] again. And again we suffered. We didn't have anything. Just the suitcases with our clothing. When we came back, I set up my workshop in the Avenida Perú. At that time, my husband had promised he would dance in Laja, and he told me: "Let's go and dance in the fiesta. It will be nice. They will give you clothing to sew, and you can earn something." I accepted because I wanted to earn some money. Then he went and agreed to sponsor the fiesta! He did it for no reason at all. He was drunk. I said: "How can you accept such a large sponsorship?" But he answered: "No, we have to accept it and do what we can." That fiesta costs a lot of money. Of course, the people help, but it still is a lot. We came back Franciscan poor. We had nothing to begin with. We had to sell whatever we had. This man really has done terrible things to me. We suffered a lot and then he drank a lot, hitting me when I accused him [with words like], "Why did you accept it? This is for the rich."

So, one day I escaped to Árica [Chile] with my two daughters and worked for a seamstress. I didn't know anyone there. I chose Árica because it was close. I lived in a place where the women who deal in contraband goods stayed. My oldest daughter went to school, and they gave her lunch, notebooks and pencils. But then my husband called for me through the newspapers and sent the international police after me, and I preferred to return rather than risk being returned to the border by force. [Also I was molested by a man, and I was afraid of the corrupt people.] When I came back, my husband hit me even more. So I escaped once more, this time to my brothers in Santiago. One of my brothers bought a large, well-stocked store and told me: "We will share the profits equally. I will give the capital and you the work." But my youngest daughter cried a lot for her father, and she became ill. The doctor told me: "She misses her father a lot. You must return to your husband." So I had to return here, and things continued as before.

Rita's mother urged her to divorce Federico, but she didn't. She returned to her husband under the condition that she would make the major decisions from then on. She continued working in the shop in the Avenida Perú. At one point—just as his in-laws had done on an earlier occasion—Federico's brother offered the young couple an apartment rent-free. Rita slowly furnished it with secondhand furniture that she bought with her savings; but after some time, they had to move out precipitately and had no place to put their furniture. Then, she managed to purchase a small, four-room house. She said to herself: "At least it will be my own. I will have it enlarged when the time comes."

The Two Daughters

Mrs. Gutierrez: My [older] daughter [Ruth] has studied to be a secretary as well as an accountant with computer skills. She has also studied French at the French Alliance, but she had to leave that because we could no longer pay for her classes. Then she studied automobile mechanics. She has a diploma in that too. In sum, she does all sorts of things. She is bright. I think that, with all that, we are going to do alright.

Ruth: When I was a little girl, there was a lot of fighting going on in our house--drinking, quarreling. All this traumatized me. I felt very bad. Perhaps because he didn't have money or because of all the problems he had in his childhood, my father was a always cantankerous. He was very mean to me. Sometimes he would hit me very hard, even when he was sober. I even tried to commit suicide. I was only able to overcome my hatred of him last year with some psychological help. My mother was both the woman and the man of the house. She worked, took care of us, fed and clothed us. She gave us everything. Not my father! He was very irresponsible with respect to his home.

When I went to school I felt happy, because in the school I found what I did not have at home. My parents separated [for a short time] when I was seven or eight. I didn't miss my father at all because he always brought turmoil. It was a happy time. I was in school; I studied; I was the best student. School was everything for me. I was the president of my class. I was happy, happy, happy in school. My teacher would call my mother in to congratulate her. I had a beautiful experience in school.

Then, in fourth grade, I told my teacher that I was going to jump a grade. My teacher didn't want me to leave. They always placed me on the honors' list every year. [That was] the maximum honor one could get; for, at the time, there were no diplomas for the best pupils. But that year there were diplomas. So that I wouldn't think that I was the best and [so that I] wouldn't leave the school, my teacher did not give me the diploma. She gave it to someone else. I felt terrible. My classmates had told me that she would call me [to the podium] during the *hora cívica* [civic hour]. I shed bitter tears. I ran out and hid in the bathroom. I left the school [anyway] and jumped two grades--from fourth grade to the first grade of high school. I only went to see the teacher I had loved so much once more. I never saw her after that; it had been such a bad blow.

I was always a tomboy. My mother would say, "My daughter is like a boy. She does everything." I took care of my sister. I did all sorts of things that men do: I nailed things, fixed things in the home. I still like to do things like that: nail, hammer, cut, work like a man.

Time passed. I went to night school. I was the youngest in the

school. The others worked. [Many] were already ladies. I couldn't have
skipped two grades in regular school, but since my uncle [father's
brother] had an acquaintance who was the director of the [night]
school, I was able to jump the grade. Apart from this, I was taking
private lessons during the entire vacation. I was happy doing this. The
other girls were much older and often up to all sorts of mischief, and
they would do all sorts of things to me because I was just a little girl-
-still very innocent. They would steal the money for salaries and would
blame me for it. So I investigated who was stealing and found them
out. They were expelled. Perhaps it was my way of getting revenge.
Then I went to a day school and I loved it. I liked my friends, I liked
to play. . . . Then I entered *ciclo medio* [middle school]. I studied hard.
I always wanted to excel. Most of all, I wanted to show my father. He
used to say that he had not had an education because he was an
orphan. And I wanted to show him that it was not essential to have
parents. Because for me, he didn't exist at all. Another thing that made
me angry was that when I came home with a report card with
excellent grades, my father would refuse to sign it. He was envious.
Only my mother would sign it. She would always give me prizes
when I came with my report card; we would go places. She was good,
my mother was. I always had the best experience that one can imagine
with her. And it continues today.

Once I went to a science fair in my school. I won the first prize
and advanced to the interschool competition. Each school sends its
three best students. That was wonderful. A beautiful experience. They
gave me diplomas, everything. My "invention" received the first prize.
First I wanted to make an eraser and that didn't work out. I tried for
a whole month, but something was missing. So then I made Chinese
ink, and it came out fine. I had read books that my mother had. I
liked to invent things like that.

Q: Did your father help you?

No, not really. I don't talk much to him. He continued to hit me.
And when I was fifteen, I left home. I went to live with some cousins
and my uncle, the architect. My uncle finally convinced me to return
home. But after a month or two, things continued the same way. In
the third grade of middle school [*tercero medio*], I rarely was at home.
I couldn't stand the constant criticism. I would return from school, eat
and leave again. And I would return at night. I would go to the
library or visit my friends, and we would study together. I also had
some bad friends but got over that too. Then came the fourth grade,
and I was about to get my high-school diploma [*bachiller*]. In school,
I was quite annoying. I would get all my teachers angry. I always
came up with ideas of how to do mischief, and the others would take
them up. I even succeeded in getting rid of the director of the school.

[Among other things, the director tried to fire good teachers and replace them with her cronies.]

That year, I also went to the science fair. My school won that year, too, with a project that our group did. We presented a project on embryonic development. I gave my father a drawing, and he made a container that looked like a cake form in the shape of a fetus [and had] partitions. If one pushed buttons, different parts lit up. I didn't know anything about electricity, so I shorted my creation several times when I connected the wires. It was brightly painted. Everybody liked it. Then came graduation, and my mother didn't want me to go on the graduation excursion for fear that I would get into some mischief. But my teachers convinced her. How could I not go? I was the class president!

The following year, I wanted to enter the university. I really would have liked to study architecture. I liked everything associated with construction: making things that men do. But that would have been very expensive. So I studied economics instead. But then the university closed. There was nothing that year. I studied accounting at an institute. But I lost a lot of time. In 1981, the university was still closed. Then I studied to become a secretary. After that, following the suggestion of a friend, I went to study at the university, [when it opened again]. Now I am continuing there. In a year and a half I will get my degree in public relations. I am losing my enthusiasm because my father doesn't help me. I felt bad about it.

In December, after classes ended, I traveled to the Chapare [a tropical valley near Cochabamba] and bought a parcel of land with money I had earned selling furniture that I ordered from Santa Cruz. The land was far away, some five hours on foot. I sowed rice. Then, I returned here in January, left again after two weeks and transported truckloads of rice I bought in the villages and [then] resold. I earned well. Then, I came here and took some four dozen watches along [to the Chapare]. It is a place with a lot of money, and people don't get out too frequently. But I only earned enough to pay for the fare. At that time there was a transportation strike, so I took advantage and brought in bread and chickens by taxi. They sold like hotcakes because there was nothing to be had down there. I earned a lot during that month. I paid for the university and I still have some money left over. I no longer ask my father for anything. I would like to finish the semester at the university, then leave, earn some money and start a business. I would like to open a snack shop and a disco like in *Flashdance*. I have some capital but not enough.

I have some furniture arriving soon; that's my capital. I also sell other things. I have a friend in Santa Cruz. Now I am having furniture sent from Cochabamba, where I also have a friend who has a furniture factory. I came to her house quite by accident. I had to get in contact with a particular woman, and her telephone had changed. So I looked up the address and came to the girl's home. I left my knapsack there.

When I still didn't find the house of the friends I was to stay with, the girl's family prepared a bed for me. It turned out that they had a large furniture factory. They became my friends as a result.

The younger daughter wanted to study interior decoration in Chile, where she has been invited to live with her maternal uncles. When we interviewed her in 1984, she was still recovering from a nervous breakdown she suffered after she was sexually assaulted. As we shall see, her experiences with men were much more positive in the following years.

The Gutierrez Household

The Gutierrez family approximates the ideal of the Bolivian cholas and lower middle class de vestidos in which all members of the household allocate labor and earnings to a joint pot from which the senior female, usually the mother, distributes the shares according to the needs of each individual and the collective household. Men are often accused of wasting their wages on drink, women or feasts. As Mrs. Gutierrez tells it:

My husband is a heavy drinker and that has harmed us a lot. . . . He used to earn [well enough], but he never gave us [much]. He gave us [only] a hundred pesos a week because he liked women a lot, the taverns, friends. I have suffered a lot because of him, but I am tolerant. I come from a good family [i.e., decent, moral and conservative]. My mother always said when the husband is bad and has no money, one has to bear it quietly. . . . For a short while [during the economic crisis], when he didn't work, he was fine; but when he is working, he is awful. Now he has no work, and he is meek; he stays at home. Before it was *quite* different.

Since the contribution of husbands to the support of the family is generally regarded as erratic at best, women make sure to guard their own assets. Both Mrs. Gutierrez and her daughters made it clear that they regarded the home as the mother's. She bought it and added on to it with savings from her dressmaking atelier, and she had established the business with money given to her by her mother. Other women also tried to distinguish their own assets, which were often working capital and portable wealth, such as jewelry and clothes. So the women in some ways hold contradictory views. They stress the economic interdependence of family members, but at the same time, they resist gender dependence.

Commitment to the Family

As the passages above indicate, the women in the Gutierrez family (and generally) shared with working-class women elsewhere a commitment to the family as a unit of self-help (Westwood 1985:236,238). However, the commitment of these women to family and kinship is not just about survival but is also about sentiment and subordination. As Westwood writes, "Apart from the ideological push they receive in this direction, it is quite clear that working class women are committed to the family because it is an experience and a space which offers them some degree of autonomy over their lives and the warmth, support and affection from a group of people who matter and who in turn make a woman feel that she is important and valued. It is not that they do not know about the underside of family life or the way that unemployment affects the contributions that members of families can make" (1985: 236). In a similar vein, Sachs writes that "it is important to begin seeing family-kin relations as about love, money, and power simultaneously" (1984:16).

Our own work suggests that we need to look at multiple relations of gender over generations to understand the complex relationship between economic need, attachment and hierarchy. Comparing more than one person's view of a relationship or significant event over time allows one to capture the inconsistencies, ambiguities, and multidimensionality of family and kin relations within patriarchal and capitalist systems. To unravel the dynamics of gender, it is necessary to go beyond the relationships within the nuclear family. Thus, we would misunderstand Mrs. Gutierrez's relation to men if we looked only at her relation to her husband or his relation to her. Her relationship to him is a function of her relationship to her brothers and father, just as her relationship to her daughters reflects her own relationship to her mother.

Mrs. Gutierrez denounces the physical and psychological abuse she (and her daughters) have received from her husband. She attributes some of the abuse to the current economic crisis and some to the fact that her husband was orphaned. She also stresses the differences in their class origin, to his detriment. Her own family once owned land, while his family was based in urban artisanry. These differences lie at the base of some of their conflicts. She relates bitterly how her husband prevented her from attaining her educational goals.

You know, I would have liked to study psychology--to have a profession--social worker or psychologist, in order to orient and help people. I was studying when I married. I could have afforded it, but my husband was very egotistical. He never allowed me to continue. For example, when I had my little girl, my husband threw me out of the house with my 8 month old. He said: "You aren't going to your classes. If you want to go, go with the baby." So I had to go to class with my little one, and the boys helped me hide her under the desk. . . . He never wanted me to achieve more--to be someone. . . . But I tell you, if I could have studied, I would have left my husband!

Mrs. Gutierrez recognizes that such educational differences would have exacerbated the friction between the spouses. He would not have accepted that because he is a man and a husband, and he would want my submission and his dominance. . . . We would have separated years ago. But since I'm not educated, I have adapted to his ways, his capricious ways. . . . I think my husband realizes this, and that is why he didn't want me to study; but that is also why I want my daughters to be more than I, that they become professionals. My mission was to be a good wife and mother, but I want my daughters to be otherwise. That is the way I think at times, but at other times I say to my daughter: "We all have some advantages and some disadvantages, and God rewards all." The one way he has rewarded me is through my daughters, who perhaps will do better than I.

Depending on the context, Mrs. Gutierrez blames herself, her husband, mother, or brother for her present circumstances. She acknowledges that she married her husband on a stubborn whim. She blames her mother for not allowing her to study. And she feels that her brother did not really want her to come to Chile when her parents sent her there. I went to Chile, but I longed for him [my husband], and so I returned and married him and I had my little girl. . . . But afterwards I often regretted my marriage. *She has, indeed, been close to despair more than once.*

Mrs. Gutierrez's mother was inconsistent in her advice to her daughter. She tried to prevent the marriage; then once her daughter was married, she counseled patience. But on the occasion when Mrs. Gutierrez was severely beaten, her mother urged her to leave her husband. The mother's reaction to her daughter's troubles reflects her own marital history. She had also suffered from familial disapproval and from the her husband's bouts of drinking. His alcoholism became so severe that he had to give up the running of a successful bar and return to the less lucrative occupation of carpentry.

However, Mrs. Gutierrez remembers her father with a great deal of unalloyed affection. During her childhood, he seems to have favored her over her six brothers. Later, although he had some doubts about doing so, he tried to mediate between his daughter and son-in-law. Once, when the latter threatened to commit suicide, the father urged his daughter to return to her husband. He has also tried to be supportive in other ways. He came to their financial aid--by giving them the down payment for their first home.

The relationship between Mrs. Gutierrez's family and her husband has also been wrought with more serious conflict. One of the most severe rifts came during and after her husband's sponsorship of the Fiesta of the Virgin of Laja (see Chapter 10). This sponsorship is considered the most expensive and prestigious for the urban lower and middle class. Mrs. Gutierrez and her family, who are not involved in the same civil-religious hierarchy as Mr. Gutierrez, were appalled at the expense associated with this sponsorship for food, drink, costumes and decorations. Individuals, including even many of Federico's kin, who regard themselves as solidly middle class and who do not depend on personal ties with lower-class individuals for a living, regard the fiesta system merely as an economic drain and not as a means to demonstrate superior social status and consolidate a network of personal connections. The recent trend for migrants from rural areas to assume major sponsorships in what are regarded as urban fiestas[4] has contributed to the view of involvement in the fiesta system as declassé by some old-time Paceños who would have supported it a generation earlier.

Sponsoring the fiesta left the family "Franciscan" poor, according to Mrs. Gutierrez. It also led to a bout of alcohol-related violence. Her husband threw her out of the house, whereupon she left for Arica with the children. On another similar occasion, she went to Santiago, Chile. Both times, her brothers rescued her financially and emotionally. The first time, her younger brother avenged the unsolicited attentions of a male stranger by going to Arica and setting the man's house on fire. The second time, her older brother provided her with shelter and work in Santiago. Yet Mrs. Gutierrez decided to go back to her husband once again, even when she had the option of marrying a widowed engineer with two houses, a car and a good salary.

As the life history shows, the pressures she felt to leave the marriage were countered by pressures to return: Her husband both threw her out of the house and sought energetically for her return. He once refused to let her go to Chile alone and insisted on accompanying her. Another time, he sent the police out after her; and a third time, he put psychological pressure on her father to intervene. According to his account, he told her father that if she wanted a divorce, so be it. But he, the husband, did not want to see his wife cry and his daughters hate their grandfather for destroying the family by encouraging a divorce.

Mr. Gutierrez thinks of himself as a skilled, hardworking, self-made man who has not enjoyed many opportunities. According to him, workers do not have much of a chance in Bolivia. He feels that he has always had to be on guard against potentially unscrupulous relatives who would deny him his just rewards. Drink, for him, is an escape from the injuries of class and family.

From his description of his youth, it is quite clear that he always intended to marry a woman with some money. Such a marriage would help him out of his economic straits. He speaks with considerable pride about his wife's accomplishments. He relates how her two Chilean degrees, in dressmaking and hairdressing, enhanced their status in the eyes of her snobbish relations. He seems to feel genuine regret that his wife could not take advantage of a chance to study haute couture in Paris. He also bemoans the fact that he alone among his siblings was unable to continue his education because of his mother's untimely death. Further, he claims that his wife is as free as he to come and go as she pleases. He acknowledges that she controls the family's finances.

The daughters' relationships to men are flawed by violence and tempered by support. They both express hatred for their father, who they claim ignored them and beat them. The father seems unaware of his daughters' pain and anger. He considers himself a strict father, and he is particularly concerned about his daughters' freedom of movement. But he claims to be willing to listen to explanations about "misdemeanors."

The older daughter has been able to establish good relationships with male colleagues and with male relatives on her mother's side. She seemed to get along very well with her male boss, who appreciated her knowledge and efficiency. In 1984, although she admitted to quarreling with her new student-husband because their lack of resources forced them to continue to live apart, she fully expected the relationship to continue. However, by 1988, the couple was divorced, and Ruth's mother was helping to take care of Ruth's small daughter. She seemed fond of and grateful to her uncles--her mother's brothers--in Chile, who sent her textbooks and who have asked her to transfer to the Catholic University in Chile, where they would pay her fees.

Until she met and married her husband, the younger daughter's relationships with men were much less fortunate. First she suffered at her father's hand, and then she was raped by a stranger. But she seems to have recovered sufficiently from those horrible experiences and, in 1988, was happily married.

In this case, we see that the women in the family, in the generations of the grandmother, mother and daughters, were subjected to sexual violence by males who also controlled their labor power. In all three generations, they were able to circumscribe or curb male power by leaving the men in question for the shelter of other kin, male and female; by maintaining control over their own inherited or earned resources; by appropriating their children; and by reaffirming in words and actions the importance of family ties to economic and personal/social survival.

Exercising a Profession: Federico Gutierrez

Federico manufactures a wide array of products. His mainstay have long been molds of various types and sizes for popsicles and other foods. He makes feeders for chicken farmers, roof gutters, stove hoods for restaurants, and ventilation systems for small industries. He has made signs out of bronze for a bank and larger ones out of corrugated metal for import firms, as well as bird cages, metal crucifixes, Viking helmets for theater productions, a large bottle out of sheet metal for a beer brewery, and masks for dance groups. Frequently he prepares all sorts of toys that are sold during the Alasita fair. In 1981, for example, he was planning to prepare miniature chicken feeders. He also considers himself an accomplished plumber and has worked in this capacity in both small and large jobs. And he has engaged in foundry work. Sidelines include shoemaking and tailoring.

Mr. Gutierrez generally works alone, although his nephews and his older daughter have helped him when he has required assistance installing bulky ventilation systems. At his workshop, which is in his home, he works by himself, occasionally calling his wife or a daughter to hold something for him. His daughter says her lack of involvement in his work has more to do with the way he treats her than with any lack of aptitude on her part.

Federico has had constant problems with clients who have failed to pay him. For example, dance group members would give their leaders rings to pass on to him as a guarantee of payment for his services in making costume accessories for them. But he often found that some of the rings were worthless and that the dance group leaders had absconded with most of the rest. The end result would be that he would often receive little or nothing for a major contract.

Mr. Gutierrez is very touchy about his social position: One bad thing around here is the fact that people are generally not trained, and so those of us who do have titles are not recognized. They treat us all the same. Some do recognize differences in speech between lower- and middle-class people. For example, they will tell a servant to bring me food on a tray: "Take this out to the *maestro* who is working in the patio." And I have to find some place to eat my meal. They tell me: "No, not here; go in the back there." They think that you are an animal. They may send you to a smelly place. Here they treat workers like lepers. [There are exceptions.] In one neighborhood I worked for someone who addressed me [politely]: "Excuse me, please be seated at our dining-room table." And she and her husband and their children sat down too, and I took my cap off in order not to get things dirty. But she was [one of] the only persons who served me the way one should: without humiliation. During my entire career, there were [only] some six persons who treated me like that. What does it cost to offer a chair and say: "*Maestrito*, serve yourself" and not to deal with us like servants?

A major problem for Federico is finding a suitable outlet for his products. Until the early 1980s, he continued to sell tin objects in the family store tended by his nephews, who sold weavings in an adjacent shop. The latter also took orders. However, he had constant disputes with his nephews. They would forget to notify him about an order for gutters until it was too late to fill it on time, or they would fail to properly record the measurements of a ventilation system.

He sometimes thinks of opening his own store, but it is difficult and risky to borrow money. He is afraid of using the house as collateral for a loan because the lenders might appraise it at much less than its real value, and if something happened to the store they would lose the house as well. He had the following to say about his experiences in trying to borrow money to develop an idea:

They [the lenders] require you to present your invention in the presence of a lawyer or an accountant. Then they tell you to come the next day or the following day or in a week, and when they finally return it, they have rejected your request. However, they have already copied your idea. . . . That's why the workers die with their ideas, while others die as alcoholics because they were not given any opportunities in life.

The fear of being taken advantage of permeates Mr. Gutierrez's entire narrative. Thus, speaking about his plans for making innovative miniatures for the competition at the annual fair of Alasita, he said: The problem is that you make marvelous things, and if they would at least compensate you for your work it would be fine. But the first prize is only 5,000 pesos. But if you figure the time you have invested and the fact that the city hall keeps what you have made [it's not worth your while]. You go out with a friend, and you drink the money up.

Similarly, he finds that clients have no compunctions about forcing a craftsman to waste time on a project by failing to be at home at an agreed-upon meeting time. Since artisans are not paid by the hour, they suffer from such a lack of consideration: People don't want the poor to prosper; instead, they try to humiliate them. Someday I am going to rise from my misery, even if I am already an old man.

The Importance of Multiple Occupations

Irrespective of their formal or informal origin, the acquisition of what may appear as an inordinate number of skills is, in fact, a rational response to present circumstances in Bolivia. As we argued in Chapter 3, due to the uncertain economic conditions, artisans cannot necessarily expect to work in the same occupation during their entire lives. They must be prepared to exercise a number of trades consecutively, simultaneously or both.

Mr. Gutierrez has engaged in nine different types of work: printing, baking, tailoring, shoemaking, fireworks manufacturing, working in a plasticine factory, plumbing, acting as an assistant to a topographer, and tinsmithery. Similarly, the relative who taught Federico many of his skills was well versed in everything from making fireworks to radio electronics, carpentry, forging metal, to automobile repair and truck driving. Technical skills enabled Federico's pharmacist brother to finance his studies, while his chemist's training was put to good use in the manufacture of fireworks. Finally, Rita exercised her hairdressing skills for a short while but then concentrated on sewing, which could be done at home. And her sister-in-law learned occupations ranging from nursing to radio electronics.

One of the few strategies that may make it possible to accumulate some savings is to practice multiple occupations concurrently. Thus, because the salary Mr. Gutierrez earned in Chile was insufficient to allow the couple to save for any kind of major purchase, they began to make salteñas *in their free time. The extra income enabled them to improve their standard of living and allowed Federico to buy some equipment and consumer goods to take back to Bolivia. Multiple skills are also important because of the seasonal nature of many artisan activities. Adobe construction and hence the demand for metal*

gutters are limited to the dry season. The demand for items for fiestas, such
as metal masks, depends on the ritual calendar as does the manufacture of
miniatures for the annual Alasita fair.

In some ways, Mr. Gutierrez was more fortunate than other artisans. He
never had to share the lot of the informally employed worker who could be
fired at will without compensation. When he was forced to leave his work as
a typesetter because of his leg injury, he received an indemnity of one month's
salary for every year he had worked there, and in his job in Chile, job security
was no issue. Workers from poorer families often live more precarious lives.
But, Mr. Gutierrez's livelihood was not always assured when he was an
independent producer. He depended on the goodwill of his siblings to permit
him to work and do business in the family store, and when his business
prospered they humiliated him by locking the shop door so he could not work,
which was one of the reasons why he finally decided to leave for Chile.

Social Networks and the
Exercise of an Artisan Trade

Mr. Gutierrez's career demonstrates the importance of kin ties and social
networks in general in the exercise of a trade. The history of his interaction
with kin also shows that such ties often have major drawbacks but may be the
only viable alternative in a situation or at least may present a reasonable
option.

Just as they had been influential with respect to his learning various skills,
Mr. Gutierrez's siblings and parents-in-law had a major influence on the way
he exercised those skills. At various times, they provided lodgings, work space
and work. Mr. Gutierrez worked in the family shop as a tinsmith and
metalworker, he worked in his brother-in-law's factory in Chile, he was
employed by his engineer brother in construction, and he sold his wares
through his nephews in the centrally located, erstwhile family store. These
nephews also took special orders from customers for him. Members of the
extended family provided one another with a variety of services. Rita made the
wedding gown for Federico's nephew's bride and the dresses for her sisters.
Federico has installed bathroom fixtures in his siblings' homes, while his sister
repairs his radios. Finally, his brother furnished the land for the construction
of his home.

The extent of the cooperation of the family members could lead one to
believe that interpersonal relationships in Mr. Gutierrez's extended family are
generally harmonious. However, this is in fact far from true. During the
initial interview and in the first two hours of our second interview with him,
Federico painted a positive image of his siblings. But this was followed by
increasingly bitter attacks. His brother's magnanimity in providing free
lodgings was offset by his exploitation of Federico on the job, which took the
form of late payment of his wages, some of which are still outstanding after
many years. Indeed, Federico's request to his brother for construction materials
was an attempt to extract at least part of the outstanding debt. A loan he
made to his brother was repaid in devalued currency, and perhaps because the

brother was ashamed of Federico's lowly economic status, he treated him on the job like any ordinary worker rather than like a brother. Also, the brother failed to offer Federico meals when he worked for him, although he did offer meals to some of his other clients.

Similar occurrences took place in Chile. There his brother-in-law not only failed to honor his work contract but also took advantage of him in an arrangement they had for making Christmas ornaments. Their agreement was for the brother-in-law to contribute the materials and he the labor and for the profit to be shared equally, but the brother-in-law ultimately cleared at least three times as much as he did. The following year, he made the ornaments on his own and had his wife sell them.

His kin also treat him with condescension. To this day, he has not been invited into his brother's home. Sometimes he would take his older daughter along to help him in his brother's workshop, and she would ask: "Why does he treat you like his other workers? He doesn't treat you like a brother." And he would mumble something about there being no need to talk at work. But she was not fooled.

Mr. Gutierrez's relationship with his older sister soured when in a fit of envy she refused to let him use the family shop. Also, there were inheritance squabbles and tensions with the nephews, whom Federico regards as irresponsible. He feels they earn a high commission without contributing much work.

At present Mr. Gutierrez prefers not to ask his siblings for any favors, particularly monetary support, and his daughters refuse any gifts of money from their paternal uncle. In contrast, one of his daughters was planning to go to Chile to study computing and was likely to live with her maternal kin there.

Exercising a Profession: Rita Gutierrez

When I came back [from Chile with my husband] I had a small room in the Avenida Perú that my father rented for me through an *anticrético* arrangement[1] for 3,000 pesos. I had my bed there, a small table, a chair and a sewing machine that my father bought me.

Of course, I couldn't charge much--some 20,000, 10,000, for a dress. I had a lot of work though. People would bring me wedding dresses to make, and I would charge 50,000. I didn't spend everything. Some of it I put in a bank. [Later when we had the apartment in Miraflores] I no longer lived in the same location where I worked. I had a sign [that said] "SEAMSTRESS" and "GUARANTEED WORK" on the door, and wealthy people came. Some of them were doctors. I made a wedding gown for one of them.

I have always worked alone. I have always disliked paying others; I wanted to earn everything myself. That's why I never had a cook, servant or laundrywoman. I wanted to keep as much as possible. In addition, my husband didn't give us much money. He measured out everything he gave us, and so I wanted to have enough for food, to dress my daughters and to put away. I said to myself that I would be without money if I hired help. Also, I figured that if I hired a seamstress, I might be tempted to pay her very little, and someday she might complain about me. I didn't have the heart to cheat. I see no point in exploiting people--having someone work hard and earn little. No, I would want her to earn the same as I. Also, [in dressmaking] sometimes there is work and sometimes not. . . . Some weeks I sewed eight outfits, others three. But, the thing that gave me the most satisfaction was that all my customers were pleased. No one ever complained. . . . They always said, "Oh, how pretty." I was never disappointed with my own work. I always felt happy. I earned well as a seamstress. The clients were wealthy and liked to dress well, so they didn't mind paying.

When I was little, I had no friends; but when I established my atelier I began to enjoy friendships. They [the clients] always told me their problems. I don't know why they confided in me. We talked as I sewed. I didn't feel tired or anything. I suffer a bit now. I don't go out much; I don't talk to people in the neighborhood; I am stuck inside cooking, washing and ironing. . . . I would like to return to work, but I have a cataract that I would like to have operated. Then I would like to open some kind of store--a grocery, textile or book store that might be less demanding. When one has one's own workshop, one has to be very responsible and always finish on time. . . .

Unlike her husband, who has difficulties collecting his fees from his customers, Mrs. Gutierrez thought of herself as lucky in that regard. In my work, no one tried to take advantage of me. In fact, they often gave me more for having finished on time. For Christmas, they brought me wine, presents, telephoned me and wished me well. I was happy in my atelier. I felt secure. When I saw something in a store window, I would say, "Oh, how pretty!" and I would buy it. Now that thought doesn't even cross my mind--I don't even have enough for food. Before, there was enough for everything. . . .

For cholas and lower middle-class de vestidos, central to the meaning of work are pride in work skillfully accomplished, economic independence and the satisfaction of supportive female relationships. Rita and the others working in textiles, metal, leather, printing, and food were conscious that they were engaged in dignified labor, producing items of quality, which required a great deal of dexterity, attention and artistic talent. The emphasis on skill reflects the resistance to "de-skilling" that capital uses to control labor. Working alone without supervision develops independence and responsibility. Such work was essential to their emotional and financial well-being. The case history supports Westwood's suggestion that women's work culture may be seen as a "resistant and creative attempt to overcome the stultifying aspects of capitalist labor process," but as we also found, this "creativity has bound itself securely to an oppressive version of womanhood" (1985:6).

The Forms of Work:
"We Are Now into Everything"

As many others have noted, the boundaries between women's work in the home for the family and their paid or unpaid work "outside" the home for capitalism are often blurred (Glazer 1983; Beneria 1982; Sachs and Remy 1984; Westwood 1985). The women in the nineteenth and early twentieth century working-class families described by Sachs (1984), just like those we interviewed in Bolivia, often combined waged work, homework and miscellaneous entrepreneurial activities, such as the taking in of boarders and the provision of laundry and food for others. The multiplication of tasks in both eras and settings was particularly true for periods of economic depression. The case history illustrates how waged work and other activities were combined in one family. Mrs. Gutierrez regards the earnings from dressmaking and rents as part of the household resources, which also include the gains from her husband's tinsmithery and repair shop, the wages and other contributions of the daughters, and charity.

In the mid-1980s, when dressmaking and tinsmithing declined by 85% because no one could afford new clothes or hardware and when her eyesight deteriorated, Mrs. Gutierrez, with the aid of her daughters, constructed an addition to her house, which she later rented out to "hippie tourists." She said that renting rooms "saved us." The hippies, who came to Bolivia as tourists, sold jewelry on the streets and did not want to spend much money on anything. They don't want to go out to eat. . . . So I put in a kitchen with plates and pans and everything. *They also have a small living space and two furnished bedrooms. At the time of our interview with her in 1984, three couples lived there who seemed to get along well with one another, sharing food and lodgings. One couple was Argentinean, another French and the third Chilean. For their lodgings, they paid about a third of the cost of a cheap hotel.* They come and go as they please and no one knows they are here. The neighbors think they are our daughter's friends. *In fact, the first set of renters were friends of their daughter's friends at the university.*

In addition to contributing their labor, the two daughters contribute their earnings to the family. As we noted above, both helped haul stones and mix adobe for the additional rooms. At one point, the older daughter assisted her father in his workshop and her mother in the atelier. But she claims that her father paid her miserable wages and that she did not possess the patience necessary for sewing. This married daughter, who studied French, accounting, computers, and mechanics, later worked outside the home for a car rental agency. She also engaged in trade and service in the Chapare. She brought rice and chickens to the area and also cooked expensive meals for persons involved in the production and trade of narcotics. She has invested her profits in land in the lowlands and in American clothing. She is also involved in selling furniture manufactured in a prison in Santa Cruz and in selling liquor. The proceeds from these various activities help offset the cost of college fees and other joint household needs.

The older daughter took care of all kinds of household chores, including cooking, cleaning and shopping, and worked part-time as a laundress for private families and as a market vendor for clothing. She was also a part-time university student. (All students in Bolivia are part-time by necessity. The university is often closed because of political conditions. Students also often have to interrupt their studies for financial reasons.)

Mrs. Gutierrez has taken a number of actions to help make ends meet. She bought a pressure cooker to speed up cooking, which would, in turn, make time for other work. She has also changed her family's diet to cope with the persistent high cost of food and shortages of staples. She and her daughters take turns standing on line for bread, and when bread is unavailable they try to get rolled oats, which are distributed by Caritas (a Catholic relief organization) in all neighborhoods for a reasonable price. Oatmeal might then take the place of bread for the morning meal. For other meals, she often substitutes bananas, yams, yucca and oca for potatoes, and though many of their meals are now meatless, she tries to vary their content by adding some eggs, cheese or fish. Such changes in diet are a real sacrifice for Bolivian families, whose meals have typically consisted of bread, meat and potatoes. However, Mrs. Gutierrez maintains that they no longer find the diet so foreign or strange. Some see these dietary changes as symbolic of the general collapse of the nation, while for many others the problem is not merely food substitution but dire hunger.

Mrs. Gutierrez: [When I came to live in this house] I continued working. I had a fashion shop in the Calle Yungas and Corrales. But I was unhappy with the arrangement. I would leave in the morning with lunch already prepared. I returned at one for lunch, went back to work at three, and sewed till eight or nine in the evening. But then I would say to myself, "Why go home so early?" and so I would perhaps finish a suit by eight and decide to make a skirt still, in order to earn some more. So I would stay on till one or two a.m. I would then have to walk home because there wouldn't be any public transportation any more, and I would always meet some drunkards around here. It was always full of drunkards. I would not be able to sleep because I was afraid that they might break in until they left at five or six in the morning. But then I would have to get up and clean the house and leave again by seven without having slept. So, finally I got sick of it and said to myself: "Why should I work to earn a living while [my husband] wastes his money? It's better not to have a workshop." Now I regret [giving up the shop] because we could use the money. My daughters are growing older, and they ask for clothing, and I can't buy them any.

After I bought this house in 1975, I continued working until 1980. I was having the house fixed up. We slept downstairs, the part where we are now didn't exist. I continued to work all night to pay for construction materials and for the workmen. When it rained, my daughter and I would go down to the stream and wash sand, and I would carry stones. We suffered a lot to make the house. I made this stone wall with my daughter in order not to have to pay the workmen. My daughter and I cemented the rooms down below all by ourselves. I learned by observation. In the beginning, the workers would ask [my husband]: "Pay us, mister." "No," he would answer, "I am not the owner of the house. Ask my wife to pay you; she is the one who knows." He said this so that he wouldn't have to pay out of his own pocket. He is lucky because other women like me wouldn't have put up with it. Nowadays, women are more self-centered. They figure what they are getting and don't contribute anything themselves.

Mrs. Gutierrez's practical expertise is not limited to sewing, hair-dressing and construction. She is knowledgeable about a number of industrial processes as well. For example, she has watched her brother experiment with all sorts of plastics, cosmetics, floor polishes and soap powders:

I loved to watch my brother grind Arabic gum into powder, mix it with alcohol and pour the mixture into kegs [to make nail polish]. He would keep it covered for two days to soak the gum, and finally he would burn off the alcohol to get rid of the odor. Then he would add myrrh, which gave the polish a pleasant smell, and finally he would fill it into small plastic containers that he had purchased.

Rita also learned that such entrepreneurial activities were risky, for as soon as her brother was selling the goods he produced for half the price of the competition, the powerful importers would come and threaten him with jail sentences for patent infringement.

Change: 1988

The years between 1984 and 1988 brought further hardship to the Gutierrez family. To be sure, they had been able to make substantial improvements to their house and had furnished it nicely, thanks largely to Mrs. Gutierrez's inheritance. But the country's involvement in the production and trade of cocaine had struck their family as well. Rita was deeply worried about her older daughter, Ruth, who had been caught using and sharing cocaine with her friends and who was detained in a detoxification center. Between 1984 and 1988, Ruth had suffered a series of misfortunes from commercial ventures on the "wild border" with Brazil and in the coca-growing valley of Chapare, had caught malaria and had lost a considerable sum of money in the process. Moreover, her husband had initiated a divorce, and she was left with a small daughter who was being raised largely by Mrs. Gutierrez. The latter was still hopeful that Ruth would finish her studies and launch a new life. Fortunately, the Gutierrezes' younger daughter, Juana, was happily married into a very supportive family. Since her husband is an only child, her father-in-law promised that he would pay for her studies. Juana planned to finish high school and then learn how to machine knit garments or to bake pastries.

In the years since we talked to him in 1984, Mr. Gutierrez had established himself in a small, covered market just a block away from his home, where he repaired kerosene burners. Clients also came to order ventilation hoods, and he continued to work as a plumber. However, many of the items he was still making in 1984 were now being imported from other countries, and he could no longer compete. Even his wife and daughters had substituted plastic pails and tubs for metal ones. He had never seriously entered the market for fiesta items, objects his wife associates with persons of Indian descent and the cholada (i.e., Pazeños who retain some of the Indian traditions). But now she spoke wistfully that if her husband had been a costume maker he would be earning a much better living. Federico's brother had been forced to close his construction-materials business because the city opened its own facility a block away, and he had turned to importing equipment and supplies for dentists.

In 1988, Mrs. Gutierrez had just begun to sew again after a period in which she was so preoccupied with her daughter's predicament that she was incapable of working. Even her enterprise of renting rooms to hippie tourists had turned sour. She stopped renting to hippies when a group of them held a young woman virtually hostage for several months in order to be able to live from the remittances she received from her parents. So she was renting to permanent renters again. She was finishing additional rooms to rent out but kept a room for her salesman brother.

This brother (presumably the one who has been a salesman in Chile) was importing a wide range of goods from Chile. After several unsuccessful attempts at striking it rich, he finally made a killing by capturing the market for tapioca. Commerce was the name of the game. Even Mrs. Gutierrez invested some of her money in her brother's ventures and in the goods that her daughter attempted to sell on the Brazilian border. Perhaps in an attempt to emulate the success of some of her clients, she was also thinking of using her husband's tiny market stall to sell dry goods and other items. Indeed, there had been a shift in her clientele:

The richer people are now buying ready-made clothing sold in the fashionable boutiques in the new shopping galleries, while those who keep me busy are the people from the Calle Buenos Aires who have their dry-goods stores, micro-buses and large buses. They are not *de vestido* [i.e., they do not wear European-style clothing]; they are *costumbristas* [people who follow the traditional customs]. They go from fiesta to fiesta. They celebrate weddings, baptisms and sponsor saints' fiestas. And so, since they have money and compete [for prestige], they would be criticized if they bought their clothing ready-made in the markets; so they have their clothing made. They don't have time to come here because they have to tend to their stores or travel, and so I go to their homes.

Mrs. Gutierrez's Dreams

Do you want me to tell you about my dreams?[6] I often have dreams at night. In those dreams, I am not married. I never dream about my husband nor about my daughters. I dream that I am still unmarried and a small girl, that I am always studying. I have beautiful dreams; I never have problems in them. For example, I frequently dream that I am buying very pretty porcelain figures. I also buy shoes in my dreams and dresses in bright and cheerful colors. I dream about flowers, never about ugly things, and always about being a small girl, never a grown woman. I dream that I am flying, and I visit a house, always to the same house, but I can't remember where the house is. In my flight, I always pass by a river and trees. And then a car chases me, a white car. And the car climbs the hills to catch and kill me. So I run to escape it. . . . I have dreamt that I was on a stage and people were praising the way that I was reciting, but again as though I was a child. It is a high school with 15-year-old girls. And I dream that I have to take exams and that I am very afraid of the teacher. But when I am dreaming of the civics hour, everything is beautiful. I dream that I have to recite things and that the girls are applauding. That's how I dream. Sometimes I think that perhaps I have not been very happy, but in my dreams I am very happy. What I want to say is that I think that in my dreams I am compensated by happiness; the dreams are another life for me. I live a happy life in my dreams. So I resign myself to having to suffer, because God also compensates, even though it may only be in one's dreams.

Notes

1. He was probably Federico's mother's cousin.
2. The copious free drinks at all the fiestas where he prepared the fireworks probably also contributed to Pedro's alcoholism.
3. While the sisters did at least finish primary school, they did not receive much professional training until later in life, when at least one of Mr. Gutierrez's sisters accumulated diplomas in several fields, including television repair.
4. The fiesta that Federico sponsored was actually in a small town on the altiplano, but because it is the site where the city of La Paz was originally founded, it has become the locus of a fiesta whose prestige, at least traditionally, has surpassed that of all fiestas held in the city itself.
5. In such an arrangement, the owner cedes the rights to real estate in return for an interest-free loan to be repaid to the lessee at the end of the lease.
6. We had not broached this very personal subject with Mrs. Gutierrez; perhaps in consonance with her interest in psychology, she brought it up on her own.

12

Conclusion

By now it will have become apparent why we have not adhered to any narrow definition of "microenterprises," "informal economy" and so forth. The inclusion of some larger firms in our sample highlighted the arbitrary nature of strict categories. Through a review of those firms, we saw that some of the problems faced by smaller enterprises, such as the dependence on imported equipment, raw materials and intermediate goods, and the reduction of consumption during crises, also affect larger ones. In addition, many characteristics of firms are only vaguely correlated with one another, making it difficult to fit them neatly into narrow categories.

In La Paz, the municipal government distinguishes between establishments with fewer than five workers and those with more than five workers. Those in the first category are subjected to flat tax rates, the level of which depends on rough estimates of invested capital, and those in the second category are taxed according to monthly revenues. These categories are based on capital as well as on the number of workers the establishments employ.

Official studies of the "formal" and "informal" sectors of the La Paz (e.g., Bolivia 1980a & b) assume that registered small-scale firms constitute an upper stratum of the "informal sector." From this one could conclude that even though some small enterprises could be considered as legal entities, illegality would still be correlated to size. In actual fact, this is by no means the case. We found that while some two-person operations are legally constituted, many larger firms hire a part of their labor force informally. It is the more visible producers and vendors and those that are more dependent on state-controlled, rationed or subsidized raw materials that are the enterprises most likely to be registered. Those that are less visible or more mobile are less likely to be registered. In fact, as Dandler (1986)[1] and others have argued, in Bolivia one of the activities that is most lucrative and central to the national economy--the manufacture and trade of cocaine--is illegal. Informality, Dandler maintains, constitutes a broad strategy or set of strategies rather than a definable sector of the economy.

Small-scale production has also not been studied with the same rigor or frequency as larger scale production because some of the work involved has not been considered important for many of the same reasons that women's work is denigrated in economic analysis. It is often regarded as involving activities that an individual would engage in only if formal employment were not available or activities engaged in merely to complement the income of the primary worker. It is frequently not spatially separated from the home, a location considered outside the parameters of formal economics. At the same time, it does not follow rigid schedules, and it may even lack a clearly definable set of persons who engage in these activities separate from their reproductive work or from their education. In fact, this form of production may often not be separable from seemingly radically different activities, such as religious observances.

The studies that *have* focused on small-scale production have often adopted some of the same stereotypical notions. For one, they have assumed that activities situated in different spatial and temporal frameworks are separable from one another. Therefore, they have not paid sufficient attention to the interlinkages. By refusing to limit our sample to narrowly defined categories, we were able to show the complex interaction of more dispersed and more concentrated activities. Such an approach also led us to ask a different set of questions. By focusing on questions of how one can survive, secure an acceptable livelihood, and flourish in a climate of economic and political uncertainty rather than arbitrarily defining types of "sub-economies" and then concentrating on one of them, we were able to reveal both strategies that are particular to small-scale producers and those that are more universally applicable. Some of the strategies we have examined in this book are independent of firm size and legal status, however defined; others are more closely linked to or have manifestations sui generis in smaller firms. In general, the strategies are consonant with situations of economic and political uncertainty. Simultaneously, in some cases, they respond to specific economic niches in the local, national and international economy: culturally influenced strategies, like the production of fiesta-related goods, Alasita miniatures, or--in the international arena--exotic goods or the fashions of particular groups; and geographically influenced ones, like the production of goods that are bulky to transport over long distances.

This systemic approach also allowed us to determine how gender, ethnicity and class influenced these behaviors. But these latter factors were not viewed in an essentialist manner. They were placed in the larger political and economic context of the city, the nation and global conditions.

Our study suggests that small-scale enterprises may well remain a major and indispensable component of Third World economic niches that large industries find too risky and that they generate links among different activities to promote new types of enterprises. We discovered that an orthodox Marxist model that views "simple commodity production" as a vestige of a precapitalist past, destined to disappear under the pressure of advanced capitalism, was inadequate to describe the Bolivian situation. Instead of seeing an inexorable unilineal evolution toward greater and greater capitalization and increasing loss of autonomy on the part of the worker, we found a mutual accommodation among firms of widely varying nature. Development did not proceed from independent producer to dependent worker. Capital generated by the wages of a dependent worker may be invested in small-scale production. Thus, individuals who began their careers as workers in large factories (the formal sector) used their accrued benefits to establish owner-operated industries. Even bureaucrats could become artisans, and professionals could become managers of small firms.

Firms were interconnected through putting-out systems; the rental or borrowing of space and machinery; the complex division of labor among otherwise independent producers based on differences in skills and access to means of production; and partnerships involving various kinds of arrangements. Consequently, in order to understand the development of firms, we found it imperative to trace the inter-dependencies of firms both of similar and of different sizes.

In analyzing the *internal* structure of firms, we had to focus on the role holders rather than concentrate narrowly on the roles themselves. Particular producers may engage in a number of different aspects of production, i.e., they may at the same time be managers, engage in skilled, more highly remunerated aspects of production, and engage in relatively unskilled, low-margin work. They are thus simultaneously exploiters of the labor of others as well as exploiters of their own labor and that of other members of their families.

Marxists often assume that highly capitalized industries are necessarily more centralized in terms of the control over the labor of others. However, we found that relatively highly mechanized industries could permit relatively decentralized production. Thus, lumberyards rented their expensive machinery to carpenters by the hour. The rates were probably not much higher (and, under the present conditions of falling exchange rates, perhaps even lower) than the amortization costs of a privately owned machine. Some informants cited convenient access to machinery rather than returns on capital and labor as their reason for wishing to acquire their own machinery. The progression from smaller to larger firms postulated by orthodox Marxist as well as developmentalist models is also far from universal. In fact, the dissolution of a large firm often was the basis for the creation of a number of smaller ones because long-term employees received pieces of equipment in lieu of severance pay and set up their own shops with them. At the time of our 1984 revisit, this process had been accelerated by the economic downturn that forced larger firms to lay off large numbers of workers.

In some ways, the mechanisms that operate in the Bolivian situation are analogous to those analyzed by Piore and Sabel in *The Second Industrial Divide* (1984). In his earlier work (Berger and Piore 1980), Piore viewed small scale production as an adjunct to mass production. Small-scale enterprises manufacture for small, specialized markets but also can retain the unstable portion of larger markets by shifting production to fit demand. He argued that, frequently, such activities occur in a dependent relationship to mass production, which is geared toward longer runs, higher volume and a stable market requiring specialized machinery and a pronounced division of labor. By acquiring machine tools and putting out production of goods with an uncertain demand to flexible, small-scale firms, large-scale factories minimize their risk.

Berger and Piore (1980) found that the size of the small-scale sector depends on the particular history of each economy and on the relative stability of the market at a given time. Those countries and regions with cultural traditions amenable to craft production and political institutions that support them are more likely to develop such symbiotic systems.

Recent events affecting the world economy have led Piore and Sabel to reconsider the continued dominance of the mass-production paradigm (1984). The social unrest of the late 1960s followed by the abandonment of fixed exchange rates, the first oil shock (1973) and the Russian wheat deal, the second oil shock and concomitant high inflation (1979), and the high interest rates instituted to fight inflation, world recession and the debt crisis led to a reduction in the size of the market and an increase of uncertainty. One solution has been to reduce the fixed cost of multinationals by shifting the burden of risk to the workers of the Third World. In Southeast Asia, industrial development was largely self-financed but was predicated on a continued low living standard and labor peace enforced by totalitarian regimes. Alternatively, risk can be reduced by avoiding direct investment in industry and by lending money, guaranteed by creditor nations, at interest rates determined largely by the economic vagaries of the First World, such as the high public-deficit spending in the U.S. (Pastor 1986). In countries of the industrial periphery, like Brazil, export-led development is helping to service debt but at the cost of long-term environmental degradation, low wages and unfavorable terms of trade, especially for required imports of capital goods. In poor, geographically isolated countries, such as Bolivia, loans intended for ventures promoted by the government with little chance of long-term success, like loans for large-scale export-oriented agro-industry, have often been diverted by entrepreneurs into land for cattle haciendas, urban real estate and reinvestment abroad. The rate of default has been high.

Piore and Sabel (1984), however, envision a more constructive solution to the mass production crisis than its transfer to the Third World, i.e., a solution that would permit small-scale producers to overcome the limitations of and low wages in craft production while retaining their major advantage--flexibility. Such production would entail multipurpose (numerically controlled) equipment, a skilled work force with broadly defined tasks, and flexible arrangements among clusters of small firms.[2] In this scenario, Piore and Sabel expect a continuation of the status quo in the relationship of the periphery to the core, i.e., the periphery would still provide the raw materials and perhaps now the assumption of mass production, too. But, they also foresee the possibility that Third World countries would engage in flexible production facilitated by a form of "international Keynesianism," specifically, the transfer of the debt to a vastly expanded International Monetary Fund, the reduction of interest rates and new long-term loans. While the first scenario merely compounds the past problems of the dependent producers with the new uncertainties in mass production, the second would seem to be an attractive alternative for such smaller, poorer, geographically more isolated economies like Bolivia.

Interestingly, such economies are in some ways more analogous to those of the industrial core than to those of the industrial periphery, in the sense that large industries consider both types unfavorable, albeit for entirely different reasons. Bolivia cannot engage in either capital- or labor-intensive mass production because of the small size of its population and internal markets, its low consumption rates and its poorly developed infrastructure. Further, the attempt to enlarge markets by participating in regional consortia has failed because the larger and geographically favored economies of neighboring states dictate the terms of trade and subvert any such agreements with impunity.

Some of the preconditions of flexible production of goods for specialized markets are indeed present in Bolivia. Despite the inroads of cheap, mass-produced imports (both official and contraband), skilled production of a wide variety of goods organized along craft production lines has occurred in Bolivia throughout recorded history and today maintains itself by catering to specialized local cultural needs (such as the ritual cycle and elite tastes for customized goods) and by undercutting imports with the use of cheap labor and local or foreign recycled raw materials and lower transportation costs. At the same time, small entrepreneurs make booming businesses with modern, moderately priced equipment. They set up copiers in tiny rooms in accessible locations or employ personal computers for printing. A few conditions for increasing craft productivity, such as the sharing of equipment through rental and other arrangements, are also already in place. The tendency for the exploitation of small-scale producers by unscrupulous middlemen may be mitigated by the establishment of marketing cooperatives. There are also plans to provide working and selling space in central locations in La Paz to an array of artisans in order to stimulate innovation and sales. And a further expansion of bank credit at reasonable rates initiated by a few non-governmental organizations such as PRODEM (and already under way in 1990) may lessen the dependency on loan sharks.

However, further development along the path of flexible specialization will face major obstacles in Bolivia even in times of relative prosperity. Financial policies continue to discourage small-scale producers from applying for credit. Banks favor agricultural over industrial investments, larger over small enterprises. Credit is given for equipment and not for other means of production. Only real estate, or a physical plant, qualifies as collateral, and substantial cash flows must be demonstrated in addition. An established reputation for reliable production or acknowledged skills do not count. Often, elite connections are also necessary.

Additional impediments are the governmental policies that control the flow of raw materials. These policies fail to recognize the potential of craft production to add value. The lack of state interest in craft production is also reflected in the small, underfunded and inadequate training programs it provides and in the poor assistance it grants for export marketing. Indeed, state agencies often compete with private producers, vendors and exporters.

During periods of economic and political crises, the further development of the technological component of Piore and Sabel's flexible specialization becomes impossible. The lessons learned in periods of crises carry over to those of relative prosperity. Just as a biological system must be adapted to the most adverse circumstances in a natural cycle (Liebig's Principle), so a system of production has to be able to withstand the troughs in economic cycles. Without the ability to influence the world monetary system or the terms of trade that would accompany a true internationalization of finance, the Bolivian economy will remain subject to deep periodic crises. These require a degree of flexibility on the part of individual investors which may well surpass that provided by flexible specialization. Bolivians often opt out of particular industries altogether and move into speculative commercial ventures or into real estate. This is one of the reasons why industrialists/ artisans prefer to use their own capital for equipment that can be amortized quickly and to limit the time and effort they spend in skill acquisition.

The unwillingness of producers to invest too heavily in any one technical skill contributes to the devaluation of skills in general and to the tendency to move up into managerial roles and relegate production to less fortunate former colleagues--a problem that is not unique to Bolivia. The division of labor thus engendered results in unequal shares of the rewards to enterprises. The resultant differential weight of capital and labor is not adequately addressed even in the ideal flexible-specialization model.

The successful implementation of Piore and Sabel's model in Bolivia and many other parts of the Third World, then, would presuppose a new system of international finance in addition to a restructuring of the terms of trade and internal political realignment.

The above considerations led us to reanalyze social class distinctions and their role in production in terms of a processual model. We examined situations where people, who by arbitrary criteria would be classified in different categories, in fact struggle together to reach a goal and where people who would be lumped together compete. In the case of Doña Flora's woolen-goods enterprise, an illiterate second-generation rural-urban migrant with strong ties to her home community collaborated with her son-in-law, a well-educated long-term resident of La Paz.

A processual view of social class also revealed that there were different avenues to upward mobility. We found a multiple stratification system—or, rather, multiple parallel cognitive frameworks—of upward mobility:

1. one based on rural-urban migration and continued network ties with the place of origin
2. another based on identification with certain activities: especially small-scale production, marketing and transportation
3. and a third centered on both traditional and "modern" middle-class and elite cultural values that are also emulated by poorer people

The first two systems are largely compatible with the exception that energies expended in one may detract from advancement in the other. These avenues are characterized by the involvement in an elaborate ritual system including fiesta sponsorships. For women, clothing style, derived from earlier colonial fashions, is an important means of expressing social status. They are involved in a finely nuanced system of symbolic stratification based on the type of material used in, and the quality of, their garments.[3] Among first- and often second-generation migrants, upward mobility is achieved through continued contacts with the place of origin manifested in continued land ownership there and/or in participating in and sponsoring rural fiestas and providing material assistance to more recent migrants from the one's place of origin. The stratification system based on occupation places greater emphasis on urban fiestas and participation in urban producers' and vendors' organizations.

In the third system, rituals are more hidden from public view and, except for Catholic masses, are less connected to saints' days, conforming to more generalized Latin American patterns symbolized most saliently by European-style women's dress.

Differences in class manifest themselves in the struggles against what is perceived as abuses of power by government officials. Unions, that are in fact associations of owners of small-scale enterprises, nevertheless couch their struggles to obtain government benefits in class terms, identifying with the working class. Alternatively, however, they also view their relationship with the government as well as with foreigners, who might be useful in securing foreign orders, in patronage terms.

Class is experienced differently according to gender. As we have already noted, class-based styles of dress are far more important for women than they are for men. There may be major differences in class affiliation even within households. In the case of the Gutierrez family, Federico was oriented toward an urban tradition in which fiestas played a significant role, while his wife's family rejected fiesta sponsorship as an expression of social standing. Federico was also looked down upon even by his own brother, who refused to acknowledge any kin relationship when Federico was working for him. Finally, an individual may switch frameworks if he or she finds it advantageous to do so. Thus Lucía, who had been wearing modified modern-style clothing, decided to switch to *chola* dress in order to facilitate social interaction in rural fairs and street markets. Social stratification, then, is enormously complex and cannot be accounted for by any single model.

To conclude, this book will have succeeded in its purpose if we have been able to convey a sense of the myriad decisions that small-scale producers have to make in the extraordinarily fluid situations they must cope with. Far from the unitary phenomenon implied by such concepts as "the informal sector," small-scale production in Bolivia is an extraordinarily varied phenomenon, whose shape, at any given time, is molded by the vagaries of national and international economics and politics and also by past experiences and traditions. Far from constituting an isolable phenomenon, it is inextricably intermeshed with production in middle-sized and larger firms both at home and abroad. And it is intricately linked with small- and large-scale internal and international commerce and with municipal and national government bureaucracies. In an economic climate that "economic intelligence reports" have routinely written off as impossible,[4] Bolivian small-scale producers have managed to survive thanks to an admirable resourcefulness attained through a long history of dependency and informed by long-standing indigenous, colonial and republican traditions.

Notes

1. Dandler is quoted in Doria Medina (1986).
2. It should be remembered, however, that intermediary forms are possible between the two types of production (a fact implicit in Piore and Sabel's work but insufficiently developed by them) and that, at least in modern contexts, each type depends on and entails elements of the other.

3. It should be noted that, at least in the late 1960s, differences of dress within the *de pollera* symbolic system could also denote very specific backgrounds: a *chola sin sombrero,* i.e., a woman who wore wide skirts but no bowler hat, for example, indicated by her dress her origin as the owner (or former owner) of a very small hacienda or an enterprise in a small town.

4. See, for example, the *Bolivia Country Profile,* an annual report of the Economist Intelligence Unit, where paragraphs describing the unfavorable industrial climate are reprinted verbatim from year to year.

Appendix:
Land Tenure Arrangements

The following examples will give an idea of the range of possible land tenure arrangements. Tiburcio had two sons, Benjamin and Teodoro, and a daughter, Josefa. When Benjamin, the eldest son, married, he established his own compound and Tiburcio permanently divided each of his plots into two equal parts. Nevertheless father and son continued to work the entire parcel together, planting the same crops. At the same time, Isodoro, the second son, was living with Anastasia whom he expected to marry the following year. He had built a house of his own but was still eating with his father. He expected to inherit the remaining share when his father died. Josefa was married to a man from Jank'o Amaya and moved into that community. However, she and her husband came over to help Tiburcio in the fields and therefore received *chiquiñas*. Anastasia, Teodoro's future wife, received special treatment from her eldest brother, Pedro, who had been able to secure for himself a portion of land directly from the *patron* in hacienda times. As Pedro knew that his sister would need money for the wedding, he made the following provisions concerning his own seven plots of land:

a: 1/3 of this parcel was given to his father who gave it to his sisters and 1/8 to his mother-in-law.

b: Out of 60 furrows planted in habas (broad beans), 7 went to his father, 1 went to his wife's mother and 1 to his wife's eldest sister. Some onions planted in the same plot went to his father.

c: Here he planted habas, ocas, and potatoes, in uneven proportions. He planted 48 furrows of potatoes, which yielded 6 1/2 cargas (a carga = 150 lbs). His three living sisters received two furrows each, corresponding to one carga of produce. In the same parcel the family planted 30 furrows of ocas. Of these the father received the produce from four, the youngest sister Anastasia, two, and his wife's sister, one furrow. They also planted half of the parcel with *habas* which yielded 18 callchas.[1] The father received five furrows corresponding to one callcha of *habas*.

d: Pedro gave this parcel to his compadre for a time, to plant onions. The compadre provided the seed and the yield was shared equally between the two partners.

e: Pedro gave this entire parcel to Anastasia to cultivate barley.

f: In this parcel he planted onions in three spots: two for himself, the third for Anastasia. In another place he planted 48 furrows of habas of which 16 went to his sisters and brother-in-law. In still another which he also planted in habas, the two younger sisters received 2 furrows each out of a total of 38 furrows. In addition, four went to the brother-in-law (husband of Pedro's deceased eldest sister) and four to the father.

g: Finally, in this plot planted in habas, the father received 1/3 to share with Anastasia, while the other 2/3 went to Anastasia alone.

Although Pedro could afford to be generous to his relatives because he had been working outside the community for many years previously, was working as the interpreter of one of us during that year, and his wife might not have been able to cultivate the land alone, his is simply an extreme case of more routine arrangements exemplified by Tiburcio's case.

Six other peasant families made the following arrangements. One cultivated all the plots for himself after his FZ and two Zs, one of which lived in Llamacachi had died. Another gave his sister *chiquiñas*, another gave his son who was living in Arica at the time a houseplot and *chiquiñas*, and *chiquiñas* to the wife of a son who had died. Another rented some of his land to his godfather while share-cropping another plot with an unrelated Compeño. Finally, one worked his land jointly with a son.

The *chiquiñas* are more or less fixed locations which may continue to be apportioned to a relative for a number of years. When apportioned to male relatives, however, *chiquiñas* are usually interim arrangements made until the land is divided up permanently. Thus Rufino has three to twelve furrows in 7 plots while his brother Apolinario has 4 to 7 in 6 plots. Furthermore, each brother has received a plot of his own. Rufino also owns a houseplot, while his brother constructed his home on a plot given to him by his father-in-law. However, the brothers expected a permanent partition soon.

1. A callcha is a good armload of habas plants stacked in the shape of a pyramid at harvest time.

Glossary

Alasita: A fair held in honor of Ekeko, a supernatural venerated for his power to concede the wishes represented by the miniature objects sold at the fair. In La Paz, the fair is held in the last week of January.

ambulantes: Street vendors without a fixed sales site.

bayeta: Handspun and Handwoven woolen cloth.

cabeza: Dance group sponsor.

caseras: Favored regular clients.

chiquiñas: A specified number of furrows in each plot owned by a family conceded in usufruct.

cholas: Urban-born women who continue to dress in the traditional garb that includes the *pollera* (skirt), *manta* (embroidered shawl), and felt bowler hat.

comadre: Term used to designate the godmother of one's child; term usd by the godfather/godmother to designate his/her godchild's mother.

compadre: Male counterpart of *comadre*.

comuneros: Individuals residing in a *comunidad*.

comunidades: Communities that were free from large landowners even before the agrarian reform.

de vestido: Woman wearing European-style dress.

de pollera: See *cholas*.

Ekeko: God of plenty venerated during Alasita.

fulbito: A form of soccer with only six players per team, played on a small   field.

juntar: Acting as an intermediary by purchasing goods for resale from a large number of producers.

manta: Embroidered shawl worn by a *chola*.

mercado artesanal: A market for crafts. The best known one is next to the Church of San Francisco in the center of La Paz.

obrajes: Artisan workshops during the colonial period where workers were forced to work for little pay and under terrible physical conditions.

paisano: Person from the same community of origin.

pasanaku: Rotating credit union popular among Bolivians from a wide range of social backgrounds.

Pazeño(a) (noun): La Paz-born man (woman).

pazeño(a) (adjective): From La Paz; of La Paz.

polleras: The traditional gathered and pleated skirts worn by rural and urban Aymara women.

pollerera: *Pollera* manufacturer.

preste: Principal sponsor of a fiesta.

presterío: Fiesta sponsored by an individual.

puesto: Market site.

relacionadores: Market coordinators (under military regimes after 1970).

salteña: Spicy meat-turnover.

sindicatos: Producers' organizations; also labor and market unions.

supermercado: Street market for consumer goods; supermarket.

utawawa: "Children of the house," who have received land from a peasant family; also, adopted children.

Bibliography

Abu-Lugod, J.
    1988   "Migrant Adjustment to City Life: The Egyptian Case." In *Urban Life: Readings in Urban Anthropology*. 2d ed., edited by G. Gmelch, and W. Zenner. Prospect Heights, Ill.: Waveland.

Alarcón A., J., ed.,
    1925   *Bolivia en el primer centenario de su independencia 1825-1925*. New York: University Society.

Albó, X.
    1979   *Achacachi, medio siglo de lucha campesina*. Cuaderno de Investigación CIPCA, No. 19.

Albó, X., T. Greaves and G. Sandóval
    1981   *Chukiyawu: La cara aymara de La Paz. I. El paso a la ciudad*. La Paz: Cuadernos de Investigación CIPCA, No. 20.

    1982   *Chukiyawu: La cara aymara de La Paz. II. Una odisea: buscar "pega."* La Paz: Cuadernos de Investigacion CIPCA, No. 22.

Albó, X., and M. Preiswerk
    1986   *Los Señores del Gran Poder*. Centro de Teología Popular, Taller de Observaciones Culturales. La Paz: Editorial Alenkar.

Arensberg, C.
    1972   "Culture as Behavior: Structure and Emergence." *Annual Review of Anthropology* 1:1-26.

Basch, L., N. Glick Schiller, and C. Szanton
    1990   *The Transnationalization of Migration: New Perspectives on Ethnicity and Race*. New York: Gordon and Breach.

Benería, L.
    1982   *Women and Development: The Sexual Division of Labor in Rural Societies*. New York: Praeger.

Benería, L., and G. Sen
    1981   "Accumulation, Reproduction, and Women's Role in Economic Development: Boserup Revisited." *Signs* 7:279-299.

Berger, S., and M. Piore
    1980   *Dualism and Discontinuity in Industrial Society*. Cambridge: Cambridge University Press.

Bolivia
1976   *Resultados del censo nacional de población y vivienda 1976.* Vol. 2:
        Departamento de La Paz. La Paz: Ministerio de Planeamiento y
        Coordinacion: Instituto Nacional de Estadística.

1980a   *Empleo en el sector informal de la ciudad de La Paz.* La Paz: Ministerio
        de Trabajo y Desarrollo Laboral: Dirección General de Empleo.

1980b   *Sector Formal de la ciudad de La Paz: los trabajadores y sus familias.*
        La Paz: Ministerio de Trabajo y Desarrollo Laboral: Dirección
        General de Empleo.

Brush, S.
1977   *Mountain, Field, and Family: The Economy and Human Ecology of an
        Andean Valley.* Philadelphia: University of Pennsylvania Press.

Buechler, H.
1966   *Agrarian Reform and Migration on the Bolivian Altiplano.* Ph.D.
        dissertation, Ann Arbor Microfilms.

1980   *The Masked Media: Aymara Fiestas and Social Interaction in the Bolivian
        Highlands.* The Hague: Mouton.

1983   "A Poor Man Must Die with His Ideas: The Life and Perceptions
        of a Bolivian Tinsmith." Paper presented at the annual meeting
        of the Northeastern Anthropological Association, Syracuse.

1986a   "Adaptations, Holding Actions, and Economic Decline: Small In-
        dustries in La Paz, Bolivia, in 1981 and 1984." Paper presented at
        the 85th annual meeting of the American Anthropological Associa-
        tion, Philadelphia, December 3-7.

1986b   "Dealing with the Economic Depression in Bolivia: Male Strategies
        in Small Firms." Paper presented at the XIII International Congress,
        Latin American Studies Association, Boston, October 23-25.

1988   "Doña Flora's Network: Work Relations in Small Industries in La
        Paz, Bolivia." In *Urban Life: Readings in Urban Anthropology.* 2d ed.,
        edited by G. Gmelch and W. Zenner. Prospect Heights, Ill.:
        Waveland.

1989   "Apprenticeship and Transmission of Knowledge in La Paz,
        Bolivia." In *Apprenticeship: From Theory to Method and Back,* edited
        by Michael Coy Albany: State University of New York at Albany
        Press.

Buechler, H., and J.-M. Buechler
1971   *The Bolivian Aymara.* New York: Holt, Rinehart, and Winston.

1981   "Government Policies and Small-Scale Firms." Paper presented at
        the American Anthropological Association meeting, Cincinnati.

1982a   "Small-Scale Production and Late Capitalism in La Paz, Bolivia."
         Paper delivered at the International Congress of Americanists,
         Manchester, England.

1982b   "Small Trades Do Better in Bolivia." *The Geographical Magazine* 54
         (September): 518-519.

1984   "Inter-Ethnic Relations in Small-Scale Manufacturing in La Paz,
         Bolivia." paper presented at the 83rd annual meeting of the
         American Anthropological Association, Denver, Colorado,
         November 14-18.

1986   "The Potential for Flexible Production in La Paz, Bolivia." Paper
         presented at the 85th annual meeting of the American Anthropo-
         logical Association, Philadelphia, December 3-7.

Buechler, J.-M.
1972   *Peasant Marketing and Social Revolution in the Province of La Paz,
         Bolivia.* Ann Arbor, Mich.: University Microfilms.

1976a   "Negociantes contratistas en los mercados bolivianos." *Estudios
         Andinos* 5:57-77.

1976b   "Something Funny Happened on the Way to the Agora: A Com-
         parison of Bolivian and Spanish Galician Migrants." *Anthropological
         Quarterly* 49:62-69.

1978   "The Dynamics of the Market in La Paz, Bolivia." *Urban
         Anthropology* 7:343-359.

1985a   "Women in Petty Commodity Production in La Paz." In *New Direc-
         tions in the Study of Sex and Class in Latin America,* edited by J.
         Nash and H. Safa. Boston: Bergen and Garvey.

1985b   "The Burden of Debt on Petty Commodity Producers in Bolivia."
         Paper presented at the American Ethnological Society/Canadian
         Ethnological Society meetings, Toronto, May 9-12.

1986   "Gender Ideology and Politics: The Case of Bolivian Petty Com-
         modity Producers." Paper presented at the session, Women in the
         Americas: Relationships, Work and Power. 85th annual meeting of
         the American Anthropological Association, Philadelphia, December
         3-7.

Cámara de Comercio e Industria Boliviano Peruana
1981   *Directorio Industrial Boliviano.* La Paz: Ministerio de Industria,
         Comercio y Turismo.

Cámara Nacional de Industrias
1981   *Guía Directorio de la Industria Boliviana.* La Paz.

Canelas, O.
   1966   *Mito y Realidad de la Industrialización Boliviana.* La Paz: Amigos del
           Libro.

Carter, W.
   1964   *Aymara Communities and the Bolivian Agrarian Reform.* Gainesville:
           University of Florida Monographs, Social Sciences No. 24,
           University of Florida Press.

Casanovas, R.
   1985   "Los trabajadores por cuenta propia en el mercado de trabajo: el
           caso de la ciudad de La Paz." In *El sector informal urbano en los
           países andinos,* edited by Carbonetto. Quito: ILDIS and Guayaquil:
           CEPESIU.

Casanovas, R., and S. Escobar de Pabón
   1988   *Los trabajadores por cuenta propia en La Paz: Funcionamiento de las
           unidades económicas, situación laboral e ingresos.* La Paz: CEDLA.

CEDLA
   1986   *El sector informal urbano en Bolivia.* La Paz: CEDLA, FLACSO.

Chaplin, D.
   1967   *The Peruvian Industrial Labor Force.* Princeton: Princeton University
           Press.

Cooper, E.
   1980   *The Wood-Carvers of Hong Kong: Craft Production in the World
           Capitalist Periphery.* Cambridge: Cambridge University Press.

Dandler, J.
   1986   *Apuntes generales sobre economía informal y su importancia en Bolivia.*
           La Paz: CERES.

De Soto, H.
   1989   "Structural Adjustment and the Informal Sector." In *Microenterprises
           in Developing Countries,* edited by J. Levitsky. London: Intermediate
           Technology Publications.

Doria Medina, S.
   1986   *La economía informal en Bolivia.* La Paz: Editorial Offset Boliviana
           Ltda.

Doughty, P.
   1968   *Huaylas: An Andean District in Search of Progress.* Ithaca: Cornell
           University Press.

Dunkerley, J., and R. Morales
   1986   "The Crisis in Bolivia." *New Left Review,* 155:86-106.

Eames, E., and J. Goode
1977   Anthropology of the City: An Introduction to Urban Anthropology.
        Englewood Cliffs, N.J.: Prentice-Hall.

Eckstein, S., and Hagopian, F.
1983   "The Limits of Industrialization in the Less Developed World:
        Bolivia." Economic Development and Cultural Change 32:63-95.

Economist Intelligence Unit
1986-   Peru, Bolivia Country Profile. London: The Unit.

Eder, J.
1968   Inflation and Development in Latin America: A Case History of Inflation
        and Stabilization in Bolivia. Michigan International Business Studies,
        no. 8. Ann Arbor: University of Michigan.

Escobar de Pabón, S., and H. Maletta
1981   La Paz 1980: Población, migraciones y empleo: resultados preliminares.
        Serie Resultados 1. La Paz: Proyecto Migraciones y Empleo Rural
        y Urbano (OIT/FUNAP).

Estes, V.
n.d.   "Factories and Families: Urban Working Women in La Paz, Bolivia:
        A Very Preliminary Report." La Paz.

1981   "Patrons and Clients, Owners and Workers: Changing Social
        Relationships in a Bolivian Factory." Paper presented at the 80th
        annual meeting of the American Anthropological Association, Los
        Angeles, December 6.

1984   Factories and Families: Urban Working Women in La Paz, Bolivia. Ann
        Arbor, Mich.: University Microfilms.

1988   "These Days, to be a Bolivian is to Die Slowly: Women Factory
        Workers in La Paz." In Lucha: The Struggles of Latin American
        Women, edited by C. Weil. Minnesota Latin American Series, no.
        2. Minneapolis: The Prisma Institute, Inc.

Fröbel, F., J. Heinrichs and O. Kreye
1980   The New International Division of Labour. Cambridge: Cambridge
        University Press.

García, B., H. Muñoz and O. de Oliveira
1982   Hogares y Trabajadores en la Ciudad de México. México: El Colegio
        de México/UNAM.

Gisbert, T.
1980   Iconografía y Mitos Indigenas en el Arte. La Paz: Gisbert & Cia.

Glazer, N.
1983   "Servants to Capital: Unpaid Domestic Labor and Paid Work,"
        Review of Radical Political Economics 16:61-89.

Gmelch, G., and W. Zenner, eds.
  1988   *Urban Life: Readings in Urban Anthropology*, 2d ed. Prospect Heights,
          Ill.: Waveland.

Gomez, W.
  1976   "Bolivia: Problems of a Pre- and Post-Revolutionary Export
          Economy." *Journal of Developing Areas* 10:461-484.

Harding, P., and R. Jenkins
  1989   *The Myth of the Hidden Economy: Towards a New Understanding of
          Economic Activity*. Philadelphia: Open University Press.

Hopkins, D.
  1983   *The Colonial History of the Hacienda System in a Southern Peruvian
          Highland District*. Ann Arbor, Mich.: University Microfilms.

Irvin, G.
  1979   *Planning Investment in Bolivia: The Changing Role of the Public Sector*.
          Research Report Series, no. 6. Institute of Social Studies. The
          Hague: Institute of Social Studies.

Jacobs, J.
  1984   *Cities and the Wealth of Nations: Principles of Economic Life*. New
          York: Random House.

Johnson, C.
  1979   "Dependency Theory and the Capitalist/Socialist Process." Working
          Paper no. 25. Montreal: Center for Developing Area Studies, McGill
          University.

Kelley, J., and H. Klein
  1981   *Revolution and the Rebirth of Inequality: A Theory Applied to the
          National Revolution in Bolivia*. Berkeley: University of California
          Press.

Kirsch, H.
  1977   *Industrial Development in a Traditional Society: The Conflict of Entre-
          preneurship and Modernization in Chile*. Gainesville: University of
          Florida Press.

Klein, H.
  1969   *Parties and Political Change in Bolivia, 1880-1952*. Cambridge:
          Cambridge University Press.

Laclau, E.
  1971   "Feudalism and Capitalism in Latin America." *New Left Review* 67
          (May-June).

Levitsky, J.
  1989   *Microenterprises in Developing Countries*. London: Intermediate
          Technology Publications.

Lomnitz, L., and M. Perez-Lizaur
1987   A Mexican Elite Family, 1820-1980. Princeton: Princeton University
        Press.

Long, N., and B. Roberts, eds.
1978   Peasant Cooperation and Capitalist Expansion in Central Peru. Austin:
        Institute of Latin American Studies, University of Texas at Austin.

Long, N., and B. Roberts
1984   Miners, Peasants and Entrepreneurs: Regional Development in the Central
        Highlands of Peru. Cambridge: Cambridge University Press.

McEwen, W.
1975   Changing Rural Society: A Study of Communities in Bolivia. New
        York: Oxford University Press.

McFarren, W.
1985   "Antonio Viscarra: O Construtor de Máscaras." In 18a Bienal
        Internacional de São Paulo/ Outubro-Dezembro 1985: Sala Especial "O
        Turista Aprendiz," edited by M. Bisilliat. São Paulo: Editora Abril.

Manwar, A.
1990   Social Structure of Capital Formation in Bangladesh: A Micro-Level
        Study in the Village Community. Ann Arbor: University Microfilms.

Marsh, M.
1928   The Bankers in Bolivia: A Study of American Foreign Investment. New
        York: AMS Press.

Milkman, R.
1976   "Women's Work and Economic Crisis: Some Lessons of the Great
        Depression," The Review of Radical Political Economics 8: 73-97.

Mörner, M.
1985   The Andean Past: Land, Societies, and Conflicts. New York: Columbia
        University Press.

Müller y Asociados
1988   Estadísticas Econômicas 1988. La Paz: Instituto Latinoamericano de
        Investigaciones Sociales.

Nash, J.
1979a   We Eat the Mines and the Mines Eat Us: Dependency and Exploitation
        in Bolivian Tin Mines. New York: Columbia University Press.

1979b   "Anthropology of the Multinational Corporation." In The Politics
        of Anthropology from Colonialism and Sexism: Toward a View from
        Below, edited by G. Huizer and V. Mannheim. The Hague: Mouton.

New York Times
        2/4/85; 5/21/87.

Pastor, M.
   1984   "The International Monetary Fund & Latin America, Core-
           Periphery & Capital-Labor Aspects to Fund Policy." Ph.D.
           Department of Economics, University of Massachusetts.

   1986   "Long Shadow of Global Debt." In *Economic Report of The President
           People*, 185-207. Center for Popular Economics. Boston: South End
           Press.

Peñaloza, L.
   1953   *Historia Economica de Bolivia*. vols. I & II, La Paz: Amigos del Libro.

Piore, M., and C. Sabel
   1984   *The Second Industrial Divide: Possibilities for Prosperity*. New York:
           Basic Books.

Portes, A., M. Castells and L. Benton, eds.
   1989   *The Informal Economy: Studies in Advanced and Less Developed
           Countries*. Baltimore: Johns Hopkins University Press.

Preston, D.
   1978   *Farmers and Towns: Rural-Urban Relations in Highland Bolivia*.
           Norwich (England): Geo Books.

Redclift, N., and E. Mingione, eds.
   1985   *Beyond Employment: Household, Gender and Subsistence*. Oxford: Basil
           Blackwell.

Rhyne, B.
   1991   "Bolivian Bank Targets Microenterprises." U.S. Agency for
           International Development, *Front Lines* 31:6-7.

Sabel, C.
   1982   *Work and Politics: The Division of Labor in Industry*. Cambridge:
           Cambridge University Press.

Sachs, K.
   1984   Introduction, "Generations of Working Class Families." In *My
           Troubles Are Going to Have Trouble with Me: Everyday Trials and
           Triumphs of Women Workers*, edited by K. Sachs and D. Remy, 1-
           39. New Brunswick, N.J.: Rutgers University Press.

Sachs, K., and D. Remy, eds.
   1984   *My Troubles Are Going to Have Trouble with Me: Everyday Trials and
           Triumphs of Women Workers*. New Brunswick, N.J.: Rutgers
           University Press.

Sandóval, G., X. Albó and T. Greaves
   1978   *Ojje por encima de todo: Historia de un centro de residentes ex-
           campesinos en La Paz*. La Paz: Cuaderno de Investigación CIPCA,
           No. 16.

Schoop, W.
1978   "Industrialization and Regional Planning in Bolivia." Center for Latin American Research and Documentation, Amsterdam: Mimeograph.

Simiç, A.
1988   "The Adaptation of a Rural Family to Yugoslavian Urban Life." In *Urban Life: Readings in Urban Anthropology*. 2d ed., edited by G. Gmelch and W. Zenner. Prospect Heights, Ill.: Waveland.

Stein, W.,
1961   *Hualcan: Life in the Highlands of Peru*. Ithaca: Cornell University Press.

Trager, L.
1988   *The City Connection: Migration and Family Independence in the Philippines*. Ann Arbor: University of Michigan Press.

Tyrer, R.
1976   "The Demographic and Economic History of the Audiencia of Quito: Indian Population and the Textile Industry, 1600-1800." Ph.D. diss., University of California, Berkeley.

Uzzel, D.
1980   "Mixed Strategies and the Informal Sector: Three Faces of Reserve Labor." *Human Organization* 39:40-49.

Wall Street Journal
8/13/85.

Weaver, F.
1986   "Recent Scholarship in Industrial Growth in Latin America." *Latin American Research Review* 21:173-187.

Westwood, S.
1985   *All Day, Every Day: Factory and Family in the Making of Women's Lives*. Urbana: University of Illinois.

Whiteford, S.
1981   *Workers from the North: Plantations, Bolivian Labor, and the City in Northwest Argentina*. Austin: University of Texas Press.

Wolf, E.
1982   *Europe and the People Without History*. Berkeley: University of California Press.

Ybarra, J.-A.
1989   "Informalization in the Valencian Economy: A Model for Underdevelopment." In *The Informal Economy: Studies in Advanced and Less Developed Countries*, edited by A.Portes et al. Baltimore: Johns Hopkins University Press.

Zapata, C.
    1978   *Las cooperativas artesanales de Bolivia.* La Paz: Universidad Católica Boliviana, Departamento de Estudios Económicos.

Zondag, C.
    1966   *The Bolivian Economy, 1952-65.* New York: Praeger.

Index

Abu-Lugod, J., 292
Achacachi, 49, 86, 87, 89-91, 200, 231, 235, 237, 292
Advertising, 53, 54, 185, 199, 200, 202, 225, 231
Agrarian reform, 39, 41, 46, 50, 60, 89, 90, 184, 291, 293, 295
Alasita, 55, 57, 95, 96, 188, 189, 192, 225, 267, 269, 279, 291
Amortization, 20, 80, 171, 280
Apprentices, 4, 40, 41, 83, 96-98, 105, 115, 117, 140, 142, 159, 165, 171, 175, 214
Apprenticeship, xvi, 7, 83, 86, 88, 96, 98, 100, 101, 127, 135, 139, 293
Arensberg, C. 24, 36, 292
Artisan fairs, 29, 55, 188, 190, 207, 209, 210, 229
Artisans
  bakers, 25, 26, 30, 31, 41, 42, 47, 49, 53, 57, 58, 81, 132, 137, 138, 141, 149, 158-160, 166-170, 173, 175, 195, 212, 221, 238, 242, 243
  blacksmiths, 89, 245, 246, 250
  bus body builders, 56, 58, 176
  cabinetmakers, 139, 144, 145, 190, 218, 221, 222. See also Artisans, furniture makers
  candle makers, 47, 57, 85, 96, 152, 154, 184, 219
  carpenters, 2, 4-6, 12, 17, 20, 42, 72, 75, 86, 92, 120, 130, 135, 136-138, 143, 145, 146, 148, 159, 160, 180, 202-204, 218, 221, 234, 235, 250-252, 280
  cookie makers, 26, 28, 29, 53-55, 57, 58, 138, 156, 158, 159, 165, 166, 170, 178, 186, 200
  costume makers, 1, 87, 90, 91, 178,

179, 200, 231, 235-237, 276
dressmakers, 3, 26, 55, 249, 263, 266, 273
flute makers, 1, 88, 89
furniture makers, 30, 31, 52-54, 57, 96, 178-180, 186, 187, 190, 191, 218, 219, 234. See also Furniture factories
furriers, 28, 143, 145, 170-173, 177, 195
goldsmiths, 28, 102, 137, 139, 198, 202, 218, 233
hatmakers, 29, 97, 99, 136, 146, 187, 235
jewelers, 7, 9, 12, 41, 47, 57, 58, 98, 101, 102, 135, 137, 138, 140, 142, 146, 147, 151, 159, 179, 196-198, 201, 212, 222, 233, 234
knitters, 27, 28, 30, 31, 53, 57, 58, 59, 68, 85, 86, 109, 112, 114, 118, 123, 131, 136, 140, 147, 153, 227, 229, 230
lamp makers, 99, 115, 136, 144, 198
leather workers, 54, 136
mask makers, 92, 93, 95, 96, 108, 231
mechanics, 1, 9, 30, 35, 52, 55, 56-58, 94, 102, 103, 108, 120, 124, 137, 139-141, 171, 173, 174-176, 217, 240, 247, 248, 260, 273
metal-lathe operators, 4, 30, 136, 173
metalwork(ers), 1, 7, 9, 55, 94, 103, 108, 124, 137, 139, 173, 175, 176, 217, 240, 246, 248, 260, 270, 273

producers of musical instruments, 52, 96, 209, 210. *See also* Artisans, flute makers

producers of wall hangings, 84, 85, 112, 172

rug makers, 88, 89, 145, 172, 198, 209, 2,12, 213

sandal makers, 88, 91, 151, 186, 188

seamstresses, 4, 6, 19, 75, 111, 171, 184, 199, 200, 231, 242, 254, 259, 271, 272

shoemakers, 42, 97, 142, 145, 146, 157, 159, 187, 192-194, 211, 227, 235

sign painters, 53-55

silversmiths, 1, 96-98, 240

skirt makers, 3, 5, 86, 87, 161, 162, 165, 166, 173, 180, 192, 199, 291

spinners, 115, 116, 123, 131

tailors, 1, 5, 7, 8, 40, 42, 48, 50, 53, 86, 97, 98, 136, 142, 146, 163, 166, 168, 170, 173, 187, 192, 200, 219, 231, 237, 248, 252

tinsmiths, 1, 20, 48, 95, 96, 106, 108, 152, 157, 237, 242, 245-248, 250, 269, 270, 273, 293

upholsterers, 30, 103, 221

weavers, 47, 84, 85, 91, 92, 111, 114, 115, 123, 145, 227, 300

wood-carvers, 51, 57, 90, 95, 145, 187, 194, 223, 225, 295

Baking industry, 9. *See also* Artisans, bakers

Balance of trade, 150

Bank for International Development credit for artisans, 146, 202

Bank loans, 142, 143, 145, 147. *See also* Credit, from banks

Benton, L., 299

Bribes, 14, 149, 154, 174, 202, 234

Brush, S., 60, 293

Candy makers, 9, 10, 123-131, 146, 179, 181, 192-194

Canelas, O., 23, 295

Capital, 1, 2, 5-8, 12, 14, 15, 19, 20, 29, 32, 33, 35, 50-52, 55, 56, 59, 63, 65, 69, 71, 74, 75, 77-80, 86, 99, 104, 119, 123, 133-137, 139, 140, 141-143, 145, 147, 148, 150, 152, 154, 156-161, 165, 166, 167, 170-173, 175, 176, 182, 183-185, 187, 191, 194, 198, 201, 204, 205, 207-209, 211, 214, 217, 221, 225, 227, 237, 259, 262, 263, 272, 278, 280-283, 297-299

Careers, 2, 20, 37, 41, 49, 51, 52, 56, 66, 87, 93, 97, 100-102, 122, 126, 134, 135, 137, 138, 141, 148, 182, 237, 250, 268, 270, 280

Carter, W., 46, 295

Casanovas, R., 37, 156, 165, 166, 295

Caseras (caseros), 33, 35, 114, 116, 131, 291

Castells, M., 14, 299

Chain migration, 40, 41, 43

Chola, 7, 25, 87, 142, 152, 157, 161, 187, 188, 192, 197, 199, 201, 202, 204, 215, 263, 272, 285, 286, 291

Circulatory migration, 38

Clandestine producers, 18

Class, 2, 4, 8-10, 12, 14, 16, 18, 25, 28, 30, 31, 34, 57, 58, 63, 68, 75, 76, 78, 87, 89, 91, 96, 99, 103, 106, 107, 116, 121-123, 131, 140, 141, 165, 166, 170, 177-180, 185, 186, 190, 192, 197-201, 204, 205, 215, 227, 245, 255, 256, 260, 262-266, 268, 272, 273, 279, 284, 285, 294, 300

Clientele, 2, 7, 30, 44, 70, 75, 89, 102, 103, 140, 156, 169, 178, 197, 198-201, 231, 276

Clothing manufacturers, 53, 161

Cochabamba, 10, 26, 65, 85, 91, 94, 100, 109, 112-117, 131, 169,

180, 181, 188, 189, 192, 194, 196, 197, 231, 238, 244, 262
Coffee processors, 120, 121, 127, 131, 137, 143, 151
Commercialization, 19, 84, 178, 180, 196, 224
Competition, xv, 2, 6, 14, 19, 57, 69, 70, 73, 75, 85, 96, 98, 103, 106, 109, 116, 123, 148, 150, 156-158, 164, 173, 176, 181, 193, 199, 201, 205, 208, 214, 216, 223-225, 233, 237, 253, 261, 269, 275
Compi, xv, 18, 39-44, 47-50, 60, 87, 163, 164, 231, 232, 237
Construction industries, 4-6, 17, 36, 37, 42, 57, 71, 75, 84, 86, 106, 128, 129, 156, 249, 262, 269, 270, 274-276
Contraband, 6, 11, 33, 57, 79, 101, 154, 158, 176, 186, 212, 215, 233, 259, 282
Cooper, E., 98, 295
Cooperatives, 19, 31, 47, 49, 86, 92, 101, 105, 118, 145, 167, 170, 177, 193, 206, 215, 216, 219, 222, 225-227, 244, 283
Corporations, 2, 13, 66, 69, 79, 130, 149
Crafts markets, 86, 186, 190, 218, 283
Credit, 4, 6, 10, 12, 13, 22-24, 30, 32, 33, 35, 49, 52, 53, 59, 64, 73, 74, 76, 79, 80, 94, 104, 120, 121, 131, 133, 134, 137, 140-149, 161, 162, 175, 177, 182, 183, 190, 191, 194, 195, 204, 207, 209, 211, 215, 216, 219, 229, 237, 268, 270, 277, 281-283, 291
  from banks, 4, 6, 12, 30, 73, 104, 131, 133, 134, 141-144, 147, 209, 283
  collateral to obtain, 73, 133, 134, 142, 143, 146, 147, 240, 268, 283
  commercial, 52, 133, 134, 137, 141-144, 147, 162
  to consumers and wholesalers, 33, 35, 74, 101, 175, 190, 191, 194, 195, 204, 209, 211, 237
  from kinsmen, 134, 161, 182, 183
  lines for artisans, 144, 145
  from non-governmental organizations, 13, 145, 146, 283
  from the World Bank, 144, 145,
Credit unions, 49, 59, 291

Dance groups, 43, 45, 90, 93, 187, 188, 192, 231, 232, 235, 237, 238-241, 267, 268, 291
Dandler, J., 278, 279, 285, 295
De Soto, H., 21, 295
Debt crisis, 22, 23, 32, 35, 65, 281
Dependent workers, 20, 116, 117, 131, 134, 139, 142, 157, 194, 280
Devaluation, 6, 11, 12, 27, 35, 36, 59, 142, 154, 160, 283
Development, xvi, 1, 2, 13, 19, 20, 24, 29, 62-65, 68, 74, 79, 83, 100, 105, 107, 118, 121, 134, 143, 146, 151, 215, 217, 226, 228, 262, 280, 281, 283, 292, 293, 296-299
Division of labor, 18, 20, 63, 94, 98, 105, 107, 173, 179, 181, 280, 281, 283, 292, 299
Doria Medina, S., 285, 295
Doughty, P., 38, 296
Dual economy, 13
Dunkerley, J., 31, 296

Eames, E., 38, 296
Eckstein, S., 296
Economic crisis, 11, 16, 20, 24, 50, 55, 100, 114, 145, 148, 155, 165, 170, 175, 188, 206, 207, 208-211, 237, 264, 278, 281, 283, 298. *See also* Debt crisis
Economic diversification. *See* Multiple occupations
Economic policies, 16, 23, 150, 155, 166, 168, 208, 283, 294
Economic strategies, 16, 32, 38, 49, 76

Economic strategies, 16, 32, 38, 49, 76
Eder, J., 76, 127, 128, 296
Education, xv, xvi, 1, 5-10, 12, 13, 15,
    16, 18-20, 23-26, 38, 39, 41, 44,
    47, 48, 50, 52-59, 62, 75, 76, 83,
    87, 91, 92, 94, 96, 101, 102, 103,
    106, 112, 117, 119, 121, 122, 126,
    132, 140, 149, 155, 161, 162, 165,
    166, 168, 173, 176-178, 183, 184,
    186, 193, 196, 199-202, 205, 225,
    227, 228, 239, 242-254, 256-266,
    271, 276, 277, 279, 294, 298
  high school, 55, 102, 252, 254, 260,
    276, 277
  university, 8, 9, 12, 52, 54, 57, 117,
    118, 120, 171, 205, 246, 249, 252,
    253, 258, 262, 267, 273, 274,
    292-301
Employer-employee relationships, 77,
    109, 123, 125, 130
Entrepreneurs, 64, 70, 72, 79, 80, 104,
    105, 120, 281, 282, 298
  foreign, 79, 80
Equipment, 17, 21, 30, 53, 55, 70, 71,
    72, 74, 83, 87, 94, 97, 99-101,
    133, 135-141, 143, 147, 148, 150,
    151-153, 156-160, 163, 171, 174,
    175, 197, 207, 214, 217, 245, 246,
    253, 269, 276, 278, 280, 282, 283
  imported, 70, 153, 214, 276, 278
  improvisation of, 139, 148, 150,
    159, 253
  renting of, 17, 137-138
  as severance pay, 21, 137, 280
  sharing of, 53, 94, 97, 135, 137-138,
    141, 282
  theft of, 136. 159, 160
Escobar de Pabón, S., 37-39, 60, 156,
    295, 296
Estes, V., 120, 126, 127, 129, 296
Exchange rates, 20, 23, 27, 30, 31, 32,
    33, 76, 80, 128, 149, 154, 155,
    164, 207, 208, 211, 214, 280, 281
Export(s), 6, 9, 19, 23, 27, 31, 36, 64,
    65, 69, 76, 78, 85, 86, 89, 112,
    114, 116-120, 131, 137, 143, 151,
    153, 170-172, 176, 193, 196, 197,
    203, 204-211, 213, 216,
    224, 226, 229, 240, 281,
    283, 297

Factory workers, 5, 32, 42, 100,
    106, 118, 123, 124, 126, 168,
    171, 212, 296
Family history, 2, 5, 19, 242
Fiestas, 3, 4, 6, 8, 11, 19, 30, 34, 38,
    43, 44, 47, 48, 51, 55, 57, 61,
    68, 86, 89, 90, 93, 96, 129,
    162, 166, 173, 175, 185,
    187-189, 191-193, 199, 200,
    214, 218, 221, 222, 226, 230,
    231-243, 247, 255, 259, 265,
    269, 276, 277, 279, 284, 285,
    291, 293
  production for, 96
  sponsors of, 45, 89, 125, 192,
    200, 231, 232, 234, 237-241,
    243, 255, 259, 276, 291
Flexibility, 15, 16, 32, 36, 44, 57,
    103, 104, 107, 132, 136, 143,
    148, 157, 175, 282, 283
Foreign buyers, 109, 115, 131, 203,
    204, 206
Foreign clients, 36, 109
Foreigners, 9, 27, 53, 62, 63, 66, 71,
    72, 75-81, 84, 92, 93, 97, 99,
    100, 102-104, 131, 158, 168,
    169, 170, 189, 201, 202, 206,
    246, 250, 285. *See also* Skills,
    transmitted by foreigners
  historical roles of 63-66, 69
Foreign firms, 13, 62, 71, 72, 75,
    76, 78, 80
Foreign manufacturers, 63, 66, 68,
    69, 70, 76, 77, 79
Formal sector, 6, 13, 20, 155, 280
Formality, 14, 15
Furniture factories, 50, 66, 72-76,
    99, 100, 103, 127, 137, 143,
    180, 190, 191, 193, 202, 262,
    263

Garment industry, 41, 108, 109,
    118, 119, 170, 233

Gender, 2, 16, 155, 176, 262, 263, 279,
    285, 294, 299
Gisbert, T., 297
Glazer, N., 273, 297
Glick Schiller, N., 292
Gmelch, G., xvi, 60, 292, 293, 297, 300
Gomez, W., 23, 72-77, 79-81, 143, 151,
    297
Government, 2, 4, 11-13, 16, 19, 20,
    23, 24, 30, 31, 33, 34, 52, 59, 64,
    65, 68, 69, 73, 75-77, 79, 91, 103,
    120, 124, 131, 132, 136, 144, 148,
    151, 153, 154, 156, 157, 166, 168,
    169, 171, 175, 177, 184, 186, 188,
    190, 195, 202, 204, 206, 208, 209,
    210, 212, 214-217, 219, 221-225,
    278, 281, 285, 294
  agencies, 13, 15, 202, 206, 215, 223
  bureaucracy, 2, 285
  contracts, 52, 73, 77
  control, 166, 208
  policies, 16, 150, 168, 283, 294
  regulations, 2, 19, 36, 131, 132, 208
  subsidies, 23, 76, 128, 205, 206, 278
  See also Training programs,
    governmental
Greaves, T., 42, 292, 300

Hagopian, F., 296
Harding, P., 15, 297
Hazards
  occupational, 8, 139, 158, 159
Heinrichs, J., 296
Home work(ers). See Putting-out
    system
Hopkins, D., 297, 299, 301
Household economy, 38, 44, 58
Hyperinflation, 5, 24, 25, 32, 74, 134,
    154, 208, 211

Imports, 1, 6, 10, 23, 30, 31, 36, 65, 66,
    71, 79, 80, 152, 154, 156, 158,
    175, 203, 207, 210, 221, 281, 282
Independent workers, 37, 165, 166
Industrial development, 24, 68, 107,
    281, 297
Industrialization, 24, 37, 62, 78, 107,

    296, 300
Industries
  large. See Large industries
Inflation, 4, 6, 12, 22, 24, 27, 31,
    32, 33, 35, 59, 73, 76, 134,
    142, 143, 147-150, 154, 164,
    211, 281, 296
Informal economy, 13, 15, 278,
    299, 301
Informal sector, 14, 16, 278, 285,
    295, 300
Informality, 14-16, 279
Inheritance, 44-46, 59-61, 183, 246,
    253, 271, 275, 288
Intermediaries, 25, 88, 131, 178,
    186, 187, 188, 193-195, 197,
    198, 212, 215, 216, 225, 229,
    230
Intermediate goods, 143, 147, 150,
    151-154, 210, 214, 278
International economy, 63, 279
Investment, 6, 8, 33, 41, 50, 56, 59,
    62, 69-71, 74, 77, 87, 99, 100,
    113, 132, 135, 136, 137, 147,
    148, 187, 200, 209, 281, 283,
    297, 298
  in machinery, 6, 10, 19, 20, 119,
    135, 136, 138, 140, 146, 148,
    196
Irvin, G., 65, 80, 127, 128, 297

Jacobs, J., 79, 297
Jenkins, R., 15, 297
Johnson, C., 63, 297

Kelley, J., 297
Kin
  assistance from, 7, 8, 51-53, 87,
    89, 93, 105, 139, 140, 141,
    183, 257, 270, 271, 274, 288,
    289
  involvement in workforce, 107,
    108, 109, 111-114, 117, 119,
    121, 130, 131, 163, 166, 170,
    172, 178, 179, 180-182, 205,
    243, 246-248, 267, 270
  learning from, 7, 57, 84-86, 90,

91, 92, 94, 95, 100, 102, 105,
   161, 170, 173, 182-184, 243,
   247-250, 275
 ties with rural, 43, 44, 47-49
Kirsch, H., 120, 297
Klein, H., 297
Koreans, 62, 66, 68, 71, 72, 74, 75, 77,
   79, 101, 119, 153, 156, 157, 194
Kreye, O., 296

Labor costs, 171, 172, 175
Laclau, E., 298
Land
 access to, 38, 44-51, 58-60, 87, 164,
   231, 284, 288, 289, 292
Land tenure, 43, 45, 47
Large industries, 13, 15, 51, 62, 80,
   108, 120, 123, 126, 130, 134, 136,
   155, 278
Learning a trade, 51, 83, 139, 245-247,
   249, 254, 276
 in factories, 103, 124, 168
 informally, 88, 246
Lending agents, 16, 134
Lending policies, 13
Levitsky, J., 13, 295, 298
Living conditions, 11, 16, 24, 62
Llamacachi, xv, 18, 40, 42, 47, 60, 199,
   289
Local market, 33, 36, 64, 121, 176,
   183, 225
Lomnitz, L., 59, 298
Long, N., 298
Lumberyards, 4, 20, 30, 49, 50, 66, 87,
   136, 198, 199, 280

Machines, machinery, 4, 6-8, 10, 17,
   20, 30, 31, 35, 52, 53, 58, 68, 85,
   86, 95, 97, 111, 112, 119, 120,
   127, 131, 135, 136, 137-142, 143,
   145-147, 153, 154, 157, 161, 162,
   165, 168, 171-173, 177, 181, 185,
   186, 196, 199, 226, 229, 239, 240,
   253, 254, 271, 276, 280, 281
 credit for, 141, 142, 143, 145, 147,
   162, 226, 229
 imported, 1, 4, 6-10, 35, 53, 131,

139, 147, 152, 153, 168,
   185, 221
 rented, 4, 6, 20, 52, 137, 138,
   253, 280
 second hand, 75, 135, 136, 140,
   152, 153, 161, 165
 as severance pay, 120, 137
 sharing of, 199
Maletta, H., 17, 37-39, 60, 156, 296
Manufacturers
 foam rubber, 74
 furniture, 72, 74
 furnitures, 73
 lamp, 76
 plastics, 77, 176
 polyurethane foam rubber, 73
 sausage, 70, 71
 textile, 74
Manwar, A., 13, 298
Market vendors, 18, 26, 33, 44, 47,
   115, 116, 139, 145, 147, 149,
   165, 178, 182, 183, 195, 204,
   207, 217, 233, 274
Markets
 internal, 1, 69, 153, 203, 204,
   216, 282
 national, 2
 regional, 2
 urban, 26, 32, 52, 95, 96, 171,
   180, 182, 183, 187, 195, 197,
   212, 232, 234, 274
Marsh, M., 298
Marxist models, 20, 280
Master-apprentice relationship,
   98, 99, 101
McEwen, W., 60, 298
McFarren, W., 92, 93, 298
Microenterprises, 13, 15, 146, 278,
   295, 298, 299
Middle class, 8, 14, 25, 28, 30, 31,
   57, 75, 89, 91, 99, 103, 106,
   121, 131, 140, 166, 170,
   177-180, 185, 190, 192,
   197-199, 201, 204, 205, 215,
   227, 263, 265, 268, 272, 284
Middlemen, 31, 32, 39, 114, 115,
   118, 120, 194-196, 204, 282

Middlewomen, 39, 118
Migrants, xv, 5, 8, 18, 37-44, 46-52,
    60, 62, 63, 66, 68, 70, 71, 76-81,
    83-92, 96, 100, 101-103, 105, 109,
    115, 117, 121, 126, 131, 138, 140,
    143, 156, 157, 163, 182, 183, 187,
    199, 227, 231, 232, 235, 237, 265,
    284, 292, 294
  contribution of, 37, 38, 40, 51, 83,
    84, 86, 88-90, 182, 187, 265
  role in fiestas, 231, 232, 235, 237,
    240
  rural-urban, 37, 41, 44-46, 48, 50,
    51
  and skill acquisition, 51, 83, 84,
    85-87, 96, 100, 104, 105
  specialization of rural-urban, 40
  ties to community of origin, 18,
    38, 41, 43, 47, 49-51, 88, 115,
    231, 235, 284
  ties with, 5, 18, 38, 41, 85, 86, 88,
    105, 183, 199, 231, 235, 237
Migration, 1, 18, 28, 37-41, 43, 44, 58,
    60, 62, 68, 78, 104, 183, 284, 292,
    293, 300
  abroad, 28
  history of, 39-41
  importance of kin for, 5, 38, 43,
    44, 47, 48, 51, 84, 85, 87, 89,
    100, 105, 140, 183
  reasons for, 40
  rural-urban, 1, 2, 5, 18, 37, 41, 58,
    83, 86, 104, 109, 111, 115, 126,
    157, 163, 183, 199, 200, 227, 284
  to Australia, 34, 113
  to U.S.A., 115, 209, 240
Military regimes, 27, 117
Milkman, R., 34, 298
Mingione, E., 13, 299
Modern sector, 13
Monopolies, 10, 86, 104, 111, 148, 150,
    152, 153, 214
Morales, R., 22, 31, 92, 93, 296
Multinational firms, 62, 69, 77, 78, 79,
    80, 115, 206, 281, 299
Multiple occupations, 37, 57-59, 73,
    112, 127, 136, 148, 269, 273

Nash, J., 65, 77, 294, 299
National economy, 15, 63, 80, 164,
    279

Oligopolies, 14
Outwork(ers). *See* Putting-out
    system

Paisanos, 41, 43, 85, 88, 159, 291
Partnerships, 9, 68, 70, 72, 74, 112,
    136, 141
Parts, 11, 20, 74, 113, 141, 280
Pasta factory, 136, 146
Pasta industry, 11, 32, 126
Pastor, M., 22, 23, 242, 247, 281,
    299
Paternalism, 11
Patronage, 2, 200, 285
Paz Estenssoro, 4, 23, 32, 33, 74,
    103, 158, 210
Personalism, 11, 129, 131
Piecework(ers), 87, 171, 181
Piore, M., 116, 281-285, 293, 299
Plastics industry, 176
Portes, A., 14, 299, 301
Preiswerk, M., 192, 234, 235, 237,
    241, 292
Preston, D., 38, 47, 299
Printers, 52, 56, 57, 94, 95, 108,
    120, 136, 138, 157, 178, 185,
    192, 200, 246, 252, 269, 272,
    282
Producer organizations, 19
Public enterprises, 19
Putting-out system, 7, 8, 13, 16,
    20, 29, 77, 109, 114, 119, 126,
    134, 163, 166, 178, 193, 196,
    197, 280

Rationalization of production, 29,
    30, 124
Raw materials, 2, 5, 7, 10, 12, 19,
    23, 28, 30, 31, 35, 50, 53, 63,
    64, 66, 73, 74, 76, 80, 95, 99,
    101, 104, 111, 118, 133, 134,
    142, 143, 145, 147, 148, 150,
    151-154, 156, 158, 173,

203, 204, 209, 212, 214, 219,
221, 224, 226, 278, 282, 283
imported, 31, 76, 150, 154
national, 150, 151
recycled, 151, 152
Recession, 8, 23, 27, 44, 148, 281
Red tape, 14, 36, 70, 100, 144, 202
Remy, B., 273, 300
Renting equipment, 137-139
Retailing, 7, 27, 65, 66, 70, 73, 100,
109, 119, 123, 172, 185, 190, 191,
193, 194
Rhyne, B., 146, 299
Rites of passage, 19, 43, 231
Ritual, 43, 46, 96, 111, 114, 214, 237,
253, 269, 282, 284. *See also* Rites
of passage; Fiestas
Ritual kin, 43, 46
Roberts, B., 38, 100, 298
Rural areas
ties to, 25, 38, 43, 51
Rural crafts, 51
Rural fairs, 87, 92, 182, 187, 285
Rural-urban migration, 39-41, 45

Sabel, C.,, 116, 281-285, 299
Sachs, K., 264, 273, 300
Santa Cruz, 4, 10, 34, 35, 66, 74, 75,
81, 87, 91, 100, 115, 116, 142,
161-163, 169, 186, 188, 194, 203,
205, 217, 220, 262, 273
Scarcity, 2, 6, 27, 30, 35, 73, 150, 153,
154, 170, 195, 212, 221
Schoop, W., 69, 300
Seasonal production, 173, 191, 192
Self-employed, 17, 116, 156, 182
Self-financing, 135
Service industry, 6, 17, 25, 28, 37, 65,
85, 111, 112, 118, 120, 127, 128,
135, 142, 147, 148, 173, 175, 273,
281
Severance pay
as source of startup capital, 21,
120, 121, 124, 126, 127, 136, 137,
280. *See also* Equipment, as
severance pay
Shirt factory, 127, 148

Shoe industry, 97, 127, 158
Sindicatos, 19, 217, 292
Skill(s), 5, 6, 12, 20, 28, 35, 37, 50,
51, 55, 71, 73-75, 78, 83, 84,
85-88, 95-105, 115, 116, 118,
119, 127, 130, 139, 157, 170,
176, 182, 183, 185, 190, 196,
197, 199-201, 223, 225, 245,
247, 250, 258, 260, 269, 270,
272, 280, 283
acquisition of, 83
commercial, 86, 87, 182
generalized, 84-87
rural, 51, 85, 88-90, 92, 104
specialized, 88, 103
transmitted by foreigners, 71,
75, 78, 84, 92, 96, 170
Skilled workers, 14, 72, 92, 101,
104, 105, 118, 155, 171
Soccer, 2, 11, 43, 125, 129, 193,
221, 233, 234, 244, 246, 255,
291
Social marginality, 14
Social mobility, 2, 11, 19, 104, 116,
123, 284
Social networks, 2, 19, 37, 38, 43,
51, 53, 59, 83, 85, 113, 114,
116, 231, 249, 270, 284
Social revolution, 39, 49, 294
Social security, 100, 140
benefits, 2, 4, 19, 20, 23, 33, 65,
75, 100, 124, 125, 127, 128,
129, 132, 168, 193, 194, 215,
219, 223, 226, 280, 285
Social stratification, 12, 19, 92,
116, 121, 197, 246, 252, 256,
261, 264, 268, 269, 271, 284,
285
Social welfare legislation, 14
Soft-drink factory, 136
Speculation, 26, 31, 153
Stabilization, 33, 124, 127, 156,
208, 210, 296
Standard of living, 55, 155, 162,
163, 269, 281
lowering of, 25, 30, 156, 164,
274

State enterprises, 152
Street markets, 186
Szanton, C., 292

Taxes, 6, 17, 32, 65, 128, 142, 149,
    154-157, 163, 167, 171, 174, 177,
    185, 207, 214, 215, 217, 219, 222,
    225, 278
Technology, 79, 156, 176, 295, 298
Textile factories, 68, 93, 136, 152, 252
Theft, 55, 158-160, 202
    and recession, 9
Tools, 6, 12, 14, 63, 83, 97-99, 101,
    135, 137-139, 141, 143, 148, 153,
    157, 159, 174, 190, 247, 281. *See
    also* Equipment; Machines
    lending of, 138
Tourists as consumers of handicrafts,
    26, 29, 36, 50, 57, 84-86, 89, 91,
    106, 109, 112, 116, 157, 172, 179,
    181, 185, 186, 188, 189, 193, 197,
    198, 208, 210, 215, 223, 246, 273,
    276
Trade schools, 103, 176, 245, 246, 249,
    258-260
Trager, L., 38, 300
Training, 8, 55, 76, 78, 84, 94, 98, 103,
    106, 121, 124, 217, 249, 250, 269,
    277, 283
Training programs
    governmental, 103, 106, 121, 215-
    217, 249, 283
Transportation costs, 1, 66, 69, 79,
    153, 193, 203, 282
Tyrer, R., 300

Under-employment, 9, 37, 53
Unemployment, 12, 37, 53, 226, 264
Unions, 11, 12, 26, 34, 39, 49, 59, 123,
    124, 129, 130, 145, 167, 211, 215,
    217-219, 221, 222, 231, 233, 234,
    285, 291, 292
Uzzel, D., 33, 300

Vendors, 4, 6, 15, 18, 26, 31-33, 44, 47,
    48, 52, 55, 89, 95, 96, 111, 115,
    116, 138, 139, 145, 149, 171,

    179, 180, 182, 183,
    185-189, 195, 197, 198,
    204, 207, 212, 217-219,
    225, 232-234, 239, 243,
    274, 278, 283, 284, 291

Wage
    minimum, 128
Wages, 5, 11, 12, 16, 20, 23-25,
    30-33, 36, 53, 64, 73, 75, 79,
    97, 101, 115, 116, 121, 123,
    124, 127-129, 135, 136, 148,
    155, 167, 168, 171, 172, 176,
    181, 208, 211, 212, 214, 217,
    245, 258, 263, 270, 273,
    280-282
    in kind, 128
Westwood, S., 263, 264, 272, 273,
    301
Whiteford, S., 33, 301
Wholesaling, 10, 55, 65, 136, 182,
    187, 193, 195, 196, 227
Wolf, E., 63, 64, 301
Women, 4, 6, 7, 9, 25, 30, 33, 34,
    44, 45, 47, 48, 54, 59, 60, 84,
    85-87, 92, 108, 111, 112, 116,
    118-123, 126-128, 132, 138,
    147, 157, 165, 178, 180, 181,
    182, 183, 187, 193, 198, 212,
    215-217, 222, 226-228, 230,
    233, 235, 249, 259, 263, 264,
    267, 272, 273, 275, 279, 284,
    285, 291, 292, 294, 296, 298,
    300, 301
    and access to land, 45, 48, 59
    and collective action, 215, 216,
    226, 228
    commitment to family, 34, 264
    contribution to household, 25,
    30, 165
    exploitation of, 59, 226, 267
    factory workers, 120, 121, 123,
    126, 127, 128
    and household budgeting, 263
    and independence, 272, 275
    as intermediaries, 39, 41, 118
    leaders, 222

migrant, 86, 87, 111, 227
and skill acquisition, 84, 118
and social status 284, 285. *See also*
  Chola
roles in artisan production, 29, 30,
  84-87, 92, 108, 111, 112, 116,
  138, 157, 165, 180, 193, 230, 235
training of, 217
vendors, 9, 30, 44, 47, 86, 92, 116,
  147, 178-180, 182, 183, 222, 233,
  259
Work conditions, 9, 11, 40, 123,
  126, 131, 139
Work hazards. *See* Hazards,
  occupational

Work histories, 18, 19, 101
Work relationships, xvi, 2, 11, 16,
  75, 77, 107, 113-115, 117, 120,
  129, 130, 293
World Bank, 22, 24, 144-146, 229
World system, 2

Ybarra, J-A., 301

Zapata, C., 170, 187, 301
Zenner, W., xvi, 60, 292, 293, 297,
  300
Zondag, C., 301